EVERYDAY WORDS ANI
PROSE IN NINETEENT

M000286661

Everyday Words is an original and innovative study of the stylistic tics of canonical novelists, including Austen, Dickens, Trollope, Thackeray, and Eliot. Jonathan Farina shows how ordinary locutions such as "a decided turn," "as if," and "that sort of thing" condense nineteenth-century manners, tacit aesthetics and assumptions about what counts as knowledge. Writers recognized these recurrent "everyday words" as signatures of "character." Attending to them reveals how many of the fundamental forms of characterizing fictional characters also turn out to be forms of characterizing objects, natural phenomena, and inanimate, abstract things, like physical laws, the economy, and legal practice. Ultimately, this book revises what "character" meant to nineteenth-century Britons by respecting the overlapping, transdisciplinary connotations of the category.

JONATHAN FARINA is Associate Professor of Nineteenth-Century British Literature at Seton Hall University, New Jersey, where he is Director of the Center for Humanities and the Public Sphere and an Associate Director of the Honors Program. He is Associate Editor of *The Wordsworth Circle*.

CAMBRIDGE STUDIES IN NINETEENTH-CENTURY LITERATURE AND CULTURE

General Editor
Gillian Beer, *University of Cambridge*

Editorial Board
Isobel Armstrong, *Birkbeck, University of London*
Kate Flint, *University of Southern California*
Catherine Gallagher, *University of California, Berkeley*
D. A. Miller, *University of California, Berkeley*
J. Hillis Miller, *University of California, Irvine*
Daniel Pick, *Birkbeck, University of London*
Mary Poovey, *New York University*
Sally Shuttleworth, *University of Oxford*
Herbert Tucker, *University of Virginia*

Nineteenth-century British literature and culture have been rich fields for interdisciplinary studies. Since the turn of the twentieth century, scholars and critics have tracked the intersections and tensions between Victorian literature and the visual arts, politics, social organization, economic life, technical innovations, scientific thought – in short, culture in its broadest sense. In recent years, theoretical challenges and historiographical shifts have unsettled the assumptions of previous scholarly synthesis and called into question the terms of older debates. Whereas the tendency in much past literary critical interpretation was to use the metaphor of culture as 'background', feminist, Foucauldian, and other analyses have employed more dynamic models that raise questions of power and of circulation. Such developments have reanimated the field. This series aims to accommodate and promote the most interesting work being undertaken on the frontiers of the field of nineteenth-century literary studies: work which intersects fruitfully with other fields of study such as history, or literary theory, or the history of science. Comparative as well as interdisciplinary approaches are welcomed.

A complete list of titles published will be found at the end of the book.

EVERYDAY WORDS AND THE CHARACTER OF PROSE IN NINETEENTH-CENTURY BRITAIN

JONATHAN FARINA

Seton Hall University, New Jersey

CAMBRIDGE UNIVERSITY PRESS

CAMBRIDGE
UNIVERSITY PRESS

University Printing House, Cambridge CB2 8BS, United Kingdom

One Liberty Plaza, 20th Floor, New York, NY 10006, USA

477 Williamstown Road, Port Melbourne, VIC 3207, Australia

314-321, 3rd Floor, Plot 3, Splendor Forum, Jasola District Centre, New Delhi - 110025, India

79 Anson Road, #06-04/06, Singapore 079906

Cambridge University Press is part of the University of Cambridge.

It furthers the University's mission by disseminating knowledge in the pursuit of education, learning and research at the highest international levels of excellence.

www.cambridge.org
Information on this title: www.cambridge.org/9781316632789
DOI: 10.1017/9781316855126

First published 2017
First paperback edition 2019

A catalogue record for this publication is available from the British Library

ISBN 978-1-107-18163-2 Hardback
ISBN 978-1-316-63278-9 Paperback

For Jennifer, every day

I've been telling you what we said – repeating the phrases we pronounced – but what's the good? They were common everyday words – the familiar, vague sounds exchanged on every waking day of life. But what of that? They had behind them, to my mind, the terrific suggestiveness of words heard in dreams, of phrases spoken in nightmares.

– *Joseph Conrad,* Heart of Darkness *(1899)*[1]

[T]he primary object is character, which is, as all know, of a mingled woof, good and evil, virtue and weakness, truth and falsehood, woven inextricably together.

– *G. H. Lewes,* Life and Works of Goethe *(1855)*[2]

The crown and glory of life is Character ... That character is power, is true in a much higher sense than that knowledge is power.

– *Samuel Smiles,* Self-Help *(1859)*[3]

Contents

Acknowledgments

I am forever grateful to Mary Poovey for believing in me and in this project from its earliest stages and also for her exquisite scholarship, which still inspires my thinking. She is as awesome a teacher as an intellectual. Marilyn Gaull has been an indefatigable friend, a model writer and speaker, our profession at its happiest. At NYU, where this book began, I also thank Patrick Deer, John Guillory, Phil Harper, the late Paul Magnuson, and John Maynard: all generous, genuine teachers. Susan Harlan has read more of this book in its worst first drafts and ramblings than anyone else: her friendship and conversations are a great gift, and I wish they too were in print.

Other colleagues have been extraordinarily generous with their time and attention: Nicholas Dames, Dino Franco Felluga, Kate Flint, William Galperin, Deborah Denenholz Morse, and John Plotz all read and commented on substantial portions of the book. This text, and my career, is much better because of them. For comments on papers, invitations, encouragement, and advice of all sorts, I also thank James Eli Adams, Tanya Agathocleous, Rae Greiner, Anne Humphreys, Gerhard Joseph, Mark Knight, Meredith Martin, Kyle McAuley, Andrew Miller, Adrienne Munich, Jesse Rosenthal, Jason Rudy, Jonah Siegel, Rachel Teukolsky, Carolyn Williams, Danny Wright, Alex Woloch, the Center for Cultural Analysis and English Department at Rutgers University, Columbia University, the University of Toronto, and the many NAVSA and especially NVSA conferences where this book came alive.

Seton Hall has been altogether encouraging and collegial: Angela Weisl, Karen Gevirtz, Mary Balkun, Donovan Sherman, and Martha Carpentier, in particular, have made writing this first book a joy. Before them, Allison Schachter, Ben Tran, András Kiséry, Dahlia Porter, and Gabe Cervantes, my colleagues at Vanderbilt, helped redirect where this book was headed (and we had a lot of fun together), and I thank Jay Clayton and Carolyn Dever for the opportunity to teach there.

I want to thank Linda Bree and Gillian Beer at Cambridge University Press for their faith in this project, my excellent copy-editor, and my two anonymous, enormously beneficial readers, who were both provocative and charitable.

I am most fortunate and grateful, however, for my congenial, generous, and witty family, who make it all worthwhile, whatever I write: Mom and Dad, Anj and Mike, Joseph and Caroline, Mikey, Mackenzie, Matt, the Overbecks (Sir, Kate, and JO), my wonderful Ethan and Felicity, characters who put my reading skills to the test every night, and most of all Jennifer, who makes me happy everyday.

***

Much shorter, early versions of Chapters 3 and 4 appeared as "Dickens's 'As If': Analogy and Victorian Virtual Reality," *Victorian Studies* 53.3 (Winter 2011): 427–36 and "*Middlemarch* and 'that Sort of Thing,'" *RaVoN: Romanticism and Victorianism on the Net* 53 (February 2009): www .erudit.org/revue/ravon/2009/v/n53/029903ar.html. A tiny portion of Chapter 1 derives from a longer article, "Flash Reading: The Currency of Knowing in *Tom & Jerry*," *The Wordsworth Circle* 41.3 (Summer 2010): 150–54. And a shorter version of Chapter 5 appeared as an article with the same title in *Victorians* 128 (September 2015): 138–61. I thank all of the editors for their help and permissions to reprint that work here.

Preface

Everyday Words expatiates on a cluster of rudimentary words that are especially common in nineteenth-century British print: "turn," "attention," "as if," "but," "something," "that sort of thing," "particular," "general," and "character," which is the multivalent keyword around which all of the others coalesce. Many novels foreground these everyday words as mediums of characterizing personages, but writers, then as now, readily ascribed character to things other than people and fictional personages – things as diverse as furniture and the financial market. Character was perhaps the most prevalent of Victorian "vernacular aesthetic categories," to borrow a phrase from Sianne Ngai,[1] and the many connotations and discourses of character that now seem distinct were closely correlated throughout the nineteenth century: coincident, that is to say, were the notions of character as a psychological identity, personality, and reputation; a fictional personage or theatrical role; an amorphous moral and aesthetic value, embracing sincerity, perseverance, industriousness, and courage as well as interest, originality, and marked distinction (a room with character or a person who is a character, as in "a card"); and, finally, a taxonomical feature identifying the nexus of genera and species, general affinity and specific difference. Samuel Smiles's exalted sense of character as "moral order embodied in the individual" (314) thus coincided with Charles Darwin's sense of character in the *Origin of Species* (1859) as an "inflection" or "manner" of physiology:

> Man can act only on external and visible characters ... We care not how trifling a character may be – let it be the mere inflection of the angle of the jaw, the manner in which an insect's wing is folded, whether the skin be covered by hair or feathers – if it prevail throughout many and different species, especially those having very different habits of life, it assumes high value; for we can account for its presence in so many forms with such different habits, only by its inheritance from a common parent. (*OS* 76, 337)

xi

Everyday Words restores the connotative multiplicity of *character* and treats the signature stylistic tics of nineteenth-century writers as *characters* in the natural historical sense Darwin invokes in this passage.

The everyday words I describe can appear "trifling," but they prevail across so wide a range of genres and situations that they bespeak a common epistemological, aesthetic, and moral objective. This objective – character – designated not the definitive essence of a person or thing, but a manner of relating persons or things. Darwin does not treat "external and visible characters" as symptoms of an underlying cause or interiority, but as the means of fitness – the means by which an organism adapts to the ambient world and relates to other organisms. Everyday words likewise indicate neither the definitive essence (or function) of a topic nor the thematic focus of a text, though some of the novels I discuss here do indeed thematize common words, but its "external and visible character" – that is, its style: its manners and attitudes toward its subjects, referents, and readers. *Characters*, as I describe them, thus produce the texture of prose as it implicates or addresses the reader and as it negotiates between its many subjects and objects. Characterization was a means of articulating meaningful superficiality.

Poststructuralism hampered *character* as a critical category by exposing it as a medium of ideology and as a fantasy of coherent selfhood,[2] but it has since resurged as an object of critical interest.[3] Deidre Lynch recounts the emergence of an "economy of character" in which cultivating and affecting intimacy with and deep knowledge of literary personages circulated as a kind of cultural capital.[4] Alex Woloch describes how the depth of such personages emerges as a function of "the definitively circumscribed form of a narrative" and the subordination of secondary characters in "a character system."[5] And Susan Manning, recognizing that character "is verbally and conceptually *relational*," rekindles the eighteenth-century discourse of moral correspondence – analogy, comparison, fitness, sympathy, exemplarity, and allegory – to animate "a comparative criticism that supplements sequential historical narrative (with its implied linearity and progressive or regressive trajectory), with rhetorical structures able to hold competing or antithetical 'truths' in tense simultaneity" – rhetorical structures modelled on character relations.[6] These studies inspire much of the work that follows, but they remain attached in different ways to an equation of *character* and personhood, psychologically realistic personages, and the moral values associated with them. But as even Lynch admits, "individuated, psychological meanings did not come naturally to British writers and readers" in the Regency period (9).

Recognizing character less as personhood than as ethos, Amanda Anderson describes it as the premier category by which Victorians tautologically ascribed form and value to those modern practices that specifically seemed to threaten the principle assumptions of character: scientific reason, liberal critique, and objective detachment, all of which resurface in the succeeding chapters.[7] Yet, these modern practices and the ideal of deep, secret subjectivity were perceived by many Victorians as additional impositions on the extant paradigms of a more social and external epistemology of character. As David Kurnick writes, many nineteenth-century novelists were rather reluctant to embrace the interiority for which they subsequently became famous: even, he says, as domestic fictions "push inward they fantasize about collective responses to the isolations of privacy" and exhibit "a frustrated will to performative exteriority and collectivity," an "allergy to interiority."[8] Following Kurnick, *Everyday Words* restores a prose aesthetic that was more prevalent for much of the nineteenth century than the depth model of character that has since dominated studies of character but from which literary studies began to turn in the 1970s. As Michel Serres put it, "what is essential is neither the image nor the deep meaning, neither the representation nor its hall of mirrored reflections, but the system of relations."[9] Thinking of everyday words as the stylistic correlatives to epistemological assumptions and social manners, this book describes characterization accordingly as a grammar of relations.

The everyday words studied here all perform the taxonomical work of concomitantly affiliating and disaffiliating entities: like natural historical characters, they gesture at an affinity to a familiar genera of some sort even as they mark an individuating departure from that genera; they gesture at a known referent even as they deviate from it. Like manners, they accommodate individuality to social conventions even as, like mannerisms, they depart from them. Everyday words thus endow the prosaic with a frisson of tact and contact, an aesthetic affect produced by interactions of different sorts – friction, contingency, apposition, and affinity.

Character thus names a unit of knowledge that at times rivaled, at times supplemented, but formally differed from what Mary Poovey has described as the modern fact. Poovey describes the modern fact as "a mode of representation that seemed to be transparent," a deracinated particular that seemed to represent accurately the object to which it refers and yet whose validity depended reciprocally upon its integration – as evidence – in systematic knowledge of some kind.[10] Where facts proffered impassive, purportedly unmediated knowledge whose veracity was guaranteed by tangible or visible referents and upheld by "[jettisoning] the ornamental excesses associated with rhetoric" (Poovey 13), *character* promised a markedly oblique relation to its objects. *Character* applies to prose that mediates its content aslant, prose that is mildly awkward or intriguing, at once appealing but unfamiliar. By "prose," I should note, I do not exclude verse or poetry, which share the idioms this book details, but invoke and revise Hegel's sense of a distinctly modern form of ironic description. However, where Hegel ascribed disenchantment or alienation to prose, many Victorians ascribed character; they felt a connection.

Writers like Hegel presume prose to be predominantly referential, but distinguishing the stylistic signatures of characterization reveals how regularly nineteenth-century prose refutes or complicates direct reference. George Levine has observed that "there was no such thing as naïve realism – simple faith in the correspondence between word and thing – among serious Victorian novelists," and his claim still bears repeating, for realism is still too regularly reduced to an aspiration toward photographic mimesis.[11] Each of my subsequent chapters details how a different everyday phrase – and its synonyms and variants – disavows the referential correspondence that writers have most consistently associated with the prosaic and with realism and instead installs a formal discrepancy between representation and referent, people and things, interiority and exteriority. *Character* was the value ascribed to these kinds of performative deviations, which manifested in a range of discrete modes: turns, attentions, inductions, conditional conjectures, liberal abstractions, and tactful rebuttals. Characterization evoked a disposition distinguished by its ability to adhere to conventions even as it departs from them, a disposition defined by minute but iterative acknowledgments and dismissals of expectations, assumptions, and empirical facts.

This tension with mimesis had its moral analogue: moral character traditionally denoted sincerity, authenticity, and honesty, the correspondence between external expressions (emotions, physiognomies, clothes, actions, manners, words) and interiority. As Smiles writes in "Character – the True Gentleman," the concluding chapter of *Self-Help*, "Integrity in word and deed is the backbone of character; and loyal adherence to veracity its most prominent characteristic. ... A man must really be what he seems or purposes to be" (317–18). But both the realism and the charm of fictional personages owes to their deviations from expectations, types, and probability, as to the discordance between their appearance and their interiority. Over the course of the nineteenth century, discordance between categories – internal and external, particular and general, actuality and ideal – came to index truth via irony, free indirect discourse, and other formal features. Dazzlingly dissimulative personages such as Becky Sharp and Lizzie Eustace, or even Frankenstein's Creature, whose monstrous exterior and murderousness belie his potentially loving inner child, exemplify character precisely because character legitimated formal hypocrisy as a medium of moral and epistemic truth, whatever the morality of its contents. Realistic personages appear – to others as to themselves – differently than they prove to think or feel or otherwise be on the inside. Everyday words writ this irony small but distributed it throughout Victorian prose, affording all sorts of objects and abstractions a glimmer of the aesthetic interest of these personages.

If novels are not now routinely respected as epistemology per se, they are the pre-eminent medium of characterization, and they record routine assumptions about the relations between things in the world. I take novels here, then, as exemplary repositories of an epistemology of character than extended well beyond fiction into other genres and domains. Michael McKeon traces the epistemological negotiations of the novel as it justified its non-referential content as a form of "concrete virtuality," knowledge that can be realized in actual particulars although it refers to none in particular.[12] This "concrete virtuality" applies but is not restricted to fictional personages. McKeon points out that the disaggregation of two modes of fictionality – falsity and fabulation, dishonesty and artistry, "made up" and "made" (109) – originated in modern empiricist epistemology that insisted on actuality, history, factuality, and concreteness. *Character* marks where prose shades from description into abstraction, generality, possibility, or fiction. The epistemology of character I describe resisted the hegemony of facts and utility, but also helped realize and moralize modern abstractions that facts could not wholly depict, abstractions such as the factory system and the financial market, the links between radically disparate organisms, the materiality of ephemeral mental life, the practice of science, and the extension of social etiquette into professional domains.[13] Characterization was essential to realizing the ideas behind modernity.

Natural historians, other non-fiction writers, and novelists alike performed analogous modes of characterization, then, by isolating individual features (characters) that could be said to articulate individuality and typicality, eccentricity and exemplarity, materiality and abstraction. For natural historians, these characters were instantiated in features such as opposable thumbs, the bumps on an earlobe, and the vestigial femurs and pelvic bones embedded in a whale's sides; for novelists and critics they were, to be sure, instantiated in imaginary persons such as Jane Eyre but

also in diction, in the very language of exposition used to depict the
interrelations of those personages and the things around them. Such
characters were the natural historical correlatives to manners, but even
natural history has its manners, its "epistemological decorum," as Steven
Shapin calls it, and everyday words served this decorum on the level of
style.[14]

Decorum describes an attitude that ensured that proper procedures were
being followed, and, as Nicholas Dames explains, "the sense of the novel as
a process rather than a structure was a fundamental part of Victorian novel
theory."[15] Victorians thought of novels and character both as processes
rather than fixed contents. So prose was of course the performative medium of characterization, part of the habitus of a person with character. Like
Ngai's categories, character was both performative and descriptive: character accrued as much to the assertion of its presence (this building or that
poem has character) or the iteration of the proper everyday words (the play
was typical, but interesting; she has a certain something about her, as if
I knew her already), as to any fixed attributes or properties belonging to
a given person or thing.[16] Victorian readers and writers tacitly adhered to
an epistemology of character according to which character was produced
by a repertoire of appropriate expressions, by the decorous treatment of
subjects rather than by any innate or essential property of the subjects
themselves.[17] That the style of a text could bear the weight of its moral,
aesthetic, scientific, and political character, independently of the character
of its content and its author, is consonant with the emergence of what
Elaine Hadley calls "liberal cognition" and "abstract embodiment" –
modes of liberal subjectivity that purported to liberate individuals' characters from their money, their estates, their ancestry, their gender and class,
their nationality and locality, even the received ideas of a political party.[18]
Like manners, everyday words liberated them also from interiority, as they
put the onus on relation, interface, and action rather than identity. In this
sense, *Everyday Words* echoes D. A. Miller's compelling description of the
"open secret" of "secret subjectivity," "a subject who can thus continue to
affirm his subjectivity *as a form* even where it no longer has a content of its
own."[19] Beyond the familiar components of "liberal cognition" itemized by
Hadley – "disinterestedness, objectivity, reticence, conviction, impersonality, and sincerity" (9) – and the disciplinary interiority described Miller,
I describe forms of asserting character via attention, inference, deference,
difference, self-reference, and suggestion, which are all tangential to direct
reference.

I turn to everyday words as my evidence for at least three reasons, the first two of which are historicist. First, my approach approximates a nineteenth-century reading practice. Nineteenth-century Britons were rapt with philology of all sorts, and extracting phrases – slang, dialect, pithy quotations, taglines, puns, neologisms – as parcels of self-evident, affective knowledge was rather more fundamental to their mode of reading than was anything that we would recognize as interpretation or critique. However necessarily inflected by the institution of modern academic literary scholarship, my process strikes a chord with this largely overlooked mode of reception.

Second, turning to everyday words also makes evidentiary sense because the history of reading is embedded in form: at once remarkably prevalent and yet more often than not unremarked upon, these are the words that most readers take for granted, and therefore they might best evidence the attitudes, moods, manners, and assumptions that their culture took most for granted. I describe many nineteenth-century essays that explicitly ascribe *character* to texts and attend to philological peculiarities, but most acts of reading leave their trace in style rather than explicit accounts. "The history of reading," Dames writes,

> could be discovered not (solely) in records of individual reading acts – marginalia, journal reviews, histories of criticism, commonplace books, and autobiographies – but ossified in the very form of texts themselves, in the genetic code, so to speak, of genre itself, which evolves in a reciprocal relation with the reading modes they determine and are in turn determined by. (29)

Everyday words "ossify" the epistemology of character accordingly, though character was not restricted to any one set of genres. Publishers, universities, associations, and the reading public expected books of all kinds to have character and to promote character in readers.[20] *Everyday Words* addresses many genres, but each chapter focuses on a particular novelist who parodies, questions, or otherwise foregrounds a particular stylistic tic as a medium of characterization affiliated with a specific form of mediation. They bear witness to how writers obliged the prescription for character without explicitly personifying their objects in the form of personages or didactically moralizing them.

Third, however, my approach respects the allure of the present. While the everyday words in this book had a specific historical valence in nineteenth-century Britain, whose reading practices were attuned to the epistemology of character that has been eclipsed, as I've said, by the double turn of Modernism toward psychological models of deep character and away from morality, they nevertheless remain common, and commonly taken for granted, features of everyday English prose. My attention to Dickens's "as if," for example, was accidentally prompted by a professor indulgently repeating "as it were" in a discussion of *Little Dorrit*, and plenty of television shows document the alacrity with which people ascribe "character" to houses, meals, commodities, and individuals. Everyday words retain their affordances as forms, as Caroline Levine might put it, even though the ideological heyday of character has passed.[21] Everyday words mark how historical assumptions, manners, and aesthetics inflect everyday life in the present, and so my methodology here also marks how historicism can responsibly intersect with presentism at the level of form, without forfeiting historical difference or reducing literary study to thematic comparisons.

My formal presentism with historical content shares Nietzsche's faith in slow philological reading as a moral, political, and enchanting practice requisite to "an age of 'work', that is, of hurry, of indecent and perspiring haste."[22] Nietzsche appraises this slowness – "*lento*," as he puts it – above conclusiveness, determination, and positive knowledge. The epistemology of character and *Everyday Words* are both about harboring "reservations, doors left open" (Nietzsche, 5) – forms of reading, writing, and being whose *lento* matters more than their takeaway, product, or accuracy of reproduction.

Is this close or distant, deep or surface reading?[23] I think it combines them all: it achieves distance by treating words that permeate nineteenth-century print and suggesting that my sustained interpretations tell us about all that print and not just individual novels; it attends to the surface by appreciating a surficial model of character as relations, manners, and processes, rather than the depth model of character, and more so by attending to the kind of artifact that Victorian readers tended to appreciate. Still, my readings certainly assume that deeper meanings – an epistemology, social conventions, moral ideology, and tacit aesthetic tastes – lie beneath and behind these words, and I do indeed privilege certain novels over the expansive corpus of nineteenth-century print. But I do not affect to expose or unveil some hidden identity. I aim to appreciate superficiality – manners, style, the prosaic – as mediums of an important, meaningful, moving form of knowledge that still affords us ways of negotiating a world that threatens to become too utilitarian and positivist. The idiom of characterization might help us responsibly legitimate our truth claims for fiction in a world all too liable to trade in blatant falsehoods and in universities all too bent on positivist, pragmatic, or commodifiable knowledges. Many of the chapters that follow touch upon how Victorian literary critics, at the advent of modern literary study, employed everyday words to characterize their work as genuine knowledge production in a world that seemed obsessed with facts and useful knowledge.

The latest appeal to positivism in literary studies comes via the Digital Humanities, which offer faster ways of gathering more data than actual reading. I merely make cursory use of searchable digital texts here to confirm the prevalence of words whose extraordinary frequency I noted the old-fashioned way, by slow reading; but I hope this book nevertheless models how technologically savvy data mining might serve interpretative ends without reducing literary scholarship to data and graphs, as if these numerical and visual representations were the only respectable forms of knowledge. Without interpretation and without respect for the kinds of knowledge inscribed within the formal rhythms and twists of prose, we risk forfeiting the now already tenuous epistemological value of the literary and the justification of our discipline. Prose produces meaning that is irreducible to numbers or to accurate correspondence to extra-textual reality, as Francis Galton discovered the hard way in "Hereditary Talent and Character" (1865), an essay which ineffectually attempts to explain originality of character by way of statistics culled from Sir Thomas Phillips's *The Million of Facts*. Certain things, including character, can only be known in distinction from facts.[24] The following five chapters thus offer not only an alternative history of character, but also an aesthetic theory of modern English prose as a distinct medium of knowledge production.

Chapter 1, "Darwin's View from Todgers's: 'A Decided Turn' for Character and Common Words," completes the introductory work of this Preface. It first exemplifies my methodology in an analysis of the word "turn" as Dickens parodies it at Todgers's boardinghouse in *Martin Chuzzlewit* and as it recurs in *Jane Eyre* and *The Mill on the Floss* but also in Darwin's *Origin of Species* and *Descent of Man*. These writings all mobilize *turn* as a figure of affective shock, rhetorical metabasis, histrionic gesture, and taxonomical relation that performatively evokes moral character and epistemic credibility. The chapter canvases the dizzying array of overlapping connotations at play in nineteenth-century uses of *character* and concludes by demonstrating its philological reading practices. Nineteenth-century writers such as Pierce Egan, Walter Pater, and George Meredith all raise inconspicuous locutions to the level of visibility and associate them with character.

My second chapter, "Inductive 'Attentions': Jane Austen in 'particular' and in 'general'," describes how Austen's fiction translates the idiom of induction from natural philosophical discourse, whose moral and epistemic credibility was indexed by its purportedly Baconian abstraction of generals from particulars, into a medium of social relations. Austen socializes *particular* and *general* in the form of *attention*, an everyday word that encompasses manners, affections, tastes, and degrees of interaction. The consilience of these various *attentions* – like the consilience of inductions later described by William Whewell – aptly explains the character that Austen's early reviewers ascribed to her fiction, whose realism is the effect of competing frequencies or scales of representation. I frame the discussion of Austen with accounts of the idiom of induction in eighteenth- and nineteenth-century natural philosophy and the emergent field of literary and aesthetic criticism. Critics such as Hazlitt, Horne, Pater, Masson, and others justified their writing as genuine knowledge production by affiliating it with induction and with characterization. The idiom of induction allowed them all to translate the epistemological problem of induction – how to generate empirically valid abstractions – and the modern problem of overwhelming data into an aesthetic value and a signature of credible intellectual labor.

Chapter 3, "'Our skeptical as if': Conditional Analogy and the Comportment of Victorian Prose," addresses the role of the conditional analogy in Victorian fiction and science writing. Looking first at Charles Lyell's *Principles of Geology*, it describes the way early Victorians legitimated regulative analogy as real knowledge in a culture skeptical of conjecture and wary of constitutive analogies. It then examines how Dickens ambivalently marshals *as if* as a principle medium of characterization, a medium for articulating how characters recognize but overwrite the factual world with their own fictional but no less real experience. Dickens's *as if* exemplifies how Victorian prose stands in relation to its subjects. It assumes not just an Adam Smithian sympathy, according to which we can only ever approximate knowledge of others, but also a regulative notion of experience. Concluding with a discussion of John Tyndall, the chapter shows how *as if* reconciled relativism, modernity, and empiricism with the demands of sympathy and sociality.

Chapter 4, "'Something' in the Way Realism Moves: *Middlemarch* and Oblique Character References," attends to missing referents in nineteenth-century literature, particularly George Eliot's *Middlemarch* (1872), which highlights *something* and *that sort of thing* as the signature features of both Mr. Brooke's flatness and Dorothea's depth. The idiom of *things* characterizes Eliot's world as poised between referentless detachment and the freedom of liberal self-representation. She shares this idiom with many novelists who employ *something* to stand in for the nexus where people and things, including prose and its readers, meet and are moved. After surveying a range of novels that also employ *something* to stand in for emotional contact, I turn briefly to the nineteenth-century discourse of realism, where Victorians employ *something* to account for the way prose moves them.

Finally, Chapter 5, "'Whoever explains a 'but'": Tact and Friction in Trollope's Reparative Fiction," describes how Anthony Trollope, above all novelists the one most affiliated with everyday life and with a documentary realism, employs *but* and other adversatives as a medium of tactful rebuttal. Trollope's *buts* allow him to touch upon without shamefully exposing his personages, whom he presents as "dual in character," as prone to good as bad. Trollope's style is therefore "reparative," in Eve Sedgwick's sense, to the extent that it finds interest in and affinity with all but its most egregiously immoral personages instead of delighting in shaming them. Adversatives extend this tact to everything in Trollope's fiction: they abet his productivity by tacking on clauses that contradict, qualify, or rebut the thrust of the preceding claims. Without rubbing anyone (except for maybe Henry James) the wrong way, Trollope's adversatives yield a frisson, a texture that resolves friction into ease. Given Trollope's reception and the wider use of *but* by Thackeray and others, this frisson seems to have been the feeling of everyday life, the prose correlative for the feeling of character in nineteenth-century Britain.

Abbreviations

Frequently referenced works are identified in parenthetical citations by the abbreviations below. Full references appear in the bibliography.

AA	*An Autobiography*
AB	*Adam Bede*
BH	*Bleak House*
BT	*Barchester Towers*
DC	*David Copperfield*
DM	*Descent of Man*
DT	*Doctor Thorne*
E	*Emma*
ED	*The Eustace Diamonds*
FP	*Framley Parsonage*
HT	*Hard Times*
LCB	*The Last Chronicle of Barset*
M	*Middlemarch*
MC	*Martin Chuzzlewit*
MF	*The Mill on the Floss*
MP	*Mansfield Park*
NA	*Northanger Abbey*
OMF	*Our Mutual Friend*
OS	*Origin of Species*
PP	*Pride and Prejudice*
SC	*Scenes of Clerical Life*
SS	*Sense and Sensibility*
TC	*The Three Clerks*
W	*The Warden*

CHAPTER I

Darwin's View from Todgers's
"A decided turn" for Character and Common Words

Under nature, the slightest differences of structure or constitution
may well *turn* the nicely-balanced scale in the struggle for life ... Let
us now *turn to* the nectar-feeding insects in our imaginary case.
– Charles Darwin, *Origin of Species*[1]

Whether I shall *turn out* to be the hero of my own life, or whether that
station will be held by anybody else, these pages must show.
– Charles Dickens, *David Copperfield*[2]

In the 1871 *Character*, one of a series of popular books on Puritan virtues,
Samuel Smiles seems to describe manners as legible, material symptoms of
people's real – because interiorized and hidden – self. "MANNER," he
writes, "is one of the principal external graces of character"; "A man's
manner, to a certain extent, indicates his character. It is the external
exponent of his inner nature. It indicates his taste, his feelings, and his
temper, as well as the society to which he has been accustomed."[3] Modern
readers are accustomed to interpret manners, like clothes, houses, and
physiognomies, as evidence of the secreted character of fictional personages
and real persons alike. And if we equate manners with style, correlating an
author's character with his or her manner of expression is at least as old as
Aristotle's explanation of *ethos* in *Poetics*. Hugh Blair reaffirms this correlation in his *Lectures on Rhetoric and Belles Lettres* (1783), which was reprinted
and taught throughout the nineteenth century. Indeed, Blair actually uses
"manner" and "character" interchangeably.[4] Smiles strains to emphasize
the personal individuality expressed – "to a certain extent" – by manners in
Blair's sense, but he remains cognizant that neither manners nor mannerisms are exclusive to individuals or interiority. They originate from
"society," and they are "external graces" – an "external exponent" not
because they are manifested outwardly, an exposure of privacy, but because
they are social conventions acquired from outside sources and because they
articulate the self in relation to society. Manners are generic social conventions for coordinating people and things, not for expressing individual

personality or quiddity. Accordingly, the "character" Smiles finds intimated here does not inhere in a private subject as his property, but instead
plays out at the interface of the subject and his or her culture, which makes
manners available in the first place.[5]

If manners intimate the interiority of anything, then they might be said to
intimate the interiority of the culture itself – which is to say, the shared but
unwritten assumptions that animate civil discourse and the attitudes, interests,
and mediums of contact bonding that culture as a whole. As Lionel Trilling
put it, manners are "that part of a culture which is made up of half-uttered or
unuttered or unutterable expressions of value. They are hinted at by small
actions, sometimes by the arts of dress or decoration, sometimes by tone,
gesture, emphasis, or rhythm, sometimes by the words that are used with
a special frequency or a special meaning."[6] "Our attitude toward manners,"
Trilling adds, "is the expression of a particular conception of reality" (206,
207). Steven Shapin has more recently elaborated such claims for manners in
describing what he calls "epistemological decorum": the styles of civil discourse and comportment that were requisite to producing legitimate knowledge in early-modern British culture.[7] Nineteenth-century Britain had its
own conventions of epistemological decorum, which implicitly obliged
writers to *characterize* their subjects, however non-human these seemed to
be. Characterization in this sense meant affirming that a given approach to
a subject redounded morality upon a practitioner, author, or reader, and
installing also an affinity or interest in the subject that solicited the sympathetic attention of others. Manners contributed to the production of fiction
and non-fiction alike, then, because they were, as stylistic requisites of
characterization, stylistic requisites of publication. Everyday words implied
that certain scientific and interpretive methods cultivated the "character" –
the morality, veracity, and aesthetic interest – that the same words purportedly inscribed into fictional personages. But not exclusively the familiar
deep, anthropomorphic character we have come to take for granted . . .

Turn and *character* are, in nineteenth-century British prose, "words that
are used with a special frequency," to quote Trilling once again. In a culture
obsessed with popular philology, *turn* was one of the manners by which
prose asserted its character. As characters in the natural historical sense,
everyday locutions like "a turn" concurrently refer to and differ from
a recognizable category to intimate a residual particularity, deviation, or
non-referential surplus: an inference, self-reference, deference, or difference from the generic. As a medium of characterization, *turns* enable a text
simultaneously to refer mimetically like a fact to concrete, reproducible,
familiar things, and yet at the same time to diverge discretely from the

referential to some abstract, irreproducible, or unfamiliar quirk. Where the veracity and the morality of the modern fact both depended on real-world referents as guarantors, character was a form of knowledge whose legitimacy instead owed to the manner in which it deviated from or mediated its referents – to implied induction, attention, self-reference, conditional conjecture, or tactful rebuttal. It was a form of knowledge that depended on a formal *turn* from an empirically understood reality.

Character of a "decided turn"

In *Martin Chuzzlewit* (1843–44), Charles Dickens assembles some bachelor gentlemen at Todgers's boardinghouse for Sunday dinner with the hypocritical Mr. Pecksniff and his daughters, Charity and Mercy. Evoking the opening line of the *Odyssey*, which introduces Odysseus as "a man of many turns" (*polytropos*, in the ancient Greek), Dickens individuates each bachelor by granting him "a decided turn" for one of various incongruous hobbies, habits, and tastes. These guests, he writes,

> included a gentleman of a sporting turn, who propounded questions on jockey subjects to the editors of Sunday papers, which were regarded by his friends as rather stiff things to answer; and they included a gentleman of a theatrical turn, who had once entertained serious thoughts of "coming out", but had been kept in by the wickedness of human nature; and they included a gentleman of a debating turn, who was strong at speech-making; and a gentleman of a literary turn, who wrote squibs upon the rest, and knew the weak side of everybody's character but his own. There was a gentleman of a vocal turn, and a gentleman of a smoking turn, and a gentleman of a convivial turn; some of the gentlemen had a turn for whist, and a large proportion of the gentlemen had a strong turn for billiards and betting. They had all, it may be presumed, a turn for business; being all commercially employed in one way or another; and had, every one in his own way, a decided turn for pleasure to boot. Mr. Jinkins was of a fashionable turn; being a regular frequenter of the Parks on Sundays, and knowing a great many carriages by sight . . . Mr. Gander was of a witty turn.[8]

And so on. As with Odysseus, the character of the bachelors accrues to the repetition of a kind of epithet, but whereas Odysseus as "a man of many turns" incorporates these many turns in his person, the bachelors only achieve that versatility and variety collectively. As individuals they appear atomized and myopic, not to mention shabby. Thus, Dickens diffuses the compelling adaptability of the classical, single protagonist, as if to characterize his prose rather than any of the individual personages it describes.

If the less-than-fetching bachelors even as a group seem a far cry from Odysseus, the range of historical translations of *polytropos* suggests otherwise. By the fifth century BCE the interpretation of the "the *polytropic* man," the man "of many turns," had already become controversial.[9] As the classicist W. B. Stanford explains, "Odysseus's detractors" interpreted the epithet "pejoratively as 'often changing one's character, hence unstable, unprincipled, unscrupulous'"; but Antisthenes, a student of Socrates, "rallied to Odysseus's defense" by claiming "*polytropos* . . . does not refer to character or ethics at all. It simply denotes Odysseus's skill in adapting his figures of speech ('tropes') to his hearers at any particular time" (Stanford 99). Modern classicists typically reject these early translations for an interpretation that melds plot and psychological character: Odysseus has been turned many times by circumstances from his intended course, and therefore he is defined by the detours that defer his return to Ithaca. These experiential turns constitute the plot and inflect his psyche. With this range of ostensibly disparate connotations, the famous epithet aptly condenses some of the array of connotations that Victorians ordinarily mobilized with the word *character*: various notions of dynamic and essential personality, fixed moral principle, rhetorical dexterity (turns of phrase), affective experience or the feeling of contingency, and the ethical valences affiliated with each.

Furthermore, Dickens's arch recourse to "a turn" also performs the taxonomical work of distinction and genealogy: each *turn* concurrently individuates a bachelor and likewise categorizes him as a recognizable species of the London bachelor or genus of commercial gentleman.[10] The taxonomic paradox of concomitant individuality and typicality is perhaps the most common dimension of eighteenth- and nineteenth-century character: its signature individuality is packaged and legible only in conventional forms.[11] From the classical period through the seventeenth century, types were known through the genre of the Theophrastan character, a verbal portrait or sketch of an exemplary personification of a virtue, vice, or vocation. Theophrastan characters typically begin with the phrase "such a one who."[12] Evident in Aristotle's *Rhetoric* and *Poetics*, these characters were revitalized in Jean de La Bruyère's popular *Caractères* (1688) and in books by Sir Thomas Overbury, Nicholas Breton, and Samuel Butler, all of which were in print throughout the nineteenth century. Henry Morley, for instance, published in 1891 an anthology, *Character Writings of the 17th Century*. Individuals were often conceived as combinations or variations of these types, as the bachelors combine each of their various hobbies, vocations, or habits with the nearly oxymoronic categories of commercial and gentleman, which were traditionally defined in opposition to each other. The paradox of joint individuality and typicality applies to the characterization of personages as well as objects: as it happens, Todgers's boardinghouse is "such a singular sort of place," yet, as the subsequent sentence nevertheless says, it belongs to an "odd family" of "hundreds and thousands" (*MC* 131). The recurrent *turn* thus underscores the generic form of character that the bachelors and buildings have in common: all of their ostensibly particular interests are formulaically articulated as "a turn" for this or that, and as such these tastes become legible as manifestations of character. At least at the level of prose: if the bachelors themselves seem like caricatures, character here emerges as a matter of form, a formality or manner, more than the implied content of symptomatic mannerisms.

While Dickens's characterization of the bachelors seems to climax definitively and facetiously with the bachelors' consummate "passion for gravy" – "There is no such passion in human nature," Mrs. Todgers proclaims (*MC* 135) – his savvy repetition of *turn* suggests, to the contrary, that the definitive feature of human nature is not a passion at all, but instead the formal paradox instantiated in the generic "turn" that makes humanity legible as such. Through the parody of repetition, that is to say, the dinner at Todgers's suggests that the "characters" Dickens forwards here are not so much the bachelors themselves as individual personages, but the iterative turn of phrase – the trope – that make them legible as such. "A turn" was shorthand, among other things, for such taxonomic traits: Jane Eyre, for instance, seeks in Adèle's "countenance and features a likeness to Mr. Rochester, but found none: no trait, no turn of expression announced relationship."[13] The whole novel abounds in characterological turns, including the kind that classify the Todgers's bachelors: Eliza Reed has "a turn for traffic," Mary Ann Wilson "had a turn for narrative, [and Jane] for analysis" (*JE* 38, 91). As pivot point between individuality and typicality, the iterative "turn" is a character in the natural historical sense.[14]

As Foucault writes, taxonomic characters are marks "selected to be the locus of pertinent identities and differences"; "the character, as established by natural history," he adds, "makes it possible both to indicate the individual and to situate it in a space of generalities that fit inside one another" (140, 159). In the domain of natural history, then, character names a physical feature that usefully instantiates "the relation between visible structure and criteria of identity," for the objective of natural history "is still to determine the 'character' that groups individuals and species into more general units, that distinguishes those units one from another, and that enables them to fit together to form a table in which all individuals and all groups, known or unknown, will have their appropriate place" (Foucault 226). Natural history and novels alike were invested in characterization, inasmuch as they both sought to isolate features that could articulate individuals in relation to species. As literature and science had not yet been disaggregated into "two cultures," throughout the nineteenth century the novelistic and natural historical connotations of character more readily overlapped and evoked each other.

Form and method were theoretically inseparable from morality and epistemic validity for mainstream Victorians, because credibility was deemed a function of following methods and adhering to form. Part of the importance of the colloquialism or everyday word accrued to its habitualness, which underscored the moral valence of style. Smiles repeatedly describes character as a function of habits in *Self-Help*, and James Fitzjames Stephen writes in "The Relation of Novels to Life" (1855) that "the most important differences between men are differences of habit. What we call character is little else than a collection of habits, whether their formation is to be traced to original organic differences or to any other causes."[15] This theory of habits suggests a performative conception of character as the effect of, rather than the agency behind, gestures, behaviors, and utterances. Up until the point where such locutions become frequent enough to be noticed, and therefore to become parody as "a turn" becomes in *Martin Chuzzlewit*, they also constitute a habit of the author and therefore could bolster (or attenuate) his or her morality. However farcical, then, as a recurrent, colloquial phrase, "a turn" makes the tastes and occupations of the gentleman at Todgers's coherent as habits. This particular phrase also happens to denote a habit or tendency as well as a deviation from the norm; its repetition in a text makes it a habit, but a habit of switching track, transitioning, or adapting like Odysseus. Dickens's style suggests that the formation of such habits originates neither in organic differences – an essential self or romantic germ of identity – nor in social influences or circumstances of the sort Stephen seems to have in mind, but in everyday language itself, in the manners a writer adopts from, in order to relate to, his culture.

I have been focusing on the bachelors, but variants of "turn" turn up 310 times in *Martin Chuzzlewit*, including several instances in the well-known description of the view from Todgers's boardinghouse, a hallmark of discussions of Dickensian realism and anthropomorphism since at least the 1853 article, "Balzac and his Writing" in *The Westminster Review*. Dorothy Van Ghent made the "View from Todgers's" an iconographic image of a certain variant of realism in her influential 1950 essay of that name, which describes with Lukác's Marxist nostalgia the ironic alienation inscribed in Dickens's persistent animations of matter and reifications of personages.[16] Van Ghent describes Dickens's world as a hallucinatory, demonic, or otherwise symptomatic expression of a culture in which things are monstrously inaccessible to, and yet threatening and impinging upon, people; Dickens's continual turning of spirit into matter intimates that substance has trumped significance, excess matter has displaced meaning (424). To an extent, the idiom of turns bolsters this perspective: atop Todgers's, a hypothetical observer "turning round" restlessly abides the panoramic view and, finally "after gazing, round him, quite scared, he turned back into Todgers's again" (*MC* 133–34). Inflections of the word *turn* modulate Dickens's dizzying cartography, comprising the meandering London streets and the misshapen buildings and trees they adjoin as well as the bewildered characters that perambulate them. Another hypothetical stranger looking for Todgers's suffers "resigned distraction . . . as he trod those devious mazes, and, giving him up for lost, went in and out and round about, and quietly turned back again" (131). The modern world seems to turn away from people.

As instable and rotatory as the "revolving," "crook-backed," and "askew" chimney-pots and other architectural elements (*MC* 134), then, are the personages who turn gravely and gayly, gray and insolent, over, round, around, back, against, from, toward, away, into, down, up, out, cold, pale, dark, crimson, and deeply red throughout the novel. Whether turning a key, turning their faces, turning on their heels, turning colors, turning their overflowing and languid eyes, or turning to another; whether suffering a turn, as in a shock, or taking a turn, as in a walk; whether turning out or returning, Dickens's characters relate to each other, themselves, and their environments in terms of the word *turn*. Turning is their principle form of mediation, their principle affect and attitude. *Pace* Van Ghent, then, I think the meaning – or value – evoked by this scene resides neither in the personages nor the objects by which the persons have been alienated, but rather in the persistent turning by which these categories interact, in the trope that keeps subjects and objects in flux. Still channeling Lukács, Van Ghent observes that the moral import of Dickens's "art" comes not from characters but from the "total aesthetic occasion" in which Dickens transposes "a great deal of 'inner life' . . . to other forms than that of character" (423); but "inner life" is an inadequate, specious synonym for "meaning," moral import, and aesthetics here, where the prose privileges figurative and flexible contact, exchange, and sinuous attachment far above innerness. Nineteenth-century writers routinely insisted on recognizing these "other forms" as "character" because they did not restrict character to personages, because these other forms were modes of description expressly aligned with characterization, and because texts were expected to cultivate character in readers.

Like many nineteenth-century novelists, Dickens routinely foregrounds, even mocks the fundamental features of his more amiable and allegedly realistic characters by caricaturing them in variously disagreeable, morally and stylistically inadequate, or flat characters inhabiting the same novels. So Sairey Gamp, the tipsy midwife/nurse/mourner, exemplifies the penchant for turning in her ready adaptation to the condition of her clients but also in her "remarkable power of turning up, and only showing the white of [her] moist eye" (*MC* 303, cf. 308). Perhaps excepting only Sam Weller, Mrs. Gamp exceeds all of Dickens's characters in memorable malapropisms; and, among other idiosyncratic verbal tics, she makes a "familiar phrase" of "to turn and turn about; one off, one on," a phrase "of which she must regularly discharge herself" (729). "If you should turn at all faint," Mrs. Gamp promises to "soon rewive you" by turning: "Bite a person's thumbs, or turn their fingers the wrong way," she explains, "and they comes to, wonderful, Lord bless you!" (666). In diagnosing Sweedlepipe's brains to be "topjy turjey" (which is to say, topsy turvy), she slurs the title of Chapter 52, "In which the Tables are Turned, completely Upside down" (759). The explicit comedy of the dinner at Todgers's and Mrs. Gamp's inebriate idiom might invite us to take them merely as jokes instead of earnest, metacritical reflections on the art, affect, and epistemology of character and characterization. But I have been referring to them as parody because, as Carolyn Williams explains, melodramatic parody – whether silly, sentimental, or serious – commemorates and preserves established conventions even as it critiques them; parody, that is to say, indicates when specific generic conventions have become recognizable and usable as such, but without disabling them.[17]

The parody in the Todgers's scene and in Gamp's speech indicates that "a turn" had become so prevalent as to become recognizable to Dickens as a generic index of characterization. The manners of characterization became mannerisms in their excess. In other words, Gamp's drunken linguistic eccentricities, like those of many Victorian characters, only accentuate the quirkiness of common, sober discourse and ordinary behavior. Narrators and mundane characters alike use colloquialisms like Gamp's shorthand for convalescence, to "bring *him* round" (*MC* 440, emphasis in original); and, as I have said, everyone and everything in

Dickens's world turns and returns. Indeed, *Martin Chuzzlewit* includes an additional 315 instances of "returned," one of Dickens's favored speech tags, and 89 instances of "return," "returns," and "returning," such that the novel portrays reality as a process of parrying, exchanging, redoubling, and twisting, rather than as a fixed property or identity. As a speech tag, especially, "return" implies that dialogue is less an expression of interiority than of interaction, given that *turn* was slang for "actor." Dickensian conversation puts an emphasis on "verse." *Martin Chuzzlewit* includes a few inward turns, to be sure, but things also happen by turns and in turn. Events and people turn out one way or another. Characters suffer turns; follow turns of thought; turn incidents to account; and theatrically turn themselves every which way.

But as I have hinted with *Jane Eyre*, *turn* by no means belongs exclusively to *Martin Chuzzlewit* and its eccentrics. In *The Old Curiosity Shop* (1840–1), Kit Nubbles is "by no means of a sentimental turn," Thomas Codlin has a "misanthropical turn of mind," and Sally Brass's mind is "of a strong and vigorous turn."[18] In *Great Expectations* (1860–61), just before being "turned upside down" by Magwitch and "long before the days of photographs," before the hegemony of mimetic correspondence and mass reproduction, Pip "unreasonably derived" his father and mother "from their tombstones": "The shape of the letters on my father's," he explains, "gave me an odd idea that he was a square, stout, dark man with curly black hair. From the character and turn of the inscription, '*Also Georgiana Wife of the Above*,' I draw a childish conclusion that my mother was freckled and sickly."[19] If mature Pip retroactively belittles his "childish" conclusion, the novel nevertheless offers it as a genuine insight in which *turn* links *character* as a typographical mark to *character* as personality: the scene intimates how readers can only conjure character from the turn of Dickens's inscriptions.

The first sentence of *David Copperfield* skeptically parodies the *Odyssey*, asking "Whether [David himself] shall turn out to be the hero of [his] own life" (9). And David's becoming "such a determined character" (*DC* 445) requires him "to turn the painful discipline of my younger days to account" (439). The capitalistic *Bildung* of this turning "to account" is prevalent and ambivalent in Victorian writing. It summarily reports coming to fruition, becoming, arriving, or maturing, but often in a mechanistic sense. In *Hard Times* (1854), for example, Mr. M'Choakumchild "and some one hundred and forty other schoolmasters, had been latterly turned, at the same time, in the same factory, on the same principles, like so many pianoforte legs."[20] *Character* here again carries the double valence of mass-produced typicality and utter individuality. On the one hand, that is to say, Dickens evokes Carlyle's assertion in "Signs of the Times" (1829): "Men are grown mechanical in head and heart, as well as in hand ... Their whole efforts, attachments, opinions, turn on mechanism, and are of a mechanical character";[21] on the other hand, he underscores – like Carlyle again – how the nostalgic ideal of a natural, un-mechanized human character nevertheless depends rather mechanically on the same idiom.[22]

George Eliot employs this mechanistic ambivalence in her markedly natural historical characterization of Tom and Maggie Tulliver in *The Mill on the Floss* (1860):

> He was *one of those* lads that grow everywhere in England, – a lad with light-brown hair, cheeks of cream and roses, full lips, indeterminate nose and eyebrows – a physiognomy in which it seems impossible to discern anything but the *generic character* of boyhood; as different as possible from poor Maggie's phiz, which Nature seemed to have moulded and coloured with the most decided intention. ... Under these average boyish physiognomies [Nature] seems to *turn off by the gross*, she conceals some of her most rigid, inflexible purposes, some of her most *unmodifiable characters*; and the dark-eyed, demonstrative, rebellious girl may after all *turn out* to be a passive being compared with this pink-and-white bit of masculinity with the indeterminate features.[23]

Here in explicitly natural historical terms of "modifiable characters," Eliot suggests that the indeterminate, generic, even ostensibly homogenous character, the figure that simultaneously marks identity and difference, might have more "purpose" than what appears to be the divergent individual. The genre of boys "turned out by the gross" can conceal more power than the Bildungsroman Maggies who "all turn out" as ostensibly unique individuals.

Industrial, individual, or both, character was deemed a function of processes of production, disclosure, and transformation, rather than an inherent property. For Samuel Smiles in *Character*, turning need never produce anything complete to produce character:

> We have spoken of work as a discipline: it is also an educator of character. Even work that produces no results, because it is work, is better than torpor – inasmuch as it educates faculty, and is thus preparatory to successful work. The habit of working teaches method. It compels economy of time, and the disposition of it with judicious forethought. And when the art of packing life with useful occupations is once acquired by practice, every minute will be turned to account; and leisure, when it comes, will be enjoyed with greater zest. (110)

The content of this figurative "account" remains elusive because the *turning* matters more than any product it yields in Smiles's capitalist moral economy. The *turning* is the character.

If, as Kent Puckett has said, the form of the nineteenth-century novel relies on the "bad form" of its characters, on the various petty solecisms and social mistakes whose representation produces "a range of coherence effects at the related levels of character, plot, and narration" (4), then the colloquial or linguistic consistency between novels whose styles of representation otherwise seem rather different suggests that good form on the level of style was – in turn – requisite to the social coherence of novel-reading, and indeed reading of any sort. Put another way, if within novels such as *Martin Chuzzlewit* and *Jane Eyre* and *The Mill on the Floss* repeated everyday words acquire a sort of lyric effect as internal allusions, their repetition across different novels and indeed genres suggests that they were signatures of a coherent if tacit epistemology of character. In this epistemology, character designated not an identity, essence, or property of an individual entity, but the formal relation of multiple entities, human or otherwise, turning to and away from each other.

Darwin's Rhetorical and Affective Turns

The affiliation of character with *turns* extends beyond fiction and self-help genres to natural history, where it abounds at the level of diction and also at the level of theme. Charles Darwin, to take a notable example, has frequent recourse to "turn" in *On the Origin of Species* (1859) and *The Descent of Man* (1871), which elaborates the ways morality in its widest sense bridges humans and other animals.[24] Turning might well be a common movement, but Darwin attends so frequently to it that he seems as if he tacitly accepts the movement as a conventional signature of moral activity. He privileges turns and returns as crucial evidence of the moral life of organisms: he routinely observes the ways organisms turn about in mating rituals, express feelings with turns to and from each other and from humans, turn objects as they feed, possess physical features with turns in them, and so on. And, of course, his overarching argument explains evolutionary and metamorphic turns: phylogenic and ontological divergence and species change.

Darwin discusses all of these turns in terms of "characters," the traits selected by natural historians as pertinent sites of meaningful identity and difference. He repeats that species and varieties are entirely "vague and arbitrary" classifications (*OS* 48, 49–52), a remark which echoes how David Copperfield's mature, "determined character" manifests itself in learning the stenographical art of shorthand, with its "procession of new horrors, called arbitrary characters; the most despotic characters I have ever known" (*DC* 445, 460). The same epistemology underwrites the apparently distinct connotations of *character* as scriptural mark and taxonomic feature. Darwin makes clear that natural historical characters are not necessarily the definitive properties of an organism, not its most essential qualities, but instead those features that best orient the organism in relation to other species, varieties, or genera. I have likewise been suggesting that for Victorians character was far less a matter of content, of a person's definitive personality or interiority, a text's explicit subjects, or an object's essence or nature than posterity has assumed, and more a matter of relation or mediation implicit in specific features of style. Gleaning the character of a book or a person or a whale was not a matter of mimetically representing its most definitive features, but of selecting the trivial formal signature by which he, she, or it relates to everything else. Darwin's characters can be redundant, residual, or as useless to the organism as David's shorthand symbols appears to the things they represent. And yet both characters prove to be utterly instrumental to the work of Darwin and David: Darwin's characters evidence natural selection and the genealogy of morality; David's enable him to read character just as Dickens does, through non-essential but telling mannerisms, like Gamp's turn for a tipple.

Darwin, moreover, shares with Dickens a rhetorical investment in *turns*, as if his methodology and style evoke moral and epistemic character by recapitulating what he has to say about natural historical divergence of character and what he observes in nature. Whether writing of the origins of human life or of the matchless passion for gravy, whether by Darwin or Dickens, nineteenth-century prose aspired to have character; and that character was less a matter of consistent content, identifiable purpose, or ideology, less a matter of the delineation of personages or the definitive quiddity of things, than of manifesting the rhetorical manners and attitudes that properly addressed and arranged them. Many genres of writing include no personages at all, and yet all nineteenth-century writings were tacitly obliged to instantiate character stylistically – in their "treatment" or "manner" – especially when their content was morally suspect. Recall Henry James's insistence in "The Art of Fiction" that the morality of novels owes to their execution, not their subject matter.[25] This imperative obtained for Lyell's new geology and Darwin's development hypothesis as much as for Hardy's and Eliot's fictions of infanticide and philandering. Victorian reviews and prefaces evidence that character was an evaluative category for adjudicating all sorts of books, including scientific, philosophical, and economic works without any explicit purchase on morality or human subjectivity.[26] The character these books tender was not simply credibility and moral probity, but also an epistemic and aesthetic deviation from accepted, conventional opinion – a deviation enunciated by *turns*, among the other everyday words I discuss in later chapters. The character of a text combined how it mediated the author's ethos – its feeling, manner, and attitude to the reader – and its method of producing knowledge (turning, induction, conditional analogy, tactful rebuttal, etc.) and how this combination related to and deviated – which is to say, turned – from common sense, generic expectations, prevailing opinion, probability, and even its own suppositions or tracks of thought.

Darwin's *turn* in the *Descent of Man* is to attend to the biological, ritual, and social performances of morality that some of his contemporaries were otherwise inclined to ascribe restrictively to an interiorized will or consciousness. The characters of most interest to *The Descent of Man* are those affective features – behavioral and physical – that index analogous emotional, moral, and social feelings in humans and non-humans. If non-human organisms have interiority, Darwin excuses it from analysis because it is inaccessible, but also because he is more ardently invested in the social and inter-special relations of organisms. He was far more invested in the common than in the private, the generic more than the singular variety, because the idiosyncratic variations that mattered were those that survived into subsequent generations. Darwin's turn in *The Descent of Man* to a social and animal human genealogically and morally related to other species was the natural historical correlative to the nostalgic longing for a theatrical, public, communal life that David Kurnick registers in the novel of interiority.[27] Darwin portrays the model of moral life he inherits as a depressive, isolated descent indeed from that he describes vividly at play in the histrionic behaviors of other organisms.

So in the *Origin* "the slightest differences of structure or constitution" – which is to say the variations or mutations that taxonomists label "characters" – "may well turn the nicely-balanced scale in the struggle of life" (*OS* 77). These differences that "turn the scale" include many *turns*. Metamorphic *turns* are clearly paramount: Darwin inventories many adaptations or mutations and physical modifications that species undergo during breeding season in order to captivate and mate with others: the turn from one shade of color to another brighter color or the turn of a salmon's mouth from a defensive curve to an offensive, hooked beak. In a section of the *Origin* on transitional species and modes of transition, as if presciently offering a mascot for this revisionist account of character, he observes how, "In the Hydra, the animal may be turned inside out, and the exterior surface will then digest and the stomach respire" (159). The orientation of the turn here determines the function of the Hydra's organs; the orientation is not merely symptomatic of a causal function. Darwin elsewhere observes how some rock pigeons are "turn-crowned" (138) and later supposes "the Melipona," a stingless bee, "to have the power of forming her cells truly spherical, and of equal sizes ... seeing what perfectly cylindrical burrows many insects make in wood, apparently by turning round on a fixed point" (188). Subsequent editions of the *Origin* even revise several different phrases into variants of *turn*, as if Darwin was working to meet a quota: there are 57 instances of the phrase in the first edition and 72 in the sixth edition of 1872.

The Descent of Man (1870) does not precisely refer in Dickensian terms to primates "of a sentimental turn" or to ants with "a decided turn" for altruism and for aphids, though it does indeed say all of this in other words. And this book is also awash with related forms of "turns." It twice discusses the ostensibly altruistic way Hamadryads help each other "turn" over rocks to find insects (*DM* 70, 124). It describes the way hung-over baboons, like hung-over people, "turn" with disgust from beer or wine the day after a bender (24). It likewise discusses how some dogs "easily turn sulky" but all return the affection bestowed upon them and turn ashamed from their masters after misbehaving (90). Echoing Dickens and Eliot, Darwin quizzes an animal trainer at the Zoological Society about how he discerns "whether a particular monkey would turn out a good actor" (95). Were he actually Dickens, we might mistrust the authenticity of Professor Turner, to whom he often refers, but alas the name seems to refer to a real man.

Turning is the privileged gesture in which Darwin perceives the evolution of animal affect into erotic feeling, a libidinal gesture reproduced in varying degrees by all of the everyday words I describe herein, especially "something." Describing the courtship rituals of birds, Darwin observes how the male goldfinch "sways his body from side to side, and quickly turns his slightly expanded wings first to one side, then to the other, with a golden flashing effect" (*DM* 452). In yet another passage that describes *Thysanura*, an Order that was supposed to link winged and wingless insects,[28] Darwin quotes naturalist John Lubbock detailing two springtails "coquetting together":

> the female pretends to run away and the male runs after her with a queer appearance of anger, gets in front and stands facing her again; then she turns coyly round, but he, quicker and more active, scuttles round too ... they stand face to face, play with their antennae, and seem to be all in all to one another. (322)

In this array of examples, Darwin correlates character with dexterity and helpfulness; with shame, love, loyalty, guilt, and revulsion; with rituals of flirtation, coyness, and courtship; with evanescent interest and intensity; and with development, progression, recapitulation, and variation; all of which share the verb *turn*.

Physical turns to and from and around other creatures; returns to ancestral characters or origins; and metamorphic turns have their sociological equivalents in the remarkably gestured *turns* that novelistic characters take with each other. Consider *Jane Eyre* again, which mostly indulges in histrionic bodily turns but also invokes the sequential connotation of *turn* as part of a Puritanical moral order – Eliza Reed advises Georgiana, for instance, "Take one day; share it into sections; to each section apportion its task: leave no stray unemployed quarters of an hour, ten minutes, five minutes – include all; do each piece of business in its turn with method, with rigid regularity" (*JE* 265). To suffer a turn in *Jane Eyre* is to feel the affective shock of another's presence and difference: Rochester claims to suffer from Bertha "a turn at once coarse and trite, perverse and imbecile" (344). But the most pronounced interpersonal intensities of the novel transpire in Masterpiece-Theater-worthy sequences of affective and gestural *turns*. Jane frets that Rochester "would never once turn his eyes in my direction" (210), but in midsummer when she is avoiding Rochester's detection, he summons her to "Turn back," as if his shadow could feel (280), and stroll the laurel walk toward the notorious horse-chestnut tree. During this turn (as in walk), he proposes in an exchange replete with affective, characterological *turns*:

> "You, Jane, I must have you for my own – entirely my own. Will you be mine? Say yes, quickly."
> "Mr. Rochester, let me look at your face: turn to the moonlight."
> "Why?"
> "Because I want to read your countenance – turn!"
> "There! you will find it scarcely more legible than a crumpled, scratched page. Read on: only make haste, for I suffer" (286)

As if "turning over the leaves of [a] book" (*JE* 14, 29), which of course Jane also does, she and Rochester turn each other's actions, bodies, and faces to make "legible" their intentions and their physically embodied character. Indeed, Brontë might be said to personify the implied reader's experience of the scene as a "page-turner" in the imperative *turns* of this interaction. Rochester subsequently worries Jane will "turn cool" and asks, "Why do you smile, Jane? What does that inexplicable, that uncanny turn of countenance mean?" (292, 293). Harboring his secrets, Rochester wields a kind of hermeneutics of suspicion; he insists faces should mean and not be, and that their meaning is by definition hidden. More sincere, Jane assumes words might well conceal hidden intentions but that character will be plainly evident in Rochester's turning countenance. Whether deep or surficial, secret or symptomatic, however, character manifests for both Rochester and Jane in movement – in voluntary and involuntary *turns* to and from and about, *turns* warm and cold, white and red, uncanny, and so on.

The Mill on the Floss also exemplifies the way *turns* enact Darwinian sociality, courtship, and what we now might call affective interaction. The novel is pervaded by *turns*,[29] but one short stretch about the vacillating intentions, emotions, and uncomfortably involved bodies of Maggie, Philip, and Stephen marshals ten instances of the word in its different forms. First, Eliot describes the "turn" of an old-fashioned dance, followed by "a turn" as in a walk up and down the conservatory taken by Maggie and Stephen (*MF* 356, 357). Such *turns* are staples of nineteenth-century fiction, from Austen through Meredith, and of course Jane Eyre takes more than her fair share, as when, seeking change, "Feverish with vain labour, [she] got up and took a turn in the room" (*JE* 100–1).

But at the end of Maggie's turn with Stephen, she turns to him: "Something strangely powerful there was in the light of Stephen's long gaze," Eliot writes, "for it made Maggie's face turn towards it and look upward at it – slowly, like a flower at the ascending brightness" (*MF* 357). This phototrophic exchange, where Maggie's bloom comes as relief from the "rather dizzy work" (357) of the dance and many months of repression, concludes in an additional knot of *turns*. Their "long grave mutual gaze which has the solemnity belonging to all deep human passion" is interrupted by "the end of the conservatory," where they "were obliged to pause and turn. The change of movement brought a new consciousness to Maggie: she blushed deeply, turned away her head, and drew her arm from Stephen's, going up to some flowers to smell them" (357). The conventional *turn* of dances and walks here culminates, altogether according to convention, in the breaking of convention with a transgressive kiss. Turning bodies, turning thoughts, turning plots: the intensity of the passage derives from the density of its movements – its fluid glances, steps, inclinations, and moods.

The density of movements and the comparative paucity of direct narrative description of interiority here force character to play out in the interface between these two rather than within each separately. After the kiss, "Stephen turned away" (*MF* 358) and yet the next day occasions yet another theatrical "turn" in the lane outside Mrs. Moss's house. This passage begins with a small jolt of a turn, "a slight start, such as might have come from the slightest possible electric shock" (361), climaxes in a more fateful kiss, and throughout echoes Lubbock's courting springtails. The emotional walk includes so many *turns* to and away from each other that, comically, "Tancred, the bay horse, began to make such spirited remonstrance against this frequent change of direction" (362). With Tancred, Eliot is as sensitive as Dickens to the fine line between generic characterization and caricature, manner and mannerism, prose and parody. She laughs at the very "frequent change of direction" on which characterization depends.

Perhaps Wordsworth deserves some credit, after Homer, for establishing the *turn* as a generic medium of characterization. He was particularly influential with Darwin and Eliot, and *The Excursion* (1814), which was immensely well received by Victorian readers, indulgently iterates all of the everyday words in this book even as it forwards a notion of surficial or relational character. Indeed, the comparative disregard of *The Excursion* in the twentieth century may well owe to its preference for a surficial model of character over the psychological depth and sublimity that predominates *The Prelude* (1850).[30] By *turns, The Excursion* expresses the familiar moralization of interiority as self-reflecting germ, "the mind / Turned inward," but also the empiricist concept of the mind as the accumulation of impressions from the senses turned outward: "Nor did he fail, / while yet a child, with a child's eagerness / Incessantly to turn his ear and eye / On all things which the moving seasons brought."[31] The restless, wandering characters turn this way and that, in a geographical and theatrical sense, but also turn in the sense of "rely upon" or "resort to" things (Wordsworth II: 69).[32] "Turn" also conflates for Wordsworth the social practices of exchange, sharing, and order (taking turns) with ecological relationships of reciprocity, concerted earthly and celestial movement: "elements [that] mingle in their turn / With this commotion" (Wordsworth II: 135).[33] All of these senses meld in the transformative and Odysseus-like sense of the word: "Our life is turned / Out of her course" (II: 271). And Wordsworth moreover makes use of the phrase for rhetorical transitions from one subject to the next: "But from her I turn" (II: 216) and "Turn we then / To Britons born and bred" (II: 261).

If physical turns manifest the moral, social, and aesthetic character of Maggies and Stephens and baboons and birds, rhetorical "turns" like this last of Wordsworth's persistently manifest the moral, social, and aesthetic character of *The Origin of Species* and *The Descent of Man* as works of writing that deliberately move their readers from one subject to the next. Darwin's topical attention to turns is, in other words, subordinate only to his rhetorical recapitulation of that evidentiary investment. He has a remarkable, almost mechanical penchant for changing topics and moving between examples with variants of the phrases "Turning now to" and "to return to." He writes: "Let us turn now to the nectar-feeding insects" (*OS* 85); "Turning for a brief space to animals" (89); "Turning to the sea" (279); "Turning to the Invertebrata" and "Turning to plants" (264, 311);[34] "Turning now to the nearest allies of men" (*DM* 69); "If we turn to nature" (*OS* 93); "We will now turn to the more intellectual emotions and faculties" (*DM* 92, cf. 154); "Turning to the other kind of evidence" (*DM* 171); "if we turn to geological evidence" (192); "turn to birds" (252); or "turn to the marine Carnivora" (253). Such rhetorical recourse to *turns* was an epistemic signature of characterization, a signature trope of prose that is keenly attentive to its audience and always on the move. Etymologically, "turn" derives from "trope," and has long been associated with a deft, adaptive sense of audience, a kind of tact by which a writer negotiates his readers. As I said earlier, Antisthenes interpreted Odysseus, "the man of many turns" or *polytropos*, as a personification of rhetorical versatility.

Heavy-handed in their prevalence but subtle in their colloquial ordinariness, Darwin's *turns* mediate metabasis, or change of subject, and thereby inscribe spontaneity, experiential method, a liberal open-mindedness to new ideas, and a balance between digression and focus into his prose. Metabasis has its most prominent origin in Montaigne's *Essays*, which, with every return to their putative topics, reminds the reader that Montaigne constitutes their most important subject.[35] More than topical mobility, then, metabasis bespeaks an aesthetic foregrounding of authorial subjectivity: it marks prose defined by its engagement with and mediation of its content rather than by its putative detachment from that content. *Turns* disavow transparency in favor of no less credible, because laborious and interesting, meddling. And indeed Darwin explicitly justifies his rhetorical *turns* as both persuasive and representative of what has given him a turn: he says he "will select those facts which have struck me most, with the hope that they may produce some effect on the reader" (*DM* 86). Metabasis, however, is just as prominent in Byron's *Don Juan* (1819–24), whose character is a function of his proclivity to pursue "digression" from which he must return. Like Byron, Darwin repeatedly and unconvincingly apologizes, "To return to our immediate subject" (*OS* 89, cf. 389) and "But to return to our more immediate subject" (*DM* 135; cf. *OS* 297).[36] Such digressiveness indulges the allure of what appears to be inscrutable evidence, only to find that evidence confirm his theory; it affects empirical freedom from prescriptive theories, as though Darwin openly pursues data where it takes him, only to find by chance that it takes him back to his theory.[37] The *turns* advertise a healthy skepticism and an experiential open-ness to what happens next. With such a willingness to digress, a nineteenth-century text reaffirmed its gentlemanly disinterestedness and intellectual freedom, as well as a capacity for critique or irony, even as it demonstrated its disciplined respect for evidence.

So Darwin's apostrophic *turns* to the reader and his interlocutors, includ-ing his opponents, enact liberal open-mindedness at the level of style:[38] as if experimenting with an hypothesis, he says "If we turn to nature to test the truth of these remarks" (*OS* 93); and "Now let us turn to the other side of the argument" (367), he resolves in the conclusion to the *Origin*; and only after acknowledging and humoring his opponents, only after having "recapitu-lated, as fairly as I could, the opposed difficulties and objections," does he write "now let us turn to the special facts and arguments in favour of the theory" (369). Few might expect Darwin to write himself into a new opinion, but he appears to entertain alternatives. He persistently changes topics or changes his evidentiary sources or geography in a way that seems to make the text nimble, free-ranging, adaptive, and not overly myopic or insistent. Darwin's view of the world is therefore much more consonant with Dickens's "view from Todgers's" than posterity has generally been inclined to think: for both Dickens and Darwin, this view presented not a world of alienated objects and individuals, but a world "of many turns," a world whose meaning inhered not in discrete objects or people but in their turns into, away from, about, around, on, and off each other.

Distracted by the equation of character with characters – that is, with personages – we can miss the character of prose, the particular idiom with which it negotiates its half referential and half deviant relation to the familiar. Where the range of connotations of a *turn* all coalesce, for Charles Dickens as for Charles Darwin and many others, we can retrace the contours of character as an epistemological decorum and historical aesthetic. Character described 1) the taxonomical paradox of individuality and typicality or species and variety in the form of natural historical characters and habits (a turn for X or a personage of an X turn); 2) the liberal open-mindedness, irony, and empirical experimentalism inscribed in metabasis or recursive turns to something else (an inward turn or a turn to or from another person or topic); 3) nostalgic returns and hopeful proleptic turns that disjoin temporalities; 4) the developmental transformation, becoming, or meta-morphic emergence and its sense of moral and capitalistic payoff (turn into, turn out, and turn to account); 5) the theatrical performativity (as in a stage turn or the nickname for actors, "turns"); 6) the social ritual of retreat from the crowd to the intimacy of a semi-private walk or dance (to take a turn); 7) affective frisson, shock, sadness, or other emotional persuasion (to give or receive such a turn); and 8) successive social obligation or mannerly opportunity for action (my turn and your turn) and its logical correlative, sequence or methodical order. In all of these senses, *turn* emphasizes a break from correspondence, expectation, or stasis. Even the last connotation implies a change from one order of being or one agent to another. This dynamic relation more than any fixed catalogue of virtues or forms of thought defined character as a unit of knowledge, and one posed obliquely and in resistance to the fact, which definitively foreclosed any such deviance.

A Natural History of Character

Turn is only the most readily traceable evidence of this dimension of character. Nineteenth-century culture was saturated with synonymous characterizations that relied upon turning, like Darwin's account of grouse running "round and round in a circle . . . like a fairy-ring" (*DM* 430). By honing in on the word itself, here as in the subsequent chapters, I mean to get a specific, material grasp of what was likely a much more pervasive phenomena. But it is high time I turn to *character*. *Character* was perhaps the most indeterminate or over-determined keyword of the nineteenth century, and building character was routinely assumed to be a continuous preoccupation subtending every other ostensible objective. "Character Is Everything," in the Christian journal *Sunday at Home*, is altogether representative, if somewhat hyperbolic: "We are, every one of us, *busily employed all day long in forming our own characters*."[39] If the stuff that won Waterloo was proverbially inculcated on the cricket fields of Eton and other public schools, whose objective was to foster officers and gentlemen, Victorian writers likewise held that it should be inculcated in and by factories, fox-hunts, financial exchanges, furnishings, physics, fiction, and natural philosophy. The task of prose was to characterize a world defined, as so many from Hegel to Arnold insisted, by an increasing volume of apparently unrelated facts.

In ordinary usage *character* referred to the recognizable personality, psychology, or morality, as Victorians would say, of real and fictional personages. But it also referred to an amorphous amalgam of Protestant, chivalric, and classical civic virtues that had been familiar aspects of the English ideal of gentlemanliness since the Reformation elevated the status of work: politeness, punctuality, will power, self-discipline, passion, invigila-tion, method, perseverance, sincerity, disinterestedness or disengagement, industriousness, and vocation.[40] In 1808, the influential French socialist Charles Fourier drafted a genealogical taxonomy of 12 common passions that determined what he calculated to be 810 possible character compositions.[41] Later in the century, the philosophers and social scientists T. H. Green, Samuel Bailey, George Combe, Alexander Bain, Herbert Spencer, and John Stuart Mill all proposed or published theories of character.[42] Such ethology, as Mill called it, addressed character from ethical, philosophical, political, phrenological, and physiological approaches.

In everyday life, employers wrote testimonials that vouchsafed the genealogical backgrounds, reputations, morality, and manners of servants, as well as their fitness for a situation. The letters vouchsafed the creditability of a person and his or her suitability for a particular social position, and the spatial terminology here emphasizes how relational the concept of character was, whether it was invoked to describe the fitness of a fish or a footman.[43] These "characters," as the genre was called, underscore the public, intermediary function of character and the widespread importance of being able to read character in nineteenth-century Britain. As late as 1924, Virginia Woolf wrote "people have to acquire a good deal of skill in character-reading if they are to live a single year of life without disaster,"[44] for character remained the principle medium of social interaction as well as economic exchange.

Character, to be sure, frequently signified the essential and secreted interiority of people and the imaginary personages that represented them, but in practice this usage was subordinate to the legibility of an individual – the knowable, fungible, public persona and manner by which such a person was known and felt in relation to others. That such a one as Byron was "a character" meant that he had a known reputation in public circulation. "A character," as in "a card," designated someone known by a signature mark, habit, or feature. Thus: Isaac D'Israeli's oft reprinted and revised *An Essay on the Manners and Genius of the Literary Character* (1795), which catalogs the generic eccentricities by which writers were knowable, and "The Gallery of Illustrious Literary Characters" series of biographical sketches and accompanying caricatures in *Fraser's Magazine for Town and Country* (1830–38). George Eliot employs this sense of the word when she mocks the hypothetical Mrs. Farthingale, "a lady reader," for having tastes for "comedy, the adventures of some personage who is quite a 'character.'"[45] Of course, Eliot hereby implies that character accrues not to the radical legibility of the eccentric but to the dialectical play between the eccentric and his or her opposite: she proceeds to define Amos Barton and "so very large a majority of your fellow-countrymen" as individuals of an "insignificant stamp." For Eliot, ordinary realist personages whose "pathos" inheres "in their very insignificance" (*SC* 44) also exemplified character, in both the moral and typological sense. Amos is "superlatively middling, the quintessential extract of mediocrity" (47), so this mediocrity is his "stamp."

Such paradoxes are inscribed in the word *character*, which pragmatically reconciled a host of incommensurate values: faculty and Associationist psychology, comparative anatomies and behaviors, and republican virtues and the ostensibly incongruous attributes of Romantic individuality, Anglican Christianity, and capitalism.[46] Samuel Smiles's books, including *Self-Help* and *Character*, invariably prove the value of moral virtues by detailing how financially successful individuals turned them to account, so as to suggest that moral character, which was expressly distinguished from materialism, mattered only because it was materially productive and remunerative. Such was the case in "Evangelical social thought," as Stefan Collini explains: "economic activity was portrayed as a proving-ground of moral discipline."[47] Or, as Lauren Goodlad puts it:

> the recurrent term character [stood] for an antimaterialist concept of the individual which was deeply at odds with *homo economicus*, the hedonistic subject of capitalist ideology. To build "character" in the nineteenth century was, therefore, to resist atomization and embourgeoise-ment: whether by fortifying the republican's virtuous citizen qualities, by developing the romantic's individuality and diversity, by strengthening the Christian's moral obligations to God and community, or – as often as not – by diverse appeals to all of these ends.[48]

The manifold paradoxes of character enabled Tories and Whigs to claim that oppositional agendas both promoted character, because character and characters alike could formally accommodate nostalgia and progress. Victorians almost universally accepted that character was good, then, but many held competing ideas about what its content might be. I therefore prefer "epistemology" to "ideology" in this book precisely because the ideological associations or "contents" of character were so amorphous, contradictory, and subordinate to the verbal forms or manners by which character was articulated, whatever its particular contents.[49]

The ability for *character* to give coherence to otherwise irreconcilable claims contributed to make it what Amanda Anderson calls "the ideal pragmatic category."[50] "As opposed to identities conceived in terms of essence or nature," Anderson explains, "character is antifoundational, open-ended, and in process, the site of self-crafting and mediation between the individual actor and the wider social world" (120). Hence, Smiles's best-selling *Self-Help* subsumes every possible attribute, event, and contingency into character – "character is formed by a variety of minute circumstances, more or less under the regulation and control of the individual," he says, "Every action, every thought, every feeling, contributes" (21). Describing character in this capacious way made it a particularly convenient category by which to ascribe value to those persons and things that were not readily amenable to competing criteria of valuation such as utility or money, measurement or facticity. But "process," *Bildung*, and growth of the sort Anderson describes all coincide more or less with the depth paradigm of developmental character with which scholarship is all too familiar. Clifford Siskin has demonstrated how the rhetoric of Romanticism naturalized this model of dynamic, deep subjectivity through synecdoche and other "lyric turns."[51] Deidre Lynch also ascribes the emergence of a pragmatics of reading for deep character to the Romantic period, but her genealogy of that dominant twentieth-century practice overshadows the fascinating historical alternative that it pushed against: a once-dominant shadow economy of character attuned to telling lines, surfaces, and marks.[52] Following E. M. Forster's subordination of "flat" to "round" characters and Freud's theory of the unconscious, posterity has equated real character with psychological depth. As Elizabeth Ermarth puts it, "realistic characters, like the world they inhabit, have depths that can never be expressed fully in one heroic action nor ever fully understood except as an abstraction of consciousness."[53] But Victorians routinely retained the residual surficial model of character operative in natural historical taxonomy.

The everyday words described here were periperformative in the sense that their utterance constituted character just as practicing good manners constitutes good manners. They are not symptoms of hidden character, but open enactments of it. This historical usage originates from the word's classical etymological roots as a typographical mark, signifying line, or impression. Lynch traces the etymology through "the fine line" in William Hogarth's prints that "separates the marks that individualize the countenance from the marks that exaggerate it" (64). The Third Earl of Shaftesbury's *Characteristics of Men, Manners, Opinions, Times* (1711) was one of the first texts to manifest the connotative transition of character from this sense of the mark by which a character type is legible to a sense of the mark as symptomatic of interiority. He correlated the mark to the empiricist "impressions" by which an individual's sensory perceptions were stamped on his or her character. Later rhetoricians such as Hugh Blair and Adam Smith, invoking Aristotle's concept of "ethos," explicitly presented style as an expression of authorial character and an instrument of impressing the reader's character.[54]

This empiricist notion of perceptions typographically impressed into character survived well into the nineteenth century. In *The Prelude*, for example, Wordsworth esteems the printer-like "ministry" of genii locorum and "the agency of boyish sports" because "on caves and trees, upon the woods and hills, / [they] Impressed upon all forms the characters / Of danger or desire, and thus did make / The surface of the earth / With meanings of delight, of hope and fear, / Work like a sea."[55] Wordsworth amends George Berkeley's notion of the "book of nature" with David Hartley's Associationism, such that nature literally bears the stamps less of God than of his own sensory experiences. The "characters" of the material world impress upon Wordsworth's mind, leaving what he elsewhere describes as "collateral objects" or "images to which in following years / Far other feelings were attached – with forms / That yet exist with independent life, / And, like their archetypes, know no decay" (12, 8). For Wordsworth, "character" designates the material impressions made by contact with objects, incidents, and others. "Character" names the interface, point of contact, friction, or relation between self and world. Thus, Archibald Alison claimed the sensations produced by reading are "imprinted in indelible characters on the memory."[56] George Eliot registers this correlation between the characterological stamp, the character type, and the empiricist process of character formation in her 1879 *Impressions of Theophrastus Such*. Eliot's titular "impressions" refers to the observations or opinions of her narrator as well as to both the recognizable features of a character (the marks of the miser's avarice, the fox's cunning, etc.) and the empirical sensations ("impressions" as in "perceptions," "associations," or "suggestions") out of which the mind was thought to be formed since at least the work of John Locke.

For nineteenth-century readers, then, character signified first and foremost the impressive mark at the interface between the self and anyone or anything else. Character was the signature feature by which a person or thing impressed upon another as a metal type impresses a paper page. The most obvious of these characterological marks might appear to be the proper name, which Barthes describes in *S/Z* as "a magnetic field" collecting combinations of semes and figures into an "evolving" personality and body.[57] To be sure, no word personifies as effectively as a proper name; but we should distinguish between personification and characterization. Where proper names, anthropomorphic bodies, and voices personify, the everyday words I am describing characterize something without restricting it to personhood or its fictional avatars. Registering the impression of this kind of character seems to have been at least as important to nineteenth-century critics as identifying with or cultivating "deep" or "intimate" understandings of its named personages; it was certainly more important than interpreting the "meaning" of a text. To be sure, recall that *Culture and Anarchy* (1867–68, 1869) proclaims "sweetness and light to be self-evident characters of perfection."[58] These characters are the objects neither of our sympathy nor our identification, but of our interest.

"The Study of Poetry" (1880), the essay in which Arnold laments that "Our religion has materialised itself in the fact, in the supposed fact; it has attached its emotion to the fact, and now the fact is failing it," expressly counters facts with characters, which he presents as the objects of literary criticism. In doing so Arnold neglects interpretation, allegory, and the rhetorical work of promoting his deep insight – what Siskin calls "the work of writing" – and insists instead that character inheres in "the matter and substance" of the language.[59] "Critics," he writes,

> give themselves great labour to draw out what in the abstract constitutes the characters of a high quality of poetry. It is much better simply to have recourse to concrete examples; – to take specimens of poetry of the high, the very highest quality, and to say: The characters of a high quality of poetry are what is expressed there. They are far better recognised by being felt in the verse of the master, than by being perused in the prose of the critic. (Keating 349)

For all its well-noted snobbery, Arnold's claim here also favors the individual experience of the reader to the mediation or abstractions of a critic. In part promoting his editorial selections of Byron and Wordsworth and others, Arnold suggests that the character of a text, its impressive effect and therefore value, is contained in extractable parcels, passages that are self-evident to any reader with "tact" (Keating 347). The "special character" of a text is not for Arnold expressed in allegories, per Fredric Jameson, or by symptomatic features, per Louis Althusser, but in phrases whose style elicits concomitantly moral and aesthetic effects. The coincidence of characterological values with stylistic virtues manifests in Arnold's ethological critical idiom (strength, sweetness, light) and plays out on the surface of the text: at the same time rhetorical and moral, the affective touch of "movement," "diction," "truth," "seriousness," "style," and "manner" (349–50) collectively constitute and communicate its character.[60] As Anderson shows, Arnold aspired "to give critical reason an ethical dimension . . . by casting it as an ideal temperament or character" comprising "impartiality, tact, moderation, measure, balance, flexibility, detachment, objectivity, [and] composure."[61] In practice, however, Arnoldian "critical reason" often exclusively entails tact, a mode of decorum, manner, and touch – rather than deliberative rationalization.

Even Ruskin, whose *Sesames and Lilies* (1865) includes a pioneering close reading of "Lycidas" and who regularly espouses the signal virtues of depth, painstakingly defines the "characteristic" in taxonomical terms in *Modern Painters* (1843–60). As I discuss in the next chapter, Ruskin's discussion of reflections on water expressly ascribes character to the nexus of superficiality and depth in terms of genus and species. But for now consider how he defines the tautological aesthetic of "characteristic" truths: "those truths must be the most important which are most characteristic of what is to be told," he says; and "truths are important just in proportion as they are characteristic."[62] "Characteristic" serves here as an alternative to imitative or documentary representation. Ruskin justifies the truth of those forms of representation that do not reproduce but instead remediate their subjects. Such remediation takes the form of vertiginous toggling between generalization and particularity in this section of *Modern Painters* I, "Relative Importance of Truths." The taxonomic idiom overtly applies the natural historical sense of "characteristics" to an aesthetic that he consistently aligns with "a marked aim for *character*" (3:682), the signal virtue of modern painters.[63] "That which is first and foremost broadly characteristic of a thing is that which distinguishes its genus, or which makes it what it is" (3:151), Ruskin explains,

> that which makes the thing what it is, is the most important idea, or group of ideas, connected with the thing. But as this idea must necessarily be common to all individuals of the species it belongs to, it is a general idea with respect to that species; while the other ideas, which are not characteristic of the species, and are therefore in reality general . . . are yet particular with respect to that species, being predicable of only certain individuals of it. (3:152)

Ruskin maintains that this "so-called general idea is important, not because it is common to all the individuals of that species, but because it separates that species from everything else" (3:152). In these muddlesome though mesmerizing lines, Ruskin defends the relativity of the characteristic, its work differentiating between the particular and the general or the original and the relation, as an ethological mode of truth, distinct from factual representation or mere description. "Characteristic" affords his aesthetic a natural philosophical legitimacy that "figurative" or "symbolic" or other rhetorical terms then (as now) lacked. But it aspires also to name precisely the way art produces knowledge by turning its subject to its audience, turning from representation to relation.

The points to note are twofold: first, nineteenth-century Britons routinely conflated the moral (psychological, ethical), social (reputation, sympathy), aesthetic (interest, intensity), and epistemological (credit, taxonomy, truthfulness) senses of character such that applications of the term in different genres ordinarily evoked or cross-referenced these connotations, which posterity has typically disaggregated. Second, whereas description defers value to its objects, characterization insists that value accrues to mediation instead. Characterization diverts moral value from content to form. As an epistemology, a set of protocols for what counts as knowledge, everyday words like "a turn" underwrote the characterization of flat and round persons alike in Victorian Britain, because flatness and roundness were not yet the de facto categories by which character was recognized. Furthermore, these everyday words underwrote the characterization of things other than persons and personages. "Characters" designated an overlapping set of objects, including fictional personages and everyday words but also all other features of a text or object that manifested its "relative importance" as truth, as Ruskin put it, by turning from particularity to a more general relation. The texture of prose is marked by these characteristic, mannered departures from mimesis that appeal to the reader. Subsequent chapters will describe the forms this relation takes other than *turns* and straightforward ascriptions of *character*.

The Way They Read Then: Meredith, Egan, and the "Currency" of Philology

Consistent with ordinary language philosophy, my turn to everyday words in part owes to the way that science and philosophy enter colloquial knowledge – the way most literate people know what they know – less through meticulous, studied readings than through casual appropriations of current idiolects, neologisms, and turns of phrase. An archeology of everyday language is I think a more historically accurate gauge of general sentiment and philosophy than any traditional history of ideas, for most people do not think, feel, and act with the logical consistency of theory and practice implied by such histories. The ordinary person touches reality through ordinary language and its assumptions, not through elaborate interpretations of his or her readings. As Harry Shaw puts it, quoting J. L. Austin in a polemical defense of realism, "our 'common' stock of words ... will put us in contact with reality, not the ability of the individual, sitting alone, to devise distinctions."[64]

But my turn to everyday words is motivated also by nineteenth-century reading practices, which were highly attuned to the subtleties and significance of ordinary language as a shared medium of tact: colloquialisms, conventional locutions, slang, and common language of all sorts delimited what people knew, were interested in, and could touch. David Copperfield observes that "conventional phrases are a sort of fireworks easily let off, and liable to take a great variety of shapes and colours not at all suggested by their original form" (*DC* 497), and nineteenth-century readers of all sorts were invested in the manifold shapes and colors that conventional language took, from local dialects and slang to the alleged universality of common English. John Horne Tooke established the philology of everyday language in his influential *Epea pteroenta; or the Diversions of Purley* (1786/1805), which correlates the study of the English language to national character and cultural history.[65] Late-eighteenth-century Britons responded with an efflorescence of dictionaries, not just of Dr. Johnson's Standard English but of common speech: dictionaries of cant, flash, the lingo of professional and criminal classes and localities.[66] Wordsworth authenticates *Lyrical Ballads* as an empirical experiment by purporting to write it in the real language of real men, rather than inherited artifice, and all subsequent modes of what we now call "realism" dabble in some way with hetero-glossic representations of different dialects and actual, grammatically imperfect speech. Hardy, in particular, novelizes the affecting discordance between philology and ordinary language usage.[67] But this philological propensity reached its apotheosis in the middle of the nineteenth century when Richard Chenevix Trench, along with Herbert Coleridge and Frederick Furnivall, established what would eventually become the *Oxford English Dictionary*, an express corrective to extant dictionaries, which omitted obsolete words. Trench was convinced that a dictionary ought to offer a complete inventory of the language, because the language was the best index of a culture's assumptions, values, and knowledge.[68] Philology was of course a thriving academic discipline in the Victorian age, and talks by university philologists were popular. Trench published a series of six lectures, *On the Study of Words*, in 1852. More popular were the 1861 *Lectures on the Science of Language* by Max Müller of Oxford, who attracted all sorts of intellectuals, artists, and celebrities. Such work explicitly corre-lates the zeitgeist or character of an age to its language trends. Trench, for instance, remarks in his lectures that "it will sometimes happen that the character and moral condition of an epoch are only too plainly revealed by the new words which have risen up in that period."[69]

Respect for the epistemological import of everyday words straddled high and low cultural forms, however. Everyday words and character coalesce brilliantly in the democratic philology of Pierce Egan's 1821 *Tom & Jerry: or Life in London*, an illustrated picaresque narrative that is as much a playful dictionary of slang as a manual about "*knowledge* of 'Life,'" or "an acquaintance with *character*."[70] Engraved by George Cruikshank and published monthly starting in 1821 for a shilling an issue, *Life in London* was immensely popular amongst all classes and remained in print throughout the nineteenth century. The editor of the 1869 edition, John Camden Hotten, who contemporaneously published *The Dictionary of Slang*, introduces *Life in London* as "*the* book – *the* literature – of that period, the one work which many elder gentlemen still remember far away in the distance of their youth" (Egan and Cruikshank 1). And sure enough, recollecting his boyhood self with a book on his lap, William Thackeray recalls in *The Roundabout Papers*, "behind the great books which he pretends to read, [behind even Scott's *The Heart of Mid-Lothian*], is [*Life in London*], which he is really reading" (qtd. in Egan and Cruikshank 2). Thackeray here recounts *Life in London* literally embedded in a novel, but figuratively speaking, too, the paradigm of everyday philology and the kind of reading practices it fostered, including the equation of character with idiomatic speech, are also inscribed into the text of those canonical novels. Flash genres, including ballads, dictionaries, annotated engravings like William Coombe and Thomas Rowlandson's *Dr. Syntax* series, and Newgate and silver-fork novels underwrote the way other genres conceived character as a product of certain phrases and the ways they were consumed as repositories of quotable coinages.[71] As what people were "really reading," as the text literally and figuratively tucked inside more respectable texts, the philological characterization of *Life in London* might therefore index what features everyday nineteenth-century readers actually attended to as they read the novels we study now.

Egan explains in his dedication to George IV that we glean knowledge of character from the "Metropolis," "a complete Cyclopedia" of character (51), "by means of a free and unrestrained intercourse with society" (vi). "The grand object of this work," Egan writes, "is an attempt to portray what is termed 'SEEING LIFE' in all its various bearings upon society, from the *high-mettled* CORINTHIAN of St. James's, swaddled in luxury, down to the *needy* FLUE-FAKER of Wapping, *born without a shirt*, and not a *bit of scran* [food] in his cup to allay his piteous cravings" (52). This knowledge of character proves to be neither intimate nor psychologically deep but instead a social lubricant. Lubricant: because, more than the bonds between characters, *Life in London* privileges evanescent affinities, interests, acquaintances, and passing interactions. And acquiring "flash," a sort of verbal ball-bearing analogous to adaptable manners and ready cash, enables one to navigate different social milieus without any friction. Flash itself, the medium of social interaction, exceeds the attention devoted to any individual personage in the text. Thematically, it is the subject of country bumpkin Jerry Hawthorne's urban education. Formally, it is highlighted in varying fonts, italics, boldface, small capitals, and numerous footnotes, such that the typographical characters of the text materially advertise their pre-eminence over personages as the primary characters of the text.

Corinthian Tom and Corinthian Kate are related not by family or blood but by their orientation to the metropolis through the Corinthian idiom. They do not develop, grow, reflect, or change; their characters instead transpire in verbal exchanges of wit, flirtation, interest, and other forms of sociable banter. Noting the historical associations of *character* as the sovereign impression that legitimated a piece of currency as creditable money, Lynch explains that,

> First and foremost, "character" was a rubric that licensed discussion of the order of things in a conversible, commercial society. In designating the qualities that separated an object from some things and bound it to others, *character* in its most abstract sense was a tool geared to analysis of the basic elements of the town-dweller's contemporaneity. (35)

Everyday language was the currency of this mainstream economy of character.

The everyday words I write about here are quotidian, distant cousins of the slang of Egan; of the pronounced dialects of Scott, Eliot, and Hardy; and even of the comic Micawberisms of Dickens or the portmanteau and nonsense words of Lewis Carroll – all of which bear ostentatious stamps of class, education, sobriety, nationality, locality, gender, profession, and so on. The everyday words I describe have far thinner links to any specific demographic. Even when the novels I study mock a particular phrase in a laughable character, they still tend to use the phrase no less frequently with their earnest characters. Given that novels and other published books are my primary evidence, everyday words are to be sure the language of the literate classes, most broadly understood. They comprise what Orwell called "the then equivalent of BBC" English, like that used by Dickens's "walking gentlemen" heroes.[72] Parody like that of Dickens and Eliot above, in the cases of the Todgers's gentlemen and Tancred the horse, nevertheless reveals that nineteenth-century readers were as equally attuned to these subtle phrases as to the more pronounced dialectics of criminals, provincials, or fashionable sets. To be sure, besides *Life in London* Thackeray also relished John Leech's contributions to *Punch* (1842–86), which he collected and published together as *Pictures of Life and Character* (1886). Leech's work construes characters by punning on the most mundane turns of phrase.

Nineteenth-century Britons correlated character with parcels of everyday language in all its varieties.

Except for a few privileged exceptions like Ruskin and Pater, who both dabbled in metaphorical, interpretative, "close" reading, most Victorian critics also seem to have engaged the surface of texts in the form of "current" language. When Victorian reviewers registered some fictions as "novels of character" and others as "novels of plot," they were not simply estimating a text's relative investment in personages or events but also its implicit manner, comportment, or decorum.[73] Novels of plot tend to directly present their manifest content – their plots and characters – as what matters, whereas novels of character intimate some surplus subtext or interest that matters more than the thematic content. Nineteenth-century lay readers and professional critics alike, even otherwise disapproving critics of Dickens, had overwhelmingly philological and metonymic reading habits that homed in on idiomatic turns of phrase as marks of this character. David Masson, the first professor of English literature to write a monograph on the novel, therefore described Dickens's peculiar mode of characterization as "luminous metonymy."[74] In a sustained comparison of Dickens and Thackeray, Masson expatiates on this pervasive style and implies that Dickensian characterization, because of its extraordinary "currency," is more faithful to extra-textual reality – to the way Victorians apprehended the character of the world beyond a text – than the realisms of George Eliot or Trollope. "While it would be possible," he admits, for a churlish critic of Dickens's novels

> to draw out in one long column a list of their chief characters, annexing in a parallel column the phrases or labels by which these characters are distinguished, and of which they are generalizations – the "There's some credit in being here" of Mark Tapley; the "It isn't of the slightest consequence" of Toots; the "Something will turn up" of Mr. Micawber, etc., etc. Even this, however, is a mode of art legitimate, I believe, in principle, as it is certainly most effective in fact. There never was a Mr. Micawber in nature, exactly as he appears in the pages of Dickens; but Micawberism pervades nature through and through; and to have extracted this quality from nature, embodying the full essence of a thousand instances of it in one ideal monstrosity, is a feat of invention. From the incessant repetition by Mr. Dickens of this inventive process openly and without variation, except in the results, the public have caught what is called his mannerism or trick; and hence a certain recoil from his later writings among the cultivated and fastidious. But let anyone observe our current table-talk or our current literature, and, despite this profession of dissatisfaction, and in the very circles where it most abounds, let him note how gladly Dickens is used, and how frequently his phrases, his fancies, and

the names of his characters come in, as illustration, embellishment, proverb, and seasoning. Take any periodical in which there is a severe criticism of Dickens's last publication; and, ten to one, in the same periodical, and perhaps by the same hand, there will be a leading article, setting out with a quotation from Dickens that flashes on the mind of the reader the thought which the whole article is meant to convey, or containing some allusion to one of Dickens's characters which enriches the text in the middle and floods it an inch round with color and humor. (Masson 257–58)

Invoking the language of induction that I discuss in the following chapter, and iterating "nature," as if Dickens were a taxonomist, Masson claims that Dickens extracts generalized character in the form of mannerisms, including Micawberisms, from many particular observed instances of Micawberism diffused throughout real life. In turn, Masson implies, readers appropriate these extractions – these general characters – as commutable units of knowledge that they can employ to relate to different circumstances, as Corinthian Tom teaches Jerry Hawthorn how to employ flash to relate to London society. Readers annex Dickensian character into "current table-talk," "current literature," "pithy sayings," and "common talk" (Masson 257). Thus, for Masson the trick of Dickensian characterization is of course not the prodigious production of round, realistic, imaginary personages, so much as the prodigious production of fungible phrases fit for characterizing everyday life – prose that does not reproduce particularity exactly, but that facilitates our ability to relate with life in general. With the Todgers's bachelors Dickens offers not fictional avatars or clones of real bachelors, but instead a manner of approaching, recognizing, and appreciating such people.

Masson describes what seems to have been a popular mode of character-reading. As the (then) popular novelist John Cordy Jeaffreson self-consciously admits,

> We cannot walk without [Dickens's] leading strings, or speak without using his texts, or look out upon the world save through his eyes. Indeed, it is not our world, but his, that we gaze upon. If an incident render a morning's walk eventful, we refer to his books for a parallel, or explanation, or comment. The crowds that hurry past us in the public ways we classify in a manner he has taught us, and we christen them with names taken from his fiction.[75]

Jeaffreson correlates characters with classificatory phrases and with "manner." Dickens was of course just as often disparaged for his propensity to translate characters into phrases, and some of the disparagement affected his style: the *Quarterly Review*, for example, dubbed him "Regius Professor of Slang" (92), and he responded by editing most of the flash out of subsequent editions of *Oliver Twist*.[76] But Dickens had plenty of contemporaries who turned such models of characterization into stylized, studious fiction impugned only for being overly recondite. Elizabeth Barrett Browning's *Aurora Leigh* intricately associates "common words" with John's Gospel of Christ as the Word and the savior of common man (106, 155) and with Wordsworthian realism ("the language of real men"). The poem plays with "common talk" (209), "plain words" (222), "common phrase" (272), and "a simple word" (138), all as Aurora aspires to be the poet of common man and pretends to subordinate sophisticated language to a shared, simpler, almost physical idiom. Aurora recalls that "every common word / Seemed tangled with the thunder at one end, And ready to pull down upon our heads / A terror out of sight" (119).

Likewise, in an iconic realist rebuke to a hypothetical reader wary of trivial or common subjects, the narrator of *Adam Bede* (1859) appraises "slight words" and "unimposing words, such as 'light,' 'sound,' 'stars,' 'music' – words really not worth looking at, or hearing, in themselves, any more than 'chips' or 'sawdust,'" as the "finest language" for "they happen to be the signs of something unspeakably great and beautiful."[77] Eliot's "unimposing words" recall an unspeakable *something* that seems to refer to the embodied but unconscious memories of our childhood associations, the faint echoes of our first apprehension of language. Joseph Conrad similarly invokes common words at the climax of *The Heart of Darkness* (1899) to articulate the almost monstrous potential inscribed in ordinary words:

> I've been telling you what we said – repeating the phrases we pronounced – but what's the good? They were common everyday words – the familiar, vague sounds exchanged on every waking day of life. But what of that? They had behind them, to my mind, the terrific suggestiveness of words heard in dreams, of phrases spoken in nightmares.[78]

Here where we might expect some dramatic, poetic encounter in the form of a political or philosophical dialogue, perhaps clarifying the manifold tensions and allusions of the preceding narrative, Conrad offers the small change of everyday conversation. Adjacent to the infamous horror are everyday words, equally haunting and dreamlike in their suggestiveness and resonance. Through these words, Marlowe and Kurtz connect.

Take George Meredith for one last exemplary instance of the nineteenth-century fascination with everyday words. *The Egoist* (1879) teems with Latinate neologisms, archaic and recondite words, earnest and ironic aphorisms and maxims that advertise their irregularity rather than any aura of everydayness. *The Egoist* is also almost as awash with *turns* as the other prose I have discussed.[79] *Turning* is a staple medium of character performance for Meredith, whose personages turn away from and back to each other, take turns together on the lawn, and experience frequent turns of emotion, countenance, and opinion. But I adduce Meredith here as one last representative of the Victorian habit of reading character in phrases instead of in personages. Meredith's "Prelude" to *The Egoist*, like Arnold's work, diagnoses modernity with "the malady of sameness" and "a constant tendency ... to accumulate excess of substance, and," Meredith explains, "such repleteness, obscuring the glass it holds to mankind, renders us inexact in the recognition of our individual countenances."[80] For Meredith, the antidote for this excess substance is the generic capacity for comedy to condense knowledge into little packages that Meredith describes interchangeably as phrases and characters. Comedy, he writes, "condenses whole sections of the Book [of all the world's wisdom] in a sentence, volumes in a character" (5).

The model agent of this condensation of character is witty Mrs. Mounstuart Jenkinson, "a lady certain to say the remembered, if not the right, thing" (Meredith 10). Meredith expatiates on Mrs. Mountstuart's capacity for aptly articulating character in impressive, memorable phrases such as "*You see he has a leg*" (11, emphasis in original), which consolidates Willoughby's character. "In seeming to say infinitely less than others," Meredith explains, "Mrs. Mounstuart comprised all that the others had said, by showing the needlessness of allusions to the saliently evident" (11). As with Dickens, Mrs. Mounstuart's "word" becomes part of the county's "currency": "Her word sprang out of her ... and it stuck to you, as nothing laboured or literary could have adhered" (10), Meredith explains: "A simple-seeming word of this import is the triumph of the spiritual, and where it passes for coin of value, the society has reached a high refinement" (11). So Mrs. Mountstuart generates the currency of character, the phrases that enable people to manage life.

Meredith sustains an ostensibly ambivalent attitude toward how we ought to receive Mrs. Mountstuart's phrases. On the one hand, they demand amplification, and indeed much of the novel could be summarized as an explication of Mrs. Mountstuart's proclamation that Clara Middleton is "a dainty rogue in porcelain," an epithet which recurs and accretes import throughout the novel (Meredith 36–7, 75, 134, 212). On the other hand, the phrases are cryptic and suggestive, however much Mrs. Mountstuart protests that they are not meant for interpretation. "Like all rapid phrasers," the narrator says, "Mrs. Mountstuart detested the analysis of her sentence. It had an outline in vagueness, and was flung out to be apprehended, not dissected" (39). I could imagine the same being said of Arnold's aesthetic pronouncements. The same holds for characters as for the phrases: after affecting to think Clara "has no character yet," Mrs. Mountstuart asserts that "the solid is your safest guide; physiognomy and manners will give you more of a girl's character than all the divings you can do" (38). In theory and practice, Mrs. Mountstuart suggests that character is a form of meaningful superficiality, a matter of manner, affect, physiology, and phraseology more than motives, meanings, or other interiorized contents. And the narrator blithely agrees that "Miss Middleton's features were legible as to the main-spring of her character" (39), as if to substantiate her claim.

Yet Mr. Whitford cautions Miss Dale that it is easy "to deceive one who is an artist in phrases," because "they dazzle the penetration of the com-poser"; "That is why," he adds, "people of ability like Mrs. Mountstuart see so little; they are bent on describing brilliantly" (Meredith 255). Mr. Whitford's admonition and the novel's general ambivalence toward "rapid phrasers" might betray the erosion of the epistemology of character in which Meredith works. Meredith seems to acknowledge a rift opening between the incumbent epistemology of characteristic description and the emergent, prestigious epistemology of depth. For Whitford, knowledge implies insight, a form of seeing that he equates to "penetration." But Whitford's critique also might signal a complementarity between these paradigms of character. Judith Wilt has postulated that the subplots of Meredith's fictions – and comic fiction in general – constitute self-reflective critiques of the main plots, and that, in concert, plot and subplot, self and self-critique, narrative and its inscribed reader, all marry into the character of the novel itself as a whole.[81] Whitford works in such a marriage as the skeptical spouse of everyday characterization. But Wilt's reading also implicitly appreciates the Victorian tendency to consider aesthetic totalities as character systems defined by their internal relations (their prose style) rather than their individual parts (personages).

Earlier critics were less inclined to accept such complementarity, how-ever. Dorothy Van Ghent cites Mr. Whitford as an internal critique of Meredith,[82] and she joins Henry James and Virginia Woolf in appreciating Meredith's style only as she disparages it as indifferent, dispassionate, and alienated from the reader and from "meaning." "What we see as failure in Meredith," Van Ghent says, "is just this division of form and object, the division of the elegant pattern and splendid style of the book from potential meaning, from potential relationships between characters and thus potential relationships with ourselves" (235). The division that Van Ghent diagnoses between style and meaning only exists to the extent that meaning is defined according to a different, more modernist approach than that emblematized in Mrs. Mountstuart, an approach that privileges depth as truth and reduces style to a superficial decoration, expression, or distortion of that truth. But for nineteenth-century Britons, style and manner mattered – not as coded transmissions of meaning but as the meaning itself. "Truth," Oscar Wilde insisted in "On the Decay of Lying," his manifesto against the vulgar encroachment of facts and mimesis, "is entirely and absolutely a matter of style."[83] If Wilde is too puckish an authority, reconsider Darwin, whose *Descent of Man* openly embraces the visible external evidence of morality *as* morality instead of speculating about the invisible interiority that such externals might or might not evidence.

Meredith perhaps seems reluctant to commit to one epistemology over the other and so to humor both, but outside of these characters and their estimations of each other's character, Meredith exhibits such overwhelming attention to dense, quotable phrases. As Nicholas Dames observes, *The Egoist* "continually punctuates its elaborately periodic sentences and politely composed dialogues with single-word exclamatory bursts, minimal and nongrammatical explosions that virtually summarize a movement of plot or a psychological tendency of character without any appended narratorial comment."[84] Dames connects this art of compression to contemporary physiological or psychophysical theories that recast human consciousness as "innumerable acts of noticing difference," or as the serial sensations of "just noticeable differences," rather than an uninterrupted stream of experience (182). For Dames, then, "What binds accounts of reading Meredith and Meredith's accounts of reading is the stress they both place on the individual unit, on the small moment of sense making or comprehension" (168). Dames effectively implies that Meredith's prose divorces the physiology of character from fictional personages and deposits it in its profusion of compressed and unelaborated utterances. Reproducing the atomistic rhythm of the physiological mind, his prose awkwardly disaggregates character from characters.

Awkwardly, for several reasons: first, the epistemology of character I am describing here was for the duration of the nineteenth century competing with the allure of Romantic subjectivity that, coupled with the widespread proliferation and disaggregation of disciplines, tethered *character* more tightly to personality and thereby rendered other applications of the word to seem unsettling if not merely synonymous with "moral" or "ethical." But second, where the epistemology of the modern fact promised direct correlation between knowledge and its objects, the epistemology of character offered an oblique relation – a turn, to use an example from this chapter – that was literally awkward: prose defined by its subtle deviance from its subjects. Awkwardly, at last, then, because such prose attests to an emergent aesthetic of awkwardness, an appeal or interest produced paradoxically by an eccentricity, divergence, or incompatibility with normative social, generic, and epistemic assumptions and expectations. Like the overlapping and contemporaneous aesthetic category of the interesting, the awkward captivates even as it discomfits, and it relies on what Sianne Ngai describes, paraphrasing Schlegel on the *"interessante,"* "as the serial repetition of an encounter with difference."[85] Discomfort emerges in each of the chapters of this book when novelists notice everyday language becoming a tic, linguistic manners becoming mannerisms, and parody their own usage accordingly. Again, however, parody only reproduces that which it critiques, so everyday words like "a turn" ironically accommodate awkwardness into and as the characteristic texture of the virtuous, interesting, and true. The philological turn of nineteenth-century reading practices, prone as they were to both idiomatic speech and to excerpting, quoting, and commonplace-booking, encouraged readers to appreciate their serial encounters with trifling deviance in the form of everyday words, the characters of a culture well-disposed to awkwardness.

CHAPTER 2

Inductive "Attentions"
Jane Austen in "Particular" and in "General"

> Thus because such a particular idea is commonly annex'd to such a particular word, nothing is requir'd but the hearing of that word to produce the correspondent idea; and 'twill scarce be possible for the mind, by its utmost efforts, to prevent that transition.
> — Hume, *Treatise of Human Nature*[1]

> Miss Bennet shall receive every possible attention while she remains with us.   — Austen, *Pride and Prejudice*[2]

As Jane Bennet convalesces at Netherfield Park, her sister Elizabeth teases Mr. Bingley, whom she professes to understand "completely," that "It does not necessarily follow that a deep, intricate character is more or less estimable than such a one as [his]" (*PP* 46). Elizabeth here acknowledges the disaggregation of aesthetic and moral character. While moral character still implied correspondence between actions or appearances and interiority, aesthetic character had come to require a disjunction between these ontological levels. Notwithstanding Elizabeth's point that interest may come at the cost of moral authenticity, notwithstanding her implication that Bingley might be more estimable than his deep friend Darcy, generations of readers have no doubt invested in Elizabeth's subsequent confession that "deep, intricate" characters have the "advantage" of being "the *most* amusing" (47). Elizabeth exemplifies a modern taste for the Romantic model of character that was then gaining popularity in fiction and poetry, a model of character that emanated from depth epistemology and surfaced in other discourses, including moral and natural philosophy. This depth model of character subordinates the overt morality of figures like Jane and Bingley, whose interiority largely corresponds with their behavior and appearance, to the irony of elusive types like Elizabeth, Darcy, and, beyond Austen, Frankenstein's Creature, the ambivalent heroes of the Waverley novels, and the narrator of Byron's *Don Juan*. These latter characters, whose expression mismatches their putative interiority, are the literary correlatives to the shift Foucault describes from an episteme that recognized external resemblance to one that recognized internal functions or origins as the object of knowledge claims.[3]

As if to relegate Austen to a career only of Janes and Bingleys, wonderfully nice as they are, in an 1850 letter to W. S. Williams Charlotte Brontë memorably sneers that

> [Austen's] business is not half so much with the human heart as with the human eyes, mouth, hands, and feet. What sees keenly, speaks aptly, moves flexibly, it suits her to study; but what throbs fast and full, though hidden, what the blood rushes through, what is the unseen seat of life and the sentient target of death – this Miss Austen ignores.[4]

Whether Brontë was jealous, grossly misreading Austen, or making a sound point, her letter, like Elizabeth's backhanded compliment of Bingley, evidences a tension between competing models of character. For all the interiority articulated by her famous free indirect discourse, Austen appeared to Brontë to be invested in a belated, superficial model of characterization that we might call performative, played out as it is in physiognomies, gestures, and other visible actions. Brontë discerns something about the way Austen's prose works, although her acerbity in this case curtails her acumen. Brontë's strategic list of physical appearances relegates Austen's work to artifice, posture, and coarse physical affects, without the psychological complexity she tacitly arrogates to her own prose; but Austen inhabited a culture that still respected gesture, posture, and other enactments of manners, including everyday words, as innately meaningful performatives. Her culture did not automatically reduce every movement and utterance to evidence of some underlying and therefore meaningful personal motive because it respected collective social motives. We are perhaps accustomed to diagnose meaning that originates outside of individuals as repressive, disciplinary, or inauthentic, but Austen's manner of writing suggests, to the contrary, that she was comfortable with two epistemologies, one of which conferred truth to a certain set of mannerisms.

So we need not align so exclusively with Brontë's or with Elizabeth's prejudices. The depth model of character, as Andrea Henderson has indicated, was neither exclusive nor yet hegemonic during the Regency. Henderson refrains altogether from mentioning Austen in her account of alternative models of character,[5] perhaps because Austen's penchant for suggestive writing that intimates interiority is too well known to bear much repeating or to deny outright, but Austen's prose concurrently inhabits an altogether different spatial episteme. If, as Deidre Lynch convincingly argues, Austen played a pivotal role in the emergence of a pragmatic economy of reading for deep character, whereby readers accrue depth and cultural capital by affecting intimate knowledge of unwritten characterological depths, she likewise participated in an economy of inductive character, which redounded an aura of methodical rigor, pragmatic Englishness, social consensus, and moral extroversion upon its readers.[6] Unlike the hierarchical dialectic of surfaces and depths, this complementary episteme aligned character with induction, the dynamic abstraction of generals from observed particulars. Austen has frequent recourse to the words *particular* and *general*[7] and synonymous pairings, such as *individual* and *type*, as well as to thematic conceptualizations of particularity and generality in the form of attachment and detachment, attention and inattention, partiality and impartiality, disinterest and interest, and peculiarity and conventionality. Austen's prose habitually induces partialities or particulars to adapt to or correct a general consensus, always with a sense that meaning, truth, or moral value originate in abstract collectives external to individuals.

Clifford Siskin identifies a category of locutions that are "intended to produce in specific interrelations, through strategies of inadequacy *or* excess, an effect of fragmentation experienced by the disciplined reader as a call for interpretive activity,"[8] and *particular* and *general* might appear readily subsumable into this set of "lyric turns." But Austen's *particulars* and *generals* do not serve a sense of organic wholeness, and her *particulars* rarely function as suggestive fragments of ineffable wholes. Her coordination of *particulars* and *generals* likewise solicits *attention*, another of her everyday words, more than interpretation. In place of the organic, developmental self that Siskin describes in her contemporaries, Austen's prose posits a character defined by its occupation of two frequencies, its poise between particulars and generals as between self and social collective. Such character cannot be delimited to personages but to her prose itself, as the medium modulating these frequencies.

I call this mode of exposition "characterization," despite its independence from personages, because Austen's reviewers persistently ascribed *character* to her prose and because the idiom of induction was trebly "annexed" (to borrow Hume's phrase) to the concept of character. First, induction was shorthand for an ostensibly moral, nationalistic, and commonsense empiricism that was personified in Francis Bacon and nominally opposed to French deduction and German idealism. Induction was deemed a method, and as such it supposedly guaranteed the impartiality and orderliness as well as the Britishness of the knowledge it produced. With the idiom of induction, then, Austen's prose arrogates some of the epistemological éclat of natural philosophy to fiction. Its realism accrues as much to the natural philosophical credibility and Britishness of its idiom and to its double frequency as to its probability or verisimilitude. Second, the idiom of induction became at the end of the nineteenth century a shorthand for appraising Shakespearean characterization; critics routinely lauded Shakespeare's personages for being both individuals and representatives of classes. Third, at the level of style, Austen's fiction re-enacts the Associationist process of character development as it was described by philosophers such as David Hume, for whom perceived particulars were translated into general ideas in an endless process of inference. Adam Smith added to this tradition with his concept of sympathy, which posited an "attentive spectator" apprehending a world spread along a continuum from particularity to generality.

Austen heralds her inferential or inductive work with words such as *inducement* or *persuasion*, and most frequently *attention*, all of which mark how epistemological assumptions typically discussed with reference to natural philosophy inflect the everyday work of sociality: attention was social induction, the medium of articulating manners, affections, habits, and moods with collectives and generalities. Together, *attention, attentions, attentive, attendance*, and conjugations of *attend* (attend, attends, attending, attended) occur with remarkable consistency, proportionate to novel length, across Austen's six major novels: 71 in *Northanger Abbey*, 116 in *Sense and Sensibility*, 148 in *Pride and Prejudice*, 147 in *Mansfield Park*, 133 in *Emma*, and 76 in *Persuasion*. *Attention* occurs most frequently, including a high 69 times – more even than *character*, which occurs 64 times – in *Pride and Prejudice*.

The specific array of connotations that the word *attention* carries underscores the range of epistemological problems that character was meant to resolve. *Attentions* describes social attitudes of deference and condescension as well as social engagement in the form of flirtations, courtesies (attentions), and care (attendance) – all forms of social relation destabilized by liberalism. The title of this chapter alludes to Victorian philosopher and historian of science William Whewell's notion of the "*the Consilience of Inductions*," which describes "when an Induction, obtained from one class of facts, coincides with an Induction, obtained from another different class."[9] Austen's fictions articulate the consilience of different modes of attentions as they coalesce in characters defined by their place in society, in what Alex Woloch describes as a "character system," but also in a world teeming with stimuli. Miss Bingley does not exaggerate, then, when she assures Mrs. Bennet that Jane "shall receive every possible attention while she remains with us" (*PP* 46). Jane receives attention in the form of romantic interest, curiosity, nursing, jealousy and snobbish condescension, and genteel politeness. Indeed, the coincidence of these attentions produces Jane's character. In novels so routinely impugned for lacking sufficient incident, intensity and character in general are products of consilient attentions. Jane therefore personifies the aesthetic of Austen's prose, the feeling of everyday life.

Of course, *attentions* also connotes the cognitive or aesthetic selection of certain things to notice or ignore, to appreciate or dismiss, in a modernity that was defined by its plenitude. In *Suspensions of Perception*, Jonathan Crary diagnoses attention as a category that emerged around 1850 in concert with the sentiment that modernity was over-stimulating.[10] In Crary's genealogy, western modernity unremittingly intensifies and varies its available modes of attention and distraction and thus generates a distinctly late nineteenth-century subject defined by "a capacity for 'paying attention,' that is, for a disengagement from a broader field of attraction, whether visual or auditory, for the sake of isolating or focusing on a reduced set of stimuli" (1). Austen's idiom suggests that Regency writers had already assumed a modernity defined by its hyperabundance of data and that the category attention emerged at least fifty years earlier than Crary surmises: fiction preempted the insights of psychology, sociology, and visual aesthetics. Although character was for Austen a function of attention, in her work at the other end of the century that character did not, like Crary's, devolve upon selectivity: Austen's realism toggles between the poles of particularity and generality rather than privileging particulars or individuals from amongst the general morass of modern life. Pace Ian Watt's resonant account of the coincident rise of the novel, the epistemological repute of particularity, and the ideology of individualism, few (if any) early nineteenth-century writers unequivocally privileged particulars over generals or vice versa.[11] They depicted a scalar world, and the reality of their representations owed to the aesthetic tension they produced between the ontological levels of individual and group, concrete detail and abstraction.

A touch nostalgic for an interiority that did not become a dominant concern until the second half of the century, whose very "modernity" he defines as a longing for bygone depth, Crary writes about how "automatic" attention – the idea that subjective responses could, because material, take place unconsciously – "poses the notion of absorbed states that are no longer related to an *interiorization* of the subject, to an intensification of a sense of selfhood" (79). For a culture that accepts the possibility of automatic attention, he continues, "attention as a depthless interface simulates and displaces what once might have been autonomous states of self-reflection or *sens intime*" (79). Rather than mourning this loss, we might here appreciate "depthless interface" as Austen's ideal of frictionless sociality. What Crary ascribes to late-century visual aesthetics, the "ideal of attentive *intersubjectivity*, as opposed to modern forms of interiority, absorption, and psychic isolation" (51, emphasis original), obtains much earlier in Austen's fictions about the felicitous flow of social traffic between competing particularities and partialities and the general inclinations of what Austen summarily dubs "all the world." Hers are fictions not simply of *Bildung* in the form of self-realization and development, but fictions of being induced to be habitually inductive and therefore responsive to the social totality or system.

Of course Austen was not the first or only novelist to appropriate these terms. Frances Burney – whose preface to *Evelina* (1778) wryly supposes "Perhaps, were it possible to effect the total extirpation of novels, our young ladies in general, and boarding-school damsels in particular, might profit from their annihilation" – makes ample use of the idiom of induction, as do other eighteenth-century novelists that I mention later.[12] I focus on Austen, however, because her prose so consistently portrays character as a product of the idiom of induction and an economy of attentions. Turning to the idiom of induction in Austen's prose makes visible a repertoire of descriptive tactics and an epistemology of character that complement the psychological ideal that has long dominated literary studies and that has been used to subordinate fiction to other scientific genres of prose. In place of readings of psychological character and ethics, this chapter reveals Austen's intellectual purchase in the dominant philosophical method of her moment.

I therefore frame my discussion of Austen in this chapter with surveys of the idiom of induction in the late-eighteenth and nineteenth centuries. Outside of scientific discourse and fiction, the idiom of induction was appropriated by literary critics to characterize their prose as genuine intellectual work, rather than puffery, paraphrase, or other derivative fluff. Rather than interpretation or allegorical explanation, rather than knowledge or data, much of this criticism presents "character" as the object of its work: character in the sense neither of moral axioms nor personalities, but an abstracted manner. Nineteenth-century criticism purports to be induced to abstraction by the writings it describes poised between knotty particulars and taxonomical schematization, dilating and concentrating attention. For Austen as for these critics, such poise has a decidedly libidinal tension; it folds a mildly erotic aesthetic into the quotidian work of deportment.

The Idiom of Induction and the Character of Method

By the early nineteenth century, "general" and "particular" were almost generic requisites for non-fiction titles across Europe: Xavier Bichat's *A Treatise on the Membranes in General, and on Different Membranes in Particular* (1813); Count de Buffon's *A Natural History, General and Particular* (English trans. 1815); Edward Griffith's *General and Particular Descriptions of the Vertebrated Animals* ... (1821); Johann Spurzheim's *The Physiognomical System ... founded on an anatomical and physiological examination of the nervous system in general, and of the brain in particular* ... (1815); Samuel Cooper's *"Cooper's Surgery"* ... with separate parts on *General Surgical Subjects* and *Particular Surgical Subjects* ... (1828); Edward Chitty's *The Commercial and General Lawyer: A Plain and Practical Exposition of the Law of England in All its Departments: with a More Particular Consideration of those Branches which Relate to Commerce, Trade, and Manufactures* (1839); and so on, including works on brewing, cooking, astronomy, history, politics, and aquaria. Less rambling article titles follow suit: "War, in general, and modern French Wars in particular,"[13] for example, and "On a more general theory of Analytical Geometry, including the Cartesian as a particular case," for another.[14] If many of these titles seem to address specialized readers, equally as many appeared in mainstream periodicals; and their idiom was recognizable enough to be lampooned. In 1842, a *Punch* headline mocked the annual meeting of the British Association for the Advancement of Science (BAAS) as the "British Association for the Advancement of Everything in General, and Nothing in Particular."[15] Later in the century, Wilkie Collins penned two snarky prefaces to *Heart and Science* (1883), one "To Readers in General" and the other "To Readers in Particular," so as to address mainstream moral concerns separately from questions of legal and scientific accuracy.[16] If "particular" and "general" were requisite features of natural philosophical writing, then, they were ubiquitous enough to leverage popular satires of that writing, and to appropriate and evoke the prestige of natural philosophical method.

Abstracting general theories from observed particulars is of course induction, which Francis Bacon forwarded as the principal method of the new science; and, according to Antonio Pérez-Ramos, early nineteenth-century British natural philosophy "had to be ceremonially Baconian if it aspired to respectability."[17] To practice induction was indeed to ensure the character – which is to say the veracity, morality, and national propriety – of an individual experiment or theory. The character of modern knowledge was inscribed in its inductive form. Bacon's *The Advancement of Learning* (1605) and *Novum Organum* (1620), Thomas Sprat's *History of the Royal Society* (1667), Isaac Newton's *Principia* (1687), George Berkeley's *A Treatise Concerning the Principles of Human Knowledge* (1710): all iterate the terms "particular" and "general" as they legitimate induction as the only empirical, disinterested, practical, and therefore respectable form of knowledge production. These publications, and institutions such as the Royal Society, sought to accredit knowledge generated by individual experiments conducted in relative privacy – in country-house kitchens and libraries and parks – by presenting them as general, public, systematic, reproducible experiences instead of anomalous theories of eccentric, private genius. Inductive method formally guaranteed generalizations were impersonal, impartial, "natural" effects of observed, concrete data, and not speculations driven by personal interests or belated philosophical idealism.

Natural philosophers further legitimated induction by claiming that it was an innately English thought process. As David Simpson explains, Sprat's *History* attributes "the successes" and "glorious prospects [of the Royal Society] to the national character, to the 'general constitution' of the minds of the *English*,"[18] for Sprat correlates the constitutional freedom, disinterest, generosity, "sincerity," "simplicity," and "universal modesty" of English national character to the production of "*Experimental knowledge*" and to Baconian method (45–46). The idiom of induction thus characterized natural philosophy as a practice that incorporated individuals into general British society rather than ostracizing them from it. This jingoist notion of induction surfaced outside of natural philosophical debates: an 1843 article in *Fraser's Magazine* perfunctorily distinguishes English fiction as Baconian and inductive and denigrates French fiction, dubbed "romance," as Cartesian fabulism, prevarication, and speculation.[19]

In the eighteenth century, tensions between what we might summarily label Enlightenment universalism and neo-classicism, on the one hand, and Romantic individualism, on the other, motivated quarrels about the relative merits of particularity and generality. Properly articulating the relationship between the general and the particular was, in Ernst Cassirer's words, "the basic and central question of classical aesthetics,"[20] and M. H. Abrams has demonstrated how "In the Age of Johnson ... we find standards for art running the gamut from a primary emphasis on typicality, generality, and 'large appearances,' to the unqualified recommendation of particularity, uniqueness, and a microscopic depiction of detail."[21] Alexander Pope, Joshua Reynolds, and Samuel Johnson tended to advocate general categories such as "human nature" and to denigrate particularity as a vehicle of partiality, exclusivity, and unwanted contingency.[22] Pope cautions against the perils of over-particularity in *An Essay on Criticism* (1711) and aspires to represent universal humankind in his *An Essay on Man* (1734). In *Rasselas*, Johnson famously holds that "The business of a poet is to examine, not the individual but the species; to remark general properties and large appearances: he does not number the streaks of the tulip ... [A poet must] neglect the minuter [*sic*] discriminations."[23] Likewise, Joshua Reynolds and the Academicians variously depict the particular as monstrous, materialist, effeminate, common, or threateningly superfluous – a deviation from normativity and universal truth that the "grand style" of art ought to reflect. Reynolds repeatedly affirms that "perfect form is produced by leaving out particularities, and retaining only general ideas."[24]

Or, as William Hazlitt disparagingly puts it, writing "On the Imitation of Nature," "Sir Joshua's general system may be summed up in two words, – '*That the great style in painting consists in avoiding the details, and peculiarities of particular objects*'":[25] for each eighteenth-century advocate of generality, one might cite a contemporaneous proponent of particularity. In annotations to Reynolds' *Discourses*, William Blake infamously quips, "To Generalize is to be an Idiot To Particularize is the Alone Distinction of Merit – General Knowledges are those Knowledges that Idiots possess [*sic*]."[26] Daniel Defoe, Francis Burney, Walter Scott, and the canonical Romantics all repudiated universalism and much of its lingering philosophical idealism with individualist, empirical, materialist, and recalcitrant particulars, whose refusal to be glossed signaled their liberal politics.[27]

What matters here in such disputes is not so much the merit of the relative positions as the tension between them, which consistently provokes the repetition and therefore enforces the significance of the words *particular* and *general*: rather than settling the hegemony of one scale over the other, the debates elevated the dichotomous pairing of both terms as a signature of learned discourse. Taking a position for generals or particulars or merely muddling the two together was a performative gesture legitimating the character of a piece of prose as Baconian – which is to say, inductive and British – work. Many writers waver between the terms accordingly. Hugh Blair extols generals but then insists that "No description, that rests in Generals, can be good. For we can conceive of nothing clearly in the abstract; all distinct ideas are formed upon particulars."[28] And in a discussion expressly about characterization in *Lectures on Rhetoric and Belles Lettres*, Adam Smith hedges his advice by vaguely, if not paradoxically, prescribing an equivocal "method" of characterization: "have recourse to the more particular effects of the character ... by relating the Generall [*sic*] tenor of conduct"; have recourse to "the general method" as well as "the particular method" (Bryce 80). By the end of the Regency, writers more confidently affected, as Hazlitt says, to "proceed from individuals to generals,"[29] and explicitly promoted composite modes of description that balanced particularity with generality. I denominate this form of description *characterization* because it reproduces the natural historical work of taxonomical characters, which identify an organism by concurrently marking its belonging to and deviation from larger groups (genera, family, species, etc.) and because the subjects that garnered the most praise for felicitously combining particularity and generality were Shakespeare's characters.

Shakespeare was the pre-eminent subject of Regency character-criticism and an icon of English national character.[30] Coleridge's influential appraisal is altogether representative of what turn of the nineteenth-century British critics – Johnson, Lamb, Hazlitt, Jeffrey – wrote about Shakespeare and subsequent writers known for their prolific characterization, especially Scott and later Dickens: "no character[s] in Shakespeare," Coleridge says, "could be called mere Portraits of Individuals: while the reader felt all the light arising from the individual there was a sort of class characteristic which made Shakespeare the Poet of all ages."[31] Admiring the way Shakespeare's characters represent both individuals and types, eccentrics and commonplaces, was an altogether conventional feature of literary criticism from the late eighteenth through the middle of the nineteenth centuries. This paradigm of character wed the features by which a person is recognizable because typical – certain marks (or characters) represent certain types of people, as in Theophrastan "character types" – to the interiority that purportedly distinguishes each individual as such, the psychological, subjective, experiential surplus that was thought to exceed his or her typical characteristics.[32] The idiom of induction thereby inflected the paradox of representative individuality. So Hazlitt attests that "the leading characters in Don Quixote are strictly individuals; that is, they do not so much belong to, as form a class by themselves" (6: 110), and he describes Coleridge as "a general lover of art and science, and wedded to none in particular ... Mr. Coleridge talks of himself, without being an egoist, for in him the individual is always merged in the abstract and general" (11: 31).

Indeed, the spirit-of-the-age genre that Hazlitt popularized would seem to rely on the paradox that utterly anomalous individuals could be taken as representatives of a general zeitgeist. Formally inductive in its assumption that a set of individuals could exemplify a whole culture, *The Spirit of the Age* presents prominent figures as instantiations not only of character types, but also of a general "state of things" – what Carlyle calls a "collective

individuality."[33] As James Chandler has shown, however, Hazlitt's disin-
clination to make any one individual stand in for the age or to draw any
clear similarities between the individuals he describes indicates the emergence of modern historicism founded upon contemporaneity rather than
"the prehistoricist understanding of historical exemplarity."[34] But Hazlitt's
contradictory project also indicates the emergence of a model of character
defined by its suspension between individuality and generality. The generic
form of characterization surpasses the specific attributes of its specific
subjects. By 1832, Thomas Carlyle writes in "Biography" that "every mortal
has a Problem of Existence ... the Problem of keeping soul and body
together, must be to a certain extent *original*, unlike every other; and yet, at
the same time, so *like* every other"[35]; and at the other end of the century, in
Impressions of Theophrastus Such (1879), George Eliot jokes, "one cannot be
an Englishman and a gentleman in general: it is in the nature of things that
one must have an individuality, though it may be of an oft-repeated
type."[36]

The October 1880 catalogue of Bemrose & Sons' Publishers advertises
a book of poetry, *The Spirit of the Age, and Other Rhymes for the Times: Being
a Series of Meditations on Things in General, and More Especially on Some
Things in Particular, Social, Political, Philosophical, Scientific, Educational,
and Ecclesiastical*, authored – pseudonymously, I hope – "by one who is fast
getting 'completely mixed'."[37] The comic title and author of this entry
confirm the public legibility and endurance of the connection between the
paradox of representative individuality and the idiom of induction that
originated with Bacon. The genres mocked by the advertised book (the
spirit-of-the-age book and the systematic treatise) also highlight how the
question of characterization that seems in discussions of Shakespeare to be
focused on personages was consistently and casually stretched to accommodate everything that could be encompassed by the nebulous notions of
culture or zeitgeist. The idiom of induction was used to characterize all
sorts of subjects, that is to say, because character inhered in the method or
approach, not in the subject itself. It was a matter of form and genre.

"The problem of induction" – whether and how one could derive reliable
generalizations from observed particulars – was, as Mary Poovey puts it, "the
heart of the epistemology of the long modern period."[38] If Francis Bacon
dominated nineteenth-century discussions of natural philosophical method,
philosophers typically credit David Hume for articulating induction as
a (necessary) problem in *A Treatise of Human Nature* (1739–40), his outline
for an empirical understanding of human character.[39] In the section "Of the
inference from the impression to the idea," Hume compares the process by

which sensory impressions become ideas to the process by which past experiences explain (or anticipate) present (or future) experiences. "We remember," he writes, "to have had frequent instances of the existence of one species of objects; and also remember, that the individuals of another species of objects have always attended them, and have existed in a regular order of contiguity and succession with regard to them" (88). The associative process by which empiricism describes character formation – sensory experiences are impressed upon the mind (as typographical characters are imprinted on a page), whence they are abstracted into ideas or memories of those impressions – explains for Hume how inductive knowledge *tout court* is produced. Experiential character formation thereby prescribes for Hume the method of knowledge production in the human sciences: the mind abstracts particular experiences into the ideas or memories that constitute character, just as philosophers infer from particular observations the general laws of causality that might explain or predict future phenomena. Hume calls this inference, not induction.

Hume does not employ the word *induction* in *A Treatise*, but instead describes the analogous relations between sensation and idea or cause and effect in terms of association, imagination, inference, memory, and attendance. More certain to him than the exact relation between observed experiences and abstract knowledge, which prove impossible to determine, is that knowledge originates in experiential "particulars," a word he employs well over 500 times in *A Treatise*. Indeed, while Hume's empiricist concept of character formation was highly influential, it was less associated with the term "induction" than with the idiom of "particulars" and "generals" and the array of locutions Hume used to approximate their (rather indeterminate) "certain relations" (e.g. 89, 93). I cite one exemplary instance of Hume's habitual recourse to "particulars" as an epigraph to this chapter because it manifests how eighteenth-century moral philosophers explained the way individual words, independently of context, automatically evoked "correspondent" ideas. Employing words such as "particular" and "general" performed accordingly for eighteenth- and nineteenth-century writers: their utterance educed the epistemological authority of inductive natural philosophy as well as the correlative concept of experiential character formation. The idiom of induction was "annexed," as Hume says, to the idea of character.

"Attention" likewise served as a touchstone for induction and character. Hume's treatise includes hundreds of variants of "attention," often expressly denominating the "certain relations" between impressions and ideas, causes and effects, particulars and generals.[40] As Peter Dear points

out, Hume's codification of induction admits that "certain causal properties" were "occult," not because they did not exist but because they were
not empirically observable (18). For Hume, then, character and knowledge
alike depend on the recognition that "one species of objects" has been
"always *attended*," as in accompanied, by "another species of objects"
(Hume 88; my emphasis). Attendance stood in for the unobservable
relations between coincident or contingent perceptions and ideas. These
unobservable relations might qualify as intentions, but here attention
matters more: the attention (or suspension) of two levels or "species of
objects" signified inference in action. Whether in philosophical accounts of
human nature and the natural world or in fiction, the word *attention* in
late-eighteenth- and nineteenth-century fiction invokes a reality defined by
its ontological amplitude, a reality defined by its bifurcation between
necessary scales of particularity and generality.

Posterity has been inclined to mobilize Adam Smith's "sympathy" as the
key faculty for eighteenth- and nineteenth-century British moral philosophy, especially as it inflects fiction as the medium for linking particular
individuals with general readers.[41] But turn-of-the-nineteenth-century
Britons privileged "attention," as did Smith: "Of such mighty importance," Smith says, "does it appear to be, in the imaginations of men, to
stand in that situation which sets them most in the view of general
sympathy and attention" (80).[42] A latent expression of this tendency
resides in a passage of *The Theory of Moral Sentiments* (1759) that recasts
Stoic ethics as a matter of paying properly calibrated degrees of attention.
For Smith, the cultivated Stoical mind allocates limited capacities of
perception according to a tacit cosmological order: "By choosing and
rejecting with this just and accurate discernment," Smith writes, "by thus
bestowing upon each object the precise degree of attention it deserved,
according to the place which it held in this natural scale of things, we
maintained, according to the Stoics, that perfect rectitude of conduct
which constituted the essence of virtue."[43] Smith correlates exacting perception with comportment, fitting attention with decorum. He concerns
himself less with mimetic fidelity to a particularized actuality than with
proper scales of attention because he configures reality as distributed along
a graduated continuum from concrete particularity to abstract and inclu-
sive universality. Smith grounds truth not in concrete particulars, but in
propriety: the proper degree of attention due to any particular. Cognitive
perception registered agreement between manners and the "natural scale of
things." As Stephen Shapin and Simon Shaffer have shown, early-modern
social conventions of civility, gentility, and decorum underwrote the

credibility and production of natural philosophical knowledge, which relied on these characterological conventions to convert private experiments and personal opinions into public facts; Jan Golinski, among others, has demonstrated how these conventions pertained perhaps even more prevalently at the turn of the nineteenth century.[44] Smith suggests that by the middle of the eighteenth century this convention of natural historical knowledge production had come to underwrite the way Britons experienced and represented character.[45]

Although Smith certainly uses "sympathy" more than "attention," "attend," and "attentive," he does use these variants often, and in his initial delineation of sympathy refers to the hypothetical subject as an "attentive spectator" (5). *Particular* and *general* further saturate *The Theory of Moral Sentiments* and characterize sympathetic imagination as an inductive faculty.[46] Smith writes, for example, that:

> the general passion of anger receives a different modification from the particular character of its object, as may easily be observed by the attentive. But still the general features of the passion predominate ... To distinguish these requires no nice observation; a very delicate attention, on the contrary, is necessary to discover their variations. (Smith 477)

Delicacy of attention here is both moral and observational, emotional and epistemological, a faculty that coordinates the social and cognitive work of the individual. Whether or not Smith influenced Austen directly, I adduce *The Theory of Moral Sentiments* because it makes explicit how late-eighteenth-century writers presupposed reality to be bifurcated between particularity and generality, in all their forms, and reckoned the negotiation of that scale to be a matter of emotional, social, and inductive "attention."

Inferential Realism, Austen's Amplitude

Like natural philosophy, novels were morally suspect at the turn of the nineteenth century primarily because they lacked concrete referents and, like all print, were supposed to have emotional and political effects on readers, most of whom were deemed young and therefore vulnerable. Manners of characterization were doubly relevant to fiction, then, because characters (as in personages) were its principal subjects, the vehicles for translating individual into general experience, and because like natural philosophy it sought to assert its character (as in its moral and epistemological credibility) over and against its fictionality. Michael McKeon and Lennard Davis have established how the English novel, since its emergence as a recognizable genre, legitimated its contents by representing them as virtual realities, probable histories, or imagined truth – that is, as representative particulars or concrete abstractions. These compound categories covered the inductive gamut from observed data to general idea and made fiction seem like an induction rather than ungrounded speculation or imagination.[47] Following Aristotle and Hume, and maintaining the assumption of a modern "rise" of particularity, such work addresses the epistemology of fiction as a problem of "belief," but including attention restores decorum, sociality, and broad-spectrum awareness to the question and elucidates the tacit rationale of early prose style.

Austen's style corresponds to the definitively scalar paradigm of reality that had emerged over the course of the eighteenth century, a paradigm according to which what we call the "real" was not only a matter of recognizable mimetic fidelity, probability, and individualized experience, but also a matter of appearing distributed along a continuum of scalar intensities that encompassed individuals and social life, as well as settings and objects. Partiality and impartiality, attention and inattention, individuality and collectivity, specification and overview, peculiarity and regularity: these gradations are scarcely noticeable because they have become nearly requisite ligatures of ordinary prose.

Austen's copious *particulars* variously signify an intensity of notice or concentration (particularity); remarkable affection, taste, or interest (partiality); or idiosyncrasy or *haecceity* (peculiarity). In *Mansfield Park* (1814), for example, the Bertram daughters greet their cousin, Fanny Price, with "an injudicious particularity," an excessive attention that ironically belies their self-importance and their insensitivity to Fanny's discomfort with and inexperience as the subject of others' attentions (*MP* 14). Fanny also intuits an erotic interest – dubbed "a particularity" – in the attentions that Henry Crawford pays her (418). The narrator even wryly registers the fast and loose currency of *particular* in the novel as Mr. Yates is introduced to Sir Thomas Bertram as "'the particular friend,' another of the hundred particular friends of his son" (214). The introduction of Mr. Yates complicates the analysis of these intensities because it belies the correspondence of the words *particular* and *general* with the intensities they presume to label. What is particular friendship if it can apply to a hundred, to friends in general?

As a relative modifier denoting comparatively extraordinary intensity, "particular" and its cognates intimate a world of myriad, always ongoing but not-always-noticeable perceptions, options, emotions, and relations. Circumstances offer "particular advantage" and appear "peculiarly calculated" (*MP* 54, 421). Narrators variously elide and relate "the particulars of this conversation" (*SS* 241). Characters seek a "particular object" (*MP* 98), but often can identify "no particular reason" (*NA* 23) for their feelings or behaviors. They observe "admiration of a very particular kind!" (*SS* 268) or "any particular style of building" (*MP* 66). The list could go on vertiginously: Austen's characters are "particularly pleased" (406), "particularly welcome" (10), "particularly careful" (*E* 30), "particularly necessary" (57), "particularly gentlemanlike" (*SS* 41), and so on. Words like "particular" imply selective attention only to one of the welter of objects available in a world brimming with superfluous data, a world surprisingly crowded with incidents. The selection of intimates and of aesthetic objects such as poems or trees matters greatly, but *particularity* so thoroughly pervades Austen's fiction that it does little to distinguish specific individuals for their judicious selectivity or attention to detail, and instead constitutes a kind of baseline condition of narrative possibility. To write prose for Austen is always to remark *particularity* and therefore to lay some claim to the authority of first-hand experience and concrete specificity.

The adjectival and adverbial *particular* performs the specific work of characterization because it concurrently suggests that the attribute or thing that it modifies is a recognizable, typical attribute and amplifies the attribute or thing to an exemplary degree: the modifier at once claims that its noun is common and appropriates it as an individual example of that common class, a uniquely noticed or felt version. In other words, such *particulars* foreground the thing they modify as if it were one of many always ongoing applications and objects present in any given mood. As a relative term, then, it compactly inscribes the taxonomical work of Shakespearean characterization into routine description. When, for instance, Darcy "wisely resolved to be particularly careful that no sign of admiration should *now* escape him" (*PP* 66), "particularly" does not so much modify a freshly instituted diffidence as it instead indicates Darcy's amplification of an already ongoing reticence, an amplification of the "usual reserve" (192) that makes his character legible. In describing Darcy's resolution to amplify an already ongoing reserve, the syntax implies that his ordinary, baseline experience involves an ongoing, unconscious care, a background operation against which his will performs in relief. We might ordinarily maintain that such a rift is a figure that construes a personage divided into conscious and unconscious components. But Austen's diction clearly attests that her culture assumed character was instead spatially distributed along a gradient from particular to general attentions.

Shades of particularity likewise appear in synonyms such as "peculiar," which accentuates the oddity of a given particularity. Phrases like a "sweet peculiarity of manner" imply that a character exhibits a conventional if overdetermined attribute (here, "manner") but in a noticeably if not explicably unique way (*MP* 407): "sweet peculiarity" gestures at specific distinctions of manner that the context does not wholly flesh out, and while interpretatively inclined readers might well do so in their own ways, the syntax suggests that the formal gesture at peculiarity is more important than the content of the peculiarity itself. Actual peculiarities, that is to say, matter less than the fact that peculiarities are present and duly noted by inductive and therefore characteristic prose. Indeed, Austen's characters often appreciate not having to share particulars of this sort, as when Emma subordinates the content of Miss Bates' infamous loquacity to its form: "As a counsellor she was not wanted; but as an approver, (a much safer character,) she was truly welcome. Her approbation, at once general and minute, warm and incessant, could not but please" (*E* 275). Miss Bates' approval is altogether anticipated and unoriginal, so the pleasure it occasions owes to its degree and range – "general and minute" – rather than the acuity, justness, or insight of its content. Similarly, the uninterested Lady Middleton relieves Elinor Dashwood because she affects to visit "without feeling any curiosity after particulars" (*SS* 245). If careful readers are as intimately aware of these particulars and their pain as Elinor is, the prose here measures their importance as indices of intensity rather than labels of specific emotions and their origins. In good Derridean fashion, to refer to particulars in this sense is therefore not to particularize but to generalize: to efface actual particularity with a measurement that subordinates specific details, feelings, and objects of focus to their relative quantity.

Particularity concomitantly accentuates and eludes quotidian matters – Mr. Woodhouse's prescriptions for gruel, for example, whose redundancy and vulgarity unsettled even admiring reviewers such as Richard Whately and Walter Scott – and material interests, the socioeconomic partialities, from which genteel persons could afford to abstract themselves and against which they demonstrate their liberal disinterestedness.[48] Mansfield Park is accordingly free from the distracting economic particulars of the shambolic Price household in Portsmouth, where the gritty operations of biological life – food, bodies, children, servants, bustle, and stupidity – intrude on Fanny's acquired equanimity. Fanny observes "the shocking character of all the Portsmouth servants" who "engross her [mother] completely," and regrets the naval preoccupations that mark her father's narrow-mindedness: "he had no curiosity, and no information beyond his profession" (*MP* 445, 450); "The Bertrams" and Fanny "were all forgotten in detailing the faults of Rebecca" and in "the newspaper and the navy-list ... the dockyard, the harbour, Spithead, and the Motherbank" (445, 450).

But *particularity* nevertheless also amplifies salutary singularities: it signposts empirical precision, aesthetic interest, acute sensibility, exacting taste, refinement, and distinction in relief against the homogeneity, impersonality, inexactitude, and detachment consequent upon abstraction, as when Emma laments an evening dulled by Jane Fairfax's reserve: it was "all general approbation and smoothness; nothing delineated or distinguished" (*E* 180). Whether this general civility bespeaks an insipid lack of distinction or tactful discretion depends on the circumstances, on the source of the generalization (the focalizer) and the appropriate scale of her content (what she particularizes or generalizes). But Emma's snub at Jane accentuates a picturesque taste for particulars and generals in tandem, here for general civility punctuated with the aesthetic pleasure of private gossip or confidences.

Susan Morgan frames Austen's novels as fictions about perception and the multiplicity and contingency of truth that privilege the "meantime," the lived uncertainty that accompanies knowledge which must accumulate over time. Morgan insists that "Austen's commitment is to particulars," and that in Austen's fictions "To invoke universals is to live in a world of forms, to think with all the spaciousness and all the hollowness of preconceptions and thus to withdraw from life in its demanding and inconclusive particularity."[49] But Austen's use of *particular* as a generalization consistently belies Morgan's claim. Austen insists that generalization and generalities are integral to sociability, sanity, self-composure, and good breeding, as I show later, but Emma's dissatisfaction with the polite generalities to which Jane Fairfax restricts her also expresses Emma's expectations of what her position entitles her to and what readers presumably want: as the most powerful woman in her circle, she thinks she can afford to indulge the destructive impulse to gossip, to disclose and exchange intimate particulars.

Jane's careful adherence to generalities signals, in contrast, her recognition that she cannot survive disrupting the rules of sociability or the social hierarchy; her tenuous social position – furtively engaged, bound to be a governess – precludes her ability to exhibit character in the form of full access to general and particular knowledge. Still, at the end of *Emma* both women survive their respective social disruptions by becoming general subjects of novelistic narrative, however particularly inflected: their stories become general knowledge to Highbury, their particularities are redressed with generic desires and plots. Austen naturalizes what initially emerge as singularities by smoothing them into familiar forms. So if, as Morgan suggests, Austen inhabits the temporal "meantime," she also inhabits the liminal space between particularity and generality.

Austen's prose is as replete with "generals" as it is with "particulars," and some notable critics remark on her abstraction. Dorothy Van Ghent, for instance, has argued that Austen's "is surely one of the most abstract vocabularies in fiction, and one of the least 'image-making' of styles."[50] "General" most repeatedly registers consensus either abstracted from the details of an event or ascribed to the abstract arbiters of common sense or collective opinion that Austen often dubs "all the world": "friends in general" (*MP* 54), "people in general" (*E* 130), "the general lookers-on of the neighborhood" (45), "your sex in general" (*E* 67), "the intellects of Highbury in general" (*E* 74, 372), "our guests in general" (*E* 274), "London in general" (*E* 110), and "the world in general" (*PP* 23, *E* 67). These vague populations sustain a baseline typology, perspective, mood, or opinion against which individuals might define themselves, but which they would nevertheless do well to resemble or appease. The affective realism of Austen's "ever so generally agreeable" (*MP* 408) world is a function of such generalization. If induction is the armature of empiricism, then Austen might be said here to generate aesthetic tension by instantiating contrasting empirical perspectives. She poses the experiential particularity of characters in states of individual concern against the probabilistic tendencies of narrators and other characters in states of abstraction, some-times induced from details but perhaps more often inadequately grounded in real evidence. Given the natural philosophical connotations of the word *general*, the persistent gestures at a general audience and common sense might be said to instantiate verbally the institutional audience and con-sensus built into modern science with its staged experiments. Instead of belaboring the tension between observed particulars and unverifiable abstractions as an epistemological problem, though, Austen accommodates it as an aesthetic, as the affective character of lived experience.

Austen's adjectival "general" scarcely evokes referential exactitude so much as what Orwell described as "the woolly vagueness" of Victorian prose.[51] For Franco Moretti, as for Orwell, the "vagueness" or "fog" generated by Victorian adjectives and typical of modern prose allows the adjectives to do double duty, at once ascribing an indeterminate but certain moral significance to and – belying the principle function of adjectives – somewhat obscuring rather than clarifying the words they modify.[52] As an adverb, "generally" modifies, among other things: "speaking" (*MP* 113), "allowed" (*MP* 111), "admitted" (*MP* 177), "supposed" (*E* 67), "known" (*E* 382), and "evident" (*PP* 23) – all modalities of decentered authority or perspective. As an adjective, "general" modifies: "agreement" (*MP* 121), "silence" (*MP* 109), "unreserve" (*PP* 156), "civility and obligingness" (*MP*

40), "civilities" (*MP* 226) and "incivility" (*PP* 160), "conduct" (*MP* 108), "spirits" (*MP* 124), "opinion" (*E* 450), "light" (*MP* 147), "prettiness" (*MP* 51), "character" (*SS* 94, *MP* 129), "expectation" (*PP* 219), "rule" (*NA* 20; *E* 55, 389), "notice" (*MP* 136), and "consent" (*SS* 429) – all decentered perceptions of opinion, sensations, and manner. Austen recounts "a general diffusion of cheerfulness" (*MP* 200), "general and ordinary cases" (*PP* 54), "a general want of understanding" (*SS* 261), "general opinion" that is "usually correct" because it "is general" and "opinions in general unfixed" (*MP* 129, 233), even "a general air of confusion in the furniture" (*MP* 213). Such prose eschews hundreds of potential threads of disagreement and specificity in favor of gloss, approximation, and commonness. Its recourse to "general" bolsters what Elizabeth Deeds Ermarth has described as the "implied consciousness" coordinating the discrete perspectives of a fiction, including but exceeding the narrator.[53] "General" perfunctorily implies that this prose has its finger on the pulse of the social body, grasps the bigger picture, and respects its content as only an example of more pervasive and diverse phenomena.

Characters routinely adhere to this imperative to generalize and regularly perform a kind of inductive summation, as when Emma speaks of Elton's "general way of talking" (*E* 70). Attuned to Mrs. Bennet's inanity and the narrator's irony, readers might scoff at "the report which was in general circulation within five minutes after [Mr. Darcy's] entrance, of his having ten thousand a year" (*PP* 10), but this general report turns out to be accurate and interests Elizabeth and the narrator in the long run as much as the gossipy "general circulation" in the moment. In short, as signatures of inductive method, these gestural "generals" flout the production of novelistic knowledge even as they often obscure what that knowledge might be.

Often enough, such knowledge comes in the form of rejections of generic assumptions. In *Northanger Abbey*, for example, "general" highlights generic conventions and assumptions that the narrative parodies and ironizes: the "generally accounted for" lack of a suitable suitor (*NA* 9); the "general mischievousness" of "lords and baronets" (10); "the general distress of the work" anticipated by the reader (12); "the easy style of writing for which," Tilney jokes, "ladies are so generally celebrated" (19). Amidst all of the tongue-in-cheek attention to gothic conventions, "generality" insinuates the threat of anonymity, homogeneity, effacement, and absorption by crowds of people and generically similar novels with which Austen's competed. Sardonically, Austen thereby appropriates these conventions to contain and satirize her readers' desires. Catherine Moreland grows "tired of being continually pressed against by people, the generality of whose faces possessed nothing to interest" (14). When she meets Isabella Thorpe, "generally" works with declarative pronouns like "those" and "such" to evoke a scene so familiar that it frees Austen from the burdens of particularization: "Their conversation turned upon *those* subjects, of which the free discussion *generally* has much to do in perfecting a sudden intimacy between two young ladies; *such as* dress, balls, flirtations, and quizzes" (25, my emphasis). Catherine is thus stifled and relieved by generality as the novel moves along this ontological scale between generic familiarity and satiric deviance. *Emma* works similarly, for it explicitly presents its story as divided between "interesting particulars" (457) and generic events: Emma's story is "An old story, probably – a common case – and no more than has happened to hundreds of my sex before" (465).

Austen applauds characters who are generally agreeable and facilitate general harmony. As Mrs. Weston affirms in *Emma*, "To do what would be most generally pleasing must be our object," and yet she humorously admits the difficulty of determining such an object: " – if one could but tell what that would be" (*E* 274). Juxtapositions of particularity and generality often correspond to what we call Austen's irony, for they accentuate the disparity between a particular character's knowledge (or lack thereof) and that of some collective – the unsettling particularity grating against general opinion. This tension occurs, for example, in Miss Crawford's ambivalent description of Dr. Grant as "all kindness in general" (*MP* 68), which introduces her account of his particularly "black" response to her thought-lessly (thoughtfully) having prodded farmers for use of their carts during harvest season. Claims such as "Miss Bertram is in general thought the handsomest" (*MP* 52) prompt readers' divergence from general opinion. While Mr. Knightley serves as "a sort of general friend and advisor" (*E* 62) to Emma, who has "a sort of habitual respect for his judgment in general" (*E* 69), she first takes exception to this general rule when rebuked.

The idiom of induction comes to the fore in passages of taxonomic characterization, where personages are differentiated from their species.[54] The narrator of *Emma*, relating "all that was generally known of [Harriet Smith's] history," remarks that "her beauty happened to be of a sort which Emma particularly admired" (22), and thus classifies Harriet's beauty as a familiar "sort" even as it distinguishes that sort as Emma's particular favorite. Austen regularly makes inductive rhetorical moves whereby she focuses on a particular detail, scene, or character and then extrapolates a more general axiomatic claim or expatiates on a group or class: in *Sense and Sensibility*, Willoughby's "manly beauty and more than common gracefulness were instantly the theme of general admiration, and the laugh which his gallantry raised against Marianne, received particular spirit from his exterior attractions" (*SS* 51); in *Northanger Abbey*, Henry Tilney's jibe at Catherine –"But your mind is warped by an innate principle of general integrity, and therefore not accessible to the cool reasonings of family partiality" (*NA* 225–26) – underscores present moral action as the casuist reconciliation of general principles with particular circumstances and interests; in *Mansfield Park*, "Experience might have hoped more for any young couple, so circumstanced, and impartiality would not have denied to Miss Crawford's nature, that participation of the general nature of women, which would lead her to adopt the opinions of the man she loved and respected, as her own" (*MP* 424). Here, as in the spirit-of-the-age texts that emerged in the 1820s, particulars are presented paradoxically as representative cases.

Many contemporaneous fictions explicitly ascribed *character* to a para-doxical or felicitous modulation of particularity and generality. In *Old Mortality* (1816), for instance, Walter Scott – who, second only to Shakespeare, was lauded in his day for generating characters who were both individuals and types – has Henry Morton, "securing attention" from publican Niel Blane, register the "general character" of Blane's new clientele "as leaves upon the same tree, with the same individual difference and the same general resemblance" as those he meets much earlier in the novel to celebrate his shooting of the popinjay.[55] George Eliot's *Felix Holt, the Radical* (1866), for another instance, regularly posits a cleavage between ontological levels of generality and particularity, a cleavage that instantiates the definitive irony Lukács ascribes to the novel: the lawyer and agent Matthew Jermyn "had had to do many things in law and in daily life which, in the abstract, he would have condemned; and indeed he had never been tempted by them in the abstract. . . . he had sinned for the sake of particular concrete things, and particular concrete consequences were likely to follow" (117); meanwhile, the sarcasm of the Dissenting minister, Rufus Lyon, "was not without an edge when he dilated in general on an elaborate education for teachers which issued in the minimum of teaching, but it found a whetstone in the particular example of that bad system known as the Rector of Treby Magna" (168). Even Thomas Hughes typifies the inductive posture in *Tom Brown's Schooldays* (1857):

> it is time for us to get from the general to the particular; so, leaving the great army of Browns, who are scattered over the whole empire on which the sun never sets, and whose general diffusion I take to be the chief cause of that empire's stability, let us at once fix our attention upon the small nest of Browns in which our hero was hatched.[56]

Catherine Gallagher has made the case that such oscillations in scale, from the particular, non-referential personage to the general type, are pronounced in George Eliot's work but constitute "the heart of the novel genre."[57] For Gallagher, particular readers and particular characters find common ground in an abstract domain of generalities. Rae Greiner conjoins Adam Smith's concept of sympathy to this representation of "character formation as a triptych," in which an abstract, non-empirical fellow-feeling is generated between "two ontologically distinct sets of particulars, real individuals and fictional individuals" (Greiner 46). Similarly, for Audrey Jaffe, "*Middlemarch* positions its readers within a consciousness whose cognitive mode is relentlessly comparative, in which character emerges as a closeness to or distance from an average"; and, moreover, Jaffe elaborates how the nineteenth-century social statistician Adolphe Quetelet articulated the "Average Man" as combining "the general and the particular."[58] I concur with all of these formulations, except to the extent that they delimit our connection to personages, excluding our affinities for the prose itself. The poise between *particular* and *general* constitutes the aesthetic of Austen's prose and manner of interesting the reader.

Austen's first critics, who persistently noted her subordination of "incident" to character, extended the encomium established in Shakespeare criticism to her for endowing her characters with individuality and typicality. G. H. Lewes, for instance, writes: "out of Shakespeare it would be difficult to find characters so typical yet so nicely demarcated within the limits of their kind."[59] An 1818 review of *Northanger Abbey* and *Persuasion* in the *British Critic* likewise appraises Austen's style: "by a singular good judgment, almost every individual represents a class; not a class of humourists, or of any of the rarer specimens of our species, but one of those classes to which we ourselves, and every acquaintance we have, in all probability belong" (Southam 80). An adulatory 1843 article of Thomas Macaulay's is perhaps the most exemplary. Austen, it says, "approached nearest to the manner" of Shakespeare:

> [Austen] has given us a multitude of characters, all in a certain sense, common-place, all such as we meet every day. Yet they are all as perfectly discriminated from each other as if they were the most eccentric of human beings. . . . And almost all this is done by touches so delicate, that they elude analysis, that they defy the powers of description, and that we know them to exist only by the general effect to which they have contributed.[60]

If Austen recognized the affiliation of *particulars* and *generals* with Shakespearean character, she nevertheless extended that idiom to make her prose a medium of characterizing everything it broached. *Mansfield Park* refers to "the scheme in general" and "the play in particular" (185), for example. And, for another, as if implying that marriage institutionally ensures an inductive balance between feminine particularity and masculine generalization, Mr. Knightley facetiously announces the engagement of Harriet Smith and Robert Martin: "she will give you all the minute particulars, which only woman's language can make interesting. – In our communications we deal only in the great" (*E* 515).

As William Galperin observes, Austen's fiction holds apart two modalities of the real: on the one hand, the "probable" or "familiar" institutionalized in the plot, and, on the other hand, the actual or the "everyday" instantiated by the oppositional "possibility" inscribed in "striking" detail.[61] These modalities correspond to generality and particularity, and reviewers such as Whately and Scott aspired to reconcile them. Whately's review almost explicitly describes Austen's prose as induction. As awash in *particulars* and *generals* as an Austen novel, it consistently describes the "character" or "*philosophical character*" of new novels like Austen's as the moral yield of inducing "general rules of probability," "general principles," "general rules of practical wisdom," and so on from various particulars.[62] Even as he bemoans Austen's "minute fidelity of detail" (360), expressly noting the extraordinary particularity of her "fictitious biographies," Whately nevertheless insists such novels "present us ... with the general, instead of the particular, – the probable, instead of the true; and, by leaving out those accidental irregularities, and exceptions to general rules, which constitute the many improbabilities of real narrative, present us with a clear and *abstracted* view of the general rules themselves" (357, emphasis in original). For an insistently inductive reader such as Whately, the reading of Austen's particulars seamlessly elicits generalizations, although of course those generalizations do not appear in print. They remain implicit in the particulars of the text.

Fredric Jameson's *The Antinomies of Realism* describes realism as dialectically poised between a chronological narrative impulse and a resistant affect or bodily sense that works in an eternal present.[63] Jameson associates affect with the German *Stimmung*, a kind of mood that links the subjective and the objective (38), and this mood echoes what nineteenth-century readers such as Scott and Whately identified as *character* in Austen's prose. Like Morgan, Jameson is invested in temporality, but his description of "affect's chromaticism, its waxing and waning not only in intensity but across the very scale and gamut of such nuances" (39) and "the sliding scale of the incremental, in which each infinitesimal moment differentiates itself from the last by a modification of tone and an increase or diminution of intensity" (42), aptly describes Austen's waxing and waning *particularity* and *generality*. For Austen, this affective embodiment is not at all so ineffable as the examples Jameson describes, for her idiom identifies it squarely with the fundamental cognitive work of experiential inference described by Hume. Her prose reproduces what it feels like to live on inference.

"Some marked display of attentions": Austen's Scientific Method[64]

As early as 1777, the doctor, writer, and editor John Aikin – brother of poet Anna Laetitia Barbauld – goaded poets to practice empirical observation and use diction consistent with modern natural philosophy instead of sponging anachronistic poeticisms from their predecessors. His *Essay on the Application of Natural History to Poetry* disparages the "faint, obscure, and ill characterized" descriptions of eighteenth-century verse for their "too cursory and general survey of objects, without exploring their minuter distinctions and mutual relations."[65] Such verse is "only to be rectified," he says, "by accurate and attentive observation, conducted on somewhat of a scientific plan" (10). This proposal for a nimbler, "somewhat . . . scientific" degree of "attention" integrating generality and particularity, the "survey" and the "minute," became a tacit convention of nineteenth-century literary and cultural criticism, and is therefore fundamental to understanding the kind of knowledge or value that such writing offered. Austen hardly heeds Aikin's injunction to adopt a scientific vocabulary in the way that, say, Charlotte Smith does. But her prose nevertheless respects his appeal to an "attentiveness" marked by the "mutual relations" between particulars and generals. Austen extends the natural philosophical work of induction to the domain of social interaction and manners, where emotion and persuasion come in the form of inducements and where desire, condescension, respect, and interest come in the form of attentions. Austen occasionally leverages the social connotations of the verb "induce" – to evoke, to persuade – to accentuate the contingency of character and the inductive work of fiction, but "attention" is her privileged term for mediating particularity and generality, and it too extends the cognitive work of abstracting particulars to social intercourse, where "attentions" signify the myriad gestural forms by which individuals engage social bodies.

Northanger Abbey remarks: "attention to his words" (78), "anxious attention to the weather" (81), the inability of a play to "keep [Catherine's] whole attention" (92), moral self-reflection on having "attended to what was due to others and to her own character in their opinion" (102); Tilney's "attentions to Miss Thorpe" and, despite her engagement to John Moreland,

"Miss Thorpe's admission of them" (154). General Tilney's "anxious attention ... and civility" and "incessant attentions" or "continual solicitations" (*NA* 103, 157) foreshadow his greedy misconceptions about Catherine's fortune. Tilney fixes Catherine's attention with his Gothic parody of her visit to the abbey (164); and after Tilney exposes Catherine's supposedly preposterous suspicions of uxoricide, "he paid her rather more attention than usual" (204) to sooth her, and so on. Attention is a binding force, nearly a legally enforceable binding force: because of the extent of his attentions, Tilney feels bound to Catherine.

In *Persuasion*, Wentworth likewise finds himself nearly engaged because of the attentions he pays Louisa. In *Mansfield Park*, being an object of attention ratifies one's worth, as when William Price keeps everybody but Mrs. Norris, including even the chronically somnolent Lady Bertram, "attentive" to his anecdotes (*MP* 275). Henry Crawford registers attention among a catalog of other familiar symptoms of reader response as he admires the "lively admiration, the glow of Fanny's cheek, the brightness of her eye, the deep interest, the absorbed attention, while her brother was describing any of the imminent hazards, or terrific sense, which such a period at sea, must supply" (274). Attention in such scenes indicates a physiological charm or susceptibility to the charm of others that, because of its unconscious embodiment, operates independently and often contrary to social expectations and personal intentions, and therefore appears to index genuine, unscripted feeling. But beyond the erotic, attentions also denote care of a curatorial, educational, pastoral sort, as in *Pride and Prejudice*, where Elizabeth laments her father's "indolence and the little attention he has ever seemed to give to what was going forward in his family" (312); where Lydia elopes because of her mother and father's inattention; and where Elizabeth and Darcy afford Kitty "proper attention and management" to make her "less irritable, less ignorant, and less insipid," and hence less likely to repeat Lydia's mistake (428).

As with her *particulars* and *generals*, Austen's persistent modification of *attention* with adverbs and adjectives suggests that the performance of attention was at least as important as the objects of any given act of attention. *Sense and Sensibility* records "ready attention" and "the greatest ...," "the most earnest ...," "the most steady and submissive ...," "affectionate ...," and "careful, considerate attention" (166, 182, 184, 241, 177, 403). *Pride and Prejudice*, where Mr. Collins' insufferably sycophantic and "assiduous" "attentions have been too marked to be mistaken" (129, 118) and where the Bennet daughters vie for "their share of Mr. Wickham's attentions" (94), also accounts for the "smallest attention," "proper attention," and "such unnecessary, such officious attention" (173, 428, 218). "Accounting for such attentions" is how Austen describes the Gardiners' investigation into the Darcy party's surprising alacrity to visit Elizabeth at their inn. It assumes the form of Puritanical book-keeping, as if discovering the intentions motivating attentions was a matter of inventory not interpretation. And the modifiers duly credit *attentions* the significance of narratable events, such that nods, glances, simple commitments to listen, but mostly altogether unspecified acts of attention require as much prose as incidents do. Without quite clarifying exactly what such attentions might entail, these adjectives and adverbs conjure an aura of moral significance and aesthetic interest around *attentions*. Nineteenth-century adjectives, as Moretti observes, typically provide "less ethical clarity, but greater emotional strength; less precision, more meaning" (130). For Moretti, "this incrustation of value judgments over matters of fact" evidences a Victorian revolution in values, whereby "meaning" became "more important than precision" (130–31). Austen's prose fusses accordingly more about the distribution of attentions and their degree and value than it does about their specific form. Collecting as they do around *attentions*, the modifiers further substantiate a nebulous cluster of relations – focus, condescension, flirtation, deference, presence, induction, and all the acts by which they might be enacted – as tangible expressions of character, the vague but certain objects of reader interest.

As Crary explains, mid-century disciplines such as physiology and psychology capitalized on *attention* as an abstraction around which to produce knowledge about embodied perception, but *character* preceded such disciplines as a textual model for studying embodied perception, and early nineteenth-century Britons embraced a far more polyvalent sense of attention than Crary admits. Austen's fiction registers at least six overlapping connotations of the word. For one, it employs *attentions* to denominate flirtations, like the attentions Mr. Bingley pays Jane Bennet. *Attentions* also signifies less partial, more gentlemanly or chivalric solicitude, accompaniment, or company, as when Mr. Knightley deferentially humors Mr. Woodhouse's hypochondriacal complaints. Attendance in this regard encompasses a range of social obligations, including presence and participation at certain occasions – the "regular duties" of life in Bath demand "the Pump-room to be attended" (*NA* 17) – and the generic pleasantries and inquiries about weather and wellness exchanged by acquaintances and dance partners, empty formalities that Henry Tilney nevertheless respects as "the proper attentions of a partner" (17). However hasty characters might be to dismiss or denigrate such attentions, whose insipid content is habitually slighted by the likes of Tilney and Darcy, Austen repeatedly buttresses their formal value as requisites to social flow and as modes of novelistic character-ization. *Attentions* relatedly names officious or generous acts of condescen-sion whereby a social superior goes out of her way to "notice" a social inferior with affability, a visit, a gift, a look, advice, or conversation. Think of the innumerable attentions that obsequious Mr. Collins brags about receiving from Lady Catherine de Bourgh.

Again, *attention* also served as a synonym for Smith's sympathetic imagi-nation. Austen's usage sometimes describes the work of Smith's "attentive spectator" (5), standing in for imperfect but adequate efforts to reckon the feelings of another.[66] Of course, Austen also employs *attention* to describe concentration or focus, but more often perception that operates inferentially or inductively in line with Hume's account of human nature. To attend to something is in some sense to isolate a particular from amongst the general milieu or morass of detail. The particular objects of such attention – farm improvements, landscape features, music, chapel renovations, poems, and so on – of course indicate the relative taste and propriety of the attender, though so does the proclivity of attending only to such particulars and not to things in general. Lastly, the pervasiveness of the theater in turn-of-the nineteenth-century Britain likewise attuned readers to the performance of these manifold attentions in gestures, postures, and glances, as well as to the art of managing their own attention to a stage filled with more people than one could comprehend in its entirety.[67] The theater naturalized the feeling of being an actor in a social performance subject to the attentions of others.

Collectively, the range of overlapping connotations of *attention* suggest not only that Austenian character was subject to the attentions of others, the capacities of one's own attention span, and the relative range of demands that attention span confronts, but also that nineteenth-century prose accom-modated an aesthetic economy of attentions[68] – an "economy" because attentions are a limited resource to expend and invest and because this allocation circulated as credit and propriety. The economy of *attentions* translates the epistemological problem of induction from the domain of natural philosophy into the discourses of decorum, sensibility, sociability, and fictional character: all modes of treating character as a mutual relation between entities rather than a fixed property or set of properties belonging to any individual person or thing.

Austen's characters are subjects not just to their own capacities for attention and their willful or unconscious acts of attention and inattention, but also of the wanted and unwanted, satisfying and oppressive, welcoming and alienating inattentions of others. Overhearing two gentlemen compli-menting her looks, Catherine Moreland becomes "perfectly satisfied with her share of public attention" (*NA* 16). And inductively seguing from an individual personage to the universal reader, *Northanger Abbey* offers Catherine at the cotillion ball as representative of "every young lady" as she anxiously fends off John Thorpe's attentions and solicits Henry Tilney's: "Every young lady may feel for my heroine ... all have been, or at least all have believed themselves to be, in danger from the pursuit of some one whom they wished to avoid; and all have been anxious for the attentions of some one whom they wished to please" (72). Just when she has secured freedom to accept a dance with Tilney, she is assailed again: "Scarcely had they worked themselves into the quiet possession of a place, however, when her attention was claimed by John Thorpe" (73). The "resistless pressure" of the crowd, which threatens concomitantly to gratify or overwhelm with its attentions and to alienate or relieve by its inattentions, thankfully limits how long Thorpe "could weary Catherine's attention" (74). And yet Thorpe distracts Catherine long enough to vex Tilney, who gripes, "He has no business to withdraw the attention of my partner from me" (74). Tilney proceeds, playfully but earnestly, to compare a country dance to a "marriage," "a contract of mutual agreeableness," according to which "Nobody can fasten themselves on the notice of one, without injuring the rights of the other" (74). As Crary observes,

> attention had limits beyond and below which productivity and social cohesion were threatened ... [but] attention is the means by which an individual observer can transcend those subjective limitations and make perception *its own*, and attention is at the same time a means by which a perceiver becomes open to control and annexation by external agencies. (Crary 4–5; emphasis in original)

Inundating Catherine with unwanted attentions just when she wants desperately to attend to, and be attended by, Henry, the novel seems here to titillate the reader by frustrating his or her own desire to attend to that budding romance. Indeed, given the apostrophe to the reader, we might indulgently take Catherine here as a metaphor for the work of a young novelist looking for fair attention from a public inundated with Minerva Press gothic fictions. In correlating the proper distribution of attentions with "mutual agreeableness," however, the novel certainly privileges *attentions* as the currency of social intercourse.

Emma similarly plots the distribution of attention as the object of moral education. First Emma – "the attentive lady of the house ... the attentive daughter" (473) – misperceives Mr. Elton's general civilities as marks of particular attention to Harriet Smith, because she wants the former to love the latter (*E* 141–42); she thus fails to notice that Elton is actually paying attentions to her, and the novel blames this error on thinking deductively instead of inductively: "She had taken up the idea, she supposed, and made every thing bend to it" (145). Emma relieves Harriet of her interest in Mr. Elton with "reasonings and soothings and attentions of every kind" (288). But later Mr. Knightley reprimands her, judgmentally observing "that Jane Fairfax received attentions from Mrs. Elton which nobody else paid her," and so, because these "words dwelt with her," she resolves to "shew [*sic*] her greater attention than I have done" (314–15). Emma's tactless joke at Miss Bates's volubility on Box Hill evokes Miss Bates's (passive aggressive) gratitude for her attentions, now recognized as reluctant acts of condescension: "It will be felt so great an attention!" (253). And Mr. Knightley again admonishes Emma: "I wish you could have heard her honouring your forbearance in being able to pay her such attentions, as she was for ever receiving from yourself and your father when her society must be so irksome" (407–8). Again, Emma recognizes future, continued, earnest attentions – not an apology – as the proper redress to obviate her offense: "If attention, in future, could do away the past, she might hope to be forgiven" (410).

Sense and Sensibility likewise treats attentions as the medium of morality and immorality, tact and indecorum: the novel repeatedly valorizes Elinor as "indifferent" because she regulates how much attention she pays outwardly to anyone in particular, thereby generating an effect of neutrality and disinterestedness (172, 174, 178). John Dashwood is talked into not paying any attention – especially monetary attention – to his sisters by his wife. And throughout, Marianne has to learn to attend to general society instead of just herself and Willoughby. The delicate, restrained exchange between Lucy and Elinor affirms Elinor's superior tactical attention. She grounds her earliest suspicions of Willoughby's mendacity on his inattention to circumstances and to his indecorous or insensible indulgence of undivided attention:

> Elinor saw nothing to censure in him but a propensity, in which he strongly resembled and peculiarly delighted her sister, of saying too much what he thought on every occasion, without attention to persons or circumstances. In hastily forming and giving his opinion of other people, in sacrificing general politeness to the enjoyment of undivided attention where his heart was engaged, and in slighting too easily the forms of worldly propriety, he displayed a want of caution which Elinor could not approve, in spite of all that he and Marianne could say in its support. (*SS* 58)

Here again, Austen upholds "general" attention over "particular" attention; one must induce her particular inclinations into the inclinations of
the milieu. Elinor diagnoses Marianne similarly with an attention deficit
disorder and implores her "to treat our acquaintance in general with greater
attention" (SS 108); and the narrator likewise disparages "her usual inattention to the forms of general civility" (165). Mrs. Dashwood's contrition at
the end of the novel juxtaposes "unjust, inattentive . . . almost unkind" as
appositives, thus including attention amongst cardinal virtues.

Beyond morality, attention is yoked by free indirect discourse to Elinor's
other cognitive habits of "memory," "reflection," and "fancy" (SS 121), the
various means by which Romantic writers process experience. And the
word condenses a gamut of emotions, too, as when Elinor later hears that
Colonel Brandon has confessed to Mrs. Dashwood his love for Marianne:
"feeling by turns both pleased and pained, surprised and not surprised,
[Elinor] was all silent attention" (380). "All silent attention": even here in
this moment of intense feeling, Austen presents Elinor in relation to others,
reconciling her roiling interiority with the presence of others.

Thinking of narrative in spatial terms, Alex Woloch describes characterization accordingly in *Pride and Prejudice* – for him, the paradigm of nineteenth-
century novelistic characterization – as the dramatization of "two competing
registers of narrative attention: the five Bennet sisters *in general* . . . and
Elizabeth Bennet *in particular*, the protagonist of the novel, who
transcends the social context in which she has been placed to become
the center of the narrative in-and-of-herself."[69] To be sure, nineteenth-
century fiction poses particular characters in tension with the many, at whose
expense the protagonists' particularities come: Elinor's "silent attention"
speaks to that. Yet Austen's "competing registers of narrative attention"
profoundly exceed the bounds of characters, as in personages, primary or
secondary. Because nineteenth-century Britons routinely ascribed character
to things other than characters (personages), what Woloch calls the
"character-space" – the "*intersection* of an implied human personality –
that is, as Dostoevsky says, 'infinitely' complex – with the definitively
circumscribed form of a narrative" (13) – might to be extended to include
all of Austen's prose in general and not just her personages. Indeed, Woloch
even admits that the character-space "highlights the way that the 'human
aspect' of a character is often dynamically integrated into, and sometimes
absorbed by, the narrative structure as a whole" (15). The implication is that
character is a product of the relations between elements in the narrative, the
product of specific everyday ligatures or locutions that articulate the kind of
intersections Woloch describes as well as many others.

Elinor's rapt attention to Marianne's irritable absence of attention is the evidence on which Eve Sedgwick founds her notorious essay "Jane Austen and the Masturbating Girl."[70] According to Sedgwick, the "compulsive attention paid by anti-onanist discourse to disorders *of* attention make it a suitable point of inauguration for modern sexuality" (114), and thus "attention" was symptomatic of character precisely at the historical moment when identity begins to coalesce around a secreted sexuality and self-discipline. As Sedgwick writes, "Elinor's self-imposed obligation to offer social countenance to the restless, insulting, magnetic, and dangerous abstraction of her sister constitutes most of the plot of the novel ... it creates both the consciousness and the privacy of the novel" (117). Elinor's interiority and the consciousness of the narrative or narrator are, in other words, products of "her one-directional visual fixation on her sister's specularized, desired, envied, and punished autoeroticism," and this "one-directional ... fixation" of attention models, in turn, "the chains of reader-relations constructed by the punishing, girl-centered moral pedagogy and erotics of Austen's novels more generally" (Sedgwick 120). The (then) pathological category of the masturbator registered the libinal energies ascribed to attentions paid to the self and to the interest, inducements, and other exchanges between particulars and generalities. Relational as it was, the product of attentions paid and received, character gave a morally wholesome name to the titillating interest drawing together personages, objects, and readers. Elinor's ostensible frigid injunction to leave the bed-room and consort with the crowd strangely sponsors a desire for what we might hyperbolically describe as group sex. Austen's style wants to have it both ways.

Sedgwick observes how Marianne's masturbatory symptoms mark the emergence of essentialist gender identities, but the idiom of induction and attention, with its emphatic insistence on bidirectional movement, dilation and concentration, resisted such essentialism. Marianne becomes problematic in *Sense and Sensibility* to the extent that she behaves antisocially, too interested in her own interiority, because character in Austen's world necessitated sociality, to paying attentions to all ontological scales. At stake in Marianne's awkward attentions, then, are not only the disciplining of desire, but also the resistance to the cult of interiority for which Austen has so often been upheld, with her free indirect discourse, as a paragon. In rebuking Marianne, Elinor surely also rebukes herself, stewing as she is with her own private desires and disappointments and seeking escape in the social circle if not the crowd. The aesthetic charge of Austen's prose comes from posing these competing degrees of attention together. Marianne and Elinor, in their tension and love, might therefore be said to personify Austen's aesthetic. This aesthetic approaches what Jameson describes as the affective embodiment portrayed by realism, and in Marianne and Elinor we certainly feel the physical sense of extension in a field of inducements. "A certain sensory heterogeneity is disguised as that absolute homogeneity we call style," Jameson writes, "and a new phenomenological continuum begins to emerge, which is that of the play and variations, the expansion and contraction, the intensification and diminution, of that nameless new life of the body which is affect. Affect becomes the very chromaticism of the body itself."[71]

Recall again that Elizabeth Bennet's "keenest attention was awakened" (*PP* 275) by the picturesque, sexually charged, historically and financially endowed landscape of Pemberley and by the surprising appraisal that the housekeeper, Mrs. Reynolds, gives of Darcy. This epistemological arousal of attention combines the everydayness of a housekeeper's familiar and economic knowledge of character with the aesthetics of the picturesque, a landscape that blends neoclassical form with romantic naturalness. Elizabeth is induced not just to change her mind about Darcy, but to attune her attention to a broader, general perspective, the very perspective that narrator and presumably the reader share in regretting the Bennets' embarrassing behavior but acknowledging Darcy's allure in terms of history, property, and security. Uvedale Price and William Gilpin prescribed modes of landscape observation and representation that reconciled general impressions, broad vistas, and distant, vague objects with the striking particularity and clarity of foreground details and framing objects whose irregularity deviates from generic backgrounds. The picturesque imperative to facilitate movement between foreground, middle-ground, and background was articulated in terms of the putatively "organic" relationship of parts to wholes and eccentric individuals to representative types; and the process of perceiving this organic relationship extended the voguish ideals of German Romantic *naturphilosophie* and the natural philosophical cachet of induction and "Method" to an otherwise amateurish hobby.[72] Picturesque writing thus naturalizes – in more ways than one – a realist style whose purported "naturalness" depends on its mediation of anomalous particulars with unfocused generalizations, a chromaticism of the sort Jameson discusses.

The idiom of induction offered a verbal correlative of the ocular realism portrayed by picturesque theory. Price and Gilpin relish *particular* and *general* in their books, and may well be Austen's sources for this diction. Austen's alleged favorite, Gilpin, describes in his *Essay on Prints* (1768) an inductive impressionism that attends to general effects and feelings, and then to minutiae, and then again to a general understanding of the scene as a whole. For Galperin, Austen's prose style mimics the picturesque accommodation of pre-existing generic paradigms of the natural with irregularities that frame or punctuate and thereby actually contribute to the general harmony that they only ostensibly threaten (11). Such irregularities take the form, say, of an "old twisted tree" like that about which Edward Ferrars quizzes Marianne, or the comic scene in *Northanger Abbey* where Tilney's explicit lesson in picturesque theory moves from the specificity of oaks to forests in general. This comic scene of induction segues from oaks and forests to enclosure and politics before pausing in the relief of silence, a "general pause," only to be interrupted in turn by Catherine's announcement that "something very shocking indeed, will soon come out of London" (*NA* 113). Miss Tilney enquires about the "nature" of this shock, but Catherine is only able to respond in generalities, knowing neither the nature nor the author of the novel, only that it will be "more horrible than any thing we have met with yet" (113). This passage has an inductive logic of its own as it unravels from oaks to forests to politics to aesthetics and into general anticipation for something novel.

Next to gratitude, attention is the most important interpersonal feeling in Austen's prose. It articulates almost all of the relations between Emma and other characters. As Mr. Knightley gauges Emma's response to the news of Frank Churchill's engagement to Jane Fairfax, Emma audits her mismanaged attentions received and paid: "I was tempted by his attentions," she regrets, "my vanity was flattered and I allowed his attentions" (*E* 294). Shocked by Frank's "system of secrecy and concealment ... hypocrisy and deceit," Emma dwells on the licentiousness of his "repeated attentions": "What right had he ... to distinguish any one young woman with persevering attention ... while he really belonged to another?" (274). Here again attention appears decidedly inductive and economic: partiality (engagement or marriage) to one individual necessitates that one generalize the rest of his attentions (instead of flirting), which is precisely what Jane Fairfax does in forcing Emma to endure her banal, general civilities. Moral rectitude here exacts the price of interest: the consistency requisite to a purely moral model of character detracts from the more modern inductive model of character, whose aesthetic demands fully scalable attention no matter what level of impartiality or detachment one *ought* to maintain.

Attention likewise denominates the affective intensity of Fanny Price's experience, which often subjects her to others whose specific interests exceed her comprehension or defy easy categorization. These interests can be erotic, as when Henry Crawford shows Fanny "more prominent attention" than Edmund when trying to score her reciprocal attention and, that night, Sir Thomas "found his niece the object of attentions or rather professions of a somewhat pointed character" (*MP* 292, 286). Crawford's attentions contribute to everyone else – including Sir Thomas – learning that Fanny deserves their attention in a far more complex sense: they learn, on the one hand, that she has attractions that warrant marital interest and, on the other hand, a character, too, that warrants consideration, respect, deference, and admiration, if not mere equality. Edmund first distinguishes his superiority by recognizing Fanny "to be farther entitled to attention" (19) than his aunt and mother and sisters judge. Edmund undergoes an inductive sentimental education of his own, for he later promises to "prove himself by constant attention" to his parishioners not just to Fanny alone (288). Likewise, Fanny's reward comes not just in marriage to Edmund, but in becoming an object of general attentions, in Sir Thomas discovering her to be "the daughter that he wanted," rewarding her "with every kind attention" (546).

Fanny Price, reticent to admit that she is herself worthy of attention, knows how to pay it to others and to whom and what her attentions are due. On the ride to Sotherton, she pays attention to "all that was new . . . Her own thoughts and reflections" and, with georgic relish that evokes the poetry of George Crabbe, "the appearance of the country, the bearings of the roads, the differences of soil, the state of the harvest, the cottages, the cattle, the children" (*MP* 94). Miss Crawford, however, "had none of Fanny's delicacy of taste, of mind, of feeling; she saw nature, inanimate nature, with little observation; her attention was all for men and women, her talents for the light and lively" (94). Mary Crawford pays attention improperly because she attends only to adult personages and not to the full array of objects and, more importantly, object relations – "appearance," "bearings," "differences," and "the state."

Mansfield Park depicts its eponymous great house as a space defined by its ability and inability to regulate attention properly. Markedly inattentive to the (otherwise central) romance plot between Fanny and Edmund, the novel concentrates on the deterioration and restitution of proper attentions within the park. Of course, nobody but Fanny pays attention to the authority of absent Sir Thomas Bertram, and nobody but the narrator consistently pays proper attention to Fanny. Mrs. Bertram selects Fanny to live with her because she is "of an age to require more attention than her poor mother can possibly give" (*MP* 6), and yet upon arrival Fanny's "feelings were very acute, and too little understood to be properly attended to" (15). But Fanny too needs a lesson in how to pay attention, and her characterization and character formation depends on this lesson. No longer convinced that "modesty had prevented her from understanding [Henry

Crawford's] attentions" (376–77), and therefore hoping to teach her the value of Mansfield Park and all it represents by distancing her from it, Sir Thomas sends Fanny back to the Price household in Portsmouth. She finds home altogether too claustrophobic, thin-walled, noisome, disorderly, and bustling to allow anyone to pay attention to each other – "nobody could command attention when they spoke" (454) – or to anything else in particular, except indeed to the ways Fanny's parents injudiciously apportion their attentions. The Prices's engrossment – their selfishness, indecorousness, narrow-mindedness, and their degrading social class – is dramatized in their ill-calibrated attentions. In contrast, the erstwhile inattentive spaciousness, privacy, and comportment of Mansfield Park now seem to foster general attention to everyone and liberal attention to things in general: "No, in her uncle's house there would have been a consideration of times and seasons, a regulation of subject, a propriety, an attention towards every body which there was not here" (*MP* 442). When order is reinstated, Fanny feels that Mansfield Park – and, by extension, *Mansfield Park* – models a regulated economy of attention and therefore teaches Fanny how to appreciate a certain mode of classed inattention as attention, as consideration.

Like the inductive method as described by Whewell, and like Gilpin's prescriptions for picturesque viewing, Austen's prose facilitates constant movement from particulars to generals and then back again, never resting on one individual or collective. General attentions, like theories, can problematically preclude attendance to particular observations and vice versa. In *Pride and Prejudice*, self-absorbed Sir William Lucas is "all attention to every body" (19), which shows his affability but also his lack of selectivity – his failure to adjudicate "the precise degree of attention," to repeat Adam Smith's words, each object "deserved, according to the place which it held in this natural scale of things" (Smith 403). While Sir William diffuses his attention too generally, Lady Catherine De Bourgh attends too sedulously to "the minutest concerns" of other peoples' lives (*PP* 190). Befuddled Mr. Rushworth ties his tongue acquiescing to Lady Bertram's taste "with the superadded objects of professing attention to the comfort of ladies in general, and of insinuating that there was one only whom he was anxious to please" (*MP* 65). Bolstering the relative appeal and disgust of individual characters by disclosing their preferred objects of attention, these attunements collectively give Austen's prose a rhythm; and given the propensity for critics to remark on Austen's ordinariness, her prosaic fictions, they suggest in turn that everyday life felt like a continuous balancing of frequencies.

Take Mr. Cole's dinner, whose guests "were too numerous for any subject of conversation to be general" and so "Emma could fairly surrender all her attention to the pleasantness of her neighbor." But this particular attention is interrupted by a "remote sound to which she felt herself obliged to attend," the "name of Jane Fairfax" (*E* 148). Mrs. Weston is at one moment "almost wholly engrossed by her attentions to [Mr. Woodhouse]" (84). Later, "[Jane Fairfax's] attention was now claimed" by the "particular compliments to the ladies" paid by Mr. Woodhouse, "according to his custom on such occasions" (203). On that same occasion, Emma feels "her attention disengaged" (210); "Mr. Weston's attention was chained" (221); "Emma returned all her attention to her father" (251). Here, prosaic life seems rather replete with demands that will surely eclipse each other. Every particular attention paid threatens to foreclose experience of the general mood or of some other particular,[73] and yet paying attention is not merely a matter of choice. Some people deserve our attention; others command it.

Attention operates independently of will, which makes it indicative of unconscious motives, and more interestingly severs the link between aesthetic appeal and moral consistency. Darcy's reluctance to pay attention to Elizabeth offers a telling case. At their awkward first meeting, Darcy "soon drew the attention of the room by his fine, tall person" while snubbed Elizabeth remains "unassailed by any attention to herself" (*PP* 16). Later, amidst a discussion of the character of desirable women, "Miss Bingley's attention was quite as much engaged in watching Mr. Darcy's progress through *his* book, as in reading her own" (60; emphasis in original).[74] When Caroline Bingley invites Elizabeth to accompany her pacing the room, Darcy looks up "as much awake to the novelty of attention in that quarter as Elizabeth herself could be, and unconsciously closed his book" (61). Inattention to books allows attention to particular individuals; distraction bespeaks attraction.[75] By the end of the day Mr. Darcy "began to feel the danger of paying Elizabeth too much attention" (64), but he cannot help himself and awkwardly confesses his intractable *attention* – a more appropriate term than "desire" in Austen's fiction, given its inscription of social expectations – in his first, rude and blundering proposal.

But Darcy manifests his excessive attention earlier in scenes, too, where Elizabeth catches him eyeing her: "Elizabeth blushed and blushed again with shame and vexation. She could not help frequently glancing her eye at Mr. Darcy, though every glance convinced her of what she dreaded; for though he was not always looking at her mother, she was convinced that his attention was invariably fixed by her" (*PP* 112). Austen's prose thus inscribes an erotic tension into the cognitive work of everyday life – an erotic tension accompanied, of course, with awkwardness. The awkwardness of unwonted attentions paid and received.

While many characters obliviously reply to Marianne Dashwood's singing with "raptures," Colonel Brandon, her admirer, "paid her only the compliment of attention; and she felt a respect for him on the occasion, which the others had reasonably forfeited by their shameless want of taste" (*SS* 41–42). Awkwardly, the exchange underscores Marianne's own shameless want of taste, failing as she does to return attention to Brandon. But the manifold awkwardness of the scene is its appeal and its purchase on the real. The character of the scene derives, that is, from slips such as when Sir John and Lady Middleton politely "wondered how any one's attention could be diverted from music for a moment" even as they "asked Marianne to sing a particular song which Marianne had just finished" (*SS* 41). Lynch explains that "character" in Austen relies on a negotiation of the personal and the impersonal, the private and the public that legitimates and articulates it (207–49). A character, she says, must act as "the engineer of a sort of white noise machine" that hears the outside world without listening to it (Lynch 212). Courteous acts of paying attention or being "mindful," as Elinor Dashwood says, allow characters to reserve their private interiority, to respect the noisy present and yet be engaged "elsewhere" (Lynch 236–37). They can function, that is to say, at once on the levels of particular, partial, individuality, and general convention or "pro forma" commonplace, attending the crowd or "all the world."[76] But this need not work out so harmoniously or decorously. Austen's prose subsumes tone deafness, tactlessness, distraction, and all forms of mistaken attention into its scalar movement as readily as it translates induction into its characterization of everyday life.

If Austen was exceptional, she was not alone. Romantic novels as diverse as Walter Scott's *Redgauntlet* (1824) and Mary Shelley's *Frankenstein* (1818) also appropriate the idiom of induction and attention. Noting "perpetual attention," "unremitting attention," and "unceasing attendance," *Frankenstein* implies that characterization involves reckoning objects and their proper degrees of attention.[77] Walton relates how Victor "attracted our attention, and diverted our solicitude from our own situation" (Shelley 12). Victor imputes his follies to his father's failure to invalidate Agrippa's philosophy and regrets how fathers too often neglect opportunities "of directing the attention of their pupils to useful knowledge" (Shelley 22–23). As in Austen and in inductive philosophy, Shelley insists attention must wax and wane. Divided attention appears as an ideal rather than a problem. Victor laments having "not attended any of the lectures given at the schools of Geneva" and thus having suffered from "most undivided attention" (Shelley 23). "My attention," Victor concludes, "was fixed upon every object the most insupportable to the delicacy of the human feelings" (34), and this fixation on "minutiæ" becomes a slavish "engrossment" analogous to that of the Portsmouth Prices (Shelley 38). Like divided selfhood, divided attention was for Shelley requisite to character. And reviewers of nineteenth-century fiction testify to this: an 1813 *Critical Review* piece on *Pride and Prejudice* remarks, for instance, how instead of investing all of the interest in one or two characters, it "very agreeably divides the attention of the reader" (Southam 43).

Gentlemanly character, Victor implies, involves not just abstaining from occult sciences and charnel-house recreations, but, more importantly, demonstrating an elastic, liberal, inductive attention. Thus, Victor praises Henry Clerval's "unbounded and unremitting" – which is to say disinterested and generous – "attentions"; and in his dying words Victor summarily accounts for his tragedy in utilitarian terms of misdirected attention: "My duties towards my fellow-creatures had greater claims to my attention, because they included a greater proportion of happiness or misery" (Shelley 43, 185). Meanwhile, the "close attention" that the Creature pays to the cottagers "induced [him] to turn towards [himself]" (Shelley 95, 96). In this way, *Frankenstein* extends the natural philosophical imperative to induce to the ethos of gentlemanly character, the disinterested abnegation of individual concerns on behalf of general welfare and outreach, even as it capitalizes on the interest generated by its motley assortment of over-particular and attentive personages, who fail to abstract themselves. The novel underscores the disaggregation of moral character from aesthetic character, for its appeal lies in its divided attentions and the failures of the personages to recognize each other in relation to general humanity.

Much of nineteenth-century prose consists of accounting for attentions paid and unpaid, particular and general, and its accounting, which balances these degrees of attention like credits and debits, resolves the epistemological problem of induction by converting it into an enchanting aesthetic object. When correspondence and sincerity became banal, like boring Bingley whose generous interiority matches his genial behavior, discordance between particulars and generals became compelling and desirable. By the beginning of the nineteenth century, mimetic correspondence failed to meet the aesthetic standards of the prosaic, whose failures to harmonize the general with the particular quickened its characteristic aesthetic appeal.

Attentive and Inattentive Reading

It ought to come as no surprise that, later in the century, one of Austen's most prolific admirers, Anthony Trollope, consistently apostrophized his ideal audience as the "kind and attentive reader."[78] Arraying a wide range of asymmetric attentions seems to be how reading prose was supposed to cultivate character. Austen thematizes this assumption by putting *attention* to work in scenes of reading. *Persuasion*, for instance, "explores what it feels like to be a reader," as Adela Pinch explains, and "it does so by connecting this feeling to what the presence of other people feels like."[79] For Pinch, *Persuasion* represents other people as pressing "influences," "ministrations," and vehicles for "submission to duty and propriety" (139), as agents and subjects demanding our attentions. This atmospheric presence – "an atmosphere," as Pinch puts it, "of continuous, unhierarchized sound" – serves like Lynch's white-noise as a backdrop or screen against which consciousness or innerness plays in relief (Pinch 149, 154). The personal thus becomes for Pinch a quotation of the feeling, mood, or sentiment that one reads about in a book or discerns in this noise. *Persuasion* models feeling as the product of selectively attending to and ignoring an atmosphere of external feelings. *Attention* recurs in Austen's prose as the buffer between reader and text, individual and crowd – by turns the amplifier and the muffler of the welter of emotions.

Pinch's history implies that character, in so far as it was the cumulative product of sentiments, was not the private property of individuals but a transaction between individuals and their context, social or otherwise. *Attention* was the clearinghouse for these transactions. To think of Austenian character as a relation is not entirely new, then. Before Pinch, Tony Tanner described Anne Elliot's impersonal character as an "in betweenness." But recasting this notion of character in terms of *attention* clarifies the ambitions that Austen's prose style implicitly assumes for its readers.[80] Austen portrays reading not merely as an accessory for cultivating interiority comfortably distinct from but respectful of outside noise, but as an inducement for what Crary calls "depthless interface." *Character* named the subtle pleasure of inhabiting the liminal zone between interiority and active sympathy with others, and as far as several Austenian scenes of reading suggest, reading for character was less about plumbing depths or developing intimate interpretations of personages or the texts than about savoring that depthless interface.

Mansfield Park explicitly defines reading in terms of *attention*. Edmund and Henry Crawford, trying to woo Fanny, remark on the "too common neglect . . . the total inattention . . . want of early attention and habit" paid to the art of reading aloud: "how little the art of reading has been studied! How little a clear manner, and good delivery, have been attended to!" (*MP* 392). This scene of histrionic reading forwards *attention* as a characterological practice, linked as it is to "habit" and "manner" and to Edmund's superiority to Henry, even as it upholds a performative notion of character – character that is read aloud instead of internalized. The scene does not suggest that good reading involves deep thought, analysis, interpretation, or moral reasoning, but only proper articulation – of words as well as of all the elements of a given situation. Thus, when the men start reading, Fanny first directs "All her attention" to her work so as to ignore Crawford's unwanted attentions, but against her will Crawford's dramatic rendition of Shakespeare galvanizes her: "Edmund watched the progress of her attention," as if it were *The Harlot's Progress* or *The Rake's Progress*. It climaxes with reciprocated attention: "Her praise had been given in her attention; *that* must content them" (*MP* 390–91; emphasis in original).

The actual subject of Fanny's attention is less Crawford, who unnerves her, than Shakespearean characterization properly mediated. That Fanny cannot help but attend to Shakespeare bespeaks her exemplary Englishness, even as it also indicates that attention was assumed to be tractable to the will but ultimately subject to social contingencies and physiological inclinations.[81] Fanny's attention to Shakespeare, who was repeatedly lauded for his production of characters who simultaneously exemplify individuality and generality, implies that attention was for Austen the faculty through which reading induced character in her readers. That the process of reading aloud impels Fanny to attend to what she would rather ignore further implies that a tacit object of reading was to induce us to forgo our preferences and attend to that which we would rather ignore. The scene suggests that each of these individuals is but a representative of a type, an actor playing a role defined by its "manner" and "delivery" "aloud," not by its unique insight into character.

Several critics have recently broached the historical associations between reading and attention. Underscoring the financial metaphor inhering in "paying attention," Patricia Meyer Spacks appropriates the word in *Sense and Sensibility* as an index of sympathetic and readerly interest.[82] For Spacks, investing attention yields aesthetic interest as a financial investment yields monetary interest. Boring cannot be made interesting without due payments of attention. Stephen Arata has likewise suggested that what we call "close reading" amounts to paying attention to that which appears interesting, and Arata refreshingly counters the presumption that attentive reading excels over inattentive reading by way of Robert Louis Stevenson's late-century prescription for distraction. Reading, Arata shows, was promoted as a medium for both concentrating and dilating attention.[83] Nicholas Dames claims accordingly that the mid-century novel facilitated "negative liberty": Victorian writers respected novel-reading for fostering inattention and, in turn, productive reverie, idle thinking about nothing in particular that enabled one to relax at the level of generality or to think about something new.[84] "Negative liberty," as Dames describes it, has an inductive vibe in that it poses the reader's abstraction from a particular text as the product of what De Certeau calls creative consumption.[85]

Dames grounds the association of attention with reading in physiological psychology. Thackeray's "complex and career-long engagement with the issue of his readers' attention spans," he explains, "tended in fact to see both tense, directed focusing and relaxed, vagrant mental drift as components of the same process: a rhythmic oscillation between attentiveness and distraction, or alertness and obliviousness, that characterized all reading, particularly all reading of novelistic narrative" (77). Writing of Herbert Spencer and Alexander Bain, Dames qualifies the overemphasis scholars and Victorian moralists alike have placed on the conscious will: "Distraction or general restful reverie is the ground of any interiority, while attention is the abdication of that set of mental processes – choice, self-communion, even the idle desire to have a desire – upon which the liberal individual bases his right to autonomy" (102). So, by mid-century, Victorians were clearly thinking about mental life as the interplay of attention and inattention that could be activated by reading.

The politics of this psychology and reading practice has a prehistory in Austen's prose, where Fanny, Elinor, Marianne, and others struggle for the right to be noticed and ignored, to attend or to be distracted. *Pride and Prejudice* specifically plots reading and rereading in terms of attention when Elizabeth spots Jane "dwelling intently on some particular passages" of a letter from Caroline Bingley, a "dwelling" that inhibits Jane from seamlessly joining "with her usual cheerfulness in the general conversation" (*PP* 130). This distraction in turn "drew off [Elizabeth's] attention even from Wickham" (130). Reading here, as in *Frankenstein*, divides attention, and this divided attention – not focus or concentration – in turn seems to be the characterological payoff of reading. Rather than learning to attend steely-eyed to this or that, whether it be a Shakespearean play, some sewing, or a letter from Caroline Bingley, Austen's prose formally and thematically liberates attention.

Stewing over Colonel Fitzwilliam's insinuations that Darcy applauded himself for saving Bingley from marrying Jane, Elizabeth rereads Jane's letters and "noticed every sentence conveying the idea of uneasiness, with an attention it had hardly received on the first perusal" (*PP* 210). Rereading in this scene recalibrates attention, restoring a properly inductive orientation that does not deductively begin with the premises Elizabeth, and presumably the reader, initially believes. In a novel so obsessed with character-reading, so rife, as Alex Woloch observes, with the word *character, attention* proves to be the fundamental medium of characterization, and that characterization capitalizes more on the surface tension between competing demands for attention than it indulges in expositions of interior life of the sort found in George Eliot and Henry James. Darcy follows his rejected (first) proposal with an apologetic letter in defense of his character, a letter in which he begs Elizabeth to "pardon the freedom with which I demand your attention; your feelings, I know, will bestow it unwillingly, but I demand it of your justice" (*PP* 218). Social conventions here compel both the private gentleman to maintain his public reputation and Elizabeth to pay that gentleman attention despite her private emotional aversions because they are subordinate to the public circulation of character and to propriety.

Of course, the celerity with which Elizabeth ardently devours the letter proves her aversion to be superficial. As she reads, "impatience of knowing what the next sentence might bring" first renders her "incapable of attending to the sense of the one before her eyes" (*PP* 226). This passionate recklessness cedes to rereading, one of many esteemed modes of revision and recollection in the novel. Elizabeth "read, and re-read with the closest attention, the particulars" (227). Hasty first-readings race for general impressions, where subsequent rereadings carefully attend to particulars. These scenes of rereading deductively unwind the induction that is implicitly inscribed into the preceding narrative about first reading. The endgame of induction is an amplitude informed by general truths, but general truths in Austen's fiction tend to be exposed as simplistic, presumptuous, or careless, and scenes of rereading tend to mitigate their inaccuracies by unearthing an amplitude that is most richly evident in Miss Bates's volubility, the snail's pace of Mansfield Park, the partial reports of Darcy's housekeeper, and a vaguer, more distant but salutary relation to oneself. In turn, scenes of rereading perhaps goad readers to reread the novel, so as to be able to attend to the particulars that they have missed in their first, hasty, and general reading. Only in rereading, Austen implies, can we be impartial and properly inductive.

Elizabeth correlates attention to discernment, self-correction, and self-searching, but also to a kind of ameliorative pain and indeterminacy:

"when this subject was succeeded by his account of Mr. Wickham, when she read, with somewhat clearer attention, a relation of events, which, if true, must overthrow every cherished opinion of his worth, and which bore so alarming an affinity to his own history of himself, her feelings were yet more acutely painful and more difficult of definition" (*PP* 226–27). The yield of reading with "clearer attention" is a clearer apprehension of Wickham's and Darcy's characters paradoxically coupled with a feeling "more difficult of definition." Paradoxically, but altogether generically: nineteenth-century writing routinely represents "real" feeling as ineffable, suggested, and abstract, especially when it is particularly moving.[86] Particular knowledge yields abstract feelings. Clear attention to the world abstracts Elizabeth to and from herself. If Austen's prose calls us to attention, then, it does not ask us to remain closely attentive or to be distracted, but to be both, to enjoy the inductive rhythm of a mind working to apprehend a world that exceeds its capacity for attention.

Afterlives of Induction: Scientific Conduct and the Character of Criticism

Induction came again to the fore in natural philosophical discussions in the decades after Austen's novels were published. John Herschel's *A Preliminary Discourse on the Study of Natural Philosophy* (1830),[87] William Whewell's *History of the Inductive Sciences* (1837) and *The Philosophy of the Inductive Sciences* (1840), John Stuart Mill's *A System of Logic* (1843), Baden Powell's *The Unity of Worlds and of Nature* (1856), and Auguste Comte's *The Positive Philosophy of Auguste Comte* (translated and popularized in England by Harriet Martineau in 1853) all aver that inductive methods credibly characterize the natural world and concomitantly redound moral character upon scientists. Of course, these metascientific writings often fiercely dispute the actual parameters of induction – whether its inferences employed a priori categories and were therefore deductive or whether generalization was itself observed and therefore purely empirical – and yet in so doing they nevertheless bolster both the epistemic aura and characterological associations of the idiom of induction.[88] Particular and general were the generic signatures of natural philosophy and of systems on all sorts of topics.

The induction debates were prompted in part by the encroachment of numerical thinking in disciplines that had emerged out of moral and political philosophy. David Ricardo, for instance, asserted that axiomatic principles and deduction were the proper instruments of a mathematical discipline of economics.[89] This premise irked William Whewell, the most prolific historian of science and promoter of induction, not only as a matter of epistemology (Whewell held that deduction merely confirmed what we already know), but also as a matter of moral responsibility. Political economy was a branch of moral philosophy and therefore ought to remain a study of character.[90] While Ricardo wished to objectify the science through mathematics and deduction, thereby disaggregating it from subjectivity, Whewell held that all science was moral and that inductive study concomitantly dilated observed particulars into conjectural generalizations and moved scientists from their particular spheres of concentration to public, communal concerns.

Natural philosophers likewise marshalled induction as an antidote to the very threats to Christian culture that natural philosophy was accused of bearing. John Herschel correlated inductive philosophy with virtues such as faith, humbleness, and open-mindedness. Induction, he says, "best becomes [a scientist's] character" because it "places the existence and principal attributes of a Deity on such grounds as to render doubt absurd and atheism ridiculous"; "it unfetters the mind from prejudices of all kinds"; and it impresses "humility of pretension" and "confidence of hope" (7–8). Because "the grand and indeed only character of truth is its capability of enduring the test of universal experience, and coming unchanged out of every possible form of *fair* discussion" (Herschel 10, emphasis in original), individuals seemed to need induction to socialize and universalize their experiences, to "form, as it were, a link between ourselves and the best and noblest benefactors of our species, with whom we hold communion in thoughts and participate in discoveries which have raised them above their fellow mortals, and brought them nearer to their Creator" (Herschel 16–17). Such arguments were common, as James Secord affirms in a discussion of the natural theology of Rev. Thomas Chalmers, who deemed science to be "not a substitute for Scripture, but a means of inculcating the humility that could lead to approaching God's Word in the correct frame of mind"; Chalmers maintained that "Baconian induction provided a template for spiritual understanding."[91] The third of the Bridgewater Treatises, Whewell's *Astronomy and General Physics considered with Reference to Natural Theology* (1833), concludes accordingly with a catalogue of "Inductive Habits" that would suit Samuel Smiles's books on character formation: "inductive ascent" promotes regular prayer and piety, cleanliness, hard work, temperance, even waking up early. Discussions of induction were thus inflected by the same hotchpotch of Christian and yet capitalist ideological motives that inflected didactic novels, self-help books, and conduct manuals. Indeed, Secord observes that the cheap format of Herschel's *Preliminary Discourse*, published as part of Dionysius Lardner's *Cabinet Cyclopedia*, suggests that it served as a conduct manual, a guide for the translation of scientific habits into everyday attitudes, rather than as a manual of scientific protocols for practitioners.[92]

Effectively, these early nineteenth-century writers translated the "problem of induction" – the question of how to legitimate the abstract generalizations generated form concrete data – into a solution, because however much they parse the nitty-gritties of if and how one could generate empirical abstractions their apprehension of inductive method as a medium of characterization converts the problem into the formal index of character, the signature of moral interest and epistemological credibility. Characterization embraced the problem of induction as the guarantee that it was not merely factual or theoretical but pragmatic, experiential, negotiating between both registers of ontology. Herschel goes so far as to naturalize induction by classifying it, like an organism, with *particular* and *general* serving double-duty with their taxonomical connotations: "perceive the high importance in physical science of just and accurate classifications of particular facts, or individual objects, under general well considered heads or points of agreement," he says,

> for by so doing each of such phenomena, or heads of classification, becomes not a particular but a general fact; and when we have amassed a great store of such *general facts*, they become the objects of another and higher species of classification, and are themselves included in laws which, as they dispose of groups, not individuals, have a far superior degree of generality. (Herschel 102)

Induction here appears not just as a mode of moral if not transcendental ascent, but also as coextensive with the hierarchy of plant and animal organisms. For Herschel, induction repeats phylogeny.

For Whewell, whose prose teems with *particular* and *general*, the idiom of induction ensures the character of the scientist, and "the Inductive Philosophy," moreover, solves perhaps the most salient problem that nineteenth-century intellectuals, including Austen, ascribed to modernity: its superabundance of data. Via induction, he writes,

> A number of facts in which, before, order and connexion did not appear at all, or appeared by partial and contradictory glimpses, are brought into a point of view in which order and connexion become their essential character. It is seen that each fact is but a different manifestation of the same principle; that each particular is that which it is, in virtue of the same general truth. (*Astronomy and General Physics* 280)

Matthew Arnold made similar claims in "On the Modern Element in Literature," which laments how the "copious and complex present" is burdened by a "vast multitude of facts."[93] "Intellectual deliverance" from this condition demands for Arnold an explicitly inductive frame of mind: "possession of the general ideas which are the law of this vast multitude of facts" (306). Scientists, novelists, and readers alike were thus implicated in what Deidre Lynch has called "the economy of character." They jockeyed not only for the distinction of deeper, more intimate knowledge of characters (as in personages), however, but also more inclusively for the distinction of managing a wider amplitude of impressions than the next person. Character redounded to the writer who attended to the overwhelming abundance, incoherence, and individuality of modern life even as he or she remarked on its reducibility to generic, coherent, and representative types.

Nineteenth-century British critics did not abandon the idiom of induction to the sciences. They lacked an adequate, specialized vocabulary for naming the knowledge they putatively produced and the knowledge allegedly found in the fiction, poetry, and art they wrote about, but the savvier critics overcame this deficit by appropriating the idiom of induction and leaning on the cultural clout and plasticity of *character* to legitimate the emergent genre of textual redescription as epistemologically and morally productive work, rather than mere judgment. In place of allegory or interpretation, these critics lay claim to being induced to abstraction by texts.

William Hazlitt, for instance, wrote about character in a handful of essays and books whose diversity bespeaks the versatility of the word as it straddled domains and genres: "On Personal Character" (*London Magazine/Plain Speaker* 1821); "On the Knowledge of Character" (*Table Talk* 1822); "On Depth and Superficiality" (*Plain Speaker* 1826); "Character of Mr. Wordsworth's New Poem *The Excursion*" (*Examiner* 1814); *Characters of Shakespeare's Plays* (1817); and *The Spirit of the Age* (1824–25). In these writings, *character* concurrently refers to human nature, individuality,[94] imaginary personages, biography, the ethos or personality of a text, the zeitgeist or spirit of an age, and a vague sense of aesthetic and moral – psychological and ethical – interest. This mutability of "character" reflects the disciplinary and generic instability of criticism in the 1820s. Jules David Law[95] has written that "'depth of character' is really a figurative measure of how well a person is *known*, rather than a description of the character in question" (182). In positing "character" as both its subject and product, criticism reoriented knowledge from the artifact under analysis to the form of its consumption or comprehension.

Hazlitt's essay "On Depth and Superficiality" presents "depth" as the effect of the interaction between a reader and a particular text. This interaction assumes a specifically inductive cast. "What," Hazlitt asks, "is meant by lying on the surface, or being concealed below it, in moral and metaphysical questions?" (12: 355). "*Depth* consists," he answers,

> in tracing any number of particular effects to a general principle, or in distinguishing an unknown cause from the individual and varying circumstances with which it is implicated, and under which it lurks unsuspected. It is in fact resolving the concrete into the abstract. (12: 355)

Depth thus signals less an interiority or hidden meaning than a call to work that capitalizes on the association between industriousness and character later promoted by Smiles.[96] Essays on "On Personal Character" and "On Depth and Superficiality" also represent induction as a labor-intensive mode of handling superabundant detail:[97]

> a task of difficulty, not only because the abstract naturally merges in the concrete, and we do not well know how to set about separating what is thus jumbled or cemented together in a single object, and presented under a common aspect; but being scattered over a larger surface, and collected from a number of undefined sources, there must be a strong feeling of its weight and pressure, in order to dislocate it from the object and bind it into a principle. (12: 355–56)

Passages like this abound in Hazlitt's work, where they represent utter abstraction as literally concrete substance with the weight and spatial distribution of a truckload of gravel.

Hazlitt's idiom gives this abstraction a moral turn and implies that inductive reading enriches character not by deepening or individuating but by abstracting it: as he writes on "The Influence of Books on the Progress of Manners" in the *New Monthly Magazine*, "man becomes by means of his studies, his amusements and his intellectual attachments, an ideal and abstracted, and therefore a disinterested and reclaimed character" (17: 326). The problem of egoism had plagued Romantic writers. Coleridge had accordingly described Shakespeare's characterization as disinterested and impersonal: "Shakspeare's [*sic*] poetry is characterless; it does not reflect the individual Shakspeare [*sic*]."[98] Coleridge had of course lauded Shakespeare's characters in the same terms: "they are not the things but the abstracts of the things which a great mind may take into itself and naturalize to its own" (Halmi 322). Hazlitt elides egoism by figuring objects as repositories of an abstract character irreducible to axiomatic, effable truths or to the expression of personal ethos. "Look[ing]," like Matthew

Arnold after him, "at an object as it is in itself" (3:258), he performed disinterestedness and objectivity by insisting that the critic does not project his own character onto things.[99] His lecture "On Thomson and Cowper" expressly praises "*abstractedness*" because such generality makes works more readily available to critical induction, sympathy, and association by readers (5: 100).[100] Intriguingly, the lecture prefers representations of things to people because of "the transferable nature of our feelings with respect to physical objects; the associations connected with any one object extending to the whole class" (5: 101).

The ideal of induced abstractedness recalls Elizabeth Bennet's attentive rereading, which yields her feeling "more difficult of definition," some painful amalgam of remorse, regret, guilt, and desire. And Richard Whatley makes congruent claims in his reviews of Austen's fiction: "Every thing . . . which tends to abstract a man in any degree, or in any way, from self, – from self-admiration and self-interest, has, so far at least, a beneficial influence in forming the character" (375). At mid-century, abstractness still thrived as a moral imperative. Consider the 1856 essay, "The Spirit of the Inductive Philosophy," by Baden Powell, Savilian Professor of Geometry at Oxford and father of the founder of the Boy Scouts.[101] "There is nothing of which we are less conscious," Powell writes, "than the acquisition of the commonest ideas by daily experience, and the successive and gradual generalization of that experience by the process of *abstraction*; and in this way we constantly obtain (without being aware of it) numberless prepossessions and convictions far stronger than any systematic demonstrations can supply" (14–15, emphasis in original). Induction for Powell is not merely an applied method of empirical science, but also the physiological process of character formation. So abstraction and character coalesce around ineffable emotion, ethical detachment, cognitive development, and scientific method. These coalescing modes of abstraction all opposed or tempered a modernity defined by egoism, determinacy, and a threatening surfeit of stimuli and data.

Richard Henry Horne mustered the idiom of induction to legitimate *A New Spirit of the Age* (1844), a collection of essays by he and E. B. Browning, as critical knowledge and not mere puffery, biography, or summary.[102] Horne's lengthy opening essay, "Charles Dickens," also applies the idiom of induction to defend Dickens from the already recurring gripes that he was a caricaturist rather than an author of real characters and that his sentimental, idealist, and exaggerating fictions lacked sufficient fidelity to reality. Dickens's style of personifying abstractions was and remains peculiarly contentious because it so frequently endows objects with the most explicit features of human characters, such as voices, anthropomorphic gestures, and interior life.[103] This characterization of everything from furniture to fogs troubled some critics because it is literal, and so even appreciative contemporaries such as G. H. Lewes denigrated his characterization as grotesque, infantile, hallucinatory, overly idealistic, or unnatural.[104] By 1844, noting this animistic habit was so common that Thackeray mocked it in his review of *A New Spirit of the Age*: "Has not everyone with a fair share of brains made the same discoveries long ago?"[105] In what is by now recognizable as an altogether generic formulation, Horne indulgently adapts the idiom of Shakespeare criticism to laud Dickensian characters: "Mr. Dickens's characters, numerous as they are, have each the roundness of individual reality combined with generalization – most of them representing a class" (22); "They are *not* mere realities, but the type and essence of real classes; while the personal and graphic touches render them at the same time individualized" (24). And, the genre of the book implies that Dickens is characteristic of his age, of a movement, not just himself. But most interestingly, Horne defends Dickens by ascribing character to elements of his style *other than* his personages – elements including his animated objects, but also more abstract, nondescript aspects of his prose.

If many of Dickens's characters and personified things fall short of verisimilitude or probability, Horne implies that his novels were, as wholes, legible repositories of character. In thus transferring the burden of characterization from personages to whole fictions, Horne echoes a critical tendency active in predecessors like Walter Scott, who wrote that the "finished up to nature" and "precision" of *Emma* "is a merit which is very difficult to illustrate by extracts, because it pervades the whole work, and is not to be comprehended from a single passage" (Southam 67). To make his case, Horne extends the Shakespearean idiom to describe Dickens's style of description tout court *as a mode of characterization*. He says that Dickens "not only animates furniture, and stocks and stones, or even the wind, with human purposes, but often gives them an individual rather than a merely generalized character" (Horne 20).

Horne also translates the questions of character and realism into matters of amplitude. Dickens's eccentric, ostensible caricatures, he contends, adequately represent the wide range of particularity manifest in modern life: the probable to the improbable, the gross to the ideal, the detail to the panorama, the eccentric and the type, the object and the subject it metonymically reciprocates.[106] Alluding extensively to Charles Lamb's oft-quoted essay "On the Genius and Character of Hogarth" (1811), which defends the "*ruling character*" of Hogarth's prints from similar aspersions of caricature and sentimental excess,[107] Horne defines modernity and its most adequate medium of representation – the Dickens novel – by its plenitude of detail. The prodigality of character Horne appreciates in Dickens's fiction includes something more than the sheer volume of characters produced by the likes of Shakespeare and Scott.[108] Lamb justifies Hogarth's "character" by invoking the "the numberless appendages of the scene," the "gratuitous doles," "the unwritten numberless little allusive pleasantries that are scattered about," and "the over-measure which [genius] delights in giving, as if its stores were exhaustless; the dumb-rhetoric of the scenery – for tables, and chairs, and joint-stools in Hogarth are living and significant things" (Lamb 109). The excessive volume of detail here appears consonant with modern life, as if exhaustlessness were equivalent to life and significance. The excess also muddies the distinction between protagonists, secondary personages, and their settings: Dickens's "profusion and prodigality of character" (20) are such that things in "the background of the scene," rather than the protagonists, "tend to establish the predominating feature of characterization displayed throughout Mr. Dickens's works, and the consequent difficulty of separating this feature from almost every other, so inwoven is it into the texture of the whole" (39). For Horne, what Woloch calls the "character system" exceeds personages altogether and extends to exposition in general:

> Neither of these great artists ever concentrates the interest upon any one great character, nor even upon two or three, but while their principles are always highly finished, and sufficiently prominent on important occasions, they are nevertheless often used as centers of attraction, or as a means for progressively introducing numerous other characters which cross them at every turn, and circle them continually with a buzzing world of outward vitality. (Horne 20)

Horne's reiteration of this claim for prodigality and decentered characterization bespeaks a transitional moment in the history of character, a moment when the residual commitment to a surficial, social model of character was ceding to the model of individualistic psychological personality. "The delineation of characters constitutes so very much the more prominent and valuable portion of Mr. Dickens's works," he says, "that it is extremely difficult to detach them from any view of an entire production" (24), which is to say Dickens characterizes everything.

Discussing Hogarth's prints, Horne observes with inductive savvy, "How very like they are to Dickens, not substantially nor in particular details, but in moral purpose and in finished execution of parts, and of the whole, must surely have been often observed" (11). But the idiom of induction, a periperformative conjuring of character, overwhelms his argument such that he could be characterizing anyone or anything. "The resemblance," Horne says in a delightfully circumlocutory passage,

> is apparent with regard to single figures and to separate groups – all with different objects, and often in conflict with the rest – and equally apparent with relation to one distinct and never-to-be-mistaken whole into which the various figures and groups are fused, and over which one general and harmonizing atmosphere expands, not by any apparent intention in the skillful hand of the artist, but as if exhaled from and sustained by the natural vitality of the scene. (Horne 11)

For Jonathan Crary, the type of confused plenitude that Horne glosses as "vitality" occasioned mid-century articulations of attention as "an imprecise way of designating the relative capacity of a subject to selectively isolate certain contents of a sensory field at the expense of others in the interests of maintaining an orderly and productive world."[109] Crary claims Freud's ideal of demotivated attention and similar faculties were "designed to impose a measure of cognitive control on an unassimilable excess of information or on the apparently chaotic syntax of dreams" (368). For Horne, *character* and the buzzwords of induction help control the otherwise "unassimilable excess" that others regarded as chaos. Where Austen demonstrates the diffusive and socializing work of attentions, Horne deploys "character" as a moralized synonym for aesthetic totality; through their diction, both contain the amplitude of reality with an inductive logic.

A New Spirit of the Age is an uneven enterprise, but some chapters follow suit in extending to all modes of prose exposition the subjective and epistemological values traditionally imputed to the characterization of personages. "G. P. R. James, Mrs. Gore, Captain Marryatt, and Mrs. Trollope," to cite one more rarefied example, reiterates the generic critical observation that "Prose fiction has acquired a more respectable status within the last half century than it held at any previous period in English literature" (127). In an almost absurdly periphrastic passage, the chapter explains that this greater respectability accrues to the inductive form of prose:

> This elevation of prose fiction to a higher rank, and . . . popularity, may be at once referred to the practical nature of the materials with which it deals, and the sagacity with which they are *selected* and employed. What Aristotle says of poetry *in general* may be applied with *peculiar* force to this *particular* form of narrative – that it is more philosophical than history; for while the latter is engaged with literal *details* of *particular* facts, which often outrage *general* probability and never illustrate *general* principles, the former *generalizes*

> throughout, and by tracing in natural sequence a course of causes and effects
> which would, in all probability, have succeeded each other in the same order,
> under similar circumstances, in real life, it exhibits a more *comprehensive picture
> of human nature,* and conducts us *upon the whole* to a profounder moral.
> (Horne 128, emphasis added)

As if invoking Hume's discussion of inference, this passage privileges the
probabilistic medium of fiction over history's positivist, archival detailism
because fiction induces particulars into generalities, induces portable morals from fixed specifics. Fiction cultivates character because, like the human
mind, it generalizes particulars and correlates causes and effects, whereas
history allegedly fails to generalize. According to this logic, novels were
"living and significant things" not because their parts could exhibit self-
referential, "organic" interrelation (of the sort James would seek), but
because their parts consistently inferred or suggested or otherwise
abstracted generalities just as the human mind necessarily did. Character
once again resolved the epistemological problem of fiction by treating the
incommensurability of observed particulars and unobservable generalizations as the signature of truth rather than a systematic or generic
problem.[110]

In *British Novelists and Their Styles* (1859), David Masson rehashes a generic
comparison of Dickens and Thackeray in similarly inductive terms.[111] Masson
implies that Thackeray's cynical realism is deductive whereas Dickens's "fes-
tive" idealism is inductive:

> Having once caught a hint from actual fact, [Dickens] generalizes it, runs
> away with this generalization into a corner, and develops it there into
> a character to match; which character he then transports, along with others
> similarly suggested, into a world of semi-fantastic conditions, where the laws
> need not be those of ordinary probability. (254)

Novels had been the subjects of books before, but Masson was establishing
them as an object of academic study, and so he leans heavily on the idiom
of induction to characterize prose as an epistemologically productive
medium with the dexterity to handle modernity's superfluity: "Walking,
as it does, on *terra firma,* and not merely poised on ascending and
descending wings, [prose] can push its way through the thick and miscellany of things, pass from generalities to particulars, and from particulars
back to generalities, and come into contact with social reality at myriad
points in succession" (25–26). Masson deliciously mystifies the relations
between simplicity and complexity, particulars and generals, and poetry
and prose:

As in the physical world there are infinite myriads of phenomena, complex and minute, on the basis of the elemental, and into the elemental may be decomposed, so on these fundamental feelings, facts, and thoughts of the moral world, are all the minuter facts of social experience piled, and over these as their basis they roll in varying whirl. These are the generalities; the rest are the minutiæ. Now, to the hundred definitions that have been given of genius, let this one more be added – that that soul is a soul of genius which is in affinity with the elemental in nature and in life, and which, by the necessity of its constitution, tends always from the midst of the complex and minute to the simple and general. (Masson 309)

The portrayal of verse as universalizing and prose as an inductive mediation of particulars and generals was a stock convention of nineteenth-century theories of the novel, but Masson reaches here to conjure a sense of prose as an experiential, fact-based, and "elemental" – which is to say empirical and pragmatic, and thereby British – medium for managing excess data and stimuli.

Perhaps the exemplary concatenation of imagination, genius, pleasure drives, and other elements of character with inductive method is E. S. Dallas's 1866 *The Gay Science*, however, for it explicitly portrays criticism as "an induction of facts" with a "scientific character."[112] The objective of all criticism, for Dallas, is to induce the "hidden soul" that he imputes to all art (I: 245). He goes so far as to explain that the unconscious operation of the imagination is inductive: imagination, he says, is "but a popular name given to the unconscious automatic action of the hidden soul," the "traffic" or "usual stride from the particular to the general" (I: 245). Humans and artworks alike are but inductive machines: "in the same free play," Dallas says, "the mind tends to generalize and totalize every individual fact that engages its attention: and hence another leading characteristic of that automatic energy which is commonly known as imagination" (I: 297). In Masson, then, we can see how the tent of organic wholeness typically traced to German Romanticism and Coleridge also had roots in the idiom of induction and critical characterization, for Masson describes the mind as compulsively inductive, "never content with a part; it rushes to wholes. Where it cannot find them it makes them" (I: 291).

Walter Pater's *Studies in the Renaissance* (1866–73), which replaces the presentism of the spirit-of-the-age genre pioneered by Hazlitt with historicist detachment, presents abstractness as an aesthetic that Carolyn Williams has described as an objective subjectivism.[113] Williams describes Pater's process as a "careful practice of *objectification*" whereby he represents the "object of art . . . as a figure for the epistemological process itself."[114] Lorraine Daston and Peter Galison have demonstrated that the modern "image of objectivity" necessarily amalgamates detail and idealization (85), particular and general, but this becomes an especially acute problem for Pater, who purports to describe objectively his subjective impression of a work of art. "The first step to seeing one's object as it really is," he says, "is to know one's own impression as it really is, to discriminate it, to know it distinctly" (xix). *Studies in the Renaissance* presents its subjects as representatives of the collective character of the age or movement, and thus professes interest in the Renaissance "not merely for its positive results in the things of the intellect and the imagination, its concrete works of art, its special and prominent personalities . . . but for its general spirit and character, for the ethical qualities of which it is a consummate type" (xxiii). Pater affects to induce a general character from the Renaissance by characterizing its individual artworks and artists, and he projects this formal assumption onto the works he studies. To take a striking example, his chapter on Luca Della Robbia distinguishes three styles of sculpture, starting with "*Allgemeinheit* – breadth, generality, universality," which "prompted [the Greek sculptors]" – like Pater himself – "to seek the type in the individual, to abstract and express only what is structural and permanent, to purge from the individual all that belongs only to him, all the accidents, the feelings and actions of the special moment" (Pater 51). Rather than a positivist, referential historicism, which might recount more of the reception history and conditions of production of these Renaissance figures and their art, Pater describes the age and its aesthetics in the form of a nineteenth-century character, balancing individuality and typicality, distinctness and generality.

General and *particular* were generic conventions of nineteenth-century British prose, signature phrases of a specifically British form of abstraction that eventually informed late Victorian and early Modernist formalist aesthetics.[115] As Suzy Anger explains, "a well-established movement for scientific literary criticism" had developed by the end of the nineteenth century.[116] Richard Green Moulton, a teacher of English literature at Cambridge University and later Professor of Literary Theory and Interpretation at the University of Chicago, introduced his *Shakespeare as Dramatic Artist* (1885) with an introductory "PLEA FOR AN INDUCTIVE SCIENCE OF LITERARY CRITICISM." Moulton pleas for a criticism like "*a scientific hypothesis, the truth of which is tested by the completeness with which it explains the details of the literary work as they stand.*"[117] Moulton literally characterizes the texts he analyzes: as Anger says, he shifts "intention" from authors to their writings in order to authorize interpretations liberated from biographical and historical determinacy.

Liberation from determinacy inflected the form of nineteenth-century prose. Fiction, natural philosophy, and criticism alike all invoked the idiom of induction to afford epistemological credibility to prose that flouted the assumed correlation between knowledge and accuracy. Where attention converted induction into socially legible acts of deference, condescension, concern, flirtation, and aesthetic interest; induction converted aesthetic appreciation into an ostensibly philosophical effort. Throughout the century, in a range of genres, the idiom of induction represented incoherence, awkwardness, tension, distraction, and disarray into evidence of truth, morality, and interest. A volley between concrete references and indeterminate generalizations, its cadence empowered prose that did not offer prescriptions, axioms, conclusions, explanations, allegories, or interpretations. With *particulars and generals*, nineteenth-century writers could thus humanize a world that was increasingly beholden to abstractions and to facts whose scope put them beyond comprehension.

CHAPTER 3

"Our skeptical as if"
Conditional Analogy and the Comportment of Victorian Prose

> When I think of it, the picture always rises in my mind, of a summer evening, the boys at play in the churchyard, and I sitting on my bed, reading as if for life. Every barn in the neighborhood, every stone in the church, and every foot of the churchyard, had some association of its own, in my mind, connected with these books, and stood for some locality made famous in them.
>
> – Charles Dickens, *David Copperfield*[1]

Charles Dickens's prose contains an extraordinary number of "as ifs": 411 in *Dombey and Son*, 393 in *David Copperfield*, 392 in *Our Mutual Friend*, 266 in the substantially shorter *Great Expectations*, and so on.[2] Dickens's elm trees sway "like giants who were whispering secrets ... tossing their wild arms about, as if their late confidences were really too wicked for their peace of mind" (*DC* 8); and Mr. Dombey looks "down into the cold depths of the dead sea of mahogany on which the fruit dishes and decanters lay at anchor; as if the subjects of his thoughts were rising towards the surface one by one" (*DS* 469). These novels are rather long, and *as if* is a common phrase that has been becoming more common since 1789, especially since the beginning of the twentieth century.[3] But *as if* recurs at significantly higher frequency in Dickens's prose than in that of most canonical novelists.[4] The phrase only appears five times each in Trollope's *Doctor Thorne* and *Framley Parsonage*, and only about a third as much, 135 times, in Thackeray's *Vanity Fair*. Gaskell and Eliot approached Dickens's frequency in some novels, but the comparative paucity of the phrase in others does not necessarily mean that the underlying epistemological assumptions motivating the recurrence of *as if* did not also underwrite their styles as well, because *as if* is just one pronounced articulation of conditional analogy and the subjunctive mood, which do indeed permeate nineteenth-century fictions in all sorts of other forms. Dickens's habitual use of the phrase allows me to trace it, however, and Dickens seems to invite such attention by parodying *as if* as a modish mannerism and mechanism of characterization. He foregrounds *as if* in jokes, in extended chapter-opening similes, and in passages of explicit characterization. He was attuned to the peculiar currency of the phrase as a medium of modernity.

As if is the verbal signature of conjectural, non-referential, and counter-factual knowledge that defied the ascendancy of mimesis and the infamous fact. Where verisimilitude and facts posit equivalence between a representation and the subject it represents, or knowledge and what it purports to know, *as if* posits conditional analogy. Over the course of the eighteenth and nineteenth centuries, the epistemology of analogy shifted. In the seventeenth century, when the metaphor of "the Great Chain of Being" still obtained for many, writers tended to suppose that analogies described actual, constitutive corre-spondences between things as diverse as the branching of trees and species and the nerves and blood vessels in the hand. As all things were allegedly created by God, they were presumed to follow meaningful patterns that would repeat across species and categories. But by the middle of the eighteenth century analogy was becoming more of a heuristic device, an instrument for drawing illustrative comparisons or generating insights, but not evidence of a constitutive relationship. The status of conjectural, conditional, comparative, or fictional representations were suspect in a culture more and more enthralled by demonstrable knowledge.

Tracing this epistemological shift from constitutive to conditional or "regulative" analogies, as Kant called them, this chapter first recounts how Charles Lyell implements and theorizes conditional analogy as a legitimate mode of producing knowledge about geological history. Lyell faced similar problems as Darwin: he aspired to tell an empirical history of events he could not see and for which he knew he had only partial evidence; he was interested in subterranean, subaqueous, and otherwise inaccessible causes that he could not see or reproduce; and he wanted to maintain his gentility even as he sought a profession as a scientist refuting received scriptural history and geology. Lyell represents conditional analogies as empirical inductions by suggesting that geological observations in the present can serve as evidence of past events, because the agents of geological change are the same. Inducing hypotheses about the geological past, in his rendering, seems just as credible as inducing hypotheses about the present. I will maintain that there is a constitutive analogy between the way David Copperfield reflects on the "association" attached to each local object in his old neighborhood and the way Lyell reflects on geological history attached to present causes.

Fictional prose depends on an oblique relation between actual, extra-textual people, objects, and events and the imagined people, objects, and events that it describes, and *as if* often instantiates that relation. Wolfgang

Iser has indeed proposed that *as if* captures the regulative attitude all fiction fosters in its readers. He says readers acknowledge that fiction neither refers to nor constitutes actual events and people, but they nevertheless indulge in the possibility that it does.[5] Iser problematically assumes a universal reader, as if reading practices and readers do not change over time, but the abundance of *as ifs* in nineteenth-century English prose give credence to his claims at least in that century and language. I align Lyell and this version of Coleridge's willing suspension of disbelief not to belie the artifice of geology, but, to the contrary, to restore the truth of fiction. In the famous passage from *David Copperfield* in the chapter epigraph, Dickens concomitantly acknowledges that David's "associations" are merely his associations and insists that these associations govern and animate his real life; Dickens concomitantly acknowledges that David recounts merely reading and that this reading nevertheless continues to inflect his life. David Copperfield inhabits a bifurcated reality in which everything in sight both is what it is and stands for "some association of its own." *As if* consistently referees this intersection between material perception and lived experience with all of its associative freight, its memories, imagination, and affections.

As if qualifies as a character in the epistemology I am describing because it enables personages to appropriate contingencies and other material conditions of experience as their own. Regulative analogy empowers Dickens's characters to live according to their own logics, associations, and ideologies no matter what actually happens to them. Anticipating Freud, *as if* also sometimes articulates how personages relate to themselves as secrets unto themselves. Indeed, in Lyell's and in Dickens's prose, *as if* frequently implies a hidden, latent order, agency, or animus motivating the appearance of a given observation, such as the position of a mineral deposit or the posture of a chimney. Many have noted that Dickens personifies everything and have in turn speculated why or to what effect he does so,[6] but far fewer have itemized the specific formal features his personification employs. Garrett Stewart, a notable exception, artfully shows how Dickens grammatically instantiates "divided consciousness" by recourse to syllepsis or zeugma, the device that predicates its verb in two different senses.[7] Turning to figures like *as if* and syllepsis enables us to distinguish between overt personification, which ascribes anthropomorphic features such as voices, physiognomies, and emotions to inanimate objects, and the subtler characterization, which endows objects with manners and attitudes, specific moralized relations to other things. Where personification would appear silly, characterization can pass as scientific. *As if* inscribed a decidedly moral relation because, as I show below, it also was the figure of Adam Smith's casuist sympathy: we can only know how another feels by feeling how we would feel if we were in his or her circumstances. *As if* offers things as the object of sympathy, then, rather than reproduction.

Lyell characterizes the new geology by way of the conditional analogy, which posed both the geological past and the hidden causes of present geological activity as objects of sympathy, only as knowable and only as elusive as the feelings of another. However inductive his new geology was, its departure from accepted geological narratives and from Biblical history made it vulnerable to appearing wildly speculative. *As if* redresses this moral and epistemological problem at the level of syntax. In addition to representing its intellectual work as a kind of sympathetic imagination, its conditionality also inscribes humility and skepticism into every insight it offers. It submits its ideas tentatively as possibilities open to experiment rather than brash assertions or dogmas. The simple disavowal inscribed in the "if" that follows the exuberant suppositions of the "as" inserts a hint of detachment, disinterestedness, or knowing skepticism in front of its often improbable, unverifiable, or otherwise atypical suggestions. The "if" accommodates imagination to the parameters of probability and socializes associations to the limits of common experience and decorum. Geology and fiction both met the challenge of the fact with technologies of characterization that authorized and moralized conjecture, which Dickens routinely vilifies in its principle thematic form (financial speculation).

Like Thackeray, Dickens recognized character as a manner of comporting oneself in relation to a world – fictional or real, material or ideal, comprised of people and things – that nobody could ever possibly know or want to know mimetically. Manners and their print correlatives, stylistic conventions, were more important than the identities or supposed inner lives of specific personages. In Victorian prose, *as if* routinely sustains a gap between narratives and the story they purport to tell, "as if" narrators are only speculating about the putatively real story they purport to tell but to which they seem to have only superficial or limited access. *As ifs* likewise articulate the gaps between personages and classes, like the "two nations"; gaps between sensory perceptions and emotional impressions; descriptions and the objects they affect to describe; and temporalities, past, present, and future. Victorian prose is characterized, I want to suggest, by its alternation between constitutive and regulative registers. Supplementing all the reality effects, the earnest verisimilitude, and the photographic realism of nineteenth-century prose are conditional associations that are skeptical of mimesis even as they feign to be skeptical of their own counterfactual offerings.

Victorian writers were ambivalent about *as if* and the model of character on which it depends. Dickens draws attention to this ambivalence by emphasizing the role the phrase plays in the life of antithetical characters such as Esther Summerson and Harold Skimpole, David Copperfield and Wilkins Micawber, young Pip and mature narrator Pip. The *as if* licenses as much irresponsibility as insight, as much alienation as sympathy. I suggest the extent of this ambivalence in closing the chapter with physicist John Tyndall's equivocal discussion of *as if* in his essay "The Scientific Use of the Imagination" (1870). Tyndall's essay validates how and to what benefit literary characterization underwrote Victorian non-fiction prose and scientific method. But the essay also acknowledges that embracing the *as if* threatens to undermine the authority of demonstrable knowledge. *As if* valued deviations from correspondence and the indemonstrable, and these have an allure that for good and ill surpasses that of what can be definitively known. Despite all the alleged materialism and utilitarianism of modernity, the increasing prevalence of *as if* implies that modern prose might – less knowingly than Dickens – remain invested in such an epistemology. We might do better to insist on the regulative character of our own scholarly work: rather than embracing an exclusively positivist, materialist historicism, we might better embrace fictionality not only as our subject of expertise but also as our method, if we have the courage to accept the reality and scientific utility of associative, analogical, regulative fictions.

Dispositive Motions: Lyell, Thackeray, and Regulative Realism

Platonic epistemology lingered into eighteenth-century Britain, despite the hegemony of empiricist materialism. In its simplest form, this epistemology divided the world into concrete, temporal matter, on the one hand, and ideal, timeless form, on the other. For Plato, the real or true was ideal and the concrete was only ever a partial, particular expression of it.[8] According to the Christian European variant of this paradigm, all things were presumed to be analogically related because all things were expressions of a perfect, complete God. Thus, to draw an analogy in this context was not merely to propose an illustrative comparison so much as to identify a genuine, meaningful relation between things, however diverse they might otherwise seem. Identifying analogies counted as knowledge production because locating a similar phenomenon in disparate objects or domains suggested that the phenomenon was a constitutive feature of the great chain of being, an expression of the reason animating the world. Even Francis Bacon's *Novum Organum* (1620) argues that treating all discrete objects of knowledge as analogous to each other was requisite to induction and scientific method. And, as Dahlia Porter writes,

When, following Bacon's suggestion, method became an integral component of moral philosophy and aesthetic theory, it created the sense that distinct objects of knowledge – emotions, mental operations, plants, and animals – were analogous to each other. The foundational procedure of empiricist science, in other words, gave birth to a new way of thinking about the relationship between anger and heat, fear and cold – it made linguistic relationships (those contained in phrases like "the heat of passion," "burning desire," or "cold with dread") seem like they might signify beyond the metaphorical.[9]

Such faith in analogy held through much of the eighteenth century, when David Hartley repeated the familiar book of nature argument: "All the works of God, the parts of a human body, systems of minerals, plants, and animals, elementary bodies, planets, fixed stars, &c. have various uses and subserviencies [*sic*] in respect to each other; and, if the scriptures be the word of God, analogy would lead one to expect something corresponding hereto in them."[10] Without the Christian typological rhetoric, Edmund Burke later wrote, "All the senses bear an analogy to, and illustrate one another."[11] Classical cultures that believed in constitutive analogical relationships respected similes as signatures of cosmological coherence and as knowledge rather than as ornament or illustration. Homer's similes, for instance, attest to the immanence of meaning in everything.

Over the course of the early-modern period, however, analogies ceded authority to forms of representation that corresponded more directly with what they signified. Analogies were reconsidered as symptoms of coincidence, as accidents, or as heuristic and rhetorical accessories concepts rather than as constitutive, substantial features of reality. Given the limits of human experience, cognition, and perception, empirical knowledge could only ever know an anthropomorphic, partial world. To cope with this problem, Kant proposed what he called "regulative reason," a form of reason that accepts that certain things are ultimately impossible to know with certainty but nevertheless behaves out of necessity "as if" they were true.[12] The epistemological shift from constitutive to regulative analogies began well before Kant in the rhetorical conventions of early-modern natural philosophy. Citing Touchstone from Shakespeare's *As You Like It*, Steven Shapin explains that there was "much virtue in If" for seventeenth-century natural philosophers:

> A characteristic mark of the English natural-philosophical enterprise was its vigilant protection of the factual domain combined with injunctions to speak modestly, diffidently, and doubtingly about the domain of the theoretical. It was philosophically and morally possible to do so, because the foundations of knowledge and of members' moral order were located elsewhere.[13]

Elsewhere, that is to say, in the presumed credibility of gentlemen: on the one hand, the character of a gentleman guaranteed the truth of what he presented as knowledge; on the other hand, his modest, diffident, doubting presentation of that truth rhetorically enacted his character. Somewhat paradoxically, then, the tentativeness of a piece of prose could reinforce its tenability or credibility, because that that tentativeness tacitly indicated that a philosopher was more invested in the truth than in his own rightness, theory, or persuasiveness. Recall the discussion of the performative open-mindedness of Darwin's penchant for "turning" to anomalous evidence and competing claims. Confidence and conviction evoked vanity and prejudice inimical to the character of a gentleman or a scientist. Hesitant, self-abnegating rhetoric was therefore integral to what Shapin calls "epistemological decorum" (xxix), the manner or bearing requisite to producing legitimate knowledge in a given culture.[14] Conditional analogy embeds detachment and humility into prose description by offering comparisons as mere comparisons. Even as it enables imaginative predictions, connections, and associations that transcended the limits of empirical observation, *as if* grammatically enacts a degree of skepticism and impartiality about its imaginings. It thereby protects the factual domain even as it transgresses it.

The moral valence of conditional analogy increased with its affiliation with natural theology and with the discourse of sympathetic imagination. Joseph Butler's influential *The Analogy of Religion, Natural and Revealed* (1736) affirms that all human knowledge is limited to the probable and the analogical, because existence is contingent on God's grace and on imperfect human senses. Christian character therefore accrued to those who maintained a conditional attitude to knowledge. Conditional knowledge evokes humility before God's world and constitutes, for Butler, a kind of epistemic comportment.[15] While Butler's text was first published in 1736, it remained in print throughout the nineteenth century, during most of which it functioned as a primary textbook for Anglican clergy. *The Analogy of Religion* provided some of the logic for the natural theology of the Bridgewater Treatises, which were intended to reconcile Anglican theology with cutting edge natural philosophy, and, in so doing, to reconcile useful knowledge with Christian morality.[16] Hence, Butler's notion of conditional knowledge endured into the Victorian period and habituated many educated Victorians to an affective agnosticism. Ironically, however, this manner of affecting not to know anything fully or directly licensed writers to characterize it all the more authoritatively. In practice, then, the double movement of *as if*, protecting the factual and doubting the conjectural, had inverse effects: it beset the facts with doubt and avowed faith in the conjecture.

Over the course of the eighteenth century, conditional analogy also came to inflect secular moral philosophy. Seventeenth- and early eighteenth-century natural philosophers generally considered analogies to identify actual, constitutive correspondences between different domains: animal and vegetable, human and divine, earthly and heavenly, moral and material. Reasoning from the visible to the invisible was a routine aspect of British empiricism and induction. During the second half of the century writers such as the common sense philosopher Thomas Reid implicitly reclassified all analogies as conditional, heuristic fictions. But, working in the footsteps of David Hume and Adam Smith, Dugald Stewart and other Scottish moral philosophers and historians espoused what Stewart called "conjectural history," a mode of supplementing available experiential evidence with speculative conjecture and theoretical abstraction.[17] Late-eighteenth-century botanists and natural philosophers like Erasmus Darwin aspired to define analogy as a legitimate method conformable to empiricism, and to be sure hypotheses remain fundamental to scientific method, which presumes its ideas are wrong until repeatedly proven otherwise. But philosophers constantly confronted the discomfiting proximity between analogy and allegory, imagination, and other speculative modes that were ceding epistemic authority to demonstrable knowledge. Analogy became dubious in eighteenth-century natural philosophy.

Moral philosophers naturalized this doubt, however, by integrating it into their concepts of human character. As analogy lost the epistemic authority to generate facts, it acquired the authority to generate character, and to the extent that human character came to seem structured by conditional analogy, characterizing different things with conditional analogies became less an admission of doubt than a familiar mode of morally and credibly representing things which could not be represented in facts – things like feelings, ideas, and systems. Conditional analogy would not produce the same demonstrable certainty as analogy had once had, but in turn it acquired the moral valence of fellow feeling. Adam Smith is again relevant here because he published the influential assumption that people could only know each other conditionally, conjecturally, or approximately through the hypothetical exercise that he called sympathetic imagination.[18] For Smith, an "attentive spectator" cannot know exactly how another person feels because he or she cannot wholly and precisely reproduce another's character. Feelings and characters differ to the extent that past and present experiences and circumstances differ. The attentive spectator must therefore imagine how another person feels by acting as if he or she were in that person's irreproducible circumstances. "As we have no immediate experience of what other men feel, we can form no idea of the manner in which they are affected, but by conceiving what we ourselves should feel in the like situation," Smith says.[19] Given that our senses "never did, and never can, carry us beyond our own person," he continues, "it is by the imagination only that we can form any conception of what are his sensations ... we enter as it were into his body, and become in some measure the same person with him" (3–4). "As it were": respecting the empiricist investment in experience and senses, Smith nevertheless reaffirms the conditionality and performativity of our knowledge of other people and their feelings. Even given factual, material experience, we can only ever approximate what it signifies or how it feels. So considered, sympathy applies Kantian "regulative reason" to the work of sociality. Through conditional analogy, things appear to be knowable only to the degree that other peoples' characters were knowable. Conditional analogies also suited the empiricist model of human character formation. Hume described character as the accumulation of sequential sensory perceptions that are translated imperfectly into ideas, which are in turn associated with each other based on coincidence and contingency rather than some logical reason inherent in the things causing the perceptions.[20] Hume's paradigm inadvertently legitimated coincidence and contingency as necessary (if limiting) features of human cognition, such that the kind of coincidental associations generated by *as if* seemed less like fanciful imaginings than ordinary knowledge, the way character routinely integrates perceptions. The authority of such knowledge depended not on the accuracy or reproducibility of its content but on the "propriety," as Smith says, of its sympathetic and casuistic process. Character as Smith describes it is an interpersonal practice, not a personal property.[21] It is a behavior.

This notion of character obtained in theories of fiction, where the conditional analogy was employed to make sense of "fiction," a category of representation that is ambivalently true and not-true. As Lennard J. Davis writes, eighteenth-century novels have a "constitutively ambivalent" "attitude toward fact and fiction"; "the novel is about reality and at the same time is not about reality; the novel is a factual fiction that is both factual and factitious."[22] Davis's work is consistent with Michael McKeon's meticulous account of the emergence of "the idea of concrete virtuality that is central to the modern doctrines of realism and the aesthetic" – the idea, that is to say, of a category of fiction that is neither deceit nor falsehood but instead "the aesthetic mode of truth."[23] McKeon's "concrete virtuality" expresses the way a fiction can particularize an imaginary character, a virtual person, who nevertheless exhibits features of real people in general. *As if* and other conditional analogies insinuate the ambivalence of virtual reality in the grammar of a sentence by proposing a hypothetical fiction and simultaneously disavowing it as merely hypothetical, merely fiction (as *if* rather than *as*). In *The Progress of Romance* (1785), an influential and representative theorization of the generic ideals of the novel, Clara Reeve describes readers' immersion in novels "as if" they were sympathetic investments in people or individual characters. Reeve describes "the absorptive dimension of the probabilistic novel," as William Galperin puts it, in contradistinction to romance.[24] Probable prose, she writes, conveys

> a familiar relation of such things, as pass every day before our eyes, such as may happen to our friend, or to ourselves; and the perfection of it, is to represent every scene, in so easy and natural a manner, and to make them appear so probable, as to deceive us into a persuasion (at least while we are reading) that all is real, until we are affected by the joys or distresses, of the persons in the story, as if they were our own.[25]

Reeve's description of probabilistic prose thus equates reading realist fictions to sympathizing with real people. The implicit effects of reading – of feeling the emotions of a text and accruing character from it – are condensed in the regulative act of feeling "as if they were our own." Reeve subordinates the everyday things to which fictions refer to the affective attitude or practice that they actualize in readers. This prescribes how David Copperfield could read "as if for life."

That reading fiction fosters conjecture and sympathy ought not to come as a surprise, but tracing this work in the specific locution *as if* reveals fiction at work in non-fictional genres and discloses the characterological assumptions underwriting the style of nineteenth-century prose as a medium of knowledge production. Charles Lyell explicitly and stylistically legitimates "analogy" as the methodology of the new geology in his *Principles of Geology*.[26] While almost all of its reviewers identified it as "a book of facts," as "one of the noblest accumulations of facts of modern times," most reviewers also asserted that it was a morally cultivating and interesting book, a book that enriched the character of its readers.[27] The Society for the Diffusion of Useful Knowledge would make the case that facts were intrinsically moral,[28] yet Lyell's approach intimates that moral and epistemic authority emanate from the attitude one has to facts – the "treatment" of the facts, as late-century apologists for fiction would put it – rather than the facts themselves.[29]

Lyell cultivated a prose style that could respect facts without being limited by them. He also aspired to write in a way that reconciled his character as a geologist, a professional author, and a reformist with his character as a dutiful and respectable gentleman in a Tory family. For Lyell, conditional analogy simultaneously addresses the methodological problem of producing empirical knowledge about unobservable geological phenomena and the characterological problem of moralizing and making credible that which defied received wisdom and practice. Though most Victorian novelists were familiar with *Principles of Geology*, I submit Lyell not as an influence so much as an heuristic by which to recognize the paradigmatic syntax of Victorian realism and the implicit epistemology of character that underwrites it. His turn to a distinctly fictive trope augmented the epistemic clout of fiction early in the century.

Because critics of the new geology so readily and relentlessly impugned it as an atheistic, radical repudiation of scripture, supportive reviewers had to defend books like Lyell's *Principles* as, if not compatible with Biblical history, then at least otherwise moral and politically neutral alternatives that served different but compatible purposes.[30] Advocates of Lyell insisted that he was a creditable, religious gentleman and that *Principles* cultivated the character of its readers. His audience was as interested in determining the book's moral character as they were in evaluating its description of geological processes. For example, with unabated praise and Shakespearean allusions, the *Spectator*, a liberal Whig weekly, claimed that *Principles* – "in an indirect manner" – elevated and cultivated the disposition of its reader:

> There are other investigations which more nearly affect our social happiness than the philosophy of geology, but perhaps there is none which in an indirect manner produce a more wholesome and beneficial effect upon the mind . . . After the perusal of Mr. Lyell's volume, we confess to emotions of humility, to aspirations of the mind, to an elevation of thought, altogether foreign from the ordinary temper of worldly and busy men . . . So disposed mentally, the heart overflows with charity and compassion; vanity shrivels into nothingness; wrongs are forgotten, errors forgiven, prejudices fade away; the present is taken at its real value; virtue is tried by an eternal standard. There are sermons in stones and tongues in brooks, but they want an interpreter: that interpreter is the enlightened geologist. Such a man is Mr. Lyell.[31]

The almost laughable list of effects this puff ascribes to *Principles* might appear extraordinary, but it is typical of favorable reviews: character was as important in adjudicating nineteenth-century non-fiction as fiction.[32] Books were understood not just as containers of data, whose content could be moral or immoral, but as a kind of exercise machine: reading could strengthen or degenerate character, depending on the style. Style facilitated the manner of reading, so it was considered to be as meaningful as content because it influenced readers' dispositions. Reviewers therefore heeded the "indirect manner" or "disposition" books held toward their subjects and readers. The most resonant reviews of Austen, for example, appraise her indirect approach as a refreshing turn from didacticism. Lyell's "indirect manner" redounds upon the reader, replacing the unwholesome directness of "ordinary," worldly," and "busy" minds.

Lyell's style was integral to his self-presentation as a scientist and a professional writer but also a gentleman. *As if* helped him accommodate the factual demands of the former with the disinterestedness, open-mindedness, and liberty of the latter. As James Secord writes, "Lyell hoped to raise authorship into a calling fit for gentlemen," and for Lyell "science offered an indirect way of forwarding reform without betraying his father or his teachers"; he aspired to present science "as politically and theologically neutral."[33] Of course, Lyell could not make his theoretical content neutral, because it contradicted the normative stances on scriptural history and geology, but he could write in a neutral manner.

Principles of Geology prescribes the method and manner by which a student of the natural world should apprehend physical reality. This manner involved acknowledging that no complete cosmology or narrative of the past could be asserted positively because, as Lyell reiterates, too much of the geological record is lost. "Methods of Theorizing in Geology" thus validates "analogy" "as affording the only source of authentic information" (Rudwick III: 4). Lyell distinguishes conditional analogy as a version of induction distinctly superior to the "ingenious conjectures" and "boundless field of speculation" practiced by unregulated, over-imaginative Catastrophists, Neptunists, and other millenarians (Rudwick III: 3).[34] His conjectures are credible, he says, because they originate in facts observable in the present – "Causes now in operation" – just as David Copperfield's associative recollections of *Don Quixote* and *Humphry Clinker* and *The Vicar of Wakefield* originate in the ambient objects of his narrative present. Lyell's sets conditional analogy apart from the confabulations of conjectural historians and the spurious exegetic gymnastics of natural theology and French philosophy. The analogy between past and present, for which Whewell dubbed him "uniformitarian,"[35] enabled geologists to fill in the gaps in the historical record and to narrate the geological past as a continuous and probable – which is to say realist – genealogy of the present, instead of a Romantic narrative of revolution and supernatural intervention, like those authored by Abraham Werner, James Hutton, William Paley, and William Buckland. Where these writers imagined past causes to explain the present conditions of Earth, Lyell worked from present causes to imagine past events. "Lyell's public application of his principles," Secord affirms, "was thus almost entirely regulative: that is, geologists should carry out their investigations *as though* visible causes are the same kinds as those that acted in the past, and of the same degree of intensity. Uniformity of law, kind and degree had to be assumed, Lyell argued, to make geology scientific."[36]

But belying the effect of sameness that the so-called "uniformitarian" standardization of past and present causes might be expected to produce, Lyell concomitantly insists on severing adjacent strata and other geological features. "One consequence of undervaluing greatly the quantity of past time," he explains, "is the apparent coincidence which it occasions of events necessarily disconnected, or which are so unusual, that it would be inconsistent with all calculation of chances to suppose them to happen at one and the same time" (Rudwick I: 80). The assumption of like causes actually installs vast gaps between apposite objects that otherwise seem to be closely related. As with Hume's characterological "associations," these relations prove to be coincidental and not meaningful. So in his next sentence Lyell mobilizes *as if* dismissively as a medium of superstition: "When the unlooked-for association of such rare phenomena is witnessed in the present course of nature," he explains, "it scarcely ever fails to excite a suspicion of the preternatural in those minds which are not firmly convinced of the uniform agency of secondary causes; – as if the death of some individual in whose fate they are interested happens to be accompanied by the appearance of a luminous meteor, or a comet, or the shock of an earthquake" (Rudwick I: 80). *As if* inscribes an ambivalence into the prose of *Principles*: it empowers a regulative realism that respects the parameters of probability and factual actuality with the skepticism of the conditional, which here allows him to dismiss extant geological hypotheses as "fanciful conjecture" and "prejudices" (Rudwick I: 77 and *passim*), but all the same rewrites those parameters by so frequently humoring hypothetical suppositions of its own.

For all its rigor and repudiation of superstitious conjecture, *Principles of Geology* invokes a handful of wildly Dickensian conditional analogies that disavow the verisimilitude implicit in the calming terms by which Lyell's work became known: *gradualist* and *uniformitarian*. To register "operations invisible to us" and to "[overcome] the limited range of our vision," Lyell pictures "an amphibious being" and "some 'dusky melancholy sprite,' like Umbriel," an ideal submarine observer and a subterranean observer (Rudwick I: 83, I: 82). More habitually, however, he employs rather unostentatious conditional analogies to forward his hypothetical suppositions as the truth even though that truth, as the conditional admits, differs from what common sense seems to suggest about visible data. Lyell resorts to analogies to conjure knowledge because geological "causes now in operation" prove to be as invisible as past events. The object of his science, like the objects of most modern disciplines, is an abstraction that can never be seen in its totality or essence with any of the five senses:[37] however real, natural laws and the forces of geological change are what Marx describes as "concrete abstractions," visible in various partial material expressions but invisible because virtual in their totality. For Lyell, the evident world consists entirely of circumstantial evidence, and the full geological narrative necessarily exceeds the tracks it leaves behind.[38] "The first and greatest difficulty," he admits, "consists in our habitual unconsciousness that our position as observers is essentially unfavorable, when we endeavour to estimate the magnitude of the changes now in progress, . . . we inhabit about a fourth part of the surface; and that portion is almost exclusively the theatre of decay and not of reproduction" (Rudwick I: 81). Lyell professes knowledge not merely of craters, coral reefs, mountains, and seas, but of virtual realities – *things*, he explains, "to which the eye, unassisted by art, could never obtain access" (Rudwick I: 83).[39] However linked to the speculations he rejects, then, the conditional analogy is the medium of his art.

To see the "analogous results of some former epoch," Lyell insists, we need to "recognise the analogy" with both "the reason and the imagination" (Rudwick I: 81). So, in practice, as he supplants violent with gradual change he inverts the epistemological structure of conditional analogy, such that the suppositional content becomes the truth and the conditional clause becomes a mistaken appearance.

> To a mind unconscious of the intermediate links in the chain of events, the passage from one state of things to another must appear so violent, that the idea of revolutions in the system inevitably suggests itself. The imagination is as much perplexed by such errors as to time, as it would be if we could annihilate space, and by some power, such as we read of in tales of enchantment, could transfer a person who had laid himself down to sleep in a snowy arctic wilderness, to a valley in a tropical region, where on awaking he would find himself surrounded by birds of brilliant plumage,

and all the luxuriance of animal and vegetable forms of which nature is there so prodigal. . . .

But if, instead of inverting the natural order of inquiry, we cautiously proceed in our investigations, from the known to the unknown, and begin by studying the most modern periods of the earth's history, attempting afterwards to decipher the monuments of more ancient changes, we can never so far lose sight of analogy, as to suspect that we have arrived at a new system, governed by different physical laws. (I 160)

Lyell's *Principles* is as suffused with the subjunctive mood as this passage. "*As* it would be *if* we could annihilate [and] could transfer": we can neither annihilate space nor transfer people, but Lyell implies that these virtual circumstances nevertheless make visible the real causes of geological change precisely because they do not lose sight of the analogy between past and present cases and because they bypass what the inexpert observer can see. He employs the subjunctive mood to derive truth from counterfactual premises, and in this way he characterizes geology by presenting its motive forces as knowable only to the extent that we can, according to Adam Smith, know another's inner life. Geological history could only be known to the extent another person's feelings could be known, as if we were that person. Where Smith assumes consonance between human motives, such that we can approach but not reproduce what another feels by imagining ourselves in his circumstances, Lyell assumes consonance between the motive forces animating the earth's surface now and in the past so that we can approach geological history and agency that we can never actually see.

Principles of Geology teems with both sprawling and syllogistic "if"/ "then" statements. One exemplary section at the tail end of a chapter on coral reefs incorporates 12 couplings of "ifs" and "buts," each of which draws conclusions about reef formation by speculating, and then disavowing such speculation as merely speculation, and yet implying in the end that the speculations are nevertheless true (Rudwick II: 298–301). These conditional analogies cultivate a certain "disposition," to recall the words of Lyell's admiring reviewer, precisely because they make a supposition and then affect to dispose of it; they pose an idea and then pretend to dismiss it. But, much like asking the jury to dismiss something said in court, the suppositions survive. Indeed, the very torque of the conditional by dint of its dismissal elevates the supposition as more correct than the superficial, commonsense facts that seem to disprove or preclude it.

The moral disposition of this suppositional style owes not just to its supposed humility and its formal similarity to sympathetic imagination but also to its implicative apostrophe to the reader. Engaging the ethical dimension of nineteenth-century styles, Andrew Miller explains how "the typical narrative structure of moral perfectionism takes us from skepticism to second-person relations," which is to say that, like Austen's idiom of induction, it translates "epistemological concerns into social dynamics."[40] Moral perfectionism necessitates a "second-person standpoint" (Miller 28). Lyell's grammar enacts the process of "perfecting," as Miller describes it, by announcing doubt while soliciting the reader to participate in an imaginative experiment. The second-person injunction or invitation to "suppose" directly addresses the reader and asks him or her to reproduce in his or her mind a hypothetical case precisely because the associations Lyell draws, like those David ascribes to the objects of Blunderstone, are not physically evident. Miller describes and aspires to "implicative" writing of this sort that is amendable to "perfection" in the sense that it invites the reader to "perfect" or "unfold" its implications, to experience lateral possibilities and alternatives to manifest experience (29–30). In place of conclusive or determinate prose, moral perfectionism like Lyell's acknowledges the partiality of its claims and "the existence of alternatives" to them (Miller 30).

The character of Lyell's prose therefore inheres in its disposition: in the gaps it inserts between things that are literally positioned side by side, thus severing visible appearance and virtual reality; in its preference for suppositions over positive truths; and in the moral perfectionism of its subjunctive and second-person style. The dispositional motion of the *as if* opened the space for a new kind of knowledge that replaced the correspondence implicit in the older regime of analogy, in which similarities identified manifestations of the same universal ideal or form, and in the positivist fact, which transparently reproduced manifest reality, with truth defined by its inability to be known conclusively and concretely. Unlike a legal dispositive motion, which moves to dismiss a claim entirely and avert further proceedings about it, the dispositive motion enacted by the *as if* proceeds as if the claims it has dismissed still obtains. It agrees to disagree; it disposes the reader to accept the virtual alongside the concrete.

Andrew Ure's *A New System of Geology* (1829) also includes about one hundred *as ifs* and many more conditional analogies, but the epistemic and moral authority of this regulative realism extended beyond geology to all sorts of domains, especially fiction. W. M. Thackeray – who happened to be friends with paleontologist and geologist Louis Agassiz, and with Richard Owen, who famously rearticulated the Megatherium, a sloth[41] – makes the connection between geological supposition and novelistic characterization explicit in *The Newcomes* (1853–55). As if echoing Lyell, he writes,

All this story is told by one, who, if he was not actually present at the circumstances here narrated, yet had information concerning them, and could supply such a narrative of facts and conversations as is, indeed, not less authentic than the details we have of other histories. How can I tell the feelings in a young lady's mind; the thoughts in a young gentleman's bosom? – As Professor Owen or Professor Agassiz takes a fragment of a bone, and builds an enormous forgotten monster out of it, wallowing in primeval quagmires, tearing down leaves and branches of plants that flourished thousands of years ago, and perhaps may be coal by this time – so the novelist puts this and that together: from the footprint finds the foot; from the foot, the brute who trod on it; from the brute, the plant he browsed on, the marsh in which he swam – and thus in his humble way a physiologist too, depicts the habits, size, appearance of the beings whereof he has to treat; – traces this slimy reptile through the mud, and describes his habits filthy and rapacious; prods down this butterfly with a pin, and depicts his beautiful coat and embroidered waistcoat; points out the singular structure of yonder more important animal, the megatherium of his history.
     Suppose then,[42]

Thackeray's portrayal of fictional characters as conjectural approximations of real characters that somehow precede the text is generic: the character of a complex personage was definitively presumed to be hidden within and only glimpsed in mannerisms, expressions, and action. Thackeray's rhetorical questions – "How can I tell the feelings in a young lady's mind; the thoughts in a young gentleman's bosom?" – buttress the assumption that a person's "true" or "real" character is definitively foreclosed by feigning that such character exceeds even the author's knowledge.[43] The second-person rhetorical questions and the "suppose then" construe fiction-reading as an implicative exercise in moral perfectionism, as Miller describes it. But Thackeray's pretense here also admits that realist characterization is not mimetic because character is never available to be reproduced in print. Character is, like dinosaur flesh, always conjured from partial, limited, inadequate, and circumstantial evidence. Positivism only can accept fossils, faces, facts. It takes dispositive motion to know character.
     Thackeray, whom Margaret Oliphant accused of grossly neglecting his plots on behalf of character,[44] characteristically articulates much of his prose as if he were parsing a story from scattered clues and indications instead of fabricating it all. For Dawson, Thackeray invokes the Megatherium to intimate that his ostensibly diffuse serial fiction has "an underlying organicism" (217), which chimes with this sense of a latent story. But Victorian reviewers lauded Thackeray for the character and language of his fictions,[45] rather than organic wholeness, which did not

become a dominant aesthetic desideratum until the late 1880s. He worked in the incumbent mode of serial sketches exemplified by Dickens's *Sketches by Boz* (1833–36) and *The Pickwick Papers* (1836–37), a mode comfortable with evanescent, partial portraits.[46] *The Quarterly Review* welcomed *The Newcomes* as a string of characterizations, a novelization of articles that seemed to originate in *The Spectator* and that did not need a plot.[47] Character, for many Victorians, still named a partial sketch rather than fully fleshed out personage.

The conditional tense allows him pretend that some elements of his fiction are positive representations of fact while other remarks are speculations – some "guesses," some of "the author's individual fancy" (*TN* 296–97) – filling in the evidentiary gaps; and the overall effect of this habit is a sense that a true story underlies his plot, that he is relaying an account of some pre-existing entity instead of creating something new. His point, however, is not that fiction is but a skeletal reconstruction of a fleshed out reality, but that real lived experience is always conjectural, always subject to characterization. Reality as he experiences it is virtual, the product of his associations and suppositions. However facetious, Thackeray hereby naturalizes the acknowledgment of everyday epistemological limitations as a moral disposition; he naturalizes a turn against positivism as the manner of a regular person. Conditional analogy provided the characteristic grammar of this turn.

The collusion of geological and characterological conjecture with the subjunctive mood in *The Newcomes* neatly exemplifies how the grammar of Victorian realism was skeptical of its own conjectures and yet skeptical, too, of the worth of the facts its conjectures warily and temporarily bypass. But many contemporaries drew these connections. E. S. Dallas, for one, frequently compares estimations of "the hidden soul" of art and character to Richard Owen's paleontology and comparative anatomy in *The Gay Science* (1866).[48] If most writers did not make these connections so explicit, their syntactical habits nevertheless bespeak their shared investment in an epistemology of character. "If," "yet," "could," "as," "so," "but," and "suppose": the conditional analogy inscribed dispositive motion into Victorian prose of all sorts.

Dickens's "As If" and Associative Character

If Thackeray's conditional idiom might appear subtle, Dickens's does not. Consider *Bleak House* (1852–53), which contains 311 "as ifs."[49] It begins with that "implacable" November weather: "As much mud in the streets as if the waters had but newly retired from the face of the earth, and it would not be wonderful to meet a Megalosaurus, forty feet long or so, waddling like an elephantine lizard up Holborn Hill" (5). Here, as in the epigraph from *David Copperfield*, Dickens's *as if* collapses past and present conditions, suggesting the prehistoric past correlates to present day London.[50] Dickens's indulgence in the idiomatic *as if* was less the influence of paleontology or geology, however, than the symptom of a pervasive epistemological and moral investment in regulative realism. By the 1830s *as if* was taken for granted as a convention of characterization.

"Chance people on the bridges peeping over the parapets into a nether sky of fog ... with fog all round them, as if they were up in a balloon, and hanging in the misty clouds" (*BH* 5): such similes turn up throughout *Bleak House*. They all function slightly differently, but they can be categorized. The phrase introduces clauses that animate inanimate objects and, inversely, clauses that reify animate beings; and it introduces clauses that articulate the ironic discord between the rationale of the narrative voice and the behavior, sayings, and thinking of individual personages. *As if* generates gaps between positivist descriptive actuality – things as they appear – and hypothetical possibility – things as they might or could be – and sustaining such gaps made his fictions implicitly legible as character.

An *as if* might affect that a narrator's ability to read and relate a character is limited, as when "A long-dead Dedlock" stares from the two-dimensional canvas of a painting out at Sir Leicester and Lady Dedlock, "as if he did not know what to make of it" (*BH* 142), which implies either that the narrator doesn't know with certainty that this is the reason why this portrait stares as it does, or that the narrator knows that the portrait does know what to make of it but nevertheless stares as if he did not. The eyes in some bedroom shutters likewise stare at Mr. Weevle "in his sleep, as if they were full of wonder" (255). In these passages, conditional analogies animate objects with human agency even as they disavow the possibility of such animation. And yet, the conditional mood does not always animate an object, against the acknowledged limits of literal truth, in order to present an explicit allegorical or otherwise figurative truth: to the contrary, in Dickens's prose it as often as not suggests that the figural animation exceeds the comprehension of the narrator. Perhaps the wonderment of the eyes in the painting reflect Weevle's wonder? Perhaps they embody the wonderment of the implied reader? Or perhaps they embody the narrator's own wonder at what transpires within Weevle, so as to suggest Weevle has the definitive inaccessibility that Smith ascribed to everyone? The twofold effect of this ambivalent *as if* is to generate the sense that ineffable motives and plots permeate the world of the novel and to naturalize associations as real, however indeterminate, aspects of existence.

Bleak House includes lots of indulgent, comic descriptions that exemplify the "metonymic reciprocity" that J. Hillis Miller discerns between Dickens's characters and their surroundings,[51] and *as if* often articulates this kind of metonymic reciprocity: Mr. Bagnet speaks "as if he were himself the bassoon of a human orchestra" (*BH* 343); Mr. Kenge stands "with his back to the fire and casting his eyes over the dusty hearth-rug as if it were Mrs. Jellyby's biography" (35); Mrs. Jellyby has "handsome eyes, though they had a curious habit of seeming to look a long way off. As if . . . they could see nothing nearer than Africa!" (37); and Mrs. Rouncewell "sits in her room (in a side passage on the ground floor, with an arched window commanding a smooth quadrangle, adorned at regular intervals with smooth round trees and smooth round blocks of stone, as if the trees were going to play at bowls with the stones)" (78). Such *as ifs* solicit the reader to accept these diverse objects as vehicles of characterization. They indulge the fantasy that people can own or belong to objects in physical, emotional, and otherwise meaningful ways that transcend legal ownership, exchange value, and the economies of class distinction.

Such *as ifs* also imply the indelible presence of latent, indeterminate agency or surplus significance embedded in otherwise ordinary objects. When Mrs. Pardiggle overturns a table "as if by invisible agency" (*BH* 95), for example, *as if* invests the agency of Mrs. Pardiggle's already intrusive, overbearing skirts with her intrusive, overbearing personality; and yet *as if* somewhat depersonalizes the agency by conditionally ascribing it to an invisible source instead of Mrs. Pardiggle herself. *As if* suggests, in other words, that a zeitgeist or Hegelian spirit supplements even the most quotidian aspects of even the most tertiary of characters. In Lyellian fashion, many of Dickens's *as if* clauses ascribe motives or causes to invisible agents. As conditional analogies – and often particularly ridiculous conditional analogies – these *as if* clauses disavow their content as *literally* inaccurate. But the ridiculous or otherwise counterfactual element of such analogies in turn suggests the inadequacy of literal accuracy. Far more valuable and just as true as the actual breadth of Mrs. Pardiggle's dress is the way that her bearing is so overbearing as to seem to spread beyond her; far more valuable and just as true as concrete actuality is appearance, felt experience. Characterization subordinates literal description to the associative surplus conjured by concrete objects. This surplus is associative not only in the Humean or Hartleyan sense of empiricist perception and character development, but also in the communal sense of affinity or connection: characterization affiliates things, even things that cannot possibly be related, and thereby refutes the possibility of an alienating, estranging world.

Harry Shaw imputes a similar function to select instances of the related verb "to seem." "The word can hardly be used to suggest appearances that might be deceiving," he observes, but "its function is instead to suggest that the narrator is striving to deal with difficult, potent material."[52] For Shaw, this suggestive verb models the kind of sympathetic, imaginative work that the reader ought to be doing. If "realism's basic impetus" is, as he says, not direct mimesis but "putting things in juxtaposition and leading the reader to imagine the web of relations that connects them, the conditions of possibility for a given aspect of social reality" (221), then with every *as if* Dickens is as realist as they come, and *as ifs* constitute the strings of his webs. They implicate the reader in the experience of the prose rather than offering the prose as an account of an objective experience.

"Character" more accurately particularizes some of the objectives tacitly met by Dickens's *as if* than "realism" does,[53] because Dickens so consistently employs *as if* to articulate the associative experience, self-reflectiveness, divided selfhood, and self-abnegation of his protagonists. Dickens's personages, like his narrators, have regulative relations with their worlds, even with themselves. In *Bleak House*, for instance, after Guppy's unwelcome proposal Esther recalls, "I was in a flutter for a little while; and felt as if an old chord had been more coarsely touched than it ever had been since the days of the dear old doll" (*BH* 115). This *as if* is the fulcrum mediating Esther's articulate consciousness and her inchoate, definitively ineffable unconscious. It coordinates Esther's indistinct memories, associations, yearnings, and aversions – associated with the old doll and figured vaguely by the old chord – with her more expressible feelings, ideas, and ideals; but its conditionality allows her to do so without identifying the indistinct old chord and its relation to her present self. Here the exact connotations of "an old cord" are subordinate to the reflective turn articulated by "as if." This kind of *as if* mediates the reflexivity that has been associated with complex character since at least Shaftesbury's *Characteristicks of Men, Manners, Opinions, Times* (1737), the self-reflection that Victorian writers valorized as an attribute of liberalism.[54] Thus, Esther later says that Mr. Jarndyce, whom she has loved "as if he had been my father" (436), "spoke in a regretful tone so new to me, that I inwardly repeated [what he said], as if that would help me to his meaning" (212). Esther's inward repetition of the proposal does not promise that she will perceive his meaning – the *as if* implies, to the contrary, that it will not help her to it – but she repeats it anyway because having character demands it. Her character owes to her oblique but willful relation to Jarndyce, not to her understanding of him.

Dickens consistently uses *as if* to articulate what motivates characters like Esther, particularly in passages of self-scrutiny. And yet the conditionality of *as if* nevertheless ensures that such self-scrutiny always yields an at least partially inscrutable remainder, a kernel of ineffable agency. When Esther reads Jarndyce's proposal letter, which "addressed [her] as if [their] places were reversed," she cries, "not only in the fullness of my heart after reading the letter, not only in the strangeness of the prospect – for it was strange though I had expected the contents – but as if something for which there was no name or distinct idea were indefinitely lost to me" (*BH* 537, 538). Esther only identifies her abstract loss as *something* because it would be improper to own the feeling that she loves Woodcourt, because that feeling is also still inchoate, because perhaps she has not yet recognized it, and because mid-Victorian culture did not have a term with which to adequately name "it." As I explain in the following chapter, *something* and other pronouns often substitute for such feelings. More important than naming them accurately, more important than filling the blank of the something lost, is the repetition of the gesture itself. The specific contents of feelings do not make her feel like a character so much as the regulative form of her self-relation. The conditionality of Esther's *as if* formally ensures that the phantom content that animates her character, "something for which there was no name or distinct idea," exceeds description. The "if" implies, however colloquially and subtly, that something is not actually lost to Esther. Even if readers imagine a referent for that *something*, the grammar of the sentence suggests that Esther will not or cannot acknowledge it. It is a doubly regulative analogy, then, because it functions semantically and morally. On the one hand, Esther recognizes and articulates her loss even though she cannot name it. The conditional analogy enables her to represent *something* that she cannot otherwise represent within the parameters of realism. On the other hand, the morally self-denying detachment of the conditional simile expresses her reserve. Esther subordinates the contents of the letter and the content of her feeling to the formal morality of her syntax, her manner of being. And in this manner Esther performs character. Hence, she famously disavows that she is herself the subject of the novel even though she is its primary character and one of its two narrators: "It seems so curious to me to be obliged to write all this about myself! As if this narrative were the narrative of my life!" (*BH* 27) *As if*?! Esther is of course a subject – if not *the* subject – of the narrative, and she becomes its protagonist, complex in contradistinction to characters such as Guppy and Jobling, precisely by turning to reflect on herself "as if" she weren't reflecting on herself.

As if amalgamates self-abnegation and self-knowledge for many Dickens characters. Like Esther, though with less credible false modesty, David Copperfield claims, "I feel as if it were not for me to record, even though this manuscript is intended for no eyes but mine, how hard I worked at that tremendous short-hand, and all improvement appertaining to it, in my sense of responsibility to Dora and her aunts" (*DC* 511). Elsewhere, the night before marrying Dombey, Edith Granger – split between indifference resigned to following her mother's mercenary motives and repentant, compensatory sympathy for Florence Dombey – paces her room "with an averted head, as if she would avoid the sight of her own fair person, and divorce herself from its companionship" (*DS* 475). The *as if* both articulates the manifest conflict between indifference and sympathy, and articulates Edith's defiant manner. She behaves "as if" she could separate herself into two selves. Consider Bella Rokesmith, who contemplates her baby and finds "her own dimples in that tiny reflection, as if she were looking in the glass without personal vanity" (*OMF* 736): the *as if* grants her a degree of "charming" selflessness even as it admits selfishness to be its source. Dickensian self-alienation is routinely mediated by such mannerisms.

Self-reflection, self-secreting, and self-abnegation are all enabled rhetorically by recourse to "as if." "'Esther! You to be low-spirited, you!' And it really was time to say so, for I – yes, I really did see myself in the glass, almost crying. 'As if you had anything to make you unhappy, instead of everything to make you happy, you ungrateful heart!' said I" (*BH* 212). This *as if* simultaneously acknowledges and denies that Esther has plenty to make her unhappy. *As if* allows her to have it both ways, to know and not know, to feel and express feeling while still suppressing feeling. It allows her to be at once altruistic and an individual.[55] And, moreover, it allows readers to do the work of interpretation and adjudication, to sympathize or to imagine these feelings that definitively exceed representation, but possibly – indeed most probably – simply to acknowledge them "as if" they knew what they were. Interpretation seems somewhat beside the point: this prose fosters a reading practice keener on association with the text than with decoding it.

I cannot cite every instance where the regulative *as if* articulates Esther's character, but a few more should complete the complexities the locution inscribes in Victorian characterization and manifest how Dickens routinely foregrounds it in distinct passages of characterization. Esther's convalescence, like any generic Victorian convalescence, metaphorically enables her to recognize her individual worth by documenting a transformation from a past self to a self-aware present self. This process implies developmental or dynamic selfhood, but a conditional one because she knows herself in the present by knowing what she has lost, what potential or past self she can no longer be. At this point in the novel, Esther claims to have "felt a little beside myself, though knowing where I was; and I felt confused at times – with a curious sense of fullness [*sic*], as if I were becoming too large altogether" (*BH* 390). This *as if* verbalizes the distance between the understood and the felt reality, between the expressible and the inexpressible, between two forms of actuality: literal and figurative. As in Lyell's uniformitarian analogy, Dickens's *as if* here grammatically instantiates a consistent motive, agency, or cause that sutures otherwise ostensibly discrete past and present states. The other form of representation that makes discrete, ephemeral, and dynamic feelings and thoughts cohere similarly in the recognizable form of a character is of course the proper name, but recognizing how colloquial phrases also perform this characterization will allow us to see how the modes and assumptions of literary characterization underwrote descriptions that are not so obviously personified as named characters are.[56]

Before analyzing how "regulative" characterization underwrites descriptions of things other than personages, however, consider how pervasively *as if* governs Dickensian characterization. David Copperfield, who repeatedly feels "as if he were really a stranger upon earth" (*DC* 246) and whom Steerforth treats "as if [he] were [his] property" (249), persistently recalls living his life through the lens of the conditional "as if." Thus, while he writes Agnes Wickfield of his engagement to Dora Spenlow, he recalls:

> cherishing a general fancy as if Agnes were one of the elements of my natural home. As if, in the retirement of the house made almost sacred to me by her presences, Dora and I must be happier than anywhere. As if, in love, joy, sorrow, hope, or disappointment; in all emotions; my heart turned naturally there, and found its refuge and best friend. (414)

While the content of David's "undisciplined heart" appears to be Agnes and whatever she embodies for David (a mother, a sister, a wife, a friend), the rhetorical form of his turn to that heart is certainly "as if." Such a turn likewise animates Paul Dombey. *Dombey and Son* opens playfully with little Dombey "tucked up warm in a little basket ... immediately in front of the fire and close to it, as if his constitution were analogous to that of a muffin, and it was essential to toast him brown while he was very new" (*DS* 11), but Dickens employs the form of this playfulness repeatedly to illustrate the "uneasiness of an extraordinary kind" that Dombey senior feels for his daughter Florence and, in turn, himself:

> He almost felt as if she watched and distrusted him. As if she held the clue to something secret in his breast, of the nature of which he was hardly informed himself. As if she had an innate knowledge of one jarring and discordant string within him, and her very breath could sound it. (*DS* 42)

What we call "secret subjectivity" could hardly be put more plainly: Dombey frets that he does not know himself, but he projects that self-knowledge onto Florence. The conditionality of the *as if* insists that he knows she cannot see through him, as we say, but that he nevertheless feels like she can. The same goes for Pip's childish conjectures about the meaning of his estranging, unfamiliar world in *Great Expectations*, another first-person narrative that abounds with "as ifs," and for Mortimer Lightwood in *Our Mutual Friend*, who so often turns to the dolls' dressmaker, "as if she were an interpreter between this sentient world and the insensible man" (*OMF* 720). *As if* enables these characters to sense what they cannot demonstrably know and to accord agency to motives and feelings that they cannot name. It is a medium of tempered re-enchantment. Nina Auerbach has written that "Victorian novels enchant by the implicit promise that there is always more to know, that only the attentive reader (never the narrator!) is omniscient; but the other side of this enchantment," she admits, "is the grim possibility that we have seen everything, that the uncontained abundance of character is an illusion."[57] And indeed this tenuous balance between enchantment and disillusionment is inscribed into the conditional syntax of Victorian prose, the ubiquitous *as if* that counterpoises regulative and constitutive realities. *As if* articulates what Dickens called "the romantic side of familiar things" (*BH* 4) with the ordinary side; it was the stance by which one accommodated his or her melancholy, uncanny, or extraordinary associations.[58]

The discord between the regulative reality characters sense and the constitutive reality they think they know makes Dickens's characters skeptical, prone to conditionals. But if Dickens's characters make skeptical claims to knowledge, such claims nevertheless qualify *as* knowledge (character) precisely because of the skepticism formally inscribed into them. As in *Principles of Geology*, credibility is an effect of the regulative manner or attitude with which characters and narrators relate their content. While pronounced in Dickens, this effect is evident elsewhere. John Stuart Mill, for instance, characterizes the pitch of his "dejection" through self-reflection rhetorically enabled by *as if*: "I felt as if I was scientifically proved to be the helpless slave of antecedent circumstances; as if my character and that of all others had been formed for us by agencies beyond our control, and was wholly out of our own power."[59] In Elizabeth Gaskell's *Mary Barton* (1848), for another example, Parker, the Carson family's nurse, announces the news that "Mr. Harry is brought home – " and Amy and Sophy whisper, "Brought home – brought home – how?" Parker replies "In the same low tone, as if afraid lest the walls, the furniture, the inanimate things which told of preparation for life and comfort, should hear ... 'Dead!'" (181). Parker is not afraid that inanimate things will literally hear her, but projects her apprehensions of the reaction the news will have on Sophy and Amy onto those things. She is perhaps reticent to verbalize and thereby to realize Harry's death. *As if* condenses this panoply of significations as colloquial language so often condenses and eludes full expression. It is shorthand for gesturing at complexities and discomforting thoughts that people prefer not to communicate directly and fully; shorthand for associative conjectures. In such passages, *as if* actuates the type of cognition that the text values as character above any nameable feelings or thoughts. More important than the specific passions a David or an Esther harbors is the regulative attitude those characters maintain, always indulging and undercutting the associative potential of their experience, always moved by something dispositivist, so to speak.

Suspect Similes: Skimpole, Micawber, Pecksniff, and Podsnap

As if is not restricted to good characters, however. It recurs indeed as one of the principle mannerisms by which irresponsible, uncongenial, and unfeeling characters shirk responsibility and ignore material reality. Harold Skimpole, Wilkins Micawber, Seth Pecksniff, and John Podsnap variously manifest how disavowal and conjecture combine in deleterious ways. By comically foregrounding *as if* in the characterization of these delusional, hypocritical, negligent, and otherwise discreditable characters as well as in the most endearing protagonists, Dickens underscores how *as if* made character legible as such, in any individual or object, but also how character itself was splitting into discordant aesthetic and moral categories. That is to say, Dickens's style acknowledges *as if* as an expository signature of a charismatic novelistic knowledge even as it registers the discomfiting amorality of that knowledge. Like the word "moral" itself, "character" could connote ethical goodness as well as an almost ethically neutral sense of mental life (or what we might call psychology). Almost ethically neutral: as an articulation of mental life, intrinsically social and emotional, such knowledge was implicitly ethical even in the form of bad characters. And of course bad characters had always existed. The disturbing distinction here is how Dickens makes the badness of his villains so frequently pivot on the very same turn of phrase as the goodness of his heroes and heroines. This equivocation about the moral valence of conditional analogy resonates in similarly ambivalent work with all the remaining everyday words studied in this book.

Dickens foregrounds the abuses of *as if* in Wilkins Micawber, Mr. Pecksniff, Mr. Podsnap, and Harold Skimpole. Micawber tends to be delusional and, as with so many Dickens characters, what would seem to be his most intangible characteristics often seem "as if" they were impossibly tangible, comically or even perversely reified. Confusing reading with eating, Captain Hopkins thus reads Micawber's overwrought petition aloud "as if the words were something real in his mouth, and delicious to taste" (*DC* 150); and confusing his own physiognomy, Micawber has "a certain expression of face, as if his voice were behind his eyebrows" (451). In addition to these contorted adaptations to modernity, Micawber caricatures irrational optimism. He repeatedly anticipates that he will live differently, be happy and responsible, if and when "something turns up" (154, 222, 226, 348). Micawber lives in the subjunctive mood; "I have no doubt I shall, please Heaven, begin to be beforehand with the world, and to live in a perfectly new manner," he says, "if – in short, if anything turns up" (149). Micawber habitually goes into debt because he behaves as if good fortune were probable, even inevitable, rather than living according to his actual, extant means. Micawber thus represents a human disposition to inhabit alternative, ideal circumstances instead of behaving in correspondence with reality; he represents an anti-mimetic habitus whereby he actuates his present actions with more amenable future or past conditions.

In *Martin Chuzzlewit*, Anthony Chuzzlewit identifies a similar proclivity in Pecksniff, the consummate hypocrite whom Dickens introduces as "a moral man" whose "very throat was moral" and who asserts that even eggs "have their moral" (*MC* 23–24). "The annoying quality in you," he says to Pecksniff, "is [that you] have a way with you, as if you – he, he, he! – as if you really believed yourself," and Pecksniff nevertheless replies, true-to-form, "as if he had received the highest compliments that language could convey" (123). The conditional analogy grammatically instantiates Pecksniff's ability to maintain his act, to assert the fictional character he has written for himself, no matter how other characters treat him. He effortlessly translates the consensual real – asserted by the narrator and the rest of the characters – into circumstances that suit his fantastic script. Character was not altogether correlated to sincerity – "the degree of congruence between feeling and avowal," as Trilling neatly put it – but instead to the definitive incongruence between feeling and avowal, or actuality and expression.[60] Character of the aesthetic and epistemic sort – which is to say, character that was interesting and credibly realistic – necessarily split feeling and avowal, motive and action. The proliferation of *as if* duly extends well beyond the boundaries of Pecksniff. His daughters, Charity and Mercy, open their eyes wide at the news of their new, "well-looking" boarder, Martin, with a look "as blank as if their thoughts had actually had a direct bearing on the main-chance" of marrying him (26). But Martin and Tom likewise behave according to their governing fictions of the world and their bodies, like Charity and Mercy's, correspond with circumstances as they too had "a direct bearing" on them.

Dickens's *as if* suggests that the relationship between entities – characters and objects, ideas and events, feelings and bodies – are not accidental but significant. It thus risks inscribing Pecksniffian hypocrisy into the syntax of Dickens's prose in general. Practicing a hypocrisy of its own, the narrator of *Martin Chuzzlewit* indulges liberally in *as ifs* that less ostentatiously characterize the text as something other than mimesis, as a whimsical deviation from the world as others customarily see it. Even the wind, an "impotent swaggerer," seems to have intentions that refute the natural order of things, as it "began to bluster round the merry forge, banging at the wicket, and grumbling in the chimney, as if it bullied the jolly bellows for doing anything to order" (*MC* 20). To a degree, then, Pecksniff personifies the indulgent habits of the narrator, and in doing so he is just one of many deviant and/or eccentric characters who dramatize the moral risks of Dickensian characterization. Rosemarie Bodenheimer convincingly suggests that Dickens's sometimes self-parodying style is characteristic of his embarrassed self-knowledge and concomitant desire to forget himself. Bodenheimer surmises that Dickens's sense of self depended on "another man," on other selves he anxiously imagines as possessors of secret knowledge of himself.[61] Dickens's critics harped on his habitual personification of everything as a source of his lack of realism (which they variously diagnosed as monstrosity, insanity, hallucination, and so on), but he was reproducing the specific unrealistic attitude that real people really held.

Harold Skimpole of *Bleak House* perhaps best exemplifies the particular problems that *as if* inscribed into language. With "easy negligence" of "manner" (*BH* 65), Skimpole explicitly disowns his own will and, "as if personal considerations were impossible with him" (71), holds others responsible for it: "I almost feel as if you ought to be grateful to me for giving you the opportunity of enjoying the luxury of generosity" (67), he says to thank Esther and Richard for paying his debts. Skimpole caricatures the way *as if* allows Esther to translate her own generosity into gratitude and respect toward others and enables the narrator to transpose values of any sort from one agent to another, even to objects without agency. To wit, Esther characterizes Skimpole's self-detachment as if he were an outside observer: "All this and a great deal more he told us," Esther says,

> not only with the utmost brilliancy and enjoyment, but with a certain vivacious candour – speaking of himself as if he were not at all his own affair, as if Skimpole were a third person, as if he knew that Skimpole had his singularities but still had his claims too, which were the general business of the community and must not be slighted. He was quite enchanting. (67)

Skimpole enchants Esther by becoming a narrator, detached from himself and somehow from the collective responsibility of the rest of the character system. As narrators project their associations and conjectures onto the worlds they describe, Skimpole projects responsibility for himself onto others. Although Esther affects to slight her own claims to attention and assumes responsibility for herself and for others, she consistently and willfully misrepresents herself to do so, declining to mention her interest in Woodcourt, denying her centrality to the narrative, and so on. Skimpole's detachment makes him a leach and an idler who does no work of his own; and one might therefore wonder if through Skimpole Dickens fretted about the impotence of fiction to do things in the world, fretted about the crippled conditionality of his own conjectural work as novelist. Fiction, after all, achieves its social and political ends by animating readers to act.

Passive detachment and displaced responsibility might be for Dickens the foremost dangers of analogical prose, for passivity – a deferral of responsibility and action – plagues Skimpole, Pecksniff, Podsnap, and Micawber alike. These personifications of *as if* are largely idle; they wait around, like Micawber, for "something to turn up," for someone to give them an inheritance, a reputation, a job or position, money or meaning. They defer responsibilities, like Skimpole, to other characters or, like Podsnap, to abstract causes that cannot be redressed. In *Our Mutual Friend*, a discussion of poverty and hunger between Podsnap, who represents the upper middle-class, and "the meek man" nicely dramatizes the problem as a reluctance to accept facts as facts:

The meek man was afraid we must take it as proved, because there were the Inquests and the Registrar's returns. ... The man of meek demeanour intimated that truly it would seem from the facts, as if starvation had been forced upon the culprits in question – as if, in their wretched manner, they had made their weak protests against it – as if they would have taken the liberty of staving it off if they could – as if they would rather not have been starved upon the whole, if perfectly agreeable to all parties. ... The meek man was quite willing to concede that, but perhaps it rendered the matter even worse, as showing that there must be something appallingly wrong somewhere.[62]

The meek man demurely interprets the facts with "as if," as if his utterly logical conclusions could be doubted by any reasonable person. In the face of Podsnap, the obvious truth thus degenerates into mere possibility. The meek man politely, if also sardonically, presents his inferences as debatable conjectures even as he recognizes these inferences as "proven" by the data of "the Inquests and Registrar's returns." He feigns doubt about his interpretation as much as Esther feigns doubt about being the subject of the narrative (he even shares the same indeterminate *something* that I describe in the following chapter). However correct he seems – what sane reader could question his opinion? – he fails to convince those who are predisposed to discredit his conclusions. His facts are irrelevant. If Dickens consistently undermines the brute surety personified in characters like Dombey, Carker, Gradgrind, Bounderby, and Podsnap, characters like the meek man also appear powerless, disabled by their humility, open-mindedness, and imagination.

But the conditional analogy so thoroughly pervades nineteenth-century prose that, however much it is foregrounded as a medium of character-ological ideology or self-reflection, it ultimately constitutes the character of the prose itself. Character is a relation, and the predominant relation prose held to reality was mediated by conditional analogy. Prose with character was prose marked by such a relation. Syntactically, Dickens, Thackeray, Gaskell, and others often write as if they were only speculating about a real story – the Russian *fabula* – that precedes them as prior geological epochs, subterranean and submarine fossils precede and evade Lyell. Mr. Jellyby sits "with his head against the wall, as if he were subject to low spirits ... as if he had something on his mind" (*BH* 41), all as if Mr. Jellyby actually had a real mind of his own and Dickens could not suss out what was on it. Mr. George likewise "pass[es] one of his heavy hands over his crisp dark hair, as if to sweep the broken thoughts out of his mind" (306), as if the narrator and even George do not quite know why he does so or what thoughts he has as he does it. Recurrent *as ifs* present the narrative as a string of speculations about underlying motives and meanings, causes and explanations, which purportedly transcend the narrators' cognitive capacities.[63]

Dourer writers such as Eliot and Gaskell, who belittled anthropomorphism as childishly "Dickensy,"[64] nevertheless characterize smoke, houses, trees, and weather with nearly as many *as ifs* as Dickens.[65] In *Mary Barton*: "The two men, rough, tender nurses as they were, lighted the fire, which smoked and puffed into the room as if it did not know the way up the damp, unused chimney"; "The floor was bricked, and scrupulously clean, although so damp that it seemed as if the last washing would never dry up"; and "Houses, sky, people, and everything looked as if a gigantic brush had washed them all over with a dark shade of Indian ink" (*MB* 56, 17, 42). The whispering trees of *David Copperfield* might seem to epitomize "Dickensian" prose, but they are actually a stock Victorian trope that *Mary Barton* invokes before Dickens: "the nearer trees sway gently to and fro in the night-wind with something of almost human emotion; and the rustling air makes music of their branches, as if speaking soothingly to the weary ones, who lie awake in weariness of heart" (216). And Eliot, the paragon of Dutch-painterly probability and verisimilitude, describes in *Adam Bede* "paths which look as if they were made by the freewill of the trees and underwood, moving reverently aside to look at the tall queen of the white-footed nymphs" (129). What Dickens foregrounds in its excesses and in ludicrous characters less ostentatiously permeates a lot of nineteenth-century prose. To write in this manner was to characterize the whole fiction as a compound fiction that is as regulative, as divided, self-reflexive, and speculative, as any of its individual characters. These *as ifs* constitute Dickens's world as a virtual reality, not in our current sense of an artificially reproduced reality – an artificial textual representation that seems like the real world – but in the sense that they conceptualize reality itself as virtual, as something that exceeds materiality.

"As separate as if we were in two worlds": Dickens, Gaskell, and the Grammar of Novelistic Knowledge

Characterization can mediate abstractions that cannot be represented demonstrably with facts, which count as such because they represent the accepted consensus about any given observation. As the previous chapter explains, to characterize was simultaneously to particularize and to generalize, to negotiate different scales of attention, and the conditional analogy performs similar work, negotiating or leveraging the difference between particular associations, insights, or experiences and collective assumptions. *As if* is a lexical fulcrum balancing competing ideologies, temporalities, and ontologies. It marks the difference between lived experience and the real,[66] the general way everybody else supposedly thinks or feels, though it privileges neither individuality nor normality: it identifies disjunctions between the two as the loci of aesthetic interest, the signposts of charismatic prose. In Dickens's hand as in Lyell's, experience is regulative and teeters between the fantastic and the mundane.

To illustrate, consider the way the solicitor Tulkinghorn acts as a vehicle for regulative fictions of different sorts. One of his many characteristic "impenetrabilities" is his spatial relation to the Dedlock estate: "He walks into Chesney Wold as if it were next door to his chambers, and returns to his chambers as if he had never been out of Lincoln's Inn Fields" (*BH* 514). Like a specter, Tulkinghorn behaves as if he were not subject to physical laws, which is playfully true inasmuch as he is a fictional character, but this spatial magic also signifies the collective paranoia – most acute in Lady Dedlock, but also evident in George, Guppy, and others – that Tulkinghorn knows everything. Tulkinghorn does not possess his own interiority so much as other characters worry that he, "an oyster of the old school, whom nobody can open," possesses theirs (119). Others sit in his office, heads aching, suspecting that he, like Allegory painted on his ceiling, possesses their very meaning better than they do. Tulkinghorn thus personifies Chancery and bureaucracy in general, "the legal system": his spectral ability to appear at will impersonates the unshakeable omnipresence of the law; his impenetrability impersonates the purported impersonality of the law. The law acts as if it is sound, just, and unimpugnable even in the face of utter disbelief: with a disregard for general opinion reminiscent of Pecksniff, "The Lord Chancellor, and the whole array of practitioners under him, [likewise look] at one another and at the spectators, as if nobody had ever heard that all over England the name in which they were assembled was a bitter jest" (307).

In his near ubiquity and his haunting, secretive manner, Tulkinghorn and these other practitioners function analogously to what Marx calls "concrete abstractions," because they realize a collection of attitudes, practices, and assumptions so as to make Chancery literally come alive, not just as an institution but as a real thing in the world. Reproducing the disavowal and acknowledgment enacted by conditional analogies, most characters seem to know nothing transpires in Chancery, but to think all the same that perhaps they just cannot understand what transpires therein: "Nothing that *you* would call anything has been done to-day" (*BH* 15;

emphasis in original), Tulkinghorn tells Lady Dedlock. The subjunctive form of these intimations expresses in part the anxiety that one's own character lies beyond one's control – neither in some internal unconscious nor just in the public economy of reputations – but in the files, memory, or logic of some bureaucratic office or functionary. Esther, Richard, Lady Dedlock, and others literally do require outside parties to inform them who they are and what they have.

Dickens's prose almost mechanically projects conjectural motives onto the visible actions of characters in a way that not only makes them instruments of ideology but also concretizes the abstract, indirect, or long-term effects of their behavior. In *Bleak House*, Sir Leicester passes a "capital sentence; as if it were the next satisfactory thing to having the sentence executed," and he "yields up his family legs to the family disorder [gout], as if he held his name and fortune on that feudal tenure" (*BH* 148,196). Rebuffing chance, physics, and natural laws of all kinds, Sir Leicester believes in the complete "metonymic reciprocity" between himself and the world; he takes ownership of ambient objects and accidents such that they all seem to redound upon his greatness. He gestures and speaks, moreover, with the conviction that his manners and words are what we would call performative – that his moves and utterances effect or realize what they say. Mr. Tulkinghorn likewise enjoys his wine, "As if it whispered to him of its fifty years of silence and seclusion [and] shuts him up the closer" (273). *As ifs* such as this one mediate commodity fetishism of various sorts. As Slavoj Žižek observes in *The Sublime Object of Ideology, as if* is the armature of fetishistic disavowal, the locution that enables people to concurrently believe and deny.[67] But Tulkinghorn's wine does not merely grant him cultural capital or taste as an oenophile; to the narrator it seems a reservoir of secrecy and alienation, a literal distillation of the character traits Tulkinghorn inherits from his profession and clients.

Histrionic gestures throughout Dickens's work dramatize the way personages seem to concretize abstractions. Richard Carstone's lawyer Mr. Kenge, to take a perfect example, "gently mov[es] his right hand as if it were a silver trowel with which to spread the cement of his words on the structure of the system and consolidate it for a thousand ages" (*BH* 741). Dickens's *as if* is a trowel of its own, a colloquial tool by which Dickens materializes ephemeral associations, intangible systems, and ideological effects. *As if* enables Dickens's prose, like Lyell's, to leapfrog the limitations of immediate material evidence by recognizing them as expressions of some abstraction or other. In this respect,

Dickens's *as ifs* affirm Žižek's further claim that *as if* couples observed reality with "*the 'real abstraction'*," "the support of objective-universal scientific knowledge" (18, emphasis in original)[68]; that is, *as if* couples routine physical description (observed data) to the abstract domains of modern knowledge, the domains of the market, natural and economic laws, class, the factory system, liberalism, the spirit of the age, and other subjects. Only Dickens, as a novelist rather than a social or natural scientist, rarely names the abstractions he animates. He characterizes abstractions without always specifying them by name. Just as Esther's or David's *as ifs* suggest that they are driven by or desire *something*, that the animating force of their character remains invisible, these *as ifs* characterizing the likes of Tulkinghorn and Kenge and other less "round" personages suggest that they are driven by invisible or even fantastic drives, by a virtual reality, whose effects on the world are as real as any concrete entity.

Gaskell's *Mary Barton* and *North and South* both use *as if* to articulate the disparity between the gritty experience of workers and abstract political economy. John Barton, for instance, explains the "condition of England" problem motivating *Mary Barton* – the relation between "the two nations," rich and poor – in a harangue that posits *as if* as the regulative grammar of social class:

> Don't think to come over me with th' old tale that the rich know nothing of the trials of the poor; I say, if they don't know, they ought to know. We're their slaves as long as we can work; we pile up their fortunes with the sweat of our brows, and yet we are to live as separate as if we were in two worlds; ay, as separate as Dives and Lazarus, with a great gulf betwixt us. (12)

Gaskell's *as if* here verifies the reality of fictions: physical and economic actuality, Christian doctrine, and common sense all clearly indicate that rich and poor live together in one world with the responsibility to love and respect each other, and yet the majority of the population persist in living otherwise, "as if" the two nations were literal and not virtual realities. The virtual reality of class has trumped all others.

In Catherine Gallagher's rendering, at least "the first half of [*Mary Barton*] is about the dangers inherent in various conventional ways of organizing reality,"[69] and I would include the analogical realism articulated by *as if* and cognate phrases among these dangerous conventions. *As ifs* might seem to naturalize the alienation between people and the world that Lukács identified as the fundamental historical condition of the novel.[70] But to reduce Gaskell's and Dickens's predominant syntax to alienation

would be to miss the ways it concurrently enables extraordinary connections between otherwise estranged domains. Would, could, should: the
subjunctive mood is the mood of possibility, speculation, hope, idealistic
imagination, will, intention, projection, and moral obligation. Alice
Wilson of *Mary Barton* counters the reductive and pejorative ideology of
separate spheres with her perhaps nostalgic, perhaps senile, perhaps just
old-fashioned faith, which nevertheless orients her to God with the same
grammar that orients the rich to the poor: "Whene'er I plan over-much,
He is sure to send and mar all my plans, as if He would ha' me put the
future into His hands" (70). If Alice seems quaintly, overly, irrationally
providential to some modern readers, her religion nevertheless pleases her
and helps her act charitably.

Mary Barton employs the conditional simile to affect the distance between
narrator and narrated, but this distance, in turn, introduces new insight that
seems to exceed the knowledge of the narrator or to defy his or her rules.
Indeed, at one of the climaxes of the novel, instead of direct or indirect
discourse, *as ifs* inform the reader that Mary's father is the murderer of
Carson:

> Mary took the paper and flattened it: then suddenly stood stiff up, with
> irrepressible movement, as if petrified by some horror abruptly disclosed;
> her face, strung and rigid; her lips compressed tight, to keep down some
> rising exclamation. She dropped on her seat, as suddenly as if the braced
> muscles had in an instant given way. But she spoke no word. (211)

Following Raymond Williams, critics have tended to describe *Mary Barton*
as distanced from its subject, as sympathetic sociological observation rather
than omniscient identification, and the *as ifs* might contribute to this
distance here, where they verbalize the connection between Mary's body
and her mind without access to that mind.[71] The narrator must watch and
interpret without telling us what Mary is thinking. *As if* yokes Mary's secret
knowledge – that the letter in Jem's writing was her father's property and
therefore incriminates her father for the murder of Harry Carson – and her
visible, physiognomic embodiment of this knowledge in her face and
posture. Esther's initial discovery of the wadding adds to readers' suspicion
of Jem, and that passage explicitly articulates the fuzzy distinction between
reasonable evidence and fanciful suspicion in terms of *as if*: "what terrible
thought flashed into her mind; or was it only fancy? But it looked very like
the writing which she had once known well – the writing of Jem Wilson . . .
As if only one person wrote in that meandering style!" (206). This last *as if*
adds a faint skepticism to brace against the painful truth, but its skepticism,

like the doubt embedded in all the passages other conditionals, proves false. The conjectural connections and associations prove true.

One requisite of modern knowledge is that it purports to predict or estimate future events. In statistics, finance, meteorology, medicine, even theology, the relative ability to anticipate, price, insure against, capitalize upon, and avoid otherwise unpredictable futures makes such knowledge valuable. Character, the knowledge Victorians ascribed to fiction, may or may not enable a reader to predict certain aspects of the future – the implications, say, of hiding one's identity from one's spouse, as Lady Dedlock does – but in lieu of reliable pragmatic utility it does nevertheless affect to be predictive. The irony of the *as if* is that its conditionality is consistently dismissed. Rather than disqualifying conjecture, the conditional tends to license it. Thus, Dickens's fictions often corroborate or verify the conjectural or fanciful connections that they initially broach with *as if*; what starts out to be mere Dickensian whimsy typically turns out to be literally true. His *as ifs*, in other words, are syntactic signposts of prolepsis. Esther, for instance, introduces Krook in *Bleak House* as "short, cadaverous, and withered, with his head sunk sideways between his shoulders and the breath issuing in visible smoke from his mouth as if he were on fire within" (*BH* 49). If his personality is metaphorically incendiary and his stomach literally dyspeptic, he is not yet – the "if" assures us – ablaze; but he does indeed "spontaneously" combust. I could cite many of these instances: for example, in *Our Mutual Friend* when the narrator repeatedly prods the reader to "mistrust" John Rokesmith, "the Secretary [who] was discerning, discreet, and silent, though as zealous as if the affairs had been his own" (*OMF* 193), and yet of course the affairs are his own, the novel later shows, for he is John Harmon in disguise. Such *as ifs* abound, advertising insights into upcoming developments, plot twists, and characterological revelations. A kind of internal allusion, they lend coherence to sprawling novels by securing sentences with an anticipatory logic that as readily dismisses its contents as red herrings as it forwards them as inchoate yearnings, intuitions, or instincts.

However modest with their proposals, then, Victorian *as ifs* undoubtedly privilege the very associations they disavow over and above the logical, literal, referential truths they affect only to color or enrich. Esther says Krook "looked so disagreeable and his cat looked so wickedly at me, as if I were a blood-relation of the birds upstairs" (*BH* 56), and if she is not related by family or species, Mrs. Flite affirms that Esther is related by her figural pet names, by destiny, by the chancery suit, and by the blood chancery will exact in the form of Richard Carstone's death. Likewise,

Esther explains that upon moving into Bleak House "Mr. Jarndyce, expressing his approval in his face, began to talk to me as confidentially as if I had been in the habit of conversing with him every morning for I don't know how long. I almost felt as if I had" (87–88). Of course, Esther has not literally been speaking to Jarndyce so confidentially and regularly, though he has indeed been checking up on her and intimately involved in her upbringing and care; but the *as if* here signals that the two share a familial intimacy even though they have not literally shared that history; that Esther has a real family even though she has lost her actual or original family; and, furthermore, that Esther perceives that Jarndyce feels more for her than she yet consciously knows or admits. Or consider *The Old Curiosity Shop*, where Nell feels an intense "sympathy" with Miss Edwards and her sister before really knowing them: "Here, every night, the child was too, unseen by them, unthought of, unregarded; but feeling as if they were her friends, as if they had confidences and trusts together, as if her load were lightened and less hard to bear; as if they mingled their sorrows, and found mutual consolation."[72] Affective relations and the associative relations of the novel: these counterfactual and figural connections consistently overcome their material, logical, or literal obstacles. Readers attuned to Dickens's conditional similes might therefore treat them as generic signposts of novelistic knowledge – that is to say, "meaning" that is to be taken as virtually or interpretively true if not factually precise or referentially realistic. A certain excess of this knowledge may well seem to distinguish prose as "literary," but Victorian non-fiction includes quite a bit of it and Victorians, of course, registered it as *character*.

The distance implicit in the conditional analogy is an ineluctable feature of modern knowledge and therefore the character of Victorian prose. As Michael McKeon explains, "Disembedded from the matrix of experience it seeks to explain, modern knowledge is defined precisely by its explanatory ambition to separate itself from its object of knowledge sufficiently to fulfill the epistemological demand that what is known must be divided from the process by which it is known" (McKeon 2005, xix). Conditional analogy enacts this process on the level of the clause. The conditional analogy affects not to be "realism" in the sense of direct, omniscient narrative, whereby a participant-observer narrator represents the world he or she sees, but a process of distancing us from that world we think we know, a process of defamiliarization or estrangement, in Viktor Shklovsky's sense.[73] But this estrangement takes the form of strangers in Smith's sense that everybody is ultimately strange: "As," in Smith's *Theory of Moral Sentiments*, "we have no immediate experience of what other men feel, we can form no idea of the manner in which they are affected" (Smith 3), so in Victorian prose "immediate experience" appears inadequate to apprehend a reality animated by associations, forces, and feelings accessible only by conjecture.

Well before the Kantian scholar Hans Vaihinger published his regulative or "fictionalist" *The Philosophy of As If* (1911), then, Victorians were colloquially habituated to valuing, trusting, acting upon, and respecting as knowledge "constructed" characterizations of things that they could not wholly see, measure, demonstrate, or even define. Everyday language evidenced the need to consistently conjure and imagine a world whose agents were never in plain sight. Other critics have remarked on the ways nineteenth-century fiction, even the fictions we now classify as realist, disavows reference to extra-textual reality. Ian Duncan explains how fiction cultivated an everyday authority that seemed beyond the partiality of the politically affiliated periodicals by maintaining a "strategic difference from reality – a distance or obliquity in the relation between narrative and world, a figurative disguise or darkening of the real – in contrast to the referential immediacy that charges the very premise of periodical publication."[74] Mary Poovey likewise describes the different "distancing conventions" by which writers as diverse as Austen, Thackeray, Dickens, Eliot, and Trollope all "reinforce the boundary that identifie[s] the textual world as *not* real [or] *non*referential."[75] For Poovey, this disavowal of reference redirects readers to the fiction itself, thus posing self-referentiality and autonomy and character not only as independent of actual historical events but critical, too, of the very markets that supported their production. *As if,* like the everyday words in the following chapters, was a distancing convention of just this sort: a turn of phrase that asserted the priority of associative knowledge over and above ordinary literal knowledge, but that in doing so threatened to concede its purchase on reality. Yet unlike Poovey's "distancing conventions," which include Dickens's reified flat personages and animated objects, the Victorian *as if* was trans-generic and carried its problems and advantages into domains more accustomed to make pragmatic, positivist claims about the real world – domains where personages would be out of place but "dispositive" character would be useful.

Tyndall and "our skeptical 'as if'"

I have already touched on the way Charles Lyell strategically appropriated the conditional analogy as a solution to the empiricist problem of history, but to elaborate how *as if* equivocally served across genres, let me conclude with the experimental physicist John Tyndall. Tyndall explicitly demonstrates the way *as if* translates questions of positive, physical knowledge into questions of character evaluation. He explains the problematic necessity of the conditional simile in "The Scientific Use of the Imagination," a lecture delivered before the British Association at Liverpool in 1870.[76] Incorporating two conventions common to realism – the pronounced attention to ordinary life, and the representation of real knowledge as invisible, ineffable, or otherwise abstract – Tyndall offers to reveal "some of the more occult features and operations" of the "disciplines of common life," "to take [his audience] beyond the boundary of mere observation, into a region where things are intellectually discerned, and to show you there the hidden mechanism of optical action" (Tyndall 103). Like the secret *somethings* that define Esther and David and the "natural causes" of Lyell's geology, the mechanisms of optical action are felt and physically substantial and yet imperceptible all the same. On the one hand, these mechanisms appear as mere virtual realities, because they are not perceptible by the ordinary five senses. On the other hand, that imperceptibility qualifies them as real knowledge according to the familiar epistemic shift described by Foucault in *The Order of Things*.[77]

"But how," Tyndall asks, "are those hidden things to be revealed?" His question echoes Thackeray's at the beginning of this chapter: how can we possibly know what is in any character's head or heart? Tyndall offers a catalog of concrete examples to suggest how imagination allows scientists to perceive hidden realities about which our senses can only speculate – just as the narrators above affect to speculate about the meaning underlying ambient gestures, comments, feelings, and objects, just as Lyell speculates about the gaps in the geological record. Tyndall insists that reason and imagination together have "led us into a world not less real than that of the senses, and of which the world of sense itself is the suggestion and, to a great extent, the outcome" (Tyndall 107). Tyndall's "suggestion" recalls David Copperfield's "association": these are interchangeable technical terms of Associationist, empirical philosophy; they denote the idea, image, or memory impressed on the mind by a sensory perception.[78] As such, these terms were expressly characterological: they described the cognitive process of accumulating the suggestions or associations prompted by sensory impressions into the character of an individual mind. Tyndall thus describes the work of science, as he practices it, as a characterization of material phenomena: he registers the world of sensory perceptions as suggestions of the hidden mechanisms which animate them, just as David translates his perceptions of Blunderstone in the narrative present into the associations that inform them.

For Tyndall, the process that leads to the "suggested" domain of abstraction, the implied mechanism subtending the visible world, is not induction, attention, or memory, but regulative analogy. After drawing a conclusion about light and airborne particles (a conclusion, by the way, that remains scientifically valid), Tyndall concedes, "You may urge that, although the phenomena occur *as if* the medium existed, the absolute demonstration of its existence is still wanting" (Tyndall 107; emphasis in original). Absolute demonstration remains wanting, because the very medium he describes, again like the feelings of another, definitively exceeds demonstration. The medium, like the interiority of a character, qualifies as genuine knowledge precisely because it eludes perception. Herbert Spencer (1872–73) nearly says as much in a contemporaneous discussion of social science, where he highlights "the 'incalculable complexity' of social phenomena, where the variety and the multitudinousness of influences upon any social trend makes it almost quixotic to imagine reducing them to intelligible form or doing valid analyses of them."[79] Christopher Herbert contextualizes Tyndall's and Spencer's thinking here in terms of what he dubs the Victorian "relativistic imagination." For Herbert, "To apprehend reality in a distinctively modern mode came in this period to mean, in effect, apprehending in relativistically."[80] And "Spencer," Herbert elsewhere concludes,

> articulates a new phase of thinking, one in which it is understood to be an inherent aspect of knowledge, and particularly in cross-cultural and historical studies, that it be unable to give a fully coherent account of itself, and in which scientific and scholarly investigation in whatever domain can only claim to be uncompromisingly rigorous once it has come to recognize its own necessarily indeterminate and conditional character. (89)

Herbert's use of "character" is coincidental but altogether appropriate. In the divergent genres of fiction, natural science, and sociology, the epistemic shift to relativistic knowledge, which was knowable only "as if" various imperceptible mediums existed (mediums such as Einstein's space-time continuum, which suspends objects as if it were a sheet of fabric), transpired in concert with the long emergence of modern psychological character that culminated in Freud's model of the subject who is secret unto himself. Victorian empiricists tended to be keenly aware of the subjective dimension of all empirical observation, and so it makes sense that Victorian scientific description was inflected by the rhetorical tropes for representing subjectivity: tropes of characterization.[81]

On the basis of these epistemological and linguistic connections, my use of "characterization" may well still seem like a stretch for describing Tyndall, but he also explicitly discusses *as if* as a characterological problem. He legitimates his hypothesis about light and particles by imagining a hypothetical case, a conditional analogy, about evaluating the creditability of a person. Again invoking the phrase "as if," he asks us to imagine physics as a personage. Channeling Adam Smith, he explains that physical laws could only be known to the degree that we could know this personage's putative interiority – that is, they can only be known partially and conditionally by inference or conjecture about his or her manners and appearance. We can, he says, only determine the reasonableness of fellow people to the level of "hypothesis," because they "behave as if they were reasonable." "As in the case of the ether, beyond the '*as if*' you cannot go" (Tyndall 108). What starts out as a potential problem – that our knowledge of physics is contingent, conditional, conjectural – turns out to be an advantage, for it grounds an abstract, destabilizing science in the altogether familiar discourse of sociality. To the extent that we are adept at dealing with others, we are adept at dealing with what we can only know conjecturally.

For Tyndall, "our skeptical '*as if*'" is morally and epistemologically preferable to being limited to what we can demonstrate or perceive with our physical senses. "Our skeptical '*as if*'" not only manifests the act of sympathetic imagination necessary to move from observable phenomena to the "hidden reality" of which they are allegedly the "suggestion" and "outcome," but also epitomizes a moral imperative and self-abnegating principle, the restraint operative in the proper scientist (116). As equivocal as Dickens, who characterizes David Copperfield with the same syntax as he characterizes Skimpole, Tyndall disparages the conditionality of *as if* while yet embracing the imaginative abstraction that it performs. He vacillates between optimism and humility. "[Our skeptical '*as if*'] is one of the parasites of science," he writes, "ever at hand, and ready to plant itself and sprout, if it can, on the weak points of our philosophy. But a strong constitution defies the parasite, and in our case, as we question the phenomena, probability grows like growing health, until in the end the malady of doubt is completely extirpated" (Tyndall 116). But then, doubt is not extirpated: "when duly pondered, the complexity of the problem raises the doubt, not of the power of our instrument [the microscope], for that is *nil*, but whether we ourselves possess the intellectual elements which will ever enable us to grapple with the ultimate structural energies of nature" (Tyndall 126). Self-doubt becomes a part of the knowledge he produces.

As George Levine writes, for Tyndall, "an ideal of self-abnegation, a more than Keatsian negative capability, without any self interest" constituted, in his own words, the "indirect means of the highest moral culture" and, paradoxically, the source of the "heroic, if not indeed angelic character" of the scientist.[82] Tyndall is attached, somewhat ambivalently, to the rhetoric of decorous imprecision that Shapin ascribes to the early-modern English conventions of civil conversation, which underwrote English natural philosophy even as it apprized empiricism (117–18). Natural philosophy was, Shapin shows, long underwritten by protocols, repertoires, and conventions of gentlemanly conversation and by the concomitant credibility of the scientists' characters. And, he adds (quoting Shakespeare), "For the English scientific community, as for Touchstone and the society of early-modern gentlemen, there was 'much virtue in If'" (125). In nineteenth-century prose, fictional and non-fictional, the doubt and humility inscribed by conditional syntax remained a colloquial signature of gentlemanly character and veracity, for the doubt imprinted by the conditionality evoked detachment rather than disbelief, associative insight rather than inadequate perception or evidence. Many seventeenth-century epistemic practices had long disappeared, but the decorum of conditional syntax had become integral to everyday language as well as to natural and social science, and it contoured the shape of reality for nineteenth-century Britons.[83] So colloquial as to remain unnoticeable except to the observant few, such as Dickens and Tyndall, the conditional analogy installed an implicit propriety and characterological relativity into diverse genres without relying on the definitively literary convention of the fictional personage.

Tyndall concludes with a moralistic, almost novelistic, and oxymoronic prescription for a disciplined scientific method that tempers speculative imagination with self-effacement: "The thing to be encouraged here is reverent freedom – a freedom preceded by the hard discipline which checks licentiousness in speculation" (128). Such remarks echo David Copperfield's regret over the "first mistaken impulse of my undisciplined heart"; Esther's self-abnegating "as if this narrative were the narrative of my life!" (*DC* 558, *BH* 27).

If Thackeray, Dickens, and Gaskell did not write terrifically much directly about science as a theme, then science is embedded in their style. I have juxtaposed their prose with Lyell's *Principles* and John Tyndall's essay to highlight how what might look like trivial colloquialisms, stylistic tics, or ineluctable features of the English language evidence historically specific assumptions about how to produce, evidence, and explain knowledge. Lyell and Tyndall manifest in different ways how these epistemological questions were wrought up in moral and epistemological assumptions about the form of character, as a category of being defined by its formal relation. To have, produce, or evoke character was to be related by conditional analogy, rather than direct metaphor or direct description. The intersection of Victorian fictional characterization and scientific prose in the figure of the common *as if* shows how the formal features of literary characterization were and remain relevant to understanding scientific writing and its tacit objectives. While we can still nod at Dickens for the most obvious and pervasive personificatory animism and pathetic fallacy, with Gaskell and even Tyndall in mind we should consider most instances of *as if* in Victorian writing as modes of anthropomorphic characterization. Victorians wrote *as if* they knew their world in the form of a character.

Insistently belying the reality effect or truthiness of referential description and acknowledging but transgressing the limits of positivism, the *as if* testifies to the value Victorians afforded to fiction as a disposition and not merely a genre. The discipline of literary criticism might relish this observation, for in a sense *as if* might be said to be the enabling gesture of criticism at its best: not just a positivist redescription of what a text meant or means or is, but a hypothetical and yet no less true supposition about what it might do, be, or mean. However important positivism is, it will inevitably hobble a discipline whose principle objects are fictions (in prose or verse). Dickens's *as if* might save the discipline of literary study from submitting to positivism if it reminds us of the reality of abstractions, associations, alternatives, and possibilities. The dispositive motion of Victorian prose once authorized these virtual realities as legitimate knowledge, and it might do so again.

CHAPTER 4

"Something" in the Way Realism Moves
Middlemarch and Oblique Character References

> Is not there a something wanted, Miss Price, in our language – a something between compliments and – and love – to suit the sort of friendly acquaintance we have had together?
> — Jane Austen, *Mansfield Park*[1]

> I believe I may have heard some whisper of that distant thought, in the old unhappy loss or want of something never to be realized, of which I had been sensible.
> — Charles Dickens, *David Copperfield*[2]

> Character is not cut in marble – it is not something solid and unalterable. It is something living and changing.
> There was silence. Dorothea's heart was full of something that she wanted to say, and yet the words were too difficult.
> — George Eliot, *Middlemarch*[3]

There is literally *something* in the way realism moves: writers as diverse as Austen and Stoker, Dickens and Eliot, Newman and Darwin, all tend to represent the motive energies connecting the subjects, human and inhuman, with the word *something* and its variants, including *nothing* and *things*. Like verbal magnets, these pronouns – often lacking clear and immediate antecedents, often lacking definite referents of any sort – active a field of attractions and repulsions; they afford prose an affective charge. As Adela Pinch writes, if nineteenth-century novels do not necessarily insist on the "inherent ineffability" of emotions, they do show how "aesthetically, socially, and personally" productive it can be "to see feelings as difficult to measure."[4] An English *je-ne-sais-quoi*, the word *something* and its variants situate a person or thing in the world with a bearing and a habitus, a physical and intellectual mobility.

As Richard Scholar observes, the early-modern *je-ne-sai-quoi* represented "a strategically indefinable quality," "the experience of a vital and inexplicable attraction," a "quality that remains irreducible to systems of explanation while setting them into movement," or the secret laws imputed to nature.[5]

A vernacular condensation of negative philosophy, the *je-ne-sais-quoi* inscribed into everyday language the assumption that the most intense, unsettling, and moving human encounters exceed explanation. As Scholar says, Montaigne employed the phrase as a placeholder as he sought to explain odd experiences and as a mode of articulating his intimacy or friendship with the reader, whereas contemporaries often used the phrase to designate the phantom qualities distinguishing polite, high society; Bacon, too, employed "a certain something" to validate anomalous particulars, especially ostensibly occult particulars, as phenomena undergoing or anticipating explanation; and Pascal invoked it as the *mot juste* to express the allure of Cleopatra's nose. Shakespeare also makes extensive use of the *je-ne-sai-quoi* to instantiate intense forces of sympathy and other social relations. In all these cases, the figure is poised between condensation and indeterminacy and between sublime insight and ignorance.

The popularity of the *je-ne-sai-quoi* waned, perhaps partially as an effect of enlightenment optimism given its inherent skepticism, but the idiom regained popularity at the end of the eighteenth century. It was the subject of a playful 1774 article in the *Westminster Magazine*, which describes it as an unaccountable, inexpressible charm that trumps all other features of a character: possessing it makes a person desirable irrespective of his lack or possession of traditional virtues.[6] By the early 1820s the idiom of "a certain something" was stylish or ubiquitous enough to be parodied. Pierce Egan's immensely popular personification of slang, *Life in London* (1821), attests to the currency of the idiom: Corinthian Tom feels the Marchioness of Diamonds "wanted that '*certain sort of something*,' so easy to be impressed with, yet so difficult to describe."[7] However modish and popular "a certain something" was, the phrase was nevertheless embedded deeply enough in early nineteenth-century English that Austen employed it as the figure of characterological distinction and desire throughout her fiction. Mr. Darcy, for example, explains to Miss Bingley that he esteems not just *something* in the way a woman moves – "a certain something in her air and manner of walking, the tone of her voice, her address and expressions," as Miss Bingley understands it – but also, he adds, "something more substantial, in the improvement of her mind by extensive reading" (*PP* 43). Darcy's ambiguous *something* has a double liberalism to it: grammatically, it substantiates a quality without quite specifying it; politically, it justifies Elizabeth's upward social mobility by redefining her social position in terms of her manner and reading instead of her lineage, property, and class. The vagueness of the word allows it to substantiate a perpetual process without any finite results, a way of being rather than a fixed possession or accomplishment: as Lizzy says, "people themselves alter so much, that there is something new to be observed in them forever" (*PP* 47). In a kind of erotic algebra, Byron's *Don Juan* dwells on "something wanting," by turns as a variable for "*Soul*," then explicitly as "That undefinable '*Je ne sais quoi*'," and next, with intensifying innuendo, as a "vacant part" that might be filled by "an awkward thing" that distinguishes the sexes and that is itself "A something all-sufficient for the *heart*."[8] *Something* likewise stands in for the motivating lack actuating characters such as David Copperfield, who repeatedly refers to his "old unhappy loss or want of something never to be realized" (*DC* 688 and *passim*). The prose correlative to a political representative, the word empowers personages by standing in for constituents without naming them. The constituents are realized to a degree – a *certain* something, something more *substantial* – but remain abstract – something *never to be realized*.

We might be inclined simply to allocate this *something* to the catalog of tropes by which nineteenth-century writers figure interiority, but it retains the tension Scholar describes between sublime condensation and indeterminacy or ignorance, and includes attachments far less intimate than Darcy's incipient desire for Elizabeth – attachments we might better classify with Mary Crawford as "acquaintance." Mary invokes *something* in *Mansfield Park* (1814) to broach delicately the inadequacy of terms of affection: "Is not there a something wanted, Miss Price, in our language – a something between compliments and – and love – to suit the sort of friendly acquaintance we have had together?" (*MP* 334). "Sort of friendly": Mary seeks a word to equivocate the fluid intimacy – sometimes amicable, sometimes jealous, sometimes mutually judgmental, sometimes genuinely intimate – by which she and Fanny know each other and to goad Fanny with her interest in Edmund. The joke is that *something* is precisely the "something wanted": *something* allows the text to touch upon without indecorously disclosing the uneasy subtext that tact also prohibits each character from articulating; and it allows the narrative to refer to a "sort" of knowledge, an "acquaintance," that eludes determination. *Something* further indicates how their relationship and knowledge of each other derives from their socialization in the Bertram circle. Acquaintance happens externally in the dynamics of groups, not privately.

Something thus accommodates competing demands for material specificity and abstraction, commitment and freedom. It grammatically instantiates a decidedly liberal and self-referential manner requisite to nineteenth-century character in many of its manifestations, including the novelistic description of implied personages and critical descriptions of realism as an aesthetic, but also physiological treatises on mental life. With ambiguous antecedents and referents, pronouns liberate the subjects they stand in for from a deterministic past or reified identity even as they afford those subjects concrete representation in the present. They articulate affinities less personal and intense than what Mary Crawford calls "love" and pro forma expressions such as "compliments." Given this freedom and the politics of representation, *something* and "nothing," *things* and "that sort of thing" together constituted a performative grammar of liberal characterization.

Nowhere are the epistemological problems and liberal politics of *something* more pronounced than in George Eliot's *Middlemarch* (1871–72). The novel includes 233 instances of *thing* and 314 instances of *things*, 293 instances of *something* and 290 instances of *nothing*. It is indeed a long novel and these are common words, but Eliot employs them at a higher frequency than all other notable British novelists and, as Dorothea's fatuous uncle Mr. Brooke says, "Well, there is something in that, you know" (*M* 52).[9] Eliot playfully foregrounds her usage in Mr. Brooke, who speaks in muddled tautologies and paratactic lists summarily punctuated with "that kind of thing" and "that sort of thing," but she legitimates Mr. Brooke's usage in chapter epigraphs from *The Maid's Tragedy* (5), *Measure for Measure* (413), Goldsmith's "The Traveler" (395), and untitled lyric fragments of her own (453) that tend to orbit around indeterminate *things* whose referents are often beyond the bounds of the excerpts. If Brooke's fumbling patter provides comic relief, then, it also cannily adumbrates the questions of representation and reference entailed by a literary register of *things* particularly as it intersects with the discourses of psychology, realism, and political representation.

Brooke's signature phrases are taxonomical postures implying that the ostensibly disparate and spontaneous thoughts and impressions preceding them are actually cogent, readily legible or intuitive, and coincident with those of his interlocutors.[10] If the taxonomic gesture underscores the incoherence and superficiality of Brooke's character, its cognate *something* nevertheless consistently functions as a placeholder for the otherwise unarticulated character – what we might now call the unconscious – animating and integrating the otherwise incongruent affects and expressions of more serious personages in the novel, namely Dorothea and Ladislaw. When Dorothea and Ladislaw feel or reflect with earnest, more often than not the content of that feeling or reflection is *something*. By refusing to delimit the content of such feelings, Eliot practices a performative characterization that formally enacts their intimations or sensations of selfhood. *Middlemarch* explicitly asserts that "character is not cut in marble – it is not *something* solid and unalterable. It is *something* living and changing" (454). Such change transpires not solely on the thematic level of character development or *Bildung* but also on the level of syntax, where often self-referential pronouns like *something* condense the movement of Victorian personages and prose. *Something* and *thing* are often modified by appositive clauses that approximate but do not exhaustively define their phantom referents: something like or something between this or that, something strange or grave or pleasing or wanting, something more or less. Such clauses are syntactically self-referential because they appear to refer to specific circumambient antecedents or clues embedded in the text, but to the degree that the antecedents or referents so often remain indeterminate, the process of looking for referents is open-ended. Writing of this sort syntactically transfers the moral virtue – the "character" – of self-reflective subjectivity to the prose itself, whatever its subjects.

Walter Houghton established "aspiration without an object" as a paradigmatic Victorian "frame of mind," but *something* instantiates more than ineffable objects of desire or ambition.[11] The word repeatedly stands in for the intuition of coherent selfhood in physiological and philosophical writings about the human mind. In its most resonant manifestations, Associationist philosophy explains subject formation as the accumulation of contingent, contiguous experiences held together not by narrative or memory so much as by what Hume called inference or what the influential physiologist Thomas Brown called "intuition."[12] Brown's Sketch *of a System of Philosophy of the Human Mind* (1820),[13] which was reprinted in at least nineteen nineteenth-century editions, describes "mental identity" as an indemonstrable effect of belief:

> We cannot prove our identity, then, and yet believe it irresistibly, – as irresistibly at least, as we believe the result of any demonstration. The belief flows from a principle of our constitution, which is as truly a part of it as the principle of reason itself. It flows, in short, from a principle of intuition; and in this, as in every other case of intuitive belief, it is vain to look for evidence beyond it. (30–31)

James Mill further cemented the notion in his *Analysis of the Phenomena of the Human Mind* (1829), which affirms Brown's grounding of mental identity in belief and further includes a chapter on grammatical substantives that discusses how the names of ideas intimate the existence of "something more" or "something less" than they name.[14] The paratactic contiguity of Brooke's thought process was for physiologists a constitutive feature of character. His propensity to speak in lists with an unspoken principle of coherence aptly instantiates this process by producing a character whose coherence, whose "mental identity," depends upon an intuitive, sympathetic, and consensual interlocutor or reader.

As *somethings* instantiate the acquaintance Dorothea and Ladislaw intuitively have with their defining feelings, Brooke's "that sort of thing" and "that kind of thing" instantiate his assumption that his interlocutors are acquainted with his line of thought, that they intuit the ineffable logic linking the items in his lists. However comically exacerbated by Brooke, his usage models the relation that many writers assumed to obtain between readers and characters as between readers and prose worlds whose fictionality ensures that they are never actually referential or reducible to definite explanations. If novels accustom us to intuiting character beyond the delimited scope of narrative and experience, then Brooke's lists question the extension of such practice to the rest of the world, to particulars such as frescoes and drainage tiles and philosophers. Just as personages were thought to exceed full comprehension, everyday prose of the sort exemplified by Brooke does not fail to articulate and achieve cogent ideas and ends so much as it avoids doing so. Brooke thus personifies how loose pronoun usage inscribes within prose a resistance to what for Hegel was the hallmark feature of prose: a reduction of the particular to a means to a specific end.[15]

At once concrete and abstract, reified and liberated, *something* and *that sort of thing* allow Mr. Brooke to succeed as a liberal political representative of *Middlemarch* the novel and the mode of life inscribed in its style of representation, even as he fails to become liberal MP of Middlemarch. His idiom enables characters in and out of the novel, including the narrator, to give material representation to affects that they refuse to declare or define in any determinate way. Brooke loses the election because he is inarticulate as well as because he confuses conservativism with reform. And his electoral failure in turn signals the ways that the grammar of Victorian characterization problematically rebuts the familiar Victorian paradigm of character defined by reform, the paradigm of character preached by Smiles's notorious *Self-Help* and by the *Bildungsroman*. Smiles insists that character must always be subject to – indeed, the product of – endless reformative work and self-discovery. And as Franco Moretti observes, the *Bildungsroman* works as the symbolic form of modernity because it personifies modernity in youth that, definitively transient, inevitably dissolves into maturity.[16] But to take Mr. Brooke seriously is to consider the possibility that an undisciplined individualism, a latent refusal to mature, to become, or to do is embedded in the nineteenth-century epistemology of character. What if Brooke's discontinuous utterances are more characteristic of nineteenth-century prose and its implicit object than progressive or developmental history or cogent ideas?

As Catherine Gallagher has suggested, Eliot prioritizes abstract "culture" over concrete political and social "fact."[17] At stake in Brooke's idiomatic speech are the epistemological and moral integrity of a liberal empiricism – the integrity of a realist representation of intimations, affects, and intuitions that cannot be factually known or mimetically reproduced – and the politics of liberalism as it was instantiated in everyday language.

The satiric turn of Brooke's parataxis syntactically instantiates Eliot's ambivalence about this paradigm of character. His speech juxtaposes impressions without explicating their logic, and instead presumes or solicits an "intuitive" reception from his often less than sympathetic and attentive auditors. Brooke therefore personifies a mode of being and knowing – call it "acquaintance" – that tenuously solicits intuitive reading instead of explication or interpretation. This intuitive perception of character recurs in Victorian theories of realism and character by critics such as John Ruskin, G. H. Lewes, and E. S. Dallas, who all ascribe *something* to the *character* of realist representation. This chapter will move through an explication of Brooke's problematic speech and the liberal representation of Dorothea and Ladislaw's subjectivity, to the use of *something* in other novels, and then to a reconsideration of how these critics characterized "realism" as a style of representation that, like Darcy's amatory ideal, has *something* in the way it moves. The effect of prose relies as much on its self-referentiality as does the morality of its most prized personages.

Mr. Brooke and the Politics of Intuition

> Well, now, Sir Humphry Davy: I dined with him years ago at Cartwright's, and Wordsworth was there too – the poet Wordsworth, you know. Now there was something singular. I was at Cambridge when Wordsworth was there, and I never met him – and I dined with him twenty years afterwards at Cartwright's. There's an oddity in things, now. (*M* 10–11)

"Something singular": the "oddity in things" that Brooke here infers from his dinner with Wordsworth apparently describes the coincidence of dining with somebody only twenty years after having attended university with him. Given Eliot's relish for Wordsworth's poetry, however, and given Wordsworth's penchant for the word *things*, the singular oddity also affiliates Wordsworth's and Brooke's styles.[18] Wordsworth writes of "seeing into the life of things," of "the speaking face of things," "the mighty commonwealth of things," "the tide of things," and so on.[19] His habitual usage became a hallmark feature of Victorian prose: Thomas Carlyle's fictional biography of the "Universal Professor of Things in General" in *Sartor Resartus* (1833–34), Matthew Arnold's tautological prescription to "see things as they really are," and a host of less notable instances, like David Masson's exposition of everyday life as "the thick and miscellany of things."[20] Indeed, *The Metropolitan* quipped in 1831 that "The age of things has arrived and we no longer have time to throw away upon words." Critics as diverse as G. H. Lewes, Virginia Woolf, Ian Watt, and the more recent practitioners of "thing theory," as Bill Brown has called it, all tend to register such statements as justifications of a pronounced modern attention to material objects and particularity.[21] But few nineteenth-century writers accepted a "dull catalogue of common things," as Keats derisively described the world posited by Newtonian theory.[22] As G. H. Lewes put it in *Problems of Life and Mind*, "Every Real is the complex of so many relations, a conjuncture of so many events, a synthesis of so many sensations, that to know one Real thoroughly would only be possible through an intuition embracing the Universe" (343). And therefore Lewes contends in "The Principles of Success in Literature" that realism is "something higher than waistcoats," something more than "detailism."[23] The substitution of pronouns like *things* for actual particulars rounds out the inductive habits I discussed in Chapter 2 and manifests a persistent resistance to specificity and avowal, pace Hegel's regret, that the objects of the world are not contingent and accidental but so interrelated that they can only be known in relation to each other (Hegel II, 975–77).[24] Even one of the most notable dismissals of Victorian materialism, Virginia Woolf's "Mr. Bennett and Mrs. Brown," which is an essay on characterization, summarizes Edwardian materialism as "an enormous stress upon the fabric of things."[25]

"These things are a parable," as *Middlemarch* famously says, in more than one sense: while Eliot consistently privileges characters like Caleb Garth and Adam Bede who work with their hands and exhibit a superior "grasp o' things" of a material sort, such characters – like Victorian writers – have a marked propensity to intimate a Lucretian, cosmological investment in an abstract "natur o' things." They intimate that a coherent order and meaning underwrite apparently diffuse fictions. Eliot reread *De Rerum Natura* (*On the Nature of Things*) while planning *Middlemarch*, and her use of pronouns evidences her investment in a world in flux.[26] Because people do not always plan sentences before they voice them, because people do not always know exactly how to articulate what they mean or how they feel, because people do not always know or wish to confront what they feel, they often employ pronouns to gesture at what they will not or cannot more directly represent. But beyond these pragmatic functions, equivocal pronouns resist the hegemony of mimesis, factuality, and accuracy. Pronouns can take on verbs without having clear and immediate antecedents, and therefore they can give agency and substance to intuitions, intimations, and abstractions that are not accommodated by the conventions of objective discourse. In the epistemology of character, pronouns endow their phantom referents with the formal self-reflectiveness and ineffability that were routinely associated with human character.[27]

Concentration, precision, and attention to material objects are potentially pathological character weaknesses in *Middlemarch*. Brooke justly diagnoses Lydgate and Casaubon with them: both men fail to abstract themselves from their narrow interests and accordingly attenuate their health and their gentlemanliness. Lydgate fails to extend his investigation of "the very grain of things" to the wider social and moral network, to what Bulstrode calls the "framework of things" and "the general scheme of things" (*M* 82, 99).[28] So much we already know, but Lydgate also fails to value himself as something more than the things he studies.[29] "Lydgate has lots of ideas, quite new, about ventilation and diet, that sort of thing" (*M* 59), Brooke says, parrying particularity in a novel that is otherwise peculiarly exacting with its physiological diction and thereby moderating Lydgate's insalubrious and antisocial specificity with the colloquial demands for imprecision that govern his model of character and his manner of sociability.[30]

Concentrated, specialized knowledge fares no better with Casaubon.[31] When he falls ill and Lydgate recommends that he abstain from "too eager and monotonous application" (180), Brooke soundly if gratuitously adds, "I would never give way to that; I was always versatile." He suggests that Casaubon take up "fishing . . . have a turning room, make toys, table-legs, and that kind of thing . . . shuttlecock . . . conchology," read "Smollett – 'Roderick Random,' 'Humphrey Clinker'" (180). Brooke recommends desultory hobbies and picaresque fictions because he favors freedom of movement, freedom to move from place to place, topic to topic, impulse to impulse, opinion to opinion. He thus parodies the liberal ideal of detached, abstract individualism as dilettantish and scatter-brained: at best, he exaggerates the disinterested, undisciplined knowledge of a belated ideal of gentlemanliness.[32] Brooke manifests a nineteenth-century variant of the "decorous imprecision" that Steven Shapin has described as an integral feature of the social history of truth in England.[33] As Shapin observes, "To value truth above good manners was not decorous; it was to disrupt civil conversation; it was the mark of a pedant" (308). For all of his fatuity, Brooke realizes – as Casaubon and Lydgate do not – that manner and character matter more in Middlemarch than do exactitude, scholarship, or scientific knowledge. Affable characters have a disinterested attitude to their knowledge – including even their self-knowledge.

Character was just as important an objective for politicians as it was for novelists and for natural scientists, who aspired to characterize the genus and species of organisms by identifying "characters": the features that both assimilated them with a kind and distinguished their individuality. These natural historical characters shared this paradoxical typicality and individuality with human and fictional characters. Nineteenth-century natural philosophers deliberated the ontology of species and the meaningfulness of taxonomic "characters." The Victorian historian and theorist of science William Whewell, for instance, writes:

> For in how few cases – if indeed in any one – can we know what is the essence of any Kind; – what is the real nature of the connexion [sic] between the character of the Kind and its Properties! Yet on this point we must suppose that the Divine Intellect, which is the foundation of the world, is perfectly clear. Every Kind of thing, every genus and species of object, appears to Him in its essential character, and its properties follow as necessary consequences. He sees the essences of things, through all time and through all space; while we, slowly and painfully by observation and experiment, which we cannot idealize or can idealize only in the most fragmentary manner, make out a few of the properties of each Kind of thing.[34]

Mocking Whewell's Scholasticism in A System of Logic, J. S. Mill also discusses the problematic elusiveness of character in terms of something and the "Kind of thing":

> [The Scholastic] notion of the essence of a thing was a vague notion of a something . . . which makes it the Kind of thing that it is . . . which causes it to have all that variety of properties which distinguish its Kind. But when the matter came to be looked at more closely, nobody could discover what caused the thing to have all those properties, nor even that there was anything which caused it to have them.[35]

In a novel of imperfect taxonomies, Brooke's classificatory coefficients "kind" and "sort" insistently imply that everything is underwritten by an invisible, orderly, animating agency or character: a baseline something. For nineteenth-century empiricists, poets, and novelists alike, including Wordsworth, Austen, Dickens, and Eliot – all proto-phenomenologists, in a sense – this character that animates the visible world conjoins self-knowledge with knowledge of external objects, knowledge of people and things.[36] In a study of the self-conscious subjectivity of Victorian empiricism, Peter Garratt almost has to borrow Brooke's style to affirm that empiricists as diverse as Ruskin, Alexander Bain, Herbert Spencer, G. H. Lewes, and Eliot all correlated "a certain *seeming* order, not an intrinsic or directly referential pattern" with the "real" (19). Like Mill and unlike Whewell, Eliot favored the concept that contingencies rather than innate properties or essences classified objects and organisms. Yet all of these writers shared Brooke's idiom of characterization, whether they presented taxonomy as relational or essentialist.

Eliot was not the only writer to translate this taxonomical idiom into aesthetics. In *Modern Painters*, Ruskin describes the vacillation between distinctness and indistinctness as one of the "characters" (5: 66) distinguishing great art, and he relies on *something* to do so:

> There are, indeed, certain facts of mystery, and facts of indistinctness, in all objects, which must have their proper place in the general harmony ... all good drawing must in some sort be *in*distinct. We may, however, understand this apparent contradiction, by reflecting that the highest knowledge always involves a more advanced perception of the fields of the unknown; and, therefore, it may most truly be said, that to know anything well involves a profound sensation of ignorance, while yet it is equally true that good and noble knowledge is distinguished from vain and useless knowledge chiefly by its clearness and distinctness, and by the vigorous consciousness of what is known and what is not. So in art. The best drawing involves a wonderful perception and expression of indistinctness; and yet all noble drawing is separated from the ignoble by its distinctness, by its fine expression and firm assertion of *Something*; whereas the bad drawing, without either firmness or fineness, expresses and asserts *Nothing*" (5: 60–61, emphasis in original).

For Ruskin, then, "noble" art distinctly and clearly knows and portrays the "unknown" "*Something*." In *The Westminster Review*, Eliot appraised the aptly titled third volume of *Modern Painters*, "Of Many Things," expressly for its conceptualization of realism,[37] and the same relational aesthetic, which defines truth as a function of clear and distinct apprehension of the unknown, informs Ruskin's and Eliot's realisms.

In "The Natural History of German Life" (1856),[38] Eliot idealizes a mode of knowledge that "would include all the essential facts in the existence and relations of the *thing*" (267, emphasis in original). Following Herbert Spencer, and before him Xavier Bichat (whose work inspires Lydgate), Victorians defined organic life as the relation between an organism and its medium or environment (Mason 154–55). *Middlemarch* shares the assumption that knowledge of persons or things is knowledge of their interrelations, and that such knowledge comes in the form of feeling. G. H. Lewes similarly asserts that knowledge of things amounts to how we feel in relation to things:

The only rational meaning of the question, What are things? What is their nature? is What can be known of them? how will they affect us? The terms of Knowledge being Feelings, no manipulation of those terms can evolve products which are more than symbolical representations of the ways in which the Cosmos stands related to the Organism. Knowledge may be an ideal transfiguration, but its material is Feeling, and its purpose is the guidance of action.[39]

Lewes's *Problems of Life and Mind* (1875), which George Levine has called "an important non-fictional analogue to" *Middlemarch*,[40] concedes the impossibility of knowing things as they really are and argues instead for a more ecological study of the physical, perceptual relationships between human subjects and objects (Lewes II: 27, 44, 53, and *passim*). Lewes explains that "Nothing exists in itself and for itself; everything in others and for others: ex-ist-ens – a standing out relation. Hence the search after the thing in itself is chimerical: the thing being a group of relations, it is what these are." Lewes adds that an epistemological approach that accommodates these relations is an ethical position, a form of affirming character: "the highest form of existence is Altruism," he says, "or that moral and intellectual condition which is determined by the fullest consciousness – emotional and cognitive – of relations" (2.26–27). Eliot's fiction obviously bears out this altruistic approach in its commendation of personages who manage individual with communal existence – as David Kurnick remarks, "At its most powerful Eliot's realism solicits her reader not to align himself fantasmatically with the fates of one or two privileged characters but to imagine the conditions of participation in collective life"[41] – but my point here is that this moralized epistemology is inscribed and critiqued in her vernacular, in Brooke's linguistic tics. If character is an embodied, experiential but altruistic form of knowledge that, like knowledge of the personages we call characters, respects shifting relations rather than fixating on determinate properties, then character is better mediated by variable pronouns, relative nouns, rather than determinate, referential specifics.

If Brooke's resistance to reform seems less than altruistic, he does exhibit tact by way of his vagueness, which intimates his knowingness as much as his ridiculousness. Upon Dorothea's return from her honeymoon, for example, he perfunctorily and politely chirps, "Rome has agreed with you, I see – happiness, frescoes, the antique – that sort of thing" (174). The sad, manifold joke is, first, that Dorothea's honeymoon has been a romantic and sexual disappointment, and Rome has not agreed with her. Honeymoons were routinely disappointing because of the relative strangeness and sexual inexperience of the newlyweds, the inflated expectations, and because dirty, impoverished locales like Rome fell far short of their classical images.[42] "That sort of thing" almost sarcastically undermines the eros of the "certain something" that denoted sex in early-modern and Victorian writing alike. In *Dracula*, for example, Jonathan Harker remarks in the three vampire women "something about them that made me uneasy, some longing and at the same time some deadly fear."[43] *Dracula* repeatedly invokes *something* to signal sexual desire and other physical sensations that exceed the bounds of decorum, including even the physical apprehension of Dracula, for because he is supernatural there is no natural way for characters to describe him. Second, Brooke's "that sort of thing" reduces the wonders of Rome to a list of generic expectations that in turn aligns a personal affective experience ("happiness") with incommensurate, discordant, and impersonal objects and abstractions ("frescoes, the antique"). The taxonomical gesture at kinds and sorts of thing persistently marks the discrepancy between the order of representation (ideal, genre, expectation, language, consensus) and lived experience (individual, actual) that is fundamental to many varieties of realism – including Trollope's, as the following chapter shows. Actual experience is felt as a physical departure from that which can be catalogued and referenced precisely.

Brooke senses these discrepancies, and therefore when he "has something painful to tell, it was usually his way to introduce it among a number of disjointed particulars, as if it were a medicine that would get a milder flavor by mixing" (501). Perhaps cowardly, perhaps caricaturing Matthew Arnold's cultured individual, who contemplates "the ins and outs of things ... without hatred and without partiality,"[44] Brooke broaches Casaubon's proposal to Dorothea in a preposterous flurry of sorts and kinds of scrambled things:

> he is a tiptop man and may be a bishop – that kind of thing, you know, if Peel stays in ... I said, my niece is very young, and that kind of thing. But I did not think it necessary to go into everything ... people should have their own way in marriage, and that sort of thing up to a certain point, you know. I have always said that, up to a certain point ... to be sure, – if you like learning and standing, and that sort of thing, we can't have everything ... you couldn't put the thing better – couldn't put it better, beforehand, you know. But there are oddities in things ... Life isn't cast in a mould – not cut out by rule and line, and that sort of thing ... well, you are not fond of show, a great establishment, balls, dinners, that kind of thing ... You have not the same tastes as every young lady; and a clergyman and scholar – who may be a bishop – that kind of thing – may suit you better than Chettam. (26–27)

Delicately balancing Dorothea's eccentric taste with the sensibility of everyone else, Brooke intimates his preference for Chettam – and who but Dorothea doesn't prefer Chettam? – but sketches the potential merits of Casaubon, too, and affords Dorothea the freedom to decide for herself. This cunningly parodies Arnold's argument in the essays collected as *Culture and Anarchy* (1868): "What if our urgent want now is, not to act at any price, but rather to lay in a stock of light for our difficulties?" (Arnold 73). But action here would necessitate Brooke prohibiting the marriage, like so many imperious guardians before him. At the end of the novel he solicits Chettam's advice about whether or not to change his will – testamentary and characterological, it would seem – with respect to Dorothea: "I would let things remain as they are," Chettam answers, and Brooke "was relieved by the sense that he was not expected to do anything in particular" (514). After all, Brooke has made his mistakes. "I overdid it at one time," he admits, "about topography, ruins, temples – I thought I had a clue, but I saw it would carry me too far, and nothing might have come of it. You may go any length in that sort of thing, and nothing may come of it, you know" (174). These pursuits can lead to nothing, it would seem, precisely because they have specific referents (because they lead to concrete things outside of the self) whereas Brooke's self-referential "that sort of thing" always leads back unto itself – back, that is to say, to him and the complete thought he might seem to secret.

In its disavowal of purpose or utility, Brooke's informal epistemology reproduces the ideals of liberal knowledge espoused by people such as John Henry Newman.[45] In Discourse V of *The Idea of a University* (1852), Newman prefigures Brooke's grammar by valorizing liberal knowledge for its self-referentiality. Writing of "the formation of a character" in prose awash with *something* and *things*, Newman defines liberal knowledge as a "master view of things ... capable of being its own end" (85, 78). Echoing Kant's definition of art as "purposesivness without purpose," he claims liberal knowledge is useful only insofar as it redounds upon one's character, "not merely a means to something beyond it, or the preliminary of certain arts into which it naturally resolves, but an end sufficient to rest in and to pursue for its own sake" (78):

> that alone is liberal knowledge, which stands on its own pretensions, which is independent of sequel, expects no complement, refuses to be *informed* (as it is called) by any end, or absorbed into any art, in order duly to present itself to our contemplation. The most ordinary pursuits have this specific character, if they are self-sufficient and complete; the highest lose it, when they minister to something beyond them. (81)

Newman argues that knowledge lacks "character" when it "ministers to something beyond" itself – when it ministers to some external referent. The grammar of Newman's prose follows suit with tautological *somethings* loosely identified by modifiers. Knowledge has "character" when this *something* is self-sufficient. "When I speak of Knowledge," Newman says:

> I mean something intellectual, something which grasps what it perceives through the senses; something which takes a view of things; which sees more than the senses convey; which reasons upon what it sees, and while it sees; which invests it with an idea. It expresses itself, not in a mere enunciation, but by an enthymeme: it is of the nature of science from the first, and in this consists its dignity ... this germ within it of a scientific or a philosophical process. (85)

Brooke's knowledge likewise enables him to appropriate and just as readily disavow any discourse when it threatens to become the means to an end. He consistently recalls his allegedly experimental and scholarly past to rationalize his presentist habits of spontaneity and inactivity. "I know something of all schools," he says; "it was my way to go about everywhere and take in everything"; "I have gone through all these things, but they might be rather new to you" (13, 25, 181). He thus affects to have dabbled in everything even as he dismisses it all as insufficient (because it might not be self-sufficient).

As if aspiring to embody the modern mode of abstract ownership exempt from the inhibitions and responsibilities of real property (land or gold or labor), Brooke severs his character from external, material references.[46] He thus rebukes Chettam for reading Humphry Davy "to see if something cannot be done in setting a good pattern of farming among [his] tenants":

> A great mistake, Chettam ... going into electrifying your land and that kind of thing, and making a parlour of your cow-house. It won't do. I went into science a great deal myself at one time; but I saw it would not do. It leads to everything; you can let nothing alone. No, no – see that your tenants don't sell their straw, and that kind of thing; and give them drainage-tiles, you know. But your fancy-farming will not do – the most expensive sort of whistle you can buy. (*M* 11)[47]

> You should read history – look at ostracism, persecution, martyrdom, and that kind of thing ... outlay ... that's a showy sort of thing to do, you know ... A man who does that is always charged with eccentricity, inconsistency, and that kind of thing. (*M* 240)

To be sure, these passages lampoon idleness and parsimony (Brooke is especially illiberal when it comes to expenditure), but they also exaggerate liberalism in practice: Brooke comically embodies "the aspiration to many-sidedness," that for David Wayne Thomas, "epitomizes the period's liberal ideal of cultivated agency" (26). Indeed, Brooke explicitly exalts open-mindedness: "There is something in what you say, my good friend," he says from the hustings as an effigy parrots his speech from the crowd, "and what do we meet for but to speak our minds – freedom of opinion, freedom of the press, liberty – that kind of thing" (314). When Thomas writes, however, about how *Middlemarch* valorizes "reflective individuality" (9), he does not seem to have Brooke in mind because he instinctively aligns such reflection with interiority. But Brooke is as reflective as a character can be; he reflects everyone he encounters, every subject he has encountered. If the failure to commit makes him weak, it nevertheless aligns him with the narrator, who famously asks "why always Dorothea?"

Of course Brooke is no model citizen and his reflection lacks the gravitas of Dorothea's. He appears, like Elaine Hadley's rendering of Mr. Harding of *The Warden* (1855), "often adjacent to distraction and just short of indifference" (Hadley 114), though he lacks Mr. Harding's redeeming sense and affability. For Hadley, Harding's "cognitive disorganization" is how he lives out "the dream of liberal unconsciousness"; his eccentricity is how he performs his individuality and thereby flirts with its attendant "liberal nightmare of anonymity" (121). Brooke similarly embodies the eccentric abstraction fundamental to the paradox of liberal character.[48] Whatever the content of his speech, his character *formally* asserts freedom from determination: "that kind of thing" enables him to proffer disparate keywords as if they were articulations of a cogent platform and expressions of actual convictions or opinions, expressions of character.[49] In other words, his content fits his audience's expectations because it remains largely subject to their intuition. And though readers might dismiss him – few others have written about Brooke – the ethic and narrative economy of *Middlemarch* keep him safely at the center for the novel.

Notwithstanding all its liberalism, Brooke's "floundering" campaign speech (313) conflates reform with conservative epistemology.[50] He twice says "the right thing" (312–14), as if to invoke his literary forebear, the optimistic Mr. Square of *Tom Jones*, who says "To confine any thing seems to me against the Law of Nature, by which every thing hath a Right to Liberty. . . . Can any man have a higher notion of the rule of right, and the eternal fitness of things?"[51] The "eternal fitness of things" derives from the eighteenth-century moral philosopher Samuel Clarke, who was far less sanguine about liberty. Like Voltaire's Pangloss, Clarke affirms that "things as they are" realize God's will, and therefore individuals ought to adapt to, rather than reform or rebel against, things as they are.[52] This cosmology was perpetuated by the influential empiricist, Anglican apologist, and correspondent of Clarke's, Joseph Butler, whose *The Analogy of Religion, Natural and Revealed* (1736) schooled nineteenth-century clergy and informed the Bridgewater Treatises. It inhered, too, in the ostensibly objective description and non-idealizing ethos of realism. "Great Writers," Eliot quips in "Silly Novels by Lady Novelists," think "it quite a sufficient task to exhibit men and things as they are."[53] If this risks ascribing too recondite a genealogy to Mr. Brooke's "most glutinously indefinite" mind (6), note Butler's propinquity for tautology: "Everything is what it is, and not another thing."[54]

With his "neutral physiognomy," Brooke haphazardly expounds a laissez-faire attitude that cedes agency to "everything" outside of individuals:

> It won't do, you know, breaking machines: everything must go on – trade, manufacturers, commerce, interchange of staples – that kind of thing – since Adam Smith that must go on. We must look all over the globe: – 'Observation with extensive view,' must look everywhere, 'from China to Peru' as somebody says, Johnson, I think, 'The Rambler,' you know. That is what I have done up to a certain point – not as far as Peru; but I've not always stayed at home – I saw it wouldn't do. (*M* 313)

We can laugh at his misguided invocation of "The Vanity of Human Wishes" and his ironic misattribution of it to *The Rambler*, but the painfully awkward, histrionic rambling of his speech nevertheless marks a paradigm shift in the epistemology of character. Liberated from place and from concrete referents and responsibilities, Brooke embodies a model of cognition as constant movement, a model of character as motile as "commerce," "interchange," "everything [that] must go on." The narrator describes the public's effigy of Brooke as if it was aping him, but he is already an effigy of his audience: he aptly represents the crowd insofar as he hyperbolizes the figures on which their characterization depends. He is constituted by his would-be constituents, and his idiom is the grammar of their being.

Leslie Stephen recognized this discomfiting connection. "In Middlemarch," he explains,

> We consider the higher stratum, which reads newspapers and supports the Society for the Diffusion of Useful Knowledge, and whose notions constitute what is called enlightened public opinion. The typical representative of what it calls its mind is Mr. Brooke, who can talk about Sir Humphry Davy, and Wordsworth, and Italian art, and has a delightful facility in handling the small change of conversation which has ceased to possess any intrinsic value. Even his neighbours can see that he is a fatuous humbug, and do not

care to veil their blunt commonsense by fine phrases. But he discharges the functions of the Greek chorus with a boundless supply of the platitudes which represent an indistinct foreboding of the existence of an intellectual world. (*M* 586)

In recognizing that Brooke's choral role generalizes the specific maladies of the novel's various solipsists, Stephen ultimately judges *Middlemarch* to be too uncomfortable "a satire on the modern world" (*M* 586), too uncomfortable because Brooke's "platitudes," his "delightful facility in handling the small change of conversation," caricature the signature *something* that – in more moderate doses – characterizes both the abstract substratum of realism, its otherwise ineffable sensation of an orderliness and meaning to what otherwise appears to be an alienated, disparate world, and the discursive foundation of the liberal arts, the paradoxical sense that things are both important in and of themselves but only knowable in terms of other things.

"Something" Wanting: Dorothea and the Draw of Indeterminacy

> There is something in what you say, my dear, something in what you say – but not everything – eh, Ladislaw?"   (*M* 243)

The same "small change of conversation which has ceased to possess any intrinsic value" in Brooke's "handling" is nevertheless the currency of character when Dorothea, Ladislaw, and the narrator use it.[55] Passages of self-reflection in Dorothea and Ladislaw depend on the apprehension of *something* – to repeat Mill's sarcastic tautology – to make them what they are. When Dorothea first marries, she vaguely imagines "everyday-things with [Casaubon] would mean the greatest things" (*M* 19) and wants to learn Hebrew and Greek "in order to arrive at the core of things" (*M* 41). Brooke is Dorothea's representative, then, not only as her surrogate parent but in lexical terms: his comic "that sort of thing" distracts from the repetitiveness and epistemic tenuousness of Dorothea's own vague pronominal vocabulary of feeling.

In Dorothea Eliot thus rejuvenates the implicit tension of the early-modern convention of the "unknown something" or *je-ne-sais-quoi* because "that sort of thing" mobilizes Dorothea's sympathetic altruism even as it advertises Brooke's imbecility on the other. *Something* condenses a wide array of potential emotions into one abstract intensity that most often substitutes for Dorothea's incipient sexual interests. This intensity, for all its opacity, is legible to other characters. Thus, "it seemed as if something like the reflection of a white sunlit wing had passed across [Dorothea's] features, ending in one of her rare blushes," and, in the next sentence, "For the first time it entered into Celia's mind that there might be something more between Mr. Casaubon and her sister" (*M* 30). The physiological response represented by *something* that is identified only by a succeeding simile and a residual blush recurs in the subsequent sentence as an inkling about an incipient relationship. This desirous *something* matures later in the novel, at Featherstone's funeral, where "the dream-like association of something alien and ill-understood with the deepest secrets of her experience seemed to mirror that sense of loneliness which was due to the very ardor of Dorothea's nature" (*M* 203). Still an erotic attachment to another, *something* has here intensified but remains grammatically identified only by adjectives and by way of a simile as the inverse of the loneliness Dorothea now knows. For Dorothea, desire operates like negative philosophy, mostly as a skeptical relation to the loneliness she positively feels.

These libinal *somethings* proliferate: Dorothea has "a throbbing excitement like an alarm upon her – a sense that she was doing something daringly defiant for [Ladislaw's] sake" (*M* 496). In the awkward silence following her kiss with Ladislaw, "Dorothea's heart was full of something that she wanted to say, and yet the words were too difficult" (*M* 499). At the novel's climax, she perceives "the truer measure of things" (*M* 485): "something that [Dorothea] could achieve stirred her as with an approaching murmur which would soon gather distinctness" (*M* 486). All of these instances invest physical sensations with heuristic difficulty and therefore gesture at an allegedly extra-discursive subtext or ineffable feeling. We could of course register this idiom as an easy mode of representing both interiority and embodiment, for the pronoun stands in for subjective experience that seems so private or physical that it cannot be reduced to a shared vocabulary. But the syntax of these representations of feeling has more interesting implications.

Daniel Wright details how Eliot confronts vagueness as a real property of language, "feeling, desire, and thought" that we must learn to make use of or understand "as strengthening, rather than disintegrating, our ethical lives."[56] For Wright, Eliot presents "an ethos of vagueness" – "a lived commitment or aspiration to the kind of epistemic disorientation that comes with submerging oneself in the dark places between, behind, or before clear forms" – by plotting Dorothea's development from "a pursuer of the 'distinctly shapen' idea" to a figurative agent who strives to "be clear *about* vagueness" by using metaphors (641, 38). The syntax of Eliot's prose recapitulates this plot:

whereas Brooke resolves his lists of particulars with the implicit coherence of a vague "that sort of thing," Dorothea – or the narrator working on her behalf – often pushes to modify or clarify her *somethings* with metaphors of one sort or another. But only metaphors: the iterative *something* asserts Dorothea's freedom from the necessity of naming or circumscribing her life. Neither Dorothea nor Eliot relinquishes the word.

Dorothea expressly states her concern for this liberty: when Ladislaw presses her about her despondent life at Lowick, for example, she protests, "Please do not call it by any name . . . You will call it Persian, or something else geographical. It is my life, I have found it out, and cannot part with it" (*M* 244). Dorothea assumes ownership of herself by reserving her right to remain unarticulated and by prohibiting Ladislaw from specifically referencing the "something" that constitutes her life: in other words, her self-possession necessitates her self-referentiality; the liveliness of her character precludes referential prose. Seeing *something* allows her to reflect on but not define "the ardor of her nature," "to conceive with that distinctness which is no longer reflection but feeling – an idea wrought back to the directness of sense, like the solidity of objects" (*M* 135). David Wayne Thomas ascribes Dorothea's liberalism to her embodiment of "the regulative ideal of liberal conduct" in feeling instead of maxims (12), but this liberalism extends beyond conduct to experience and to the grammar of prose itself. The iterative *something* therefore privileges embodied feeling over more conceptualized emotions, and I will suggest that *something* is the predominant vehicle for representing embodied feeling in Victorian fiction, particularly the feeling of interest in other people and things. Character is routinely perceived as a function of such interest.

Again, these passages evade referents and only qualify their *something* belatedly with adjectives and other modifying clauses. Dorothea's divided subjectivity is grammatically instantiated by a syntactic oscillation between approximate images ("the reflection of a white sunlit wing") and the pronouns they inadequately define. This deferral of referents installs a self-reflexivity and independence into the prose itself: as if eschewing the possibility of external reference to a recognizable, generic feeling, *something* retains the authority of the text, like Dorothea, to stand alone even in its expression of social interest or desire. Less important than the content of the expression is the expression itself. As Harry Shaw says, Dorothea "needs to embrace images of frustrating opacity, with a melancholic fixation and a refusal to move on, so that she will keep alive feelings for which she has no precise names, instead of defining them into the tameness of the known" (236). But where Shaw sees a metonymic historicism negotiating contingencies and cases, I see a reluctance to translate experience into meaning, a reluctance that likely echoes the practice of most readers and certainly the practice of most Victorian critics, as I explain at the end of this chapter. "Something" enables Dorothea "to conceive with that distinctness which is no longer reflection but feeling – an idea wrought back to the directness of sense, like the solidity of objects" (*M* 135), just as similar placeholders, including "character," might allow readers to acknowledge a moving encounter with a text without delineating that experience. Whereas Thomas describes Dorothea as a liberal, heroic character on the basis of how she embodies "the regulative ideal of liberal conduct" grounded by feeling instead of abstract maxims, feeling "not prior to, but consequent on, reflection" (12), Dorothea seems rather to disavow reflection for feeling that resists depth and, embracing "the solidity of objects," disports on the surface. Several Victorian writers, including Ruskin, forwarded notions of superficial truth of this kind.

For earlier nineteenth-century philosophers of the mind, *something* stood in for psychological identity and the feeling of consciousness. The Scottish philosopher James Ferrier, for instance, repeatedly employs the word in "An Introduction to the Philosophy of Consciousness," a series of articles in *Blackwood's Edinburgh Magazine* from 1838 to 1839. Ferrier, who sought to reconcile German Idealism with the empiricist Associationism of his mentor William Hamilton, maintains that "there is generally something over and above the change," or accumulation of sensations, imputed to selfhood by the empiricists. Revising John Locke, who posited that identity was an intuition or belief induced by the cumulative experience of disparate sensations, Ferrier calls this "unabsorbed something . . . the fact of consciousness, the notion and the reality of himself as the person experiencing the change."[57] However divergent in their more influential mid-century work, Herbert Spencer, Alexander Bain, and G. H. Lewes each represents consciousness as through such deferrals or negations as the residual experience left after taking out all the nameable feelings: character, in its barest sense, is something left after taking away nameable characteristics. In both *The Senses and the Intellect* (1855) and *The Emotions and the Will* (1859), Bain describes consciousness as the continuous "Discrimination, or the feeling of difference between consecutive, or co-existing, impressions."[58] This model of consciousness accords with the markedly asymptotic grammar of "something like," by which modifying clauses approximate or analogize but never define the *something* to which they refer.

If Dorothea seems too far a cry from Brooke, his protégé Ladislaw bridges the two. With a good "sense of things," a desire "to go into everything," a "sturdy neutral delight in things as they were," he dreams of some "indeterminate loftiest thing" but accepts "the common order of things" (*M* 183, 242, 286, 286). His job on Brooke's paper, *The Pioneer*, is to articulate *things*: "'you have a way of putting things. . . . I want that sort of thing – not ideas you know, but a way of putting them'" (*M* 285). Ladislaw promotes an aesthetic of vagueness: "language gives a fuller image," he says, "which is all the better for being vague" (*M* 123).[59] And his feelings also come in the form of *something*: he feels "as if something had happened to him with regard to [Dorothea]" (*M* 123); he wishes Dorothea "to know that something connected with it – something which happened before I went away, helped to bring me down here again" (*M* 496). Ladislaw, who eventually is elected MP, would seem to yoke the dissolute but easy-going character of Brooke with the earnest social feeling of Dorothea. Of course, as Franco Moretti points out, the most representative, liberal, and mature character of the novel is the narrator (222), and I'll add that this narrator's canny and discrete use of *something* and *thing* endows Eliot's prose with intimations of sympathy, desire, intuition, and interest that it liberates her from particularizing.

Scholars of *Middlemarch* tend to recognize it as a novel of interiority or psychological realism, rather than politics, and accordingly as a novel about Dorothea. Daniel Cottom writes of its "sublimation of politics in the rules of sentimental psychology."[60] For John Kucich, *Middlemarch* displaces "the site of identity away from social relations."[61] But Eliot's belabored investment in Brooke's idiom suggests that Dorothea and her totemic interiority, variously shared by the likes of Elizabeth Bennet, Lucy Snowe, and David Copperfield, appropriate a communal medium to represent, but keep secret, this putatively individuated interiority. These characters all owe some of their depth of character, their self-reflection effects, to the same "small change" of everyday conversation that Leslie Stephen ascribes to Brooke. If nothing else, Brooke's idiom externalizes the common idiom of character in a way that solicits different characters to open up, to relax, to broaden their interests, and to get along congenially without the caustic fuss of exactitude.

The obvious impulse of a realism invested in an epistemology of character instead of verisimilitude is to move readers, rather than to tell them what is already known (and therefore readily reproducible, representable). *Middlemarch* claims "character too is a process and an unfolding" (96), and it upholds this assertion in its performative style. Infamously ambivalent about everything, *Middlemarch* simultaneously appreciates the undisciplined individualism, the freedom and mobility of character enabled by equivocal pronouns, even as it laments its imprecision, detachment, and potential solipsism. We might think of this in terms of the "*mauvaise foi*," or bad faith, by which Jameson describes the "inner prestidigitation" of Eliot's characters as "always free to change and to become something different" (131–32); but where Jameson mobilizes *mauvaise foi* to show how Eliot discredits "the metaphysical and moral ideologies of evil" (137), I stress instead how Eliot's idiom of things iterates faith in the bond between people and things. Eliot's commitment to abstraction evidences her faith that everything and everyone matters, that there is an undercurrent, reason, or energy moving us to be interested in the world. As a process of unfolding, character emerges in her fiction as a method of approaching the world with the conviction that instinctual glimpses and inclinations rightly point to truth, whether we are bumbling clowns like Brooke, Theresa-like altruists like Dorothea, or hands-on actors like Adam Bede. Free from content, this character is moral to be sure in its communal impulse, but for nineteenth-century writers it was no less a matter of truth, a manifestation of experience with an empiricist faith that such experience, like experiments, contained a reason.

"Somethingological" knowledge: *David Copperfield* and Referentless Realism

The *something* that characterizes Dorothea and Ladislaw recurs in hundreds of passages of nineteenth-century prose. In *Pride and Prejudice* (1813), Elizabeth Bennet, who – according to her doting father – "has something more of quickness than her sisters" (4), looks for "something" in the "deep," "intricate characters" she prefers as "subjects" for "study" (*PP* 46–47). Lizzy's aunt, Mrs. Gardiner, discerns a wealth of *somethings* in Darcy: "something a little stately in him to be sure . . . but it is confined to his air, and is not unbecoming . . . [and] there *is* something pleasing about his mouth when he speaks"; "And," she adds, "there is something of dignity in his countenance" (*PP* 285). Mrs. Gardiner's apposition of different *somethings* with oblique referents bespeaks the necessary tautology and self-reference of the pronoun and the self-referential, elusive value it denominates: what Darcy possesses, that is to say, is as much the attraction of Elizabeth and her Aunt as anything of his own. This *something* is almost aristocratic, but it testifies to a post-revolutionary sense that the aura of aristocracy comes from the commoners who credit it.

In *Adam Bede* Eliot similarly employs "a certain something" with the proleptic freight that Austen ascribes to it with Mr. Darcy: Mrs. Poyser argues with Dinah Morris about her stubborn vocational drive to preach instead of staying at Hayslope and marrying: "There was a certain something in

Mrs. Poyser's voice just then, which she did not wish to be noticed, so she turned round hastily to look at the clock" (*AB* 477). This sentence thematizes the way "a certain something" grammatically suggests but reserves an implied truth by embodying the turn of phrase in the turn of Mrs. Poyser's head toward the clock. The passage invites readers to recognize "a certain something" as a signpost of implied meaning, but more importantly indexes the conditions for knowing character: what we know of each other is largely conjectural, foreclosed by averted faces and silences and tailored speech.

The ambivalent *something* recurs throughout *Sense and Sensibility* (1811). Mrs. Dashwood employs it to signify desirable and undesirable intangibles. She confesses to Elinor that Colonel Brandon "certainly is not so handsome as Willoughby – but at the same time, there is something much more pleasing in his countenance. – There was always a something, – if you remember, – in Willoughby's eyes at times, which I did not like" (*SS* 383). *Something* likewise serves as Mrs. Dashwood's figure for conjugal interest, for she "persuaded herself to think that something more than gratitude already dawned" in Marianne for Brandon (*SS* 386). Marianne Dashwood characterizes Edward Ferrars to her mother in a series of negations and defines his character as the cumulative lack of the recognizable, fashionable traits that she would "expect" to distinguish a man:

> Edward is very amiable, and I love him tenderly. But yet – he is not the kind of young man – there is a something wanting – his figure is not striking; it has none of that grace which I should expect in the man who could seriously attach my sister. His eyes want all that spirit, that fire, which at once announce virtue and intelligence. And besides all this, I am afraid, mama, he has no real taste. . . . He admires as a lover, not as a connoisseur. To satisfy me, those characters must be united. (*SS* 20)

The conjunction of demonstrative pronouns and indefinite articles here highlights the generic quality of Marianne's desires. "The *kind* of," "*a* something," "*that* grace," "*that* spirit," and "*that* fire" all imply that these values are familiar categorical indicators of character – of "virtue and intelligence" – that all the world recognizes and agrees upon. But Marianne stacks of all of these indicators – grace, spirit, fire, taste – as inadequate appositives to "a something wanting," the fundamental lack distinguishing Edward. Callow and romantic, Marianne regrets that Edward quite literally lacks the generic *something* that, as a connoisseur, she looks for as the signature feature of character, the lack that would later define characters such as David Copperfield and Dorothea Brooke. Marianne's education, however, involves learning to recognize that "a something wanting" is precisely what defines a desirable character and that such "a something" depends as much on her as on its alleged possessor. "Something" inheres in the relation and therefore requires her participation more than any particular qualities in Brandon.

Marianne's keener sister, Elinor, intuits that "a something wanting" actuates, rather than attenuates, Edward's character: "There was, at times, a want of spirits about him which, if it did not denote indifference, spoke a something almost as unpromising" (25). This "something almost as unpromising" prefigures Edward's previous attachment (to Lucy Steele), *something* that draws her to him not only as a jealous lover but as a sympathetic and curious narrator, as a mediator of Edward's secret history. Integrating the virtues of individual characters with the character of the novel, the novel's animating secret, *something* later articulates the emotionally moving difference between conventional expectations and the unpredictability that later became a generic feature of realism:

> Elinor now found the difference between the expectation of an unpleasant event, however certain the mind may be told to consider it, and certainty itself. She now found, that in spite of herself, she had always admitted a hope, while Edward remained single, that something would occur to prevent his marrying Lucy; that some resolution of his own, some mediation of friends, or some more eligible opportunity of establishment for the lady, would arise to assist the happiness of all. (*SS* 404)

The novel subsequently validates Elinor's (and, by extension, presumably some readers') "hope" for *something*, "some resolution," "some mediation," or "some more eligible opportunity." "Something" stands in here, not just for the *je-ne-sais-quoi* of erotic or romantic desire, but also for the admixture of generic features and deviations that can sustain narrative desire. As it turns out, Edward and Lucy are not married. But the language of *somethings* grammatically sustains these gaps between expectation and certainty on the level of the sentence, and thus diffuses some of the constitutive tension of character throughout the narrative.

As a social and narrative device, *something* is a way of saying nothing: it enables people to maintain decorous or congenial silence even as they afford agency to a feeling or idea that they cannot or would rather not specify.[62] And, inasmuch as it is a way of saying nothing – of implying and disavowing or obscuring agency – it can actuate the ways characters embody ideology. Ian Duncan illuminates how "seeing nothing" twice functions in *Emma* (1815) as a trope for acknowledging and disavowing the ideological underpinnings of the "traffic" of everyday reality,[63] the "ideological theme of a national society constituted upon a harmonious conjunction between a modern economy based on imperial trade and a traditional social hierarchy based on inherited property" (118). Emma vacantly sees the traffic of every-day Highbury commerce as *nothing*: "A mind lively and at ease, can do with seeing nothing, and can see nothing that does not answer" (*E* 192). Emma is unable to see anything that disagrees with her idea of the world. Emma later takes a walk down a Donwell Abbey path that leads "to nothing; nothing but a view . . . [of] English verdure, English culture, English comfort, seen under a sun bright, without being oppressive" (*E* 288). Embodying the nascent voice of realism, Emma looks beyond or around or through the earthy and inconvenient details of concrete reality to her own ideology, the view that fits her idea of reality. "'Nothing' refers not only to the everyday domain of traffic," Duncan writes, "it also refers, obliquely or metaphorically, to that reality's governing abstraction, embedded in naturalized forms and qualities, English verdure, culture, comfort. Nothing names the immanence of the system in an invisible cause that sustains and regulates [reality]" (118).

Passing acknowledgment of things that do not quite answer grants what we might call, with the narrator of *Emma*, a Brooke-like "ease" to Austen's fiction. Even those fictions that concertedly reject ease often depend on a colloquial capacity for seeing nothings, for negotiating a reality that definitively exceeds their knowledge. Getting through each day requires the leverage of a colloquialism that lets everything "answer," as Emma says: "There does seem to be a something in the air of Hartfield which gives love exactly the right direction, and sends it into the very channel where it ought to flow." What Duncan observes thematized in *Emma* emerges throughout the vernacular *somethings* and *nothings* of Austen's fiction,[64] but the pronoun that denominates the supplemental agency of Emma's social reality also denominates her individual self-perception. Emma's character, that is to say, depends on the same kind of pronoun that animates her reality. All of the characters, including the narrative voice, derive some of their character from the distance that this colloquial equivocation inscribes into the text: "There was something in the name, in the idea of Mr. Frank Churchill, which always interested her"; "some-thing to her advantage"; "something exceedingly precious"; "something more than human perfection of body and mind"; "something more to conceal"; "something or other"; "something about conjecturing"; "some-thing of consequence"; "something absolutely serious"; "something to feel"; "something of pleasing connexion"; "something so motherly and kind-hearted"; "a something more early implanted"; "a something of resentment"; "something wanting." In all of these instances the text refers back to itself, as if the value or quality signified by *something* were an antecedent embedded elsewhere. If Emma's "culture" is, as Duncan argues, an effect of her implicit distance from the market, her ability to disavow its traffic as "nothing," then her character and the character of the novel are effects of the implicit distance between their many indefinite pronouns and their incomplete, absent, or otherwise imprecise referents. Austen writes, "Seldom, very seldom, does complete truth belong to any human disclosure; seldom can it happen that something is not a little disguised, or a little mistaken" (*E* 297), and her prose naturalizes this incompleteness. Its character accrues to its refusal of full disclosure and to the self-reflexivity produced by internal allusions like *something*, which seems to refer back to phantom antecedents.

   In *Villette* (1853), Charlotte Brontë – who dedicated *Jane Eyre* to Thackeray because he promised to regenerate "the warped system of things" (Brontë 6–7) – employs *something* in several instances to substantiate the alienation the narrator, Lucy Snowe, feels between her and other characters, and thereby confers upon her a kind of distinction of extraordinary repression and isolation. Lucy, who like Elizabeth Bennet consistently values others for the "amusement" or "originality" they offer as "character to study,"[65] associates *something* with character-reading and the management of her own emotions. When Madame Beck's system of espionage and surveillance keeps tabs on Protestant Lucy's tête-à-têtes with her Catholic students, "An edifying consequence ensued. Something – an unseen, an indefinite, a nameless something – stole between myself and these best pupils" (84). This *something* stands in for Madame Beck and her spies, to be sure, but its vagueness extends the reference also to a keener perception on Lucy's part, an awareness of herself as the subject of the character-reading of another: "I found myself an object of study" (76), Lucy explains at the beginning of the episode. Lucy elsewhere writes of "a cold something, very slight, very transparent, but very chill," estranging her and Dr. John: "a sort of screen of ice had hitherto, all through our two lives, glazed the medium through which we exchanged intercourse" (192). The overdetermined "nun" (a crossed-dressed man sneaking in to flirt with a pupil) Lucy sees haunting the school – and the second half of the novel – first appears as "Something in that vast solitary garret [that] sounded strangely" (245), and Lucy's reticent pronoun does not go unnoticed: "Your account was quite vague, do you know?" Dr. John says. "You looked white as the wall; but you only spoke of 'something,' not defining *what*" (247). The pronoun allows her, as character and narrator, to share her experience while reserving her ideas about it. They allow her to communicate and retain secrets at the same time, a fundamental task for maintaining secret subjectivity.

In Dickens's fiction, too, *something* often conjoins the character of self-reflective characters with the character of the fiction, whose lacks and desires theoretically solicit readerly reflection. David Copperfield's feelings emerge as *something* before slowly being adumbrated in the plot. First, as a child, he recalls "Something – I don't know what, or how – connected with the grave in the churchyard, and the raising of the dead, seemed to strike me" (*DC* 43). And then, "From that night there grew up in my breast, a feeling for Peggotty, which I cannot very well define. She did not replace my mother; no one could do that; but she came into a vacancy in my heart, which closed upon her, and I felt towards her something I have never felt for any other human being" (*DC* 58). Here, Peggotty occupies a "vacancy" with anther "vacancy," a pronoun that stands in for a feeling David feels and knows but cannot define. Peggotty returns David's feeling of *something*; but, whereas David (the incipient author) articulates the ineffable with the modish *something*, Peggotty (who "ain't no scholar") divulges her feelings with "some paper bags of cakes ... a purse," and the many buttons that pop off her overstretched gown, and which David retains as keepsakes, "but not one word did she say" (*DC* 58, 59). Peggotty's nonverbal effusions might be imagined as dramatizations of what David's indeterminate *something* does and does not say. As if these indeterminate emotions were fungible, Barkis gulps down one of Peggotty's cakes, which David offers "as a mark of attention," and, discovering that Peggotty has baked them, "made up his mouth" – instead of his mind – "as if to whistle, but he didn't whistle. He sat looking at the horse's ears as if he saw something new there; and sat so, for a considerable time." The unspecified, even *un-whistled*, "something new" that Barkis sees between the horse's ears introduces his incipient marital interest in Peggotty. Barkis caricatures the modish desire of "real" characters like Copperfield (and Darcy and Elizabeth). He subsequently asks David if Peggotty has any sweethearts, and, in a Dickensian conflation of food and erotic desire, David mistakenly hears "sweetmeats," because he thought Barkis "wanted something else to eat" (61). Typical of Dickens, the passage translates sexual desire into hunger. Through a syntactical metempsychosis or transubstantiation, the care, sadness, and pride that Peggotty expresses through her cakes become "something new" that Barkis sees between the horse's ears and then again become "something else to eat," physical embodiments of his own longing for love.

Barkis is a flat character, but his particular mode of flatness, like Brooke's, only echoes the medium of David Copperfield's roundness. Dickens was far more invested in the epistemology of character I am tracing here than in the superseding depth model espoused by critics such as Forster, James, or

Lewes, who assailed him for characterizing by way of catchphrases.[66] Barkis's dialect models Dickensian characterization at large in protagonists and ancillary characters alike. And although Lewes belittled him for his attenuated realism and "*animal* intelligence" (1871, 151), we shall see that this same mode of characterization informs Lewes's defense of realism.

"Something else" if not the exact *something* about Peggotty that David finds impossible to define and Barkis finds so delicious – *something* akin to David's love for his mother and Barkis's presumably sexual interest in Peggotty – also substitutes for both the unutterable disaffection David develops toward Dora and for the duly ineffable, latent love he senses for Agnes and everything – affirming, erotic, maternal, angelic, domestic, religious, nostalgic, disciplinary, self-abnegating – that she represents. As a placeholder, *something* instantiates these overdetermined and underspecified associations as real feelings with agency throughout the novel even though they are not fully delineable until the climax, if ever. Thus, upon Betsey's financial misfortune, David "felt a vague unhappy loss or want of something overshadow me like a cloud" (*DC* 426).

This feeling recurs with additional intensity:

> The old unhappy loss or want of something had, I am conscious, some place in my heart; but not to the embitterment of my life. When I walked alone in the fine weather, and thought of the summer days when all the air had been filled with my boyish enchantment, I did miss something of the realisation of my dreams; but I thought it was a softened glory of the Past, which nothing could have thrown upon the present time. (*DC* 545)

David here speaks decorously of a "want of something" instead of too bluntly disowning Dora. As several scholars have suggested, part of David's problem with Dora is that she forces him to see the economic activity that supports the middle-class lifestyle he wants to lead. Dora makes David see the "immense account-book" and the "leaves of the Cookery-Book" (*DC* 544) and the servants – Paragon, May Anne, Mrs. Kidgerbury, and "a long line of Incapables" (*DC* 539) – who ought to remain unseen. Dora makes David see something where, like exuberantly upper-class Emma, he wants or expects to see nothing.[67]

David's "loss or want of something" affirms what he does not lack: lack itself. His missing *something* recurs so often that it becomes valuable property, his impetus, affect and characterological distinction – albeit paradoxically a distinction he shares with many Victorian characters, because it was, I argue, an epistemic convention of character itself. "What I missed," David says, "I still regarded – I always regarded – as something that had been a dream of my youthful fantasy; that was incapable of realisation; that I was now discovering to be so, with some natural pain, as all men did" (587). However much David claims to want *something*, he always possesses the want itself: a definitive lack which is a requisite asset to his character as character. David's *Bildung* involves not just a discovery of his vocation and proper wife but his taking ownership of this lack as a positive property. "I cannot so completely penetrate the mystery of my own heart," he says,

> as to know when I began to think that I might have set its earliest and brightest hopes on Agnes. I cannot say at what stage of my grief it first became associated with the reflection, that, in my wayward boyhood, I had thrown away the treasure of her love. I believe I may have heard some whisper of that distant thought, in the old unhappy loss or want of something never to be realized, of which I had been sensible. (*DC* 688)

Like Dorothea after him, David recognizes that naming or specifying this *something* with a clear referent would efface his character: "I avoided," he says, "the recognition of this feeling by any name, or by any communing with myself" (*DC* 590). Neither a melancholy concession (that he will never get what he wants) nor anything he ought to expect from some external agent (society, family, friends, charity), but instead the defining feature of autonomous, self-determined, and authorial character, "something wanting" affords David the freedom to write himself or to remain unwritten. Remember that he becomes "such a determined character" when he learns "to turn the painful discipline of my younger days to account" (*DC* 445, 439), commodifying his childhood and his "undisciplined heart" in the form of fiction. Such anonymity – a self that is defined by its nameless lack – is a standard cost of normative individualism: a degree of anonymity akin to that Catherine Gallagher describes in eighteenth-century women writers as the "exchangeable tokens of modern authorship."[68]

"Something wanting" indeed was a generic feature of the character of sensation fiction, not only in their alleged inferior personages (they were accused of subordinating character to plot) but also in their stringing together of suggestive internal allusions to generate mystery. Wilkie Collins's *The Woman in White* (1860) nicely articulates the way character conflated personages, readers, and the novel as a whole. Consider how Walter Hartright introduces Laura Fairlie:

> Mingling with the vivid impression produced by the charm of her fair face and head, her sweet expression, and her winning simplicity of manner, was another impression, which, in a shadowy way, suggested to me the idea of something wanting. At one time it seemed like something wanting in *her*; at

another, like something wanting in myself, which hindered me from understanding her as I ought. The impression was always strongest, in the most
contradictory manner, when she looked at me; or, in other words, when
I was most conscious of the harmony and charm of her face, and yet, at the
same time, most troubled by the sense of an incompleteness which it was
impossible to discover. Something wanting, something wanting – and
where it was, and what it was, I could not say.[69]

Hartright "could not say" because this "something wanting" stands in for the
fundamental mystery of the plot, the character of the woman in white and
The Woman in White. Couched in the language of suggestion, "something
wanting" here reverberates as the most perdurable content of Laura Fairlie's
character. If Hartright as narrator doubles as a surrogate reader, then "something wanting" also substitutes for the "vivid impression" (50) of reading
sensation fiction, whose effects require readers' apprehension "of something
wanting" from their understandings of the story. The repetition of the phrase
without fixed, local antecedents turns it into an internal allusion that affords
the novel a formal self-reflexivity analogous to the self-reflection ascribed to
moral character. That "something wanting" refers back to all the others, as if to
imply that they all correspond and collectively mean, well, something. Thus,
The Woman in White ultimately validates Hartright's "contradictory" "impression" as true and that "something wanting" as significant: "That 'something
wanting,'" he explains, "was my own recognition of the ominous likeness
between the fugitive from the asylum [the woman in white, Anne Catherick]
and my pupil at Limmeridge House [Laura]" (61).[70] The interchangeability of
Anne and Laura – and Walter and the novel, too – underscores the formal
homogeneity of nineteenth-century character in general.

Something characterizes many of Dickens's personages precisely by
supplementing their identifiable attributes with a certain but unnamed
value. "There was," for example, "something about [Betsey Trotwood],
notwithstanding her many eccentricities and odd humours, to be honored
and trusted in" (*DC* 180). But Dickens treats *something* with the same
ambivalence as Eliot. Mr. Micawber, for example, whose literary friend
reads his letter "as if the words were something real in his mouth, and
delicious to taste" (*DC* 150), repeatedly insists "on the probability of
something turning up" (*DC* 222, 226, 642). "Something turning up" is
indeed as identifiable a speech tag for Micawber as "that sort of thing" is for
Brooke; and to be sure Micawber is, as Garrett Stewart puts it, "the great
rival author in *David Copperfield*, a commanding stylist against whose
prose David must define his own expressive tendencies."[71]

Dickens simultaneously exploits and burlesques the capacity for pronouns with vague referents to characterize modern abstractions and human relations. In *Bleak House*, which invokes "things in general" (277, 375), "the surface of things" (330), "all things" (461), and "all manner of things" (642), Mr. Turveydrop, the residual bearer of Regency deportment, commends his son, Prince, to Esther: "'All that can be imparted, he can impart. But there are things' – he took another pinch of snuff and made the bow again, as if to add, 'this kind of thing, for instance'" (175). *Things* here presumably refers, with some lame effort at tact, to the deportment Prince lacks as well as to the irreducible notability it redounds upon his father. However much Turveydrop talks about deportment, his usage in this exchange implies that it cannot be rendered explicitly but only performed in the bow or the pinch of snuff that, like *things*, is legible only to people in the know. In turn, then, Turveydrop's usage assumes that everyone else in the conversation is in the know and adheres to his (residual and aspirational) habitus. Dickens's humor thus underscores the fundamental problem with loose pronoun usage: it assumes readers or auditors already know what sentences are going to mean, that they inhabit the same mental space as their texts or their interlocutors and therefore get what pronouns refer to, share their assumptions, without needing antecedents.

Of course, Dickens repeatedly reminds us with irony, hyperbole, and misinterpretation that we cannot so readily understand each other.[72] To wit, Tulkinghorn tells Lady Dedlock that "Nothing that you would call anything," has been done in court (*BH* 15) and thus poses chancery as a masculine, professional mystery beyond her ken. Like Emma in my earlier discussion, Lady Dedlock's genteel femininity "sees nothing" where the professional man sees something, and somehow Tulkinghorn's remark bolsters the sense that Chancery has a logic even as it suggests that Lady Dedlock is above sordid legal matters. But successful communication, like mimetic representation, is not the point: the character of prose such as this inheres in its disjunctions and failures to reproduce one meaning identically in or for another. Character accrues to prose that, like Mr. Brooke, obliquely misrepresents its constituents' intentions; it evokes not just the animating motives of secret subjectivity or hidden laws of nature and social economy, but a willful or accidental misapprehension of those motives and laws.

Humorous and sinister solecisms thus appear, as in *Middlemarch*, beside earnest passages where comparably indeterminate language acts as a proxy for vital psychological energies: again, Esther Summerson reads Jarndyce's proposal letter and cries "as if something for which there was no name or distinct idea were indefinitely lost" (*BH* 538). By turns laughable and poignant, facetious and earnest, such passages insinuate the presence of motive agencies to which the novel and its characters are subject but which no one seems able to articulate. These agencies are not restricted to psychology but diffused throughout the world of the novel, animating socioeconomic, political, and natural phenomena. Thus, Sir Leicester Dedlock complacently regards "an interminable Chancery suit" as

> a slow, expensive, British, constitutional kind of thing . . . as a something, devised in conjunction with a variety of other somethings, by the perfection of human wisdom, for the eternal settlement (humanly speaking) of everything. (*BH* 15–16)

An indubitably ridiculous passage: but one that nevertheless epitomizes how the idiom of characterization enables ideological fictions to govern human action, or, in this case, complacency. Pronouns with vague or missing referents galvanize abstractions that do not accurately represent the material conditions of the world they purport to describe. They feign knowledge of a system, law, or other rationale responsible for the apparent disorder of everyday life without disclosing that knowledge.

The stylistic investment in vernacular idioms of characterization, as I have said, complemented and sometimes reacted against the hegemony of the referential fact. Dickens overtly thematizes the tension between factual and characterological knowledge in *Hard Times* (1854). At the moment of Louisa Gradgrind's catharsis, when she enters Stephen Blackpool's home and, "for the first time in her life, she was face to face with anything like individuality in connexion with [the Coketown Hands]" (*HT* 155), *something* enables the narrative to verbalize how the statistical epistemology espoused by Gradgrind homogenizes and depersonalizes people:

> Something to be worked so much and paid so much, and there ended; something to be infallibly settled by laws of supply and demand; something that blundered against those laws and floundered into difficulty; something that was a little pinched when wheat was dear, and over-ate itself when wheat was cheap; something that increased at such a rate of percentage, and yielded such another percentage of crime, and such another percentage of pauperism; something wholesale, of which vast fortunes were made; something that occasionally rose like a sea, and did some harm and waste (chiefly to itself), and fell again; this she knew the Coketown Hands to be. But, she had scarcely thought more of separating them into units, than of separating the sea itself into its component drops. (*HT* 155)

Dickens critiques the generic commensuration of individual characters as atomistic units that can be represented as statistics by bureaucratic systems of knowledge. And yet *something* performs a double role in *Hard Times*, as in *Middlemarch*, representing inhumane abstraction as well as the abstraction requisite to individuation. The addled and belittled Mrs. Gradgrind, voicing her husband's tenets, comically beseeches her children to "Go and be somethingological directly" (24); but on her deathbed she protests, "there is something – not an Ology at all – that your father has missed, or forgotten, Louisa. I don't know what it is. I have often sat with Sissy near me, and thought about it. I shall never get its name now" (*HT* 194). Ironically, Mrs. Gradgrind's failure to remember the name of this *something* – be it love, imagination, sociality, sympathy, or a catchall like humanity – demonstrates her recognition of what matters and her character: in her forgetfulness, she proves the existence and import of knowledge that cannot be named, tabulated, or capitalized.

Mr. Gradgrind diagnoses this otherwise unnameable *something* as the problem with Thomas and Louisa. He tell Bounderby that "it would appear . . . as if something had crept into Thomas's and Louisa's minds which is – or rather, which is not – I don't know that I can express myself better than by saying – which has never been intended to be developed, and in which their reason has no part" (HT 24). He "had become possessed by an idea that there was something in this girl [Sissy Jupe] which could hardly be set forth in tabular form" (*HT* 92). Stephen Blackpool likewise describes Mrs. Pegler, Bounderby's mother, kissing his hand as a "fantastic action . . . a something neither out of time nor place, a something which it seemed as if nobody else could have made as serious, or done with such a natural and touching air" (*HT* 81). Here the representation of Mrs. Pegler's kiss as "a something" and as a "fantastic action" accentuate it as a moving refusal of referential epistemology, a refusal to live according to a system that respects only those forms of knowledge that reproduce existing material conditions as they appear.

The slurring sage of *Hard Times*, Sleary (who supplants "s" with "th"), characterizes this alternative "Ology" as "thomething" opposed to self-interestedness:

> "It theemth to prethent two thingth to a perthon, don't it, Thquire?" said Mr. Sleary, musing as he looked down into the depths of his brandy and water: "one, that there ith a love in the world, not all thelf-interetht after all, but thomething very different; t'other, that it hath a way of ith own of

calculating or not calculating, whith thomehow or another ith at leatht ath hard to give a name to, ath the wayth of the dogth ith!" (*HT* 282)

We could approximate the "thomething" modeled by Sissy and Sleary with love, sympathy, imagination, fancy, a "special inaptitude for any kind of sharp practice" (*HT* 40), but Sleary more precisely defines the "thomething" as an outward-orientated interest: interest in people and things other than oneself. People and prose with character share this outward interest. They do not merely express their selves and their subjects or interests, but through misdirection manifest interest in other selves and subjects. The form by which Dickens mediates these virtues matters more than any named virtue or collection of named virtues, that is to say, because its ambiguous proxies for virtue accommodate the novels' correspondence to many different people and things rather than fixing correspondence to a defined set. But the epistemology of character is not just another name for indeterminacy: its indeterminacies are restricted to affective and socialized relations.

I could go on citing novelists who share Eliot's idiom. Anthony Trollope's fiction makes industrious use of it, from men who "have lacked a something, the want of which has made them small and poor and dry" (*ED* 156); to "a something in [Lord Fawn] which might produce in him a desire to be relieved from" his engagement to Lizzie (*ED* 133); to the gossipy "Somebody, in speaking on Lady Eustace's behalf, and making the best of her virtues, had declared that she did not have lovers ... but there might, perhaps, be a something between her and her cousin – a liaison quite correct in its facts, a secret understanding, if nothing more – a mutual sympathy" (*ED* 136). Trollope's *somethings* facilitate tacit, decorous exchanges between people in the know, individuals sharing with the reader an intuitive or intimate body of communal but exclusive references. In *The Eustace Diamonds*, "Mrs. Hittaway was conversant with the things of the world" (120); and "The unfitness of the thing" (the un-chaperoned encounter between Lucy and Frank) appeals to Lizzie (146), who "desired to be the possessor of the outward shows of all those things of which the inward facts are valued by the good and steadfast ones of the earth" (163). And Trollope, too, seems conscious of the tact inscribed in this idiom: in *The Small House at Allington*, for instance, "there lurked behind *it all* a feeling that *it* might be safer that the *thing* should not be so openly manifested before all the world" (93, emphasis added). By plugging awkward gaps in conversation, Trollope's "that sort of thing" also allows characters to engage with one another without breaching decorum, without over-sharing, even without having anything to say.[73] These pronominal phrases are the phatic infrastructure of everyday conversation, channels of affective contact that do not need to have content in order to matter to or move us. George Meredith, whose abstruse prose appears antithetical to Trollope's, often relies upon the same colloquialisms and manifests their solidification into a tactical social currency. In *The Egoist* (1879), young Crossjay employs them to remind Clara of a promise: "'You said something?' 'What did I say, Crossjay?' 'You promised.' 'What did I promise?' 'Something.' 'Name it, dear boy.' He mumbled ' . . . kiss me.'"[74] Less obviously, Clara and the narrator apply *something* to animate Clara's inchoate character: "something is going on in me," Clara confides to Lætitia. "Lætitia took her hand, and saw and felt that something was going on. Clara said: 'You are a woman.' It was her effort to account for the something. She swam for a brilliant instant on tears, and yielded to the overflow" (131).

So there is literally *something* in the way nineteenth-century fiction moves: on the one hand, its representation of emotion relies on *something* and other inflections of *thing* with missing, vague, or tautological referents; on the other hand, it adheres to an epistemology that credits not the correspondence between representation and referent but the affective correspondence enabled between readers and characters and prose that deliberately obscures its referents. Irreducible to allegory, axioms, nameable morals, or factual information,[75] "character" accrued to prose that exceeded or downright eschewed referentiality with tactful misrepresentation and abstraction that subordinated accuracy for interest, social engagement, and investment in the worlds outside of individual interiorities. If abstraction in the form of the market, the factory system, or the social body threatens to alienate individuals, abstraction in the form of indeterminate and self-referential pronouns offers the opposite: inalienable and affective knowledge.

Touching Superficiality: Critical Acquaintances with "Realism"

> Life is for the most part but the mirror of our own individual selves. Our mind gives to all situations, to all fortunes, high or low, their real characters. . . . There is much in life that, while in this state, we can never comprehend.[76]   – Samuel Smiles, *Character*

This book maintains that *character* was the vernacular category by which Britons appreciated prose thick with everyday words like *something* and "that sort of thing," but, as the previous chapter says, Victorian critics lacked a stable and adequately nuanced critical vocabulary to describe the phenomena that they perceived in nineteenth-century culture, including fiction. Bolstering the epistemological claims for fiction as a medium of moral knowledge in a culture that was increasingly invested in scientific models of reproducible, referential truth, some critics turned to "realism" to name the same effects. These critics combine the idiom of *things* with "character" to portray "realism" not merely as virtual reality but as "something more," a moving form of representation that markedly interests, accommodates, or fits with the readers. Let me return, then, to John Ruskin, for *Modern Painters* conflates realism with character and treats them as a forms of representation that concurrently attend to truth, fidelity, experience, experiment, all the familiar nineteenth-century signifiers of mimesis or verisimilitude, and yet lack discernable or definite referents. If affirming that realist prose is especially abstract, non-referential, and indeterminate seems counterintuitive, so was the context of Ruskin's introduction of "realism" into English discourse. The first volumes of *Modern Painters* defend J. M. W. Turner's "swirling and almost abstract" paintings from contemporary critics like John Eagles by asserting that Turner – who was, as Rachel Teukolsky says, "so manifestly violating accustomed codes of the natural" – depicted more truth than the established conventions of realistic painting could.[77]

Notably, Ruskin presents "character" not as an effect of depth but as a gripping, moving, or interesting surface. Inverting the conventional privileging of depth in a discussion of Turner's style of painting water, Ruskin says that "It is the easiest thing in the world to give a certain degree of depth and transparency to water; but . . . it is next to impossible to give a full impression of surface."[78] For Ruskin, Turner's "Château of Prince Albert" exemplifies the "secret" of impressive surfaces:

> We cannot tell, when we look *at* them and *for* them, what they mean. They have all character, and are evidently reflections of something definite and determined; but yet they are all uncertain and inexplicable; playing colour and palpitating shade, which, though we recognize them in an instant for images of something, and feel that the water is bright, and lovely, and calm, we cannot penetrate or interpret; we are not allowed to go down to them, and we repose, as we should in nature, upon the luster of the level surface. It is in this power of saying everything, and yet saying nothing too plainly, that the perfection of art here, as in all other cases, consists. (Ruskin 3: 539–40)

Jules Law argues that Ruskin "believes implicitly in a correspondence between the sensations of spatial depth obtained in and from landscape, and those aspects and qualities of human experience that we figuratively describe as 'deep,'" such that portraying depth of water might redound depth upon the character of the audience of the painting – at least to the extent that the "economy of character," as Deidre Lynch calls it, trades in depth.[79] But Ruskin appeals to a more superficial yet complex notion of character. Genteel ease, composure, and decorum meld with probabilistic "nature" in his aesthetic of "repose" and "saying nothing too plainly." The description exemplifies another mode of "epistemological decorum," to again cite Stephen Shapin.[80] The "character" in Turner's paintings tactfully resists disclosure through prying analysis: "we cannot penetrate or interpret," Ruskin insists. Instead, this character manifests as "something definite and determined" while remaining "uncertain and inexplicable." Echoing Tulkinghorn's exchange with Lady Dedlock, the "character" of water emerges from owes to its paradoxical "reflection" of "everything" by "nothing."

Beyond its myriad mimetic visual terms (sketch, graphic, delineation, outline, chiaroscuro, relief, shade), all of which Victorian critics appropriated to analyze realist prose, *Modern Painters* affirms that *something* obtains between Turner's paintings and its observers. The "character" comes from surfaces that simultaneously captivate and relax the observer, surfaces that interest without involving or immersing. Such interfaces evoke definitively non-referential truth:

> Truth may be stated by any signs or symbols which have a definite significa-tion in the minds of those to whom they are addressed, although such signs be themselves no image nor likeness of anything. Whatever can excite in the mind the conception of certain facts, can give ideas of truth, though it be in no degree the imitation or resemblance of those facts. (Ruskin 3:104)

Eliot apprehends and reproduces this notion in her review: "Every one who cares about nature, or poetry, or the story of human development – every one who has a tinge of literature or philosophy, will find *something* that is for him and that will 'gravitate to him' in this volume."[81] A kind of radical reader-response theory, it suggests that the character of a text or painting belongs neither to it as an independent object nor to its readers or the subjects and objects it represents, but to the interaction between these parties, interaction that happens on the surface. The very obliqueness of Turner's referents makes them available as characters: they refer not to specific "facts" but to "a definite signification in the minds of those to whom they are addressed."

For George Lewes, *something* moving happened at the interface not of reflective surface and depth so much as that of verisimilitude and idealism. In "Realism in Art: Recent German Fiction," *something* names the "durable pleasure" and "felicity" of realism.[82] Analyzing Raphael's "Madonna di San Sisto," Lewes discerns "two exquisite angel children, intensely childlike, yet something *more*, something which renders their wings congruous with our conception of them. In the never-to-be-forgotten divine babe, we have at once the intensest [*sic*] realism of presentation, with the highest idealism of conception" (493–94). Feeling *something* once again indicates the feeling of correspondence – here "congruity" – between oneself and the text or artifact. Like Mr. Darcy musing about his ideal woman or Ruskin prosing on Turner, Lewes defines realism not by its answerable features but by this superadded relationship it seems to share with him: "something more," an intensity and memory. The representation actually becomes, "never-to-be-forgotten," commingled with his character. Registering this intensity – literally, the tension generated by his feeling himself inscribed in the painting or text – appears to be his implicit objective as a critic. He does not aspire to explicate, allegorize, or otherwise interpret its meaning. He characterizes "realism in art" by performatively enacting how they transcend his capacity to describe them, how they refer to him, "something more" than their subject.

Walter Pater writes similarly of "style," by which he denominates the way a given writer deviates from mimetic representation: "an expression no longer of fact but of [a writer's] sense of it, his peculiar intuition of a world, prospective, or discerned below the faulty conditions of the present, in either case changed somewhat from the actual world."[83] Pater explains the change effected by style as the addition of "something of his own humour, something that comes not of the world without, but of a vision within" (5). Upholding as he did an ideal of objective subjectivism, Pater does not mean that style projects the ethos or personality of an author onto the text, but instead that it imbues the text with character in general. Manifesting the characterological "tact of omission," an author ideally includes only words that add "a ponderable something" (15, 16). Pater sketches this *something* as an intuited fitness between writer and word, word and reader: the "effect of an intuitive condition of mind, it must be recognised by like intuition on the part of the reader, and a sort of immediate sense" (31). So *something* here too designates an aesthetic intensity or intuition between text and reader, and style matters because it refers a subject to the reader rather than because, like a fact, it refers to (imitates) correspondent subjects in the world.

The epitome of this critical protocol once again might be E. S. Dallas, however, for his 1866 prescription for a systemic literary criticism, *The Gay Science* (1866), repeatedly and extensively describes the pleasure of art in terms of *something* even as he professes to work scientifically.[84] For Dallas the aesthetic object of all art is "unseen," "always weird," "unknown, indescribable," "unutterable," an "incommunicable secret," a "know-not-what," and an "unknown something" (II: 111, 134–35). In places, this "unknown something" simply prefigures the Freudian unconscious and echoes the familiar trope of ineffable interiority.[85] But more consistently, *something* effervesces at the convergence of text and reader or art and audience. When Dallas interprets the fiction of Dickens and Thackeray, he does not pretend to access the personality of either novelist so much as the interiority, so to speak, of the zeitgeist or culture shared by his readers. Like Lewes (who nevertheless found *The Gay Science* laughable and scientifically inaccurate[86]), Dallas describes pleasure as an inexplicable fitness between reader and text: "the precise nature of the pleasure . . . we explain to ourselves as an agreeableness we do not know," he says, "but, nevertheless, we always revert to the sense of agreement and fitness as the only approach we can make to an explanation of pure pleasure" (II: 75). "An agreeableness we do not know": rather than the Freudian unconscious, the selves we do not know, Dallas offers an affinity we do not know. His is a thinly-veiled erotics of reception whereby the pleasure of reading dare not speak its name. The Darwinian "fitness" even adds an inkling of sexual selection to the relation. The character of art turns out to reside, then, in a style that discounts the precision or probability of its representation of its subject matter on behalf of grammatically instantiating its attraction to and relationship with its audience. Thus, Dallas's investigation purports to discover in art the same "something more" that so many nineteenth-century characters discover driving their libidinal, intellectual, and political interests. He characterizes art as Austen, Eliot, Dickens, Charlotte Brontë, and so many others characterized their personages and worlds.

Nineteenth-century novels demonstrate how the colloquial idiom of *things* and *something* allows prose to characterize everything, including prose itself, by ascribing to it the irreducible desire that was a generic feature of nineteenth-century characters, from imbeciles like Brooke and Micawber to the otherwise inimitable Dorothea Brooke and David Copperfield. This idiom translates ineffable feeling into ordinary language, intensities of fellow feeling and interest into fungible knowledge. We might consider it as a wide diffusion of the properties that Catherine Gallagher ascribes to the "nobodies" narrating eighteenth-century fiction to prose and its subjects.[87] Gallagher suggests that the emergence of fiction as a category reconciling literal truth and falsehood relied upon the production of characters with proper names who do not refer to actual people outside of the text and upon a disembodied, authorial persona (and mode of femininity) whose fungible nothingness resembled the abstract value of a commodity. By disavowing extra-textual reference and personal reputation, these nobodies affected disinterestedness and moral innocence; by their relative anonymity they welcomed many identifications from relatively diverse readers. But when character was not exclusive to persons or personages, oblique and absent referents liberated prose to characterize things other than people. With *something* and *thing*, anonymity inflects the most haunting and acute personal longings as well as the most impersonal laws of nature and society. The character – moral, epistemological, and aesthetic – of such prose inheres in its style of reflection (Ruskin) or liberal representation (Eliot) rather than in its contents. This prose is therefore "somethingological": prose not simply marked by prolific use of *something*, but also by its subordination of accuracy for free play, tact, and contact with its reader.

CHAPTER 5

"Whoever explains a 'but'"
Tact and Friction in Trollope's Reparative Fiction

> There he paused for a moment, and then looking up into her face, he
> spoke but one word more. "But," said he – and there he stopped.
> It was all clearly told in that "but."
> – Anthony Trollope, *Doctor Thorne*[1]

> [Tact is] a high polish produced on the surface of a man's character by
> constant friction with the world.
> – "Tact," *Chambers' Edinburgh Journal*[2]

> And yet in very truth the realistic must not be true but just so far
> removed from truth as to suit the erroneous idea of truth which the
> reader may be supposed to entertain.
> – Anthony Trollope, *Thackeray* (1879)[3]

In July 1849, as a Surveyor's deputy for the Post Office in Ireland, Anthony
Trollope stood witness against local postmistress Mary O'Reilly, whom he
had caught stealing a marked coin from the mail.[4] Trollope's testimony
was rebutted by the then prominent Irish barrister, Isaac Butt, an eventual
MP and founder of the Home Rule League. Butt was nicknamed "The
Rebutter" for his infamously aggressive cross-examinations.[5] To discredit
his testimony, Butt questioned Trollope's character by broaching his
unsavory portrayal of Mr. Allewinde of *The Macdermots of Ballycloran*,
one of several lawyers who viciously rebut witnesses for professional
necessity rather than the pursuit of truth, as if these caricatures under-
mined Trollope's ability to tell the truth.[6] Trollope adeptly parried Butt's
rebuttal with crowd-pleasing repartee, yet Butt's acerbic manner still
vexed him. Butt seems to have personified for Trollope how rebuttal
formally instantiates and institutionalizes the indecorous presumption
that witnesses are duplicitous and partial. Rebuttal routinizes a narrative
practice that adjudicates matters by doubting their witnesses, their characters and narrators, although they oblige the court with testimony and are
not the ones charged with malfeasance. With the institution of cross-

examinations and with lawyers like Butt, everyone involved in a matter becomes subject to doubt.

Trollope later parodied Butt with browbeating barristers such as Mr. Chaffanbrass of *The Three Clerks* (1857), *Orley Farm* (1862), and *Phineas Redux* (1873–74).[7] In *The Three Clerks*, for instance, he writes,

> The usual opening speech was made by the chief man on the prosecuting side, who, in the usual manner, declared 'that his only object was justice; that his heart bled within him to see a man of such acknowledged public utility as Mr. Tudor in such a position; that he sincerely hoped that the jury might find it possible to acquit him, but that – ' And then went into his 'but' with so much venom that it was clearly discernible to all, that in spite of his protestations, his heart was set upon a conviction. (*TC* 472)

However much cross-examination perturbed Trollope, few things resemble rebuttals so much as his own prose style. Not only does his fiction explicitly and consistently subordinate plot to character, as a cross-examination might be said to subordinate what happened to the character of the witnesses recounting such happenings, but many of his novels can be summarized as sustained rebuttals of character testimony: *The Eustace Diamonds*, to be sure, centers on the rebuttal, or the many oblique, gossipy, would-be rebuttals, of Lizzie Eustace; *The Last Chronicle of Barset* assails Josiah Crawley's character until Mrs. Arabin re-emerges with evidence to avert the trial; *Orley Farm* crosses Lady Mason in and out of court; and *The Small House at Allington* and *The Last Chronicle of Barset* subject Lily Dale to the cross-examinations of her mother, uncle, and friends, all of whom question her decision to decline Johnny Eames's proposals.

Butt's surname is even more wonderfully apposite than his nickname: as an adverb, coordinating conjunction, and preposition, *but* occurs frequently in English prose. yet much more frequently in Trollope's novels.[8] *Doctor Thorne, Framley Parsonage, The Small House at Allington*, and *The Eustace Diamonds*, in particular, include *but* about 30 percent more frequently than other nineteenth-century novels do – almost once every one hundred words, often in succession, and often enough as a noun – as in the venomous "but" above or the "whoever explains a 'but'" of my chapter title. *But* is the principle medium of Trollope's narrative rebuttal: it installs doubt into even the most mundane descriptions such that character – morality, truthfulness, and aesthetic interest – seem to be always crossing and under cross-examination in his prose.

Adversatives, including *but*, as well as *then* and *yet*, are the signature ligatures of Trollope's style. In a 1960 article, Hugh Sykes Davies aspires, against prevailing assertions to the contrary, to affirm his "hunch" that Trollope's prose has a distinct "cadence" by registering how often Trollope resorts to the word, and Davies nicely catalogs some ways *but* functions.[9] It can "introduce a qualification or exception." It can "lay bare the perplexities of motives in conflict," imply "the presence of motives not quite conscious" in characters, and "reveal indecision," and in this sense it facilitates Trollope's representation of processes of decision making.[10] It can, moreover, discriminate the difference between a character's "own estimate of himself, and the real estimate." And, finally, it can "point the discrepancy between theory and practice in moral conduct, the almost universal failure to practice what we agree ought to be preached" (Davies 78–80). I collect all of these functions under the rubric of characterization because Trollope privileged character as his highest aesthetic objective; because character connotes an aesthetic unit (a fictional personage) and affect (awkward, interesting, or touching difference) as well as the moral value of manners (tact); and because, in a culture of skepticism and rebuttal, character bears the epistemological burden of the real.

For Trollope – for many Victorians – character was less about interiority than subsequent criticism has insisted and more about tact, a category that yoked manners with aesthetic touch and contact. Often enough, rather than elaborating interiority, Trollope decorously gestures at – touches upon – it. And so R. H. Hutton and other critics genuinely and fittingly appraised Trollope for reproducing the surface of everyday life.[11] Surface matters. Trollope's prose has consistently been accepted as the epitome of referentiality, so transparent a reproduction of everyday life as to appear style-less. But that old saw remains true only if we recognize that Victorian epistemology accommodated its mimetic drive to the socio-moral assumption that people and writing ought not to refer to certain things. Some facts of everyday life simply could not be represented in the form of facts, because doing so would be tacky, if not outright immoral. And so Trollope's impeccable realism owes at least as much to his tact as to the familiarity of his subject matter, his verisimilitude, and the colloquial ease of his allegedly unstylized prose. Adversatives allow Trollope to incorporate *tacenda* (trivial things that ought not to be made public) without disclosing them; they allow Trollope to refer and defer at the same time. Because Trollope's prose was and remains so incredibly taken for granted as the nearest prose comes to transparency, it formally instantiates how integral tactful rebuttal is to modern life.

If Trollope's rebuttal is tactile in its respect and feel for surfaces and tactful in the sense of delicate, it is tactical, too, in Michel de Certeau's sense, because adversatives concomitantly append and diverge, accrete and critique. Preponderant *buts* facilitate the serial production of petty resistance and subtle individuality within the economic, generic, and sociocultural constraints and demands of Trollope's market. Inscribing a serial mutability into everyday life, they reconcile a refractory attitude and a general incommensurability of things with the dual imperative to ease social friction and to generate more writing. Trollope's prose revels in contact – in the frisson between appositive but discrepant objects, abutting but ill-suited things. His brand of realism thus assumes a world defined by unwelcome contingencies, unexpected deviations, and unconventional aspects of the otherwise utterly conventional – but it glosses this friction.

In some respects, Trollope's *but* renders the world of the novel as Georg Lukács describes it: "Art always says 'And yet!' to life. The creation of forms is the most profound confirmation of the existence of a dissonance" between concrete, lived experience and abstract, meaningful totality; "But in all other genres," Lukács explains, "this affirmation of a dissonance precedes the act of form-giving, whereas in the novel it is the form itself."[12] Writing in the Modernist moment, Lukács concludes that the novel therefore "appears as something in process of becoming" (72–3) – a genre with an "ethical intention" (72) rather than a pre-established ethic – in which characters discover that "a mere glimpse of meaning is the highest that life has to offer" (80); but Trollope with his droll disavowal of narrative surprises and secrets, which he disparages as forms of authorial dishonesty, suggests instead that ethical significance and meaning inhere not in epiphanic glimpses but in the tactful articulation of dissonance in the long periods between such glimpses.

There is no imperative here to get beyond a reasonable doubt, for reasonable doubt has become a tacit formal requisite of character. Put another way, prose that perpetually re-instantiates the dissonance of modern life converts dissonance from estrangement, alienation, or felt meaninglessness into character, the embodiment of meaning. I take Trollope's adversative style, then, as the source of what he recounts rather insipidly as "that high character" his novels "may claim to have earned by their grace, their honesty, and good teaching" (*AA* 217). His most aesthetically interesting characters are not good – "dual in character," as he calls them, they are prone to foibles, inconsistency, and dishonesty – but his prose style, as a performative medium of character, is tactical and tactful in that it touches upon but does not expose and shame this badness.

And so I submit Trollope's style as a prescient example of what Eve Kosofsky Sedgwick imagined as reparative reading.[13] John Ruskin's 1864 lecture, "Of Kings' Treasuries," identifies "tact or the 'touch-faculty,' of body and soul ... fineness and fullness of sensation, beyond reason" as both the principle aesthetic benefit of close reading and the principle character-ological failing of modern Britons.[14] By attending to the tact of Trollope's form, I aim to recover a particular historical manifestation of character as well as a readerly posture or attitude that was reasonably doubtful but neither priggish nor paranoid, committed to knowledge in the form of exposition rather than "knowledge in the form of exposure" (Sedgwick 138).

Tactical Description: Tact, Friction, and Everyday Life

Adorno describes tact in *Minima Moralia* as the dialectic frisson between emergent individualism and the residual conventions of absolutism, the coexistence of the liberal subject and residual "forms of hierarchical respect and devotion" that were bearable because "divested" of "force";[15] and this coincidence of ostensibly innocuous, residual conventionalities and rebarba-tive individualism aptly captures Trollope's political sentiments as they are personified by characters such as Archdeacon Grantly, who comfortably pairs Toryism with incorrigible independence.[16] For Amanda Anderson, this ambivalent portrayal of sincerity as both a characterological virtue and a disembodied form of liberal critique signifies his "modernity."[17] But "modernity" is embodied in "character," which comprehends for Trollope an irreconcilable tension between recalcitrant psychology and obsessive attachments to moral principles that are depicted to be no longer tenable (512) – comprehends, in other words, the problem of tact.

At the end of the eighteenth century, Dugald Stewart called tact "a quick perception of those delicate shades in character and manners, which are objects of study to the man of the world."[18] Tact was not all delicacy, though, for it mediated what Victorians called "friction." Noting the coincidence of the French "tact" with "the English prover-bial expression of *feeling one's way*," Stewart perceives what became a constitutive feature of nineteenth-century character: the manners negotiating the friction between individuals and their contingent mate-rial and social contexts. In 1843 *Chambers' Edinburgh Journal* describes tact accordingly as "a high polish produced on the surface of a man's character by constant friction with the world."[19] Stewart's notion of tact became a substantial attribute of character in Victorian discourse, where it retains its etymological affiliations with physical touch. Samuel Smiles calls tact "an intuitive art of manner, which carries one through a difficulty better than either talent or knowledge."[20] He presents tact as a principal characterological virtue, which one acquires almost osmotically from social contact (from domestic life and from business training), as well as a principal medium of characterization: both *Character* and *Self-Help* periodically suggest that "contact" with character produces character.

As if evoking Newman's definition of the gentleman as a medium of putting others at their ease, like an easy chair or comfortable fire, a similar 1866 article in *The Saturday Review* affirms tact is "the faculty of moving through the word without friction."[21] This tact, whose most salient expression was paradoxically a lubricity that all but eliminated the very friction by which it was occasioned, had its stylistic correlative in adversative turns of phrase that concomitantly register and reduce the frisson between different orders of actuality and expectation, individuality and society, and the other frictions endemic to fiction. Here tact and tactics coincide: the accretive but differential power of the adversative eases the addition of more prose by chaffing it with the friction of qualifying clauses. Consider *The Small House at Allington*, for instance: it introduces the Great House and its eponymous appurtenance with a litany of *buts* that suggests that their composite environmental and architectural details somehow do not make sense with those that precede them: "But the house itself," "there was but one window on your right hand," "but the others had been put in without regard to uniformity," "but these also were mullioned," "but this," "But outside the gardens," "but not on that account," "but I fancy," "but there is an inner gate," "but the stables" (*SHA* 7–9). This pattern segues into a reluctant sketch of the parish church: "upon the whole things were not quite as I would have had them," the narrator explains, "But, nevertheless, the place looked like a church" (10). Unlike Barthes's "reality effect" and other mimetic concepts of realism, Trollope's grammar generates the effect of realness by describing things – houses, gardens, walks, proposals, finances, elections, dinners, faces, weather – not as he supposes readers might expect them to be but slightly, even disappointingly, differently. In their profusion, adversatives diffuse graduated divergences within and between everything: they contribute to the "internal discrepancies" Christopher Herbert observes in Trollope's obsession with "caste gradations";[22] to the Darwinian, "aleatory variations and modifications" that, for George Levine, allow Trollope to survive despite "narrow plot conventions";[23] and to the "gradualness" that Roger Slakey notes in Trollope's changes.[24] Adversatives make discrepancies almost mechanically reproducible, suiting Trollope's "determination to excel, if not in quality, at any rate in quantity" (*AA* 122).

If the iterative property of this grammar affirms the propulsiveness of Horkheimer and Adorno's repetitive culture industry,[25] Trollope's pride in celerity and quantity also invokes the "quickness" ascribed to tact by Stewart, Smiles, and the periodicals. *Chambers'* says tact "is never confounded, never at a stand-still, never idle. It acts while others think, performs while others plan, has finished before others begin" (1). *The Saturday Review*, which maintains that "It is impossible to possess tact without possessing an insight into the character and feelings of one's fellow-men" (325), likewise asserts that this faculty is only maintained by constant exercise: "Tact, as its name implies, is only a fine touch, and the fineness of the touch diminishes at it ceases to be refined by constant employment and occupation. All the knowledge of character and of the world which one adds to one's store as one increases in age does not make up for the declension of sensibility" (325). Trollope counted words and esteemed "rapidity of production": "I believe," he writes, "that the work which has been done the quickest has been done the best" (*AA* 174). He deemed revision a "waste of time" and evoked a Byronic notion of spontaneous, masculine intuition: "if a man knows his craft with his pen, he will have learned to write without the necessity of changing his words or the form of his sentences" (135).[26]

Maintaining social fluidity – "live and let live," as Poppins says in *The Struggles of Brown, Jones, and Robinson*[27] – accrues a kind of moral credit even when it involves depravity. As *Chambers'* puts it: "Tact, accordingly, is rewarded for his pains by something more substantial than a sense of patriotism; and although his principles are not always to be spoken of with approbation, we may fairly allow that his tact in going *with*, instead of going *against*, the stream of popular wants and wishes, is an evidence of no mean judgment and spirit" (1). *The Saturday Review* likewise separates tact from morality, as if it were a social sensibility that somehow transcended ethical questions, and forwards it as movement or productivity:

> it is not a virtue, nor, on the other hand, is it a vice. Like many other faculties, it takes its moral hue from the circumstances of each case; but it does not of necessity imply any state of moral character at all. It is solely and purely a capacity of getting easily along, and of managing the idiosyncrasies and peculiarities of those among whom our lot is cast. (325)

Putatively as neutral, then, as the modern fact, tact connoted a kind of social objectivity that permitted one to touch on the world lightly, without being overly impressed or affected in return. So Smiles calls tact "an intuitive art of manner, which carries one through a difficulty better than either talent or knowledge" (248). Like many others, Smiles routinely describes tact as feminine and extends its purview beyond sympathy and discretion to apprehending reality at large. Henry James follows suit, for example, in valorizing Trollope's feminine touch: "women ... hold their noses close, as it were, to the texture of life. They feel and perceive the real with a kind of personal tact."[28] For James, Trollope's famously "great apprehension of the real" (5) owes to the tact of his fictions in addition to their mimetic or graphic verisimilitude: "he *felt* all daily and immediate things as well as saw them" (3). Hence, James intuits the link between Trollope's characterological tact and his realist affect: "the essence of this love of reality was his extreme interest in character" (4).

Character is known through rebuttal, and adversatives regularly enunciate actual scenes of character rebuttal in Trollope's novels. The narrator of *Barchester Towers*, for example, rebuts Mr. Arabin's self-reflection (itself flush with adversatives) about whether he loves Mrs. Bold, the widowed daughter of Mr. Harding: "But here he did not answer honestly. It was and ever had been his weakness to look for impure motives for his own conduct" (317). This rebuttal is tactful, however, inasmuch as it is qualified by a clause redeeming Arabin from his own scruples: "Eleanour's fortune put all such difficulties out of the question; but it was equally without doubt that his love for her had crept upon him without the slightest idea on his part that he could ever benefit his own condition by sharing her wealth" (317). *The Warden* dubs Archdeacon Grantly, "the reverend cross-examiner" (158), for he interrogates his father-in-law upon his resignation and his niece upon her alleged intimacy with Mr. Slope.

Obstinate contradictions and somewhat inexplicable refusals are a related staple in Trollope's fiction, where adversatives are performative agents of ambivalent politics. Grantly maintains his endearing belligerence against the Proudie party and against his son's equally defiant love for poor Miss Crawley. Mr. Harding disavows his sinecure as warden of Hiram's Hospital and turns down the deanship of Barchester, which he defers to his son-in-law to-be, Mr. Arabin, whom he must interrupt, "But! but! but –," to announce these plans (*BT* 490). This echoes the extraordinarily adversative discussion of the plans with Grantly. Harding says, "'No,' Slope has not been made Dean, "but –." Grantly replies: "But what?" The exchange proceeds with each of Harding's diffident *buts* redoubling "a modesty which almost prevented his speaking," until Grantly dissents with an incredulous, "But me no buts" (453–54). Is Trollope's tongue in his cheek here? He seems to parody his own style. Equally intractable, Johnny Eames remains jealous of Adolphus Crosbie, his rival for Lily Dale, even as Lady Julia invalidates it: "But I am – all the same" (*LCB* 343). Compare Josiah Crawley's refusal of charity and a lawyer; Lizzie Eustace's refusal to return the diamonds or to confess to misappropriating them; Alice Vavasor's double refusal of George and jilting of John Grey; and Lily Dale's chronic, infamous rejection of Johnny Eames and her rejection of Crosbie, who also jilts her. Lily eventually refuses marriage altogether. This negotiation between cross-examination and modesty is a grammatical performance of tact and, writ large, it is the source of the character-effect of Trollope's fiction.

The skeptical rebuttal and adversative obstinacy surely contribute to a liberal politics marked by insistent, willful individualism and a concomitant, almost pathological adaptability. Trollope's characters abuse and resist the way of the world even as they tactfully submit to it. *Framley Parsonage*,[29] for instance, frames ecclesiastic politics and economics: questioning whether Britons should pay for "ecclesiastical work . . . according to its quantity and quality," the narrator weighs the options on adversative fulcrums as if modeling Mill's liberal deliberation:

> but, nevertheless, one may prophesize that we Englishmen must come to this, disagreeable as the idea undoubtedly is. . . . but we know that we do so by the force of our prejudices, and not by our judgment. . . . But are there not other attributes very desirable – nay, absolutely necessary – in respect to which this time-honoured, picturesque arrangement is so very deficient? (*FP* 186)

Less than a process of logical progression, these scenes of thinking in action tend to portray various ideas neither as epiphanies nor as logical developments, but as adjacent alternatives that rub against each other until smooth. Thus, Mr. Arabin tells Eleanor, "It is the bane of my life that on important subjects I acquire no fixed opinion. I think, and think, and go on thinking; *and yet* my thoughts are running ever in different directions" (*BT* 463, emphasis added).[30] Mr. Arabin feels his way through sequentially abutting incidents, ideas, circumstances, and sensations.

Such tact requires an idiom of adjacency that allows for touching upon abutting matters without explicating or rationalizing their awkward relationship or coexistence. To wit, Mark Robarts's discomfited disclosure of the many accommodation bills he has put his name to for Sowerby: "Only to one; *and then* to that same renewed, or not exactly to that same, *but* to one which stands for it" (*FP* 238). Here Robarts's explanation of his own indebtedness reproduces the very logic of supplementarity underlying modern money as a paper substitute for a substantial substitute (gold or sterling) for some abstract value (demand, labor, cost, time, risk). At stake in this sequence of inadequate representations is of course the persistent correlation between a character's financial credibility and his personal creditability, his actions and his reputation and his intuited sense of his own value or self.

Whatever Trollope's distaste for legal rebuttal, then, his fiction marshals rebuttal as its privileged mode of characterization and its conventional mode of producing fictional "evidence," its habitual mode of cognition and representation.[31] *Doctor Thorne*, Trollope's most popular novel and the one which he takes up in *An Autobiography* to denigrate novels that privilege plot over character, foregrounds *but* by making it an explicit subject of narrative speculation (*AA* 125–26). Frank Gresham's proposal to Mary, which assumes the syntactic pattern (described in Chapter 3) of subjunctives punctuated by adversatives that negate or temper these suppositions, comes in a string of *buts*. Much like Dickens's *as if* in its conditionality, this syntactic paradigm formalizes discordance as the constitutive feature of character: "'My father I hope will approve of [the marriage],'" Frank first says; "that my mother should disapprove of it is a misfortune which I cannot help; but on this point I will take no answer from my father or mother; the question is one too personal to myself."[32] Differentiating "personal" feeling from the agonistic, homogenizing demands of society, this first *but* asserts Frank's prerogative as a liberal subject with "personal" matters free from parental determination. More *buts* follow: "Mary," Frank continues, "if you say that you will not, or cannot return my love, I will go away; – not from here only, but from Greshamsbury" (*DT* 394–95). This petulant, adolescent *but* promises – thinly – a Romantic abandonment of his inheritance and society altogether.

But an inexplicable and all-explaining *but* then intervenes:

> The poor fellow got so far, looking apparently at the donkey ears, with hardly a grasp of hope in his voice, and he so far carried Mary with him that she paused for a moment, and then looking up into her face, he spoke but one word more. "But," said he – and there he stopped. It was all clearly told in that "but." This would he do if Mary would declare that she did not care for him. If, however, she could not bring herself so to declare, then was he ready to throw his father and mother to the winds; then would he stand his ground; then would he look all other difficulties in the face, sure that they might finally be overcome. (*DT* 395)

This last "but" – prequalified as "but one word more" – tactfully condenses his hope that Mary will likewise dismiss these obstacles; it touches on an array of emotions, contingencies, and improbable possibilities that even the narrator only touches upon. Couched in the conditional "If . . . then . . . then" syntax, the all-telling *but* marks a realism defined by its rejection of probability and its preference for syllogistic, hypothetical fictions over the harshness of mimetic description; it marks a realist liberalism defined by the assertion of individual will against manifold, residual material and social constraints. Frank rhetorically rebuts all of his hypothetical propositions and implies that if Mary would do the same for him, then life would take a different turn altogether. Frank does not articulate the details of that turn, perhaps because he is afraid to hope for such a response, perhaps because they exceed his expectations, perhaps because it would be a touch presumptuous, and perhaps because his joy would be generically beyond words. The all-telling *but* therefore figures how the hypothetical case of Mary reciprocating Frank's love is generically supposed to exceed representation and realistic possibility: it condenses, among other things, the way lived experience depends on hypothetical fictions and yet also the way it reserves the right to reject these fictions, however probable they may be. Of course, nothing could be more ordinary or generic in Trollope's fiction than such wild gestures: Major Grantly, for one, risks the same with his love of Grace Crawley in *The Last Chronicle of Barset*. This syntax evidences how character formation was articulated precisely as a (generic) rebuttal of generic assumptions and demands.

Doctor Thorne also thematizes the discordances between the impulses of interiority and the reasonable dictates of social possibility. Mary's father, Doctor Thorne, has democratic tendencies and a proud investment in his profession, but he also proudly adheres to tradition, celebrates his ancient name and relation to the Thornes of Ullathorne, and respects the Greshams for their blood. With a similar "spirit of democracy," Mary likewise values "the inner reality" of gentlefolk according to "absolute, intrinsic, acknowl-edged, individual merit" at the same time as she nevertheless values the aristocratic establishment (*DT* 93). The paradoxical political sentiments of the primary characters thus reproduce the characters' formal relation to their own interiority, to others, and to the abstract social world. Everything in this novel is inflected by tact as Adorno describes it. Mary explains this funda-mental tension and her love in a pithy passage:

> Money – money; and he is to sell himself for money! Oh, Trichy! do not you talk about money. It is horrible. But, Trichy, I will grant it – I cannot marry him; but still, I love him. He has a name, a place in the world, and fortune, family, high blood, position, everything. He has all this, and I have nothing. Of course I cannot marry him. But yet I love him. (433)

Mary differentiates the reality of her love by figuring it as contrary to all of the generic categories of marriageability. Mary's love counts as real because she articulates it, as Frank articulates his own love, as autonomous in its rebuttal of what "all the world" thinks. Its rebuttal of the cultural and material conditions of Greshamsbury life signifies its emotional credibility, its genuine "character."

Formal resistance to probability comes to the fore in *The Small House at Allington* when Mrs. Dale's brother-in-law recommends Johnny Eames as a husband for Lily. The passage, like Frank's proposal to Mary in *Doctor Thorne*, generates its aesthetic torque by accreting and rationalizing conditional possibilities only to undercut them, with a "but," as nevertheless impossible:

> Every word that the squire said was true. It *would* be a healing of wounds most desirable and salutary; an arrangement advantageous to them all; a destiny for Lily most devoutly to be desired – *if* only it *were* possible. Mrs. Dale firmly believed that if her daughter *could* be made to accept John Eames as her second lover in a year or two all *would* be well. Crosbie *would* then be forgotten or thought of without regret, and Lily *would* become the mistress of a happy home. *But* there are positions which cannot be reached, though there be no physical or material objection in the way. It is the view which the mind takes of a thing which creates the sorrow that arises from it. *If* the heart *were* always malleable and the feelings *could* be controlled, who *would* permit himself to be tormented by and of the reverses which affection meets? Death *would* create no sorrow; ingratitude would lose its sting; and the betrayal of love *would* do no injury beyond that which it might entail upon worldly circumstances. *But* the heart is not malleable; nor will feelings admit of such control. (*SHA* 546–47; my emphasis)

Just as Frank Gresham's character cannot be predicted, Lily Dale's character cannot be adapted to circumstances or to the desires of readers and characters, even when – indeed, precisely because – there are no reasonable impediments to such adaptation. Lily cannot choose how to feel, to be sure, and feeling in Trollope's prose comes as an effect of unreasonable difference or friction. Later, when Johnny Eames proposes, Mrs. Dale feels, "It might be that such opportunity would avail him of nothing, but not the less should he have it of right, seeing that he desired it. But yet Mrs. Dale did not dare to get up and leave the room" (*SHA* 593). Such passages present their subject worlds as grammatically incongruent with any one character's wishes, incongruent with the narrator's or readers' wishes, incongruent with how things ought to be. Like a loose baggy monster of a secret subject, Trollope's reality contradicts or resists every character's and narrator's estimation of it.

Lily Dale might refute "all the world" most adamantly of all. She finalizes her rejection of matrimony with "But I insist" (*LCB* 353) and anchors her vacillating inclinations by inscribing "old maid" into her diary. The act emblematizes the epistemological effect of Trollope's adversatives to the extent that Victorians routinely depicted the real as a disjunction between expectations, possibilities, or abstractions and lived experience.

Lily's diary entry insists she will live out her own script, not the comedy that genres or readers might prescribe for her. Trollope infamously subjected himself to the discipline of a quota in his "taskmaster" of a diary, "with its dates and ruled spaces, its record that must be seen, its daily, weekly demand upon my industry" (*AA* 121, 120), but the exemplary instance of this diary dialectic is Matty Jenkyns' poignant account of her journal in Elizabeth Gaskell's *Cranford* (1851): "My father once made us . . . keep a diary in two columns; on one side we were to put down in the morning what we thought would be the course and events of the coming day, and at night we were to put down on the other side what really had happened."[33] The diary aptly models the non-referential paradigm of realism by which Victorian fiction countered the epistemology of the modern fact. As Mary Poovey explains, matching columns in an accountant's double-entry book formally affirmed his character (his reliability as a merchant): the formal practice or method evoked discipline and the correspondence between columns, that each debit and credit registered (referred to) a transaction, evoked credibility.[34] But the epistemology of character thematized in these diaries and enacted syntactically by Trollope's adversatives ascribes truth to disagreement, to columns – so to speak – that do not correspond. That the columns – or clauses, in the case of adversatives – do not match is what makes Matty's diary and Trollope's sentences feel so real. Sure enough, Matty quickly dismisses her tears with a *but* – "But all this is nonsense, dear!" Melding friction and smoothness, credulity and doubt, compels her to tactfully move on: "I can fancy [marriage] may be a very happy state, and a little credulity helps one on through life very smoothly, – better than always doubting and doubting, and seeing difficulties and disagreeableness in everything" (Gaskell 108).

In Trollope's fiction, events and circumstances defy the very generalizations that they would seem to exemplify: in *Framley Parsonage* the narrator remarks that the London season is usually uneventful for Lady Lufton, "but on this occasion there was a matter of vital import" (202) and Lord Lufton tries to run into Lucy regularly, "but, nevertheless, they had never come together in their old familiar way" (205). Walter Kendrick notes Trollope's "forte" for "saying opposite things at the same time,"[35] and as Frank O'Connor has said, a "favorite device" of Trollope's narrators is "to lead his reader very gently up the garden path of his own conventions and prejudices and then to point out that the reader is wrong."[36] In both cases, this process is not so much a moral rebuke of the reader as the affective drag or friction of everyday experience, a tact for the way the real definitively deviates from our expectations.

Trollope's narrators frequently affect to be obliged to relate things that disagree with their tastes or hopes or experience or leave them quizzical: "But to tell the truth openly and at once" (*FP* 152); "but, to tell honestly the truth in the matter" (*SHA* 40); "but it is not to be supposed that" (*SHA* 40); "but the truth I take to be this" (*SHA* 44); "but what could she do?" (*SHA* 45). The narrator of *The Small House at Allington* admits "It sounds sad, this sentence against her, but I fear that it must be regarded as true" (*SHA* 57); and "it is almost sad to think that such a man might have had the love of either of such girls, but I fear that I must acknowledge that it was so" (*SHA* 58). Like the trope of the "novel without a hero," which many Trollope novels invoke,[37] this posture suggests that the fictions are true because they deviate from what Trollope, the narrator, generic expectations, and readers want. "But audacity," "but yet," "but perhaps," "but never," "but still," "but they," and two instances each of "but though" and "but in truth" (*ED* 366–67) thus temper a passage of less than two pages of *The Eustace Diamonds* as if Trollope were chastening the reader and himself for over confident or rosy predictions. Noting his unappeased partialities, the narrator affects to be an objective, because self-abnegating, witness. Such self-abnegation aligns Trollope's fictions with the epistemological authority of what George Levine has described as "the narrative of scientific epistemology," a narrative paradigm according to which truth is a function of the effacement or subordination of self.[38]

Trollope's prose is so self-abnegating, through and through, that he infamously declaimed style. Good prose for Trollope was not work to the reader, but "intelligible without trouble ... and harmonious" (*AA* 234); it was easy reading or "readable" (349). Rather than generating friction with surprising or otherwise grating truths, the readable realist must ease the edge of truth with a touch of common error. As Trollope puts it in *Thackeray*, "in very truth the realistic must not be true, – but just so far removed from truth as to suit the erroneous idea of truth which the reader may be supposed to entertain."[39] Trollope describes the "natural" as a mode of speech slightly more polished and complete than real conversation and yet something less articulate and polished, less metaphorical, than avowedly literary prose. Frequently noting the presence or absence of a "touch" of this or that in Thackeray's fiction, Trollope describes realism as a kind of tactful mediation between the writer's insightful perception of reality and the readers' faulty but fixed assumptions about reality, a touch of the real tempered by a touch of the readers' misconceptions of it:

> To produce the desired effect the narrator must go between the two. He
> must mount somewhat above the ordinary conversational powers of such

> persons as are to be represented, – lest he disgust. But he must by no means soar into correct phraseology, – lest he offend. The realistic, – by which we mean that which shall seem to be real, – lies between the two, and in reaching it the writer has not only to keep his proper distance on both sides, but has to maintain varying distances in accordance with the position, mode of life, and education of the speakers. (*T* 186)

In practice, Trollope's style maintains this "proper distance," an inoffensive balance, between chafing realities or abrasive principles and blithe acceptance of common misperceptions: tact.

Of course, Trollope has been criticized as routinely as he has been praised for having no style and for being merely a transparent medium of everyday life: in Henry James's famous appraisal, Trollope's "inestimable merit was a complete appreciation of the usual," (James 100–1) and D. A. Miller quipped about a century later that his own critique recapitulated "the usual appreciation of [Trollope's] appreciation of the usual."[40] Recently, Laurie Langbauer has written of the conjunction of everydayness and seriality in Trollope's novels, and in so doing she registers the familiar litany of reports that have ascribed everydayness to Trollope's prose, including observations by Thomas Carlyle, Leslie Stephen, Nathaniel Hawthorne, William Dean Howells, George Eliot, Bernard Shaw, and J. Hillis-Miller.[41] Trollope himself proudly confessed to documenting the ordinary instead of stooping to sensationalism: of *Rachel Ray* he wrote, "I have attempted to confine myself absolutely to the commonest details of commonplace life among the most ordinary."[42] For most of my quotations, I have chosen passages that playfully foreground *but*; however, most of Trollope's *buts* go unnoticed because *but* is only rarely isolated as a noun and most characters and readers know better than to question it. Mocked for "overwhelming floods of conventionality,"[43] Trollope was particularly attuned to the style of everyday speech. His "buts," like most of his prose, seem so conventional, so generic, "almost perversely prosaic" as *The Times* put it,[44] that one naturally takes them for granted and follows Lady Glen's lead in chiding Madame Goesler for questioning them.[45] As Kendrick nicely argues, "Trollope's theory requires, and his novels assert, the complete newness of the only thing in fiction that is not language – character" (71).[46] The style of Trollope's prose directs readers not to see the assumptions on which it relies; it has been registered as a near reproduction of everyday life because it directs readers to see "character," but not the epistemological and rhetorical figures of characterization.[47]

That Trollope's style epitomized unremarkable character for favorable and unfavorable reviewers alike is remarkable, for at the beginning of the century adversatives were the medium not of common characterization but of caustic, ironic, Romantic eccentricity and depravity. Adversatives are a hallmark of Byron's poetry, particularly in *Don Juan* (1819–24), which shares impulsive productivity or serial repetitiveness and ironic narration with Trollope's fiction. *Don Juan* includes ten times the vulgarity of all of Trollope's fiction combined, but its epigram is Horace's *"Difficile est proprie communia dicere* [It is difficult to speak of common subjects in one's own way]": Byron frames the poem as matter of rearticulating and appropriating the familiar. The story of Don Juan is the common subject, but, as just about every critic agrees, the real subject of Byron's version is his speaker, who is preoccupied with quotidian concerns such as hangovers, hand-holding, and sleeping. Adversatives conjoin the quotidian consciousness of the narrator to the story of Don Juan and likewise perform the characteristic disavowals, digressive changes of subject, bathetic and ironic juxtapositions, and contradictory assertions that distinguish Byron's poem. They also articulate the components of complex but common emotions: "This may seem strange, but yet 'tis very common" (402), "Gently, but palpably" (405), "half withheld, and then half-granted" (423), "rather hard, but new" (427), "all timidly, yet rapidly" (469).

Byron famously rebuts his own authority, as Trollope was later blamed for doing in his *Autobiography*: "but what I say is neither here nor there . . . but it would not be fair . . . But scandal's my aversion / For my part I say nothing – nothing – but / *This* I will say . . . but I pass over *that* . . . Knowledge of matters – but no matter *what* . . . But this last simile is trite and stupid" (397–98); "But I have spoken of this already – / And repetition's tiresome and unwise" (464); "But to return" (465); "But to my subject – let me see – what was it?" (492); "But let me to my story" (499); "But I digress" (528); and so on. These adversatives are responsible for the sense of "cumulative" "apposition" that Jerome Christensen calls the "*Juan* effect"; they are the grammar of the poem's "non-mimetic . . . concentration of resemblance and discrepancy" and its worldly "identity rifted by discrepancy."[48] Horkheimer and Adorno argue that the capitalist culture industry encourages "a constant reproduction of the same thing" and insists that "everything has to run incessantly, to keep moving" (134).[49] Byron's aura, or "strength," as Christensen puts it, accrues to his ability to reiterate himself by perfunctorily rebutting his last utterance: "I have no more to say, but linger still, / And dare not set my seal upon this sheet, / And yet I may as well the task fulfill" (430). While Trollope dramatized his industrious morning page limit in his *Autobiography*, Byron's poem advertises his promise to produce a certain number of cantos, however repetitive or tangential that requires him to be; and his adversatives make his additions, tangents, and returns to the subject almost mechanical.

Byron was not alone in capitalizing on the flexibility the adversative affords to character. Mary Shelley's *Frankenstein* (1818), a novel about the discordance between sympathetic interiority and monstrous exteriority, individual greatness and sociable, happy anonymity, initially characterizes Elizabeth Lavenza in a passage replete with adversatives:

> She was docile and good tempered, yet gay and playful as a summer insect. Although she was lively and animated, her feelings were strong and deep, and her disposition uncommonly affectionate. No one could better enjoy liberty, yet no one could submit with more grace than she did to constraint and caprice. Her imagination was luxuriant, yet her capability of application was great. Her person was the image of her mind; her hazel eyes, although as lively as a bird's, possessed an attractive softness. Her figure was light and airy; and, though capable of enduring great fatigue, she appeared the most fragile creature in the world.[50]

Byronic adversatives allow Lavenza to have everything both ways: to be free and submissive, imaginative and practical, delicate and strong – in other words, to be so dynamic as to be beyond classification. Lavenza is adapted to the contingencies of the moment and to the desires of her beholder.

Trollope capitalizes on the same grammar for the same ends. What was the medium of shocking Romantic irony and abrasive individualism in the early 1820s, stripped of its innuendos and intrigues, became the medium of ordinary life in the 1850s, '60s, and '70s. The moral behavior called tact, as it was exhibited by fictional personages and performed by writing that touched upon but did not pry into a world defined by contingency, accommodated the manners requisite to Victorian character to the productivity, adaptation, and irony characteristic of nineteenth-century modernity. Moreover, since the early-modern period, British culture had been recognizing correspondence between representation and reality, appearance and actuality, as knowledge on the moral basis of its credibility, but by the end of the nineteenth century it had come to register discordance as a signature of truth on the moral basis of tact, which presupposed friction instead of order. Trollope's adversative style is a product of and response to these modern moral and epistemic demands.

"Dual in character" and Aesthetic Awkwardness

If Trollope's *but* was a feature of his prose style or exposition in general, he intimates that its motive was "character" not only by using it to animate scenes of character rebuttal but also by recurring to it introductory characterizations of personages and in his metafictional asides on characterization. This conflation of description and characterization is evident in D. A. Miller's incisive observation that Trollope moves the "moderate schism" or "merry warfare" of social and political conflict (plot) "into the constitution of the subject that wages it" (character). For Miller, Trollope's "characters are at war within themselves no less than they are at war with one another, and the implied politics of subjectivity are both isomorphic and continuous with the politics of the social" (124–25).[51] Mary Poovey also examines how Trollope melds characterization and plot in her account of how *The Last Chronicle of Barset* "relocated the complexities that presumably ought to belong inside a psychologized character outside the fictional individual, in the complexities of plot": understanding Josiah Crawley's character necessitates tracking the movements of a check.[52] While Miller shows how fiction internalizes social conflict, disciplining interiority from within, Poovey shows how "distancing conventions" such as Crawley's check, which ultimately matters only as an index of his character, support the fantasy of self-sufficient fiction, independent of the world to which it only seems to refer because these conventions actually refer more to passages within the novel than to actual checks. Both arguments, like Alex Woloch's *The One vs. the Many*,[53] uphold the coextension of individual character with society. But where these studies restrict "character" to personhood (secret subjectivity, personality, moral credibility, or reputation), I want to stress here how Victorians ascribed "character" to things other than people. They were able to do so because characterization was not synonymous with personification, and the tropes associated with each of these rhetorical practices were not all interchangeable.

Much of the work of characterization in his fiction serves to install not interiority but often superficial, though no less important, discordances between the features of any given subject, human or otherwise. Characteristics, for Trollope, tend to be those features of a given thing that disagree with one another. According to his model, character is precisely a function of its incoherence. Consider, for example, the introductory characterization of Amelia Roper. She appears in five see-sawing sentences teetering on "but yet not without," "but then, also," another "but then, also," "but then again," and a final "but then" (*SHA* 47). Likewise, the Dale males: updated by an "invisible magnetism," "not indeed in any case so moving him as to bring him up to the spirit of the age in which he lived, but dragging him forward," the Dales "had been obstinate men . . . but not known to be hard"; "imperious to their wives and children, but imperious within bounds"; "exacting in their ideas as to money . . . and yet not thought to be mean"; "steady supporters of the Church . . . but, nevertheless, the Dales had ever carried on some unpronounced warfare against the clergyman" (*SHA* 5). *Framley Parsonage* similarly introduces Griselda Grantly: she is "decidedly a beauty, but somewhat statuesque in her loveliness. Her forehead was high and white, but perhaps too like marble to gratify the taste of those who are fond of flesh and blood." The sequence of discordances continues:

> but they seldom showed much emotion . . . betrayed but little . . . Her nose was nearly Grecian, not coming absolutely in a straight line from her forehead, but doing so nearly enough to entitle it to be considered as classical . . . but to me she always seemed . . . But the exquisite symmetry of her cheek . . . but it lacked . . . but there were those who thought. (151–52)

Trollope introduces many of his characters similarly, including Plantagenet Palliser and Lord Chiltern (Oswald Standish).[54] Like George Eliot, he is reticent to praise anyone outright, never mind snobbish dimwits like Griselda, but the inconsistencies he delineates do not always temper qualities with faults; they just as often present mismatched alternatives. These mismatches inflect morals, habits, tastes, and mannerisms as well as physique, clothing, houses – everything, including the plot of life itself. His adversatives extend this reticence into exposition of every sort, such that his fiction altogether shares the formal shape of and thereby carries the affective freight of his characters.

A metafictional aside in *The Eustace Diamonds* privileges this grammar of discordance in the form of personages who are "dual in character." The passage favors what we might describe as a performative model of character to a model of character based on fixed identity by defending its "hero," Frank Greystock:

> Within . . . many of us, there is but one person – a man or woman, with a preponderance either of good or evil, whose conduct in any emergency may be predicted with some assurance of accuracy by anyone knowing the man or woman. Such persons are simple, single, and perhaps, generally safe. They walk along lines in accordance with certain fixed instincts or principles, and are today as they were yesterday, and will be tomorrow as they are today. . . . But there are human beings who, though of necessity single in body, are dual in character; – in whose breasts not only is evil always fighting against good, but to whom evil is sometimes horribly, hideously evil, but is sometimes also not hideous at all. (199)

This passage disaggregates moral and essentialist character from aesthetic and performative character by tacitly subordinating predictable personages, whose character – "simple, single, and perhaps, generally safe" – adheres to "fixed instincts or principles," to impulsive personages like

Frank, Glencora, and Goesler, whose capricious instincts and less categorically principled tactics grant them a fetching duality character. Synonymous with "merely," the first adverbial *but* in this passage distinguishes Greystock from those personages with "but one person" in them – characters such as Lucy Morris – even though, and perhaps because, this multiplicity involves "intermittent" devilishness. These modes of character tend to be gendered: Trollope consistently portrays women as having fewer options and less freedom than men, though Glencora and Goesler trespass these limits, and Amelia Roper and Griselda Grantly, as we saw above, have at least superficial duality. Personages like Lucy Morris, "simple, single, and, perhaps, generally safe," walk the banal, prescribed path of typology.

Frank, however, acts unpredictably. He rebuffs the ideal correspondence of theory and practice, appearance and intention, by often acting differently than he has planned or behaving differently than he wants or thinks he ought to do. He instead embodies what Michel de Certeau calls "surreptitious creativities" – ways of misusing or appropriating social infrastructure for one's own ends:[55] in matters big and small Frank dissents willy-nilly from the rules meant to fix his character.[56] He dissents from not only his best interest and his desires and the judgment of "all the world," but also from any essence that might define him. Frank's caprice, teetering between radical disinterestedness and childish impulsiveness, defies the predictability and logic that delimit creditability and sincerity, the qualities ascribed to the correspondence between who a personage "is" who he or she appears to be. Frank is scarcely Trollope's moral paragon or a pet, scarcely a Johnny Eames or even a Harry Clavering, but he exhibits in his wavering a freedom and spontaneous creativity, a charisma even, that is most characteristic of Trollope's prose. His repeated bad decisions to humor his options with Lizzie despite, and indeed because of, his commitments to Lucy exercise his right not to string along women (Trollope clearly denounces that), but to act out of character.

Aptly named, Frank Greystock is an openly – frankly – stock character because of his greyness or indeterminacy. Thus, the excerpt above culminates with a Trollopian rhetorical question about Frank's affable, gentlemanly vulnerability to intuition: "What must a man be who would allow some undefined feeling . . . to interfere with all the projects of his intellect" (200). The answer is, of course, utterly pedestrian: a run-of-the-mill Trollope man. With Frank, Trollope suggests that the primary qualification for character is neither moral probity nor sincerity, nor even immoral sincerity, but defiance of prescription and definition. With Frank,

Trollope joins Elizabeth Bennet in dismissing the Janes and Bingleys of the world on behalf of character defined by friction, resistance to identification. Trollope paradoxically underscores characterizations like these *as generic* by so often concluding them with variants of the hallmark of Theophrastan character types: "Such a one who . . .," "Of such men it is may be said," "Such men – or women may," and "Such a man was Frank Greystock" all follow the passage above, and similar turns of phrase abound in Trollope's oeuvre (199–200; cf. *SHA* 5–6). In Frank, then, Trollope personifies the "dual" character of modern prose, the necessary discord between its aesthetic and epistemological investment in grey areas and the hegemonic moral and epistemological appraisal of straightforward, honest correspondence.

Vanity Fair (1847–48), which was one of Trollope's favorite novels, presents hypocrisy as a fundamental feature of psychologically realistic characters, whether they are moral or immoral, and he employs adversatives to do so. Amelia Sedley "never, never could think of any but—but the husband whom she had lost"; and she hesitates in response to the (inaccurate) news of Dobbin's engagement: "but—but she was very happy indeed."[57] In both passages, em dashes poised between *buts* function as placeholders for withheld, unexpressed content – a feeling or thought that the reader might imagine but which Amelia does not, and that most definitely does not agree with Amelia's explicit statements or conscious admissions. *Vanity Fair* likewise makes "honest Dobbin" interesting only when he is (dishonestly) lying or concealing something his love for Amelia. Formal hypocrisy relieves his tedious uprightness:

> Conducted to the ladies, at the Ship Inn, Dobbin assumed a jovial and rattling manner, which proved that this young officer was becoming a more consummate hypocrite every day of his life. He was trying to hide his own private feelings, first upon seeing Mrs. George Osborne in her new condition, and secondly to mask the apprehensions he entertained as to the effect which the dismal news brought down by him would certainly have on her. (240)

When Thackeray writes of Dobbin "reflecting on his own consummate hypocrisy" (200), he does not impugn him, then, so much as he wryly accentuates the formal hypocrisy requisite to characterological interest. And requisite to politeness, too: tact often calls for the truth to remain unsaid or for an insincere falsehood in its place, to assuage the friction between actuality and the feelings or ideals of a particular character or milieu.[58]

The aesthetics of tact come to the fore in *The Small House at Allington* when Adolphus Crosbie learns from Squire Dale that Lily comes with no dowry, and he has to explain that they must forestall their marriage and live a lifestyle less affluent than that to which he is used. Crosbie wishes to explain still more than that. He begins, "'But now about this business. Perhaps I'd better tell you everything.' . . . 'But then you musn't understand me, and if I talk about money, you musn't suppose that it has anything to do with my love for you'" (*SHA* 125). Crosbie then initiates a tangent that he cuts short, "But, as I was saying – Let me see" (*SHA* 125). He pauses with a hanging "but – ," and his narrator takes over the description of Crosbie's self-reflection in free indirect discourse full of conditionals and *buts*:

> "Yes – all that waiting will be intolerable to me. It is such a bore to a man when he has made up his mind on such a matter as marriage, not to make the change at once, especially when he is going to take to himself such a little angel as you are," and as he spoke these loving words, his arm was again put round her waist; "but—" and then he stopped. He wanted to make her understand that this change of intention on his part was caused by the unexpected misconduct of her uncle. He desired that she should know exactly how the matter stood; that he had been led to suppose that her uncle would give her some small fortune; that he had been disappointed, and had a right to feel the disappointment keenly; and that in consequence of this blow to his expectations, he must put off his marriage. But he wished her also to understand at the same time that this did not in the least mar his love for her; that he did not join her at all in her uncle's fault. All this he was anxious to convey to her, but he did not know how to get it said in a manner that would not be offensive to her personally, and that should not appear to accuse himself of sordid motives. He had begun by declaring that he would tell her all; but sometimes it is not easy, that task of telling a person everything. There are things which will not get themselves told.
>
> "You mean, dearest," said she, "that you cannot afford to marry at once."
>
> "Yes; that is it. I had expected that I should be able, but—." (*SHA* 125–26)

Crosbie's intentions do not correspond with the conditions of his existence: Lily's uncle does not (yet) offer "some small fortune"; and Lily will be offended by his only mode of explaining his motives; and he likes her, though not enough to comprise his financial aspirations. While the free indirect discourse discloses the complexity of Crosbie's thoughts to readers, it implies that this complexity cannot be broached with Lily. The em-dashed *buts* dramatize how Crosbie repeatedly approaches the truth without ever committing it to words, how he repeatedly approaches open conversation with Lily without ever succeeding. The passage does not so much emphasize Crosbie's cowardice and disingenuousness as capitalize on the aesthetic value of awkwardness. The adversative grammar abuts characters at odd angles. "But—" signals that Crosbie understands that the missing fortune ought not "mar" his love for Lily, because it implies that he feels something more needs to be said and yet it does not say it. He cannot reconcile his intentions, his desires, Lily's feelings, and the judgment of "all the world."

Again, Crosbie is no moral paragon, but if his love for Lily is not genuine, his awkwardness in this scene most certainly is; and such awkwardness proves more fundamental to character than straightforward love. As the previous chapter explains, the genuineness of feeling was often indexed to its vagueness. Trollope complements indeterminate pronouns with em-dashed *buts* that leave feelings unsaid not only out of tact but also because leaving them unsaid guarantees their authenticity. This authenticity redounds less to the relative roundness of Crosbie as a character than to the character of the prose itself, which shares the aesthetic of awkwardness. Crosbie ultimately resorts to the passive voice to transfer agency from character to circumstance, as if it were up to *things* to "get themselves told"; and, as the narrator says, "Justice demanded that all this should be understood; but when he came to the telling of it, he found that the story would not form itself properly" (*SHA* 126). The noise that interrupts Crosbie's intentions, that rebuts his character, cannot both remain tactful and become explicit. But it evokes character precisely to the extent that it cannot be properly expressed in direct prose.

Tactful Rebuttal, Reparative Reading

The stuttered utterance of dashed *buts* – a paradigmatic feature of what Trollope calls "the ordinary talk of ordinary people" or "the slovenly inaccuracy of ordinary talkers" (*AA* 240) – often allows characters to intimate a sensitive, discreditable, more palpable than knowable, or otherwise ineffable subtext. Take *The Three Clerks* (1857), for example. In a climactic early scene, Gertrude Woodward discloses to her mother that she does not love her cousin Harry Norman, who loves her and whom her mother loves: "'Oh, mamma, I would not abuse him for worlds – I know how good he is, I know you love him, but, but – ' and Gertrude, though very little given to sobbing moods, burst into tears" (*TC* 137). Mrs. Woodward comforts her and asks what she means by this irrational resistance. Gertrude replies, "I know what you mean; I know what you wish; but – but – but, oh, mamma, you must not – must not, must not think of it anymore" (137). However aphasic, each "but – " solicits sympathy: the knowledge they articulate only can exist as tacit sympathy between these characters; it cannot be identified as an attribute of either individually.[59] Though each "but – " gestures at a tacit emotion or reason for turning Norman down, they function as appeals to Mrs. Woodward for the kind of indulgent understanding that does not require explanation. Appeals to Mrs. Woodward and appeals to the reader: once again they assume, like Mr. Brooke's "that sort of thing," that we are in the know and do not need to be (re-)told the full story. Gertrude need not expose herself for us to understand her.

Together, Gertrude's *buts* mark the threshold of what can be expressed comfortably and conventionally: that is, they touch upon a subject and establish tacit understanding without fully exposing it. Gertrude cannot denigrate Harry's impeccable character without resorting to the English *je-ne-sais-quoi, something*, that I describe in the previous chapter, or to the coarse language of her Uncle Bat, who distinguishes Alaric Tudor, her future husband, for the "gumption" that Harry lacks. The truncated adversative clauses allow Gertrude to admit that Harry's relative lack of moxie and savoir-faire matters more to her than do the constancy and scruples he possesses without saying as much and thereby shaming Harry (as a wet blanket) and herself (as one who prefers aesthetic to moral character). When Gertrude does reject Harry, Trollope assumes her style (without the sobs) and refuses to touch the awkward scene: "And so we will leave them," he says; "who could describe the intense discomfiture of that tea-party, or paint in fitting colours the different misery of each one there assembled?" (*TC* 142). Harry leaves early to visit his parents, "but the subject, by tacit consent, was allowed to pass all but unnoticed" (147). Characters and narrators alike exhibit character not by putting anyone's interiority on exhibition, then, but by having the tact to refuse to do so even as they demonstrate that nothing has passed "unnoticed."

Such tact, the equanimity of noticing everything without noting anything untoward, is idealized in the presumed legibility of modern (post-revolutionary) gentility: the gentility of a real gentleman, Trollope well believed, needed no explanation.[60] And Trollope certainly promotes tact as what Audrey Jaffe has described as "the intuitive quality of gentlemanly knowledge."[61] But this tact arises most magnificently in a cameo exchange between Lady Glencora Palliser and Madame Max Goesler in *The Eustace Diamonds*, wherein Lady Eustace's character and the attitude Glencora and Goesler maintain toward that character coalesce in the word *but*:

> "But surely Lady Eustace is very pretty."
> "Yes; – she's very pretty! nay more, she is quite lovely
>   to look at. And she is clever – very. And she is rich –
>   very. But – "
> "Well, Lady Glencora. What does your 'but' mean?"
> "Who ever explains a 'but'? You're a great deal too
>   clever, Madame Goesler, to want any explanation.
>   And I couldn't explain it."[62]

With its suggestive dash, Glencora's "But – " implies the unutterable though obvious truth that Lady Eustace has indeed purloined the diamonds she has been accused of stealing and that she is, among other things, a monstrous liar and a walking scandal. It touches upon without actually disclosing Lizzie's flirtatiousness. Implicit in the exchange is that openly avowing Lizzie's shortcomings would diminish Glencora's character as much as Lady Eustace's. She adheres to the belated injunction not to "give the lie" to a member of one's own class.[63] The novel elsewhere underscores this convention when Georgiana Fawn reminds Lucy Morris, who accuses Lord Fawn of belittling her fiancé Frank Greystock, that "in accordance with all rules of good breeding . . . people never accuse each other of untruth. No lady should use such a word to a gentleman" (*ED* 283).[64] However much Trollope openly decries lying, however much he seems to elevate Lucy as a moral touchstone, his aesthetic investment clearly lies with discretion and so Glencora personifies his prose habits, his privilege of manner over matter, behavior over identity or factual truth.

Like Gertrude Woodward with her mother, Glencora also relies upon the intimacy she shares with Goesler and, in turn, knowing readers of Trollope's fiction. Glencora need not explain her "but – " to a friend who knows her as well as Goesler knows her or to readers like us: the intimacy cultivated and implied by suggestive *buts* eludes the moral imperatives to candor that Trollope otherwise espouses. The gestural "but –" suggests that there is "something more" to Lizzie's character and indeed more to Glencora's relationship to Lizzie than meets the eye; it intimates a tangle of generically ineffable interiorities delimited by their constitutive secrecy. For Glencora to explain her "but – " would oblige her to disclose not only her judgment of Lizzie but also her sympathies with her. We might speculate that she uneasily admires Lady Eustace's dazzling duplicity; that she admires her willful refusal to succumb to the pressures of the world that pressured her into her first marriage. We might, moreover, surmise that Glencora senses in this defiance a touch of Goesler and of herself, two notably strong-willed women, and a touch too of an alternative self-gone-wrong: a Glencora who had the courage to run off with Burgo Fitzgerald for love instead of pragmatically marrying Plantagenet. Despite her magnificent wealth, does she sympathize with Lady Eustace's tenuous hold on property, a metonym for the inadequate property rights of women? What, then, is Lizzie but an exaggerated species of Lady Glen? Or of the genially rebarbative Archdeacon Grantly, the insufferable Mrs. Proudie, gruff Sowerby, or grasping Mr. Slope, all of whose appeal inheres in their friction with others rather than their often spurious morality?

Glencora cannot tastefully go so far as to applaud Lady Eustace, but her allegedly inexplicable "but –" touches on her affinities with her even as it also convicts her of promiscuity and mendacity. Glencora thus behaves like a surrogate "reparative" reader of the sort Eve Sedgwick imagines in *Touching Feeling*. Although Glencora already knows – and knows Goesler already knows – all about Lady Eustace's deviance and repute, she does not act as if rehashing that foreknowledge and reduplicating Lizzie's shame would constitute some novel information or insight for her or Goesler. An explicit recapitulation of Lizzie's shame would, like the "paranoid" reading practices Sedgwick regrets, only recapitulate what they already know. Without letting Lizzie off the hook, without either forgetting or foregrounding Lizzie's faults, Glencora's "but – " seems to "confer plenitude" on her, as if to suggest that in her deviance she offers something back, a reflection of the very gumption that makes Glencora herself so appealing (Sedgwick 144–49). Rather than recycling the suspicions she shares with "all the world" so as to shame the woman whose shame everybody already knows, Lady Glencora pauses here to admit of the possibility of assuming a reparative position whereby she might admire the richness of Lizzie Eustace that "all the world," except Frank Greystock and the narrator, are prone to ignore or subordinate to obvious moral concerns.

Given that the affinities between Glencora and Lizzie remain unwritten conjectures, to some extent Trollope literalizes how the open secret, as D. A Miller says, is that there is no secret interiority after all. Goesler – who, *Phineas Finn* (1869) assures us, will touch "anything near your heart" if anything is there[65] – checks the conventional silence on the matter of Lizzie Eustace by asking her friend to make explicit the referential content of an unfinished clause whose function is to defer content and keep it secret. She threatens not only to force exposure of the kinds of explanations I have imagined, but also to belie the pre-eminence of form over content, manner over knowledge, in matters of character. Explaining the *but* would fracture the constitutive opacity of everyday life, the opacity that made reviewers so readily align Trollope's fiction with the everyday. As Laurie

Langbauer explains, "The opacity of the everyday is crucial: it reflects the poststructural recognition that all anyone can do is gesture to the real; subjects can't experience it unmediated and untransformed by expectation, by representation, by their own attention to it" (20). For Langbauer, "Trollope's novels define the everyday not as the real ... but as a medium, a formal quality. The everyday is not so much the province of a certain social position or class, but the culture that fosters them, the glue that holds them together" (96–97). Colloquial figures such as Lady Glencora's adversative contribute to this glue. They give Trollope's prose the feel of reality because they reproduce the very specific form of touching that reality.[66] For Lady Glencora fully to explain her "but – " would be for her either to commit – to admit to her regrets, say about Burgo, or to commit to a feeling for the injustice of the world's treatment of Lizzie – and thereby fix her character to a set of positions, or to confess to the fictionality of identity, to explain the inability for character to be known because it is only a mercurial abstraction used to stand in for a performance always subject to change. This exchange suggests that character inhered in formal deferral rather than the various implied contents that any *but* might defer. The tactful turn of the *but* redounds credit upon the reader for already being in the know and too discreet to need to read its clause completed.

Glencora's "but – " reproduces the posture many readers have had toward characters such as Thackeray's fabulously roguish Becky Sharp, whom Trollope found intriguing and who influenced Lizzie Eustace. In *An Autobiography*, he characterizes *The Eustace Diamonds* in relation to Becky and with a splendid sequence of *buts*:

> But *The Eustace Diamonds* achieved the success ... not as a love-story, but as a record of a cunning little woman of pseudo-fashion, to whom, in her cunning, there came a series of adventures, unpleasant enough in themselves, but pleasant to the reader. ... the idea constantly presented itself to me that Lizzie Eustace was but a second Becky Sharpe; but in planning the character I had not thought of this, and I believe that Lizzie would have been just as she is though Becky Sharpe [*sic*] had never been described. (344)

Indeed, Lizzie might well have been the same without Becky precisely because she is but another Becky, a serial reproduction of the model of character popularized in *Don Juan* and diffused throughout Trollope's prose, a character often "unpleasant enough" to other personages "but pleasant to the reader." Of course Becky would be an awful person. Yet she makes a capital character. Trollope recognizes Becky's friction as readers' pleasure: for him, fiction replicates tact in its translation of abrasiveness into polish. The tact is so catching that it enables him to deflect his own awkward sense of cloning Becky Sharp.

Ayelet Ben-Yishai nicely delineates how the Glencora and Goesler "function in the novel purely as spectator-commentators."[67] She traces how characters discuss facts as positivist, empirical knowledge even as they practice "communal knowledge – otherwise known as gossip" (99), and explains how "the 'truth' in which one believes – the set of facts on which one draws to form an opinion – aligns the believer with one community or another" in the novel (Ben-Yishai 114). Yet, if *The Eustace Diamonds* or any other novel produces knowledge, beyond thematically representing "different processes of fact-making" (89), it does not produce facts, which are definitively supposed to be value-neutral, however validated any particulars are by the consensus of communities of gossip like "all the world"; it produces style. Goesler flirts with the imperatives of facticity when she demands an explanatory predicate to complete Glencora's conjunction, an object to correspond to her gestural clause, but Lady Glen knows she operates in a different domain of knowledge: she comfortably inhabits a world adept at subordinating content to form – a world not so unlike our own as we might like to think. Contrary to the fact confirmed by gossipy consensus, the epistemic validity of style is an effect of its departure from regular forms of understanding. The genius of Trollope's style is that it manages to make such departures reproducible and regular. Trollope's style, Lady Glen's tact: it makes knowledge out of refusals to predicate or expose the truth; it counters the referential impulse of realism with the assumption that truth inheres in fiction precisely to the extent that fiction marks a departure, deviation, or disagreement with expectation as Lady Glen disagrees with "all the world" in their public critique of Lizzie.

An Autobiography shares George Augustus Sala's description of Trollope as "pugnacious," if "somnolent," with "nothing of the bear but his skin, but whose ursine envelope was assuredly of the most grisly texture" (149), and Trollope's style epitomizes this vicarious assertion, the grizzly texture of "The Rebutter." The "ursine envelope" is an apt metaphor for his style, which is abrasive and yet soft, and less interested in content than in its form. Given Ruskin's affiliation of tact and reading, we might consider what Trollopian rebuttal might offer modern critics wary of skeptical hermeneutics. Trollope's style addresses how to inhabit a depth epistemology, grounded in exposing what lies beneath the surface, without making a habit of repetitively exposing the same sordid secrets. He no doubt populates his novels with unseemly behavior, but he cannot help but defend the most unpleasant of his subjects. He relentlessly defends even Mrs. Proudie. Sedgwick has proposed a "textural" aesthetic as the complement or antidote to the symptomatic reading (13–17, 123–51). With his adversatives, Trollope models an affective relation to a world that was more than comfortable inhabiting surfaces. His fiction revels in surficial contact between things as varied as windows and noses and vicars and undesirable narrative events, in awkward social encounters and touchy subjects.

For Sedgwick, "the prohibitive problem" in developing reparative reading "has been in the limitations of present theoretical vocabularies rather than in the reparative motive itself" (150), yet perhaps Trollope presents a practical vocabulary ready to hand: his prose makes visible the tact in the conjunctions by which we accumulate narrative and evidence, attach ourselves to others and to objects. Trollope's style mediates the affective texture of Victorian life by foregrounding its relations rather than the supposedly private properties of its objects and entities. Recognizing without muckraking secret subjectivity, the adversative accommodates friction so as to enable "additive and accretive" description; it enables the likes of Lady Glencora to "confer plenitude" on the likes of Lady Eustace, however obviously "inadequate and inimical" they may be, and thus to suggest Lady Eustace and all her avatars, all the imperfect artifacts of life, have "resources to offer" other than confirmations of our paranoid suspicions of their open secrets (Sedgwick 149). Trollope's style offers us a grammar of criticism that can limn critique and affirmation, scepticism and productivity. Foregrounding mediation, it offers a way of characterizing texts, rebutting them and touching them in terms of their manner of relation to the world, rather than browbeating them for their hidden content or delineating positivist predicates for what they only suggest or make possible. In place of the anticipatory logic of mimesis that prescribes what the world is like, Trollope's prose affectively responds to its subjects as if they always prove surprisingly different than he suspected.

"Our Universal 'But'": Retouching Mrs. Grundy

I make my evidentiary claims here, as I have throughout this book, on the simultaneous prevalence and non-eventfulness of an everyday idiom: Trollope only exaggerates an idiomatic tic and posture that already permeated his culture to a lesser degree. What Victorians said about tact also obtained for "character" in popular discourse. Writing of Samuel Smiles, Stefan Collini affirms that "the language of character could produce a certain *frisson*; it allowed a vicarious form of self-assertion, a public affirmation of one's own worth in the face of a daily experience of the condescension of the well-born and well-connected."⁶⁸ And the colloquial import of *but* as a medium of this characterological "frisson" did not go entirely unnoticed.

Trollope's preoccupation with *but* was noticeable enough to Victorians to be appropriated at least twice: Characterizing Trollope, Alexander Smith's "Novels and Novelists of the Day" in the *North British Review* – either by generic imperative or by witty parody – employs a series of *buts* to characterize the indecipherability of Trollope's fiction and everyday life:

> His mind presents no very salient point, it possesses no very special characteristic. He is witty, *but* not supremely so; he has humour, *but* no one would ever dream of speaking of him as a humourist; he can laugh at the follies in our social arrangements, *but* he is not a satirist; he can moralize prettily enough, *but* he has no claim to be a teacher; he can turn a sentence or an epigram with considerable neatness, *but* he will never be ranked amongst the masters of style. He has his share of all intellectual and artistic qualities, *but* he has nothing in excess; he inherits all the powers of the great novelists, *but* he has no very large inheritance of any one of these powers. And it is for this reason that we cannot attach any very distinctive personality to Mr. Trollope.⁶⁹

In Smith's rendering, Trollope, like the subjects of Hazlitt's *Spirit of the Age*, is characteristic of his culture insofar as he has no special characteristic; however, Smith's litany of seven *buts* either intimates to the contrary that Trollope does have a "distinctive personality," latent in his adversatives, or that the adversatives were so utterly predominant that they were coextensive with indistinctiveness, the very symptom of ordinariness.

In January 1874, *Dublin University Magazine* (which was founded, coincidentally, by Isaac Butt, although he had retired from the editorship years before Trollope wrote for it) published a leading story titled "The Universal 'But'." Written by Irish poet Catherine Hartland Inglis, "The Universal 'But'" explicitly relates the word *but* to the contradictions of character that, as far as Inglis was concerned, had become Victorian commonplaces. The first-person narrator, recounting how she has "pondered on the infirmities of mankind as a great body politic, and the avidity with which, in general, one neighbour criticizes another, comfortably unconscious that he himself is as veritable a subject for the same mental anatomy to others," is "struck ... with peculiar force" by "the terrible emphasis with which the simple little particle *But* is clothed in this neighbourly estimation of character" (58). She speculates that if we critiqued each other "with unmitigated ferocity" we would appear awkward and inspire sympathy for our victims; "But," she counters,

> to display our own unchallengeable impartiality and innate candour, and at the same time to bring home with irresistible force to the bosom of each hearer the errors of the absent delinquent, we benevolently enumerate some more or less redeeming points in the character. Now it is critically between these opposing demonstrations of amiable impartiality on one hand, and severe scrutiny on the other, that the terrible *But* takes its allotted and invariable position. (58)

Inglis portrays *but* as a grammatical instrument of equivocation that ensures the performance of both "amiable" and "severe" impartiality, appraisal and critique. "It is to be confessed," Inglis adds, "that this ominous *But* is seldom the precursor of unmixed falsehood, and is sometimes found to be the herald of nothing but truth" (58). If the correspondence between appearance and actuality used to affirm the sincerity of character – to ensure the witness's reliability, the customer's credit, the scientist's honesty[70] – this essay suggests that by the second half of the nineteenth century, assuming discordance between these categories had become de rigueur. Its light-hearted tone nevertheless presents this skepticism as altogether innocuous, as the harmless, laughable way we all rub each other the wrong way. The narrator describes a scene at her Aunt Rebecca's where gossipy spinsters glowingly characterize the suspiciously Trollopian curate, Mr. Stedfast, until "the fated *But* came muttering through the room" (59), and a clothier's shop, where a litany of *buts* comically justifies a tailor's refusal to cash a bill. "Although no external opposition appeared," the narrator explains, "yet there was quite sufficient internal opposition to evoke every possible objection to any new name proposed" to back his bill (60). These *buts* reveal nothing unique or damning; they only enable characters to reserve a respectable distance.

Thackeray's fiction exculpates *but* accordingly as an almost inevitable fulcrum between mature characters and the rest of the world. As a *Bildungsroman*, Thackeray's *Pendennis* (1848–50) practically thematizes Pen's maturation as a realization of adversative tact. At the beginning of the novel, his idleness – the "seed" of "a prodigious quantity of future crime and wickedness" – allegedly originates in his inability to properly distinguish a Greek adversative from a conjunction: "Miserable trifler!" the Doctor exclaims, "A boy who construes δε *and*, instead of δε *but*, at sixteen years of age, is guilty not merely of folly, and ignorance, and dullness inconceivable, but of crime, of deadly crime, of filial ingratitude, which

I tremble to contemplate" (52). Toward the end of the novel, however, Pen explicitly personifies *but* as an animate interlocutor through whom he mediates his contact with the world. "'A sneer, is there?" he says to Laura, "I was thinking, my dear, that nature in making you so good and loving did very well: but – '"; Laura retorts, "'But what? What is that wicked but? and why are you always calling it up?'"[71] Pen explains:

> "But will come in spite of us. But is reflection. But is the sceptic's familiar, with whom he has made a compact; and if he forgets it, and indulges in happy day-dreams, or building of air-castles, or listens to sweet music, let us say, or to the bells ringing to church, But taps at the door, and says, Master, I am here. You are my master; but I am yours. Go where you will, you can't travel without me. I will whisper to you when you are on your knees at church. I will be at your marriage pillow. I will sit down at your table with your children. I will be behind your death-bed curtain. That is what But is," Pen said. (738).

But appears here as the signature call of the real, countering the propensity to idealize experience. Disabused of the idealism that coupled him with the actress Miss Fotheringay, Pen cannot help but qualify even Laura, however impossibly she exemplifies stereotypical Victorian femininity. *But* is the fulcrum of responsible adult relations with everyone and everything, even the self-reflective relations between one's competing motivations and thoughts.

The sequel to *Pendennis*, *The Newcomes* (1853–55), further employs and draws attention to *but* as an acquired medium of social and readerly tact. Like Lady Glencora broaching the topic of Lizzie Eustace, Lord Kew explains that Ethel Newcome "is very clever, she is exceedingly handsome, she is very good to her parents and her brothers and sisters; but – ' he did not finish the sentence" (494–95).[72] Kew intimates that Ethel is a flirt or a tease, but Thackeray does not allow readers to harbor that judgment for long. True to form, Pendennis (now narrator) starts to share Kew's critique of Ethel only for a while before *but* arrests his critique and encourages a more realistic and generous estimate of her character than mainstream morality, personified in Mrs. Grundy, the fictional apotheosis of priggery and convention, would allow:

> Calling him back after she had dismissed him, and finding pretext after pretext to see him – why did the girl encourage him, as she certainly did? I allow, with Mrs. Grundy and most moralists, that Miss Newcome's conduct in this matter was highly reprehensible; that if she did not intend to marry Clive she should have broken with him altogether: that a virtuous woman of high principle, &c., &c., having once determined to reject

a suitor should separate from him utterly then and there – never give him
again the least chance of a hope, or re-illume the extinguished fire in the
wretch's bosom.

But coquetry, but kindness, but family affections, and a strong, very
strong partiality for the rejected lover – are these not to be taken in account,
and to plead as excuses for her behavior to her cousin? (694)

After more than half a page taking such excuses into account, Thackeray
exclaims:

> See! I began by siding with Mrs. Grundy and the world, and at the next turn
> of the see-saw have lighted down on Ethel's side, and am disposed to think
> that the very best part of her conduct has been those escapades which –
> which right-minded persons most justly condemn ... these are surely
> occurrences so common in young women's history as to call for no special
> censure. (694)

Pendennis promotes liberal open-mindedness, to be sure, in his change of
opinion from judgmental to generous. More importantly, he promotes
a reallocation of morality from the categorical rectitude personified in
Mrs. Grundy to the "common" misconduct exemplified by Ethel.
At once pragmatic and aesthetic, Pendennis favors ordinary misconduct
as "the very best part of her conduct" because it is both more common and
more interesting than virtuous conduct.

This aesthetic inflects all of Trollope's prose. The feeling of reading
Trollope, the feeling of everyday life, is as Michael Sadleir wrote many
years ago "a sensual rather than an intellectual experience" with an exceedingly difficult to describe effect, "at once soothing and exciting"; it is closer
to a "smell, a pain or a sound."[73] For Sadleir the "peculiar but elusive
flavour" (34) of Trollope's fiction accrues to its "acquiescence" to things as
they are or the way of the world. This acquiescence produces for Sadleir
a curious combination of effects: "a series of unsensational sensations" (37),
his books are "so featureless, so sober and so undemonstrative" and yet
"few are more enthralling" (35); they are "so drab yet so mysteriously alive,
so obvious yet so impossible of imitation" (37); "so genially disposed but
fundamentally detached" (36). All of this paradox registers as a "queer sense
of the absorbing interest of normal occupations" (37). That this feeling of
cumulative small but competing sensations corresponds to the feeling of
normalcy implies that ordinariness as such is definitively odd, off, queer,
just noticeably different enough to be felt. Paradoxically, something must
go against the grain to be felt as the proverbial grain. Sadleir writes: "Like
life, [Trollope's fictions] are diffuse, often tedious, seldom arrestingly

unusual. Their monotony is the monotony of ordinary existence, which, although while actually passing it provides one small sensation after another, emerges in retrospect as a dull sequence of familiar things" (37).

A dull sequence of familiar words: Trollope's *buts* reproduce the surface tension of everyday life and in turn translate that ordinary experience into an aesthetic and an ethic, the Victorian "vernacular aesthetic category," to borrow Sianne Ngai's term, par excellence.[74] Lady Glencora's "but – " in particular demonstrates how Victorian tact reconciled epistemological skepticism and demurral with a generous acknowledgment of the potential interest, affinity, and texture of even the most suspicious, cloying, or insipid persons or things. It is an enchanting idiom. Still, however reparative it may be, such tact certainly accommodates ethical ambivalence and affected ignorance or doubt where decisiveness seem just and true. As a medium of everyday life it remains integral to modernity's fast and loose play with the truths of fact and fiction.

Afterword: The Fate of Character and the Philology of Everyday Life

When I started this book I was invested in thing theory and in how nineteenth-century writers characterized things and in so doing revealed the most portable, least anthropomorphic features of characterization, features we had not yet noticed enough. In the process I came to question that approach, because I came to think that there are no things in writing, just writing about things. Prose was my real subject, the real agent and repository of character. I was therefore taken by the way Franco Moretti ends one of his recent books: "By now, readers of this book know that prose is its only true hero," he says. "It wasn't meant to be; it just happened, in trying to do justice to the achievements of bourgeois culture. Prose as the bourgeois style, in the broadest sense; a way of being in the world, not just of representing it. Prose as analysis ... Prose as ... work: hard, tentative, ... never perfect. And prose as rational polemic."[1] I hope to have supplied more texture to this hero in describing it in terms of character and its signature stylistic features. There are more everyday words left to explain, and perhaps more epistemologies, embedded in the contours of prose.

I want to conclude with a thought about prose not as the transparent servant of data, an invisible hand, but as a manner of being. *Everyday Words* indulges in at least one methodological ambivalence: it insists that its every-day words are both utterly historical phenomena, whose frequency, visibility, and felicitous evocation of character were uniquely pronounced in nine-teenth-century Britain, even as it admits that these same words remain altogether ordinary in the present. Although modern reading practices – and especially modern academic reading practices – vary widely from those of the average nineteenth-century reader, and our value systems have surely shifted, the connotations and grammatical functions of these words persist. If moral character seems less pressing and pervasive a concern for us than for Victorians, character lingers as a mainstream aesthetic category in our own moralized capitalist self-help genres, popular aesthetics, and commercials.

Home improvement shows relish character as a moralistic architectural value vaguely indicative of history, irregularity, care, and craftsmanship, as distinct from run-of-the-mill cheap construction. A recent television advertisement for Hennessey cognac answers the rhetorical question "What is character?" with several indecisive questions that imply character is inexplicable but self-evident – and particularly self-evident in their cognac. Character therefore remains a performative aesthetic category, generated by the articulation of certain locutions rather than by any fixed set of qualities belonging to a specific object.

The self-evidence of character refutes the epistemology of depth, for it implies that character is readily legible but bears no explanation or interpretation. Like Arnoldian sweetness and light, it is a matter of tact and touch rather than analysis. Or so the rhetoric of depth and superficiality might make it seem, but, as Ruskin observes, tact and touch also require cultivation. Recognizing character requires not merely identifying it but responding to it. The fate of the epistemology of character that I have described perhaps lies in Michael McKeon's observation that "modern knowledge is defined precisely by its explanatory ambition to separate itself from its object of knowledge sufficiently to fulfill the epistemological demand that what is known must be divided from the process by which it is known."[2] The epistemology of character ill suits modern knowledge per se, because it privileges its processes and reception over its objects. As I have shown, nineteenth-century writers employ attention, inference, difference, deference, and self-reference, and rebuttal to characterize otherwise immoral, counterfactual, and uninteresting people and things. Under the regime of knowledge production that McKeon describes, prose tends almost to disappear behind its referents and contents, behind its personages and plots. Latent in the epistemology of character, however, is the sense that prose style is its own form of knowledge and a way of being in the world that does not ignore or reject facts as they are, but which also does not become subject to or invisible behind them.

As scholars, our most tenable mode of presentism is, like the nineteenth-century novel's most tenable form of morality, not explicit, didactic, positivist prescription, but our process of reading and writing: prose as a practice, a manner, and a form of knowledge. In the *Critique of Everyday Life*, Henri Lefebvre suggests that the everyday is a domain of inarticulate, ineffable practices and objects whose redemptive potential inheres in the way they reside outside of hegemonic narratives of meaningfulness.[3] Such was, and remains, characterization at its best. As Andrew Miller well notes in *The Burdens of Perfection*, we tend to turn to criticism not for conclusive explanations, portable lessons, or positivist data so much as to be implicated in a process of thought, to share and correspond with the thoughts of another even as he or she entertains counterfactual conjectures. Moral perfectionism, he writes, "invites a criticism that acknowledges its partiality and the existence of alternatives," criticism that imaginatively develops counterfactual and "counterfictional visions" (30, 118).[4] Whately said something similar of Austen: that her novels do not explicitly moralize, but almost osmotically implicate us via style in the work of characterization. All of the everyday words and phrases studied herein work toward these implicative ends: they acknowledge and utterly respect commonsense and factual givens, but, aware of the limits of facts these phrases, turn from them, supplant them, or amend them with conjectural, skeptical, sympathetic, discretionary, or affective demurrals.

Like Dickens with his *as ifs*, I would not dream of dismissing the factuality of this book – I believe the words it selects and many of the things it says about them are historically true – but I also wouldn't reduce its value to those facts, such as they are. Its value – if it has any – inheres in its treatment of them, in its prosaic manner of thinking. Close attention, but at enough of a remove as to be able to make broad claims that are historicist but germane all the same to the present. Philology has that double benefit: it restores the *lento*, as Nietzsche called it, to reading and being, and at best implicates us in our language and the everyday assumptions, attitudes, affections, and other relations it enacts and conceals. I suspect this set of everyday words is just the really subtle tip of an iceberg and that other philological minds might find many more out, thereby implicating us in other histories and relations.

Notes

Epigraph

1. Joseph Conrad, *The Heart of Darkness*, ed. Paul B. Armstrong (New York: W. W. Norton, 2005), 66.
2. George Henry Lewes, *The Life and Works of Goethe with Sketches of His Age and Contemporaries*, 2 vols. (London: David Nutt, 1855), II, 375.
3. Samuel Smiles, *Self-Help*, ed. Peter W. Sinnema (Oxford University Press, 2002), 314, 316.

Preface

1. Sianne Ngai, *Our Aesthetic Categories: Zany, Cute, Interesting* (Harvard University Press, 2012), 17.
2. Hélène Cixous and Keith Cohen, "The Character of 'Character,'" *New Literary History* 5.2 (Winter 1974): 383–402, makes the poststructuralist case against character most clearly, but it is a part of an engaging special issue, "Changing Views of Character."
3. On this re-emergence, see Rita Felski, ed. and intro., "Character" [Special Issue], *New Literary History: A Journal of Theory and Interpretation* 42.2 (Spring 2011): v–ix, 209–360.
4. Deidre Shauna Lynch, *The Economy of Character: Novels, Market Culture, and the Business of Inner Meaning* (University of Chicago Press, 1998).
5. Alex Woloch, *The One vs. the Many: Minor Characters and the Space of the Protagonist in the Novel* (Princeton University Press, 2003), 13. "The implied person behind any character is," Woloch says, "never directly reflected in the literary text but only partially inflected: each individual portrait has a radically contingent position within the story as a whole; our sense of the human figure (*as* implied person) is inseparable from the space that he or she occupies within the narrative totality" (13). I preserve Woloch's sense of the text as a character system, but extend characters to include not just implied people but any subjects that share the performative relations articulated by everyday words.
6. Susan Manning, *Poetics of Character: Transatlantic Encounters 1700–1900* (Cambridge University Press, 2013) 14, 6.

7. Amanda Anderson, *The Powers of Distance: Cosmopolitanism and the Cultivation of Detachment* (Princeton University Press, 2001), 6–7 and *passim*.

8. David Kurnick, *Empty Houses: Theatrical Failure and the Novel* (Princeton University Press, 2012), 5–6. Kurnick insightfully delineates the nostalgic longing for public life acutely latent in novels and novelistic poems writers such as Thackeray, James, and Eliot composed out of their failed plays. The features of these fictions, latent in their other work, bespeak a reluctance to define the self through acts of disclosure and unveiling premised on a hidden, sexual identity and self who is allegedly most authentic, most real, when most alone and domesticated.

9. Michel Serres, *Parasite*, trans. Lawrence R. Schehr (University of Minnesota Press, 2007), 8.

10. Mary Poovey, *A History of the Modern Fact: Problems of Knowledge in the Sciences of Wealth and Society* (University of Chicago Press, 1998), 13, and see xi–16.

11. George Levine, *The Realistic Imagination: English Fiction from* Frankenstein *to* Lady Chatterley (University of Chicago Press, 1981), 12.

12. Michael McKeon, *The Secret History of Domesticity: Public, Private, and the Division of Knowledge* (Baltimore: Johns Hopkins University Press, 2005), 108–9.

13. On the proliferation and function of abstractions, see Mary Poovey, *Making a Social Body: British Cultural Formation, 1830–1864* (University of Chicago Press, 1995), 3–10. Expanding upon Marx's notion of "simple" or "general" abstraction, Poovey describes how institutions, technologies of representation, and other protocols for knowing "[facilitate] the perception that certain characteristics are common to a number of discrete practices [and objects]. The reified abstractions that standardized modes of knowing generate then produce effects that are simultaneously symbolic and material" (5). I elsewhere write about how Charles Dickens, Harriet Martineau, and other journalists employed techniques of novelistic characterization, including personification, secret subjectivity, and self-transformation, to represent a concrete abstraction – the factory system and its products – as repositories and inculcators of *character*. See Jonathan Farina, "Characterizing the Factory System: Factory Tourism and Factory Subjectivity in *Household Words*," Victorian Literature and Culture 35, no. 1 (March 2007): 41–56.

14. Steven Shapin, *A Social History of Truth: Civility and Science in Seventeenth-Century England* (University of Chicago Press, 1994), 65–125 on the linguistic signatures of epistemological decorum.

15. Nicholas Dames, *The Physiology of the Novel: Reading, Neural Science, and the Form of Victorian Fiction* (Oxford University Press, 2007), 11.

16. On the perlocutionary force of aesthetic categories, see Ngai 38–41.

17. Rohan Amanda Maitzen insightfully shows how Victorian moral criticism actually emphasizes the mode of "treatment" far more than the content of

literature when estimating its morality, so much of the post-Victorian dismissal of Victorian moral criticism is reductive and inaccurate. "'The Soul of Art': Understanding Victorian Ethical Criticism," *ESC: English Studies in Canada* 31.2/3 (2005): 151–86.

18. Elaine Hadley, *Living Liberalism: Practical Citizenship in Mid-Victorian Britain* (University of Chicago Press, 2010), 7–20.

19. D. A. Miller, *The Novel and the Police* (Berkeley: University of California Press, 1988), 192–220, 204.

20. See James A. Secord, *Victorian Sensation: The Extraordinary Publication, Reception, and Secret Authorship of* Vestiges of the Natural History of Creation (University of Chicago Press, 2000), 397–400.

21. Caroline Levine, *Forms: Whole, Rhythm, Hierarchy, Network* (Princeton University Press, 2015).

22. Friedrich Nietzsche, *Daybreak: Thoughts on the Prejudices of Morality*, eds. Maudemarie Clark and Brian Leiter (Cambridge University Press, 1997), 5.

23. On "symptomatic reading," see Louis Althusser, *Reading Capital*, trans. Ben Brewster (New York: New Left Books, 1970); and (as the "hermeneutics of suspicion") Paul Ricouer, *Freud and Philosophy: An Essay on Interpretation* (Yale University Press, 1970); and (as "allegorical" interpretation of "repressed" meaning) Fredric Jameson, *The Political Unconscious: Narrative as a Socially symbolic Act* (Cornell University Press, 1981), 17–102. Sedgwick describes "reparative reading" in *Touching Feeling: Affect, Pedagogy, Performativity* (Durham: Duke University Press, 2003), 123–51. Marcus describes "just reading" in *Between Women: Friendship, Desire, and Marriage in Victorian England* (Princeton University Press, 2007), 73–76. On "surface reading," see Stephen Best and Sharon Marcus, "The Way We Read Now: An Introduction," *Representations* 108.1 (2009):1–21. Heather Love recounts the "descriptive turn" in "Close but not Deep: Literary Ethics and the Descriptive Turn," *New Literary History* 41.2 (Spring 2010): 371–91.

24. Francis Galton, "Hereditary Talent and Character," *Macmillan's Magazine* 12 (1865): 157–66 (Part I); 318–27 (Part II).

1 Darwin's View from Todgers's

1. Charles Darwin, *The Origin of Species*, ed. George Levine (New York: Barnes and Noble, 2004), 76–77, 85; emphasis added.

2. Charles Dickens, *David Copperfield*, ed. Jerome H. Buckley (New York: Norton, 1990), 9; emphasis added.

3. Samuel Smiles, *Character* (New York: Harper & Brothers, 1872), 240, 241–42.

4. Hugh Blair, *Lectures on Rhetoric and Belles Lettres*, chapter 18, makes the most explicit connection between manner and style, style and character.

5. Kent Puckett, *Bad Form: Social Mistakes and the Nineteenth-Century Novel* (Oxford University Press, 2008) argues that the emergence of the autonomous genre of etiquette books in the 1830s manifests the disaggregation of ethics from manners (11). The nineteenth-century European novel, as Puckett well shows, often reproduces this separation of ethics and etiquette, as if style and manners were no longer "an index of the moral self" (11), but this was a hotly contested position – not, I will argue, because critics insisted on the moral self, but because their model of society was still imbricated in a model of civility that was at least as much moral as fashionable and classed.

6. Lionel Trilling, "Manners, Morals, and the Novel," in *The Liberal Imagination* (New York Review Books, 2008), 206–7.

7. Steven Shapin, *A Social History of Truth: Civility and Science in Seventeenth-Century England* (University of Chicago Press, 1994), xxix and 193–245.

8. Charles Dickens, *Martin Chuzzlewit*, ed. Patricia Ingham (New York: Penguin, 2004), 147.

9. W. B. Stanford, *The Ulysses Theme: A Study in the Adaptability of a Traditional Hero*. 2nd edn. (University of Michigan Press, 1968), 99.

10. On Dickens's tongue-in-cheek, see David Parker, "Dickens's Archness," *Dickensian* 67 (1971): 149–58.

11. These paradoxes of *character* are analogous to and necessarily implicated in the paradoxes of "self" and "identity" for writers as diverse as John Locke and Jacques Derrida. See Elizabeth Kraft, *Character and Consciousness in Eighteenth-Century Comic Fiction* (Athens: The University of Georgia Press, 1992), 36, 46. On the paradoxes of individuality, see also Raymond Williams, *Keywords* (Oxford University Press, 1983), 161–65.

12. See John William Sneed, *The Theophrastan "Character": The History of a Literary Genre* (Clarendon, 1985).

13. Charlotte Brontë, *Jane Eyre*, ed. Michael Mason (New York: Penguin, 1996), 165. *Jane Eyre* includes 97 uses of "turned," 57 "turn," 23 "turning," and 3 "turns," plus 66 "returned," 65 "return," 8 "returning," and 4 "returns," for a total of 323 instances of the expression in the 188,306-word novel, nevermind any synonymous locutions.

14. Michel Foucault, *The Order of Things: An Archeology of the Human Sciences* (New York: Vintage, 1994), 159.

15. James Fitzjames Stephen, "The Relation of Novels to Life" (1855), in Edwin M. Eigner and George J. Worth, eds., *Victorian Criticism of the Novel* (Cambridge University Press, 1985), 93–118, 102–3.

16. Dorothy Van Ghent, "The Dickens World: A View from Todgers's" *Sewanee Review* 58.3 (1950): 419–38. See [Anon.], "Balzac and his Writing" *Westminster Review* LX (July 1853): 199–214.

17. Carolyn Williams, *Gilbert and Sullivan: Gender, Genre, Parody* (New York: Columbia University Press, 2012), 6–7. Williams also underscores the productivity of genre as an analytic tool that interfaces literary and social conventions, xiii–xiv.

18. Charles Dickens, *The Old Curiosity Shop*, ed. Norman Page (New York: Penguin, 2000), 114, 137, 251.

19. Charles Dickens, *Great Expectations*, ed. Janie Carlyle (New York: Bedford/ St. Martin's, 1996), 23.

20. Charles Dickens, *Hard Times*, ed. Kate Flint (New York: Penguin, 2003), 14–15.

21. Thomas Carlyle, "Signs of the Times," in *A Carlyle Reader*, ed. G. B. Tennyson (Cambridge University Press, 1984): 31–55, 37.

22. "All that a man does is physiognomical of him," Carlyle asserts in "The Hero as Poet." Thomas Carlyle, *On Heroes, Hero-Worship, and the Heroic in History*, ed. David R. Sorensen and Brent E. Kinser (Yale University Press, 2013), 97.

23. In the aptly titled "The Turn of George Eliot's Realism," *Nineteenth-Century Fiction* 35 (1980): 171–92, which doesn't remark on the word "turn," John McGowan reads the *Mill on the Floss* as part of a transition Eliot makes from recognizing the inadequacy of representational realism, which relies on turning back nostalgically to a remembered self, to a metaphorical realism, which is manifest in *Middlemarch* and which privileges transformative "becoming" rather than mimetic "being." While I concur with this in principle, I think Eliot's favoring of words like "turn" and the Wordsworthian "things," which I discuss in Chapter 4, suggests that even her notion of being is unstable and contingent. Being, such as Eliot deems it, occurs in the space between characters and the world, rather than inhering within individuals.

24. Charles Darwin, *The Descent of Man*, ed. James Moore and Adrian Desmond (New York: Penguin, 2004).

25. Rohan Amanda Maitzen recounts how Victorian critics tended to emphasize the morality of treatment, manner, or style over and above the relative morality of content in "'The Soul of Art': Understanding Victorian Ethical Criticism," *ESC: English Studies in Canada* 31.2/3 (2005): 151–86. Matthew Sussman, "Stylistic Virtue in Nineteenth-Century Criticism," *Victorian Studies* 56.2 (Winter 2014): 225–49, likewise describes the rise of stylistic formalism as a development of mid-century moralistic criticism.

26. On the evaluation of the "character" of books, particularly scientific books, see James A. Secord, *Victorian Sensation: The Extraordinary Publication, Reception, and Secret Authorship of* Vestiges of the Natural History of Creation (University of Chicago Press, 2000), 397–400 and 336–63.

27. David Kurnick, *Empty Houses: Theatrical Failure and the Novel* (Princeton University Press, 2012), 1–28.

28. *Thysanura* has been since replaced by *Zygentoma*. It includes silverfish, firebrats, and bristletails. Lubbock was describing a globular springtail, *Smynthurus luteus*, but most of these insects have similar, elaborate mating rituals.

29. *Mill on the Floss* includes 128 "turned," 63 "turn," 57 "turning," and 5 "turns," plus 30 "return," 17 "returned," 17 "returning," and 3 "returns" for a total of 320 instances of the phrase in the 213,984-word novel.

30. Jonathan Farina, "*The Excursion* and 'the Surfaces of Things,'" *The Wordsworth Circle* 45.2 (Spring 2014): 99–105.

31. William Wordsworth, *The Poems*, ed. John O. Hayden. 2 vols. (Yale University Press, 1981), II, 42, 44; cf. II: 112, 138.

32. Cf. Wordsworth II: 136, 200, 225, 246, 247, 276, 281, and 289.

33. Cf. Wordsworth II: 137, 218, 275.

34. The first edition (1859), the text from which my other citations come, actually has "In regard to the Invertebrata," which Darwin saw fit to revise into "Turning to the Invertebrata," and "In the plants of the Galapagos Islands," which Darwin later revised to "Turning to plants." These 1872 revisions may well just indicate a habitual tic that intensified over time, rather than an intentional appeal to a certain epistemology, but even then it attests to the pervasiveness of that epistemology that "turning" felt right to Darwin while revising.

35. "To return to my subject": Michel de Montaigne, *The Complete Essays of Montaigne*, trans. Donald M. Frame (Stanford University Press, 1976), 152, 290, 314, 336, 358. Montaigne uses "turn" 79 times according to Frame's translation of the *Essays*.

36. *Don Juan* includes 113 "turn," 16 "turns," and 11 "turning" in 131,055 words.

37. George Levine, *Darwin the Writer* (Oxford University Press, 2011) observes similar patterns in Darwin's prose: it "foregrounds the startling nature of his subject and then, quietly, empirically, explains why it shouldn't be that startling once we think about it" (116); "Marvel gives way to plausible explanation, but the plausible explanation invokes marvelous complexity" (96), and so on. See 37–148.

38. Mill writes about the open-mindedness of liberal character, which necessitates that one has opinions but is open to adapt them in dialogue with others: "A person whose desires and impulses are his own – are the expressions of his own nature, as it has been developed and modified by his own culture – is said to have character," by which he means not that character is the result of some Romantic germ of identity, but that it has been carefully crafted by interactive adaptation. John Stuart Mill, *Mill: The Spirit of the Age, On Liberty, The Subjection of Women*, ed. Alan Ryan (New York: W. W. Norton, 1997), 87. See chapter 2 of *On Liberty* for Mill's discussion of character in these terms.

39. [Anon.], "Character Is Everything," *Sunday at Home* 463 (March 14, 1863): 164–67. Emphasis in original.

40. On the role of these virtues in the history of self-formation, see Charles Taylor, *Sources of the Self: The Making of Modern Identity* (Cambridge University Press, 1989), 143–76 and *passim*, and Lionel Trilling, *Sincerity and Authenticity* (Harvard University Press, 1972), 2–6.

41. Charles Fourier, *The Theory of the Four Movements*, eds. Gareth Stedman Jones and Ian Patterson (Cambridge University Press, 1996), xviii.

42. Samuel Bailey, *Letters on the Philosophy of the Human Mind* (London: Longmans, Green, and Co., 1855, 1858, 1863); Alexander Bain, *On the Study of Character* (London: Parker, Son, and Bourn, 1861); George Combe, *A System of Phrenology* (London: Longmans, Green, and Co., 1830); T. H. Green, *Lectures on the Principles of Political Obligation* (London: Longmans, Green, and Co., 1895), §21; John Stuart Mill, *On Liberty* (London: Parker and Son, 1859), especially 64; Herbert Spencer, *Principles of Ethics*, 2 vols. (New York: Appleton, 1892–93), especially 2: 251. See Shalyn Claggett, "The Science of Character in Victorian Literature and Culture," Dissertation Abstracts International, Section A: The Humanities and Social Sciences 67, no. 5 (Nov. 2006)/Vanderbilt University, 2005.

43. Following "eighteenth- and nineteenth-century usage," modern historian Margot Finn uses "character" as "a metonym for the fluid constellation of attributes recognised as signifiers of personal credit in the eighteenth and nineteenth centuries." Finn describes how in the eighteenth and nineteenth centuries personal character replaced the gentlemanly conventions of mutual trust that regulated early-modern credit relations. Margot C. Finn, *The Character of Credit: Personal Debt in English Culture, 1740–1914* (Cambridge University Press, 2003), 18.

44. Virginia Woolf, "Mr. Bennett and Mrs. Brown," in *The Captain's Death Bed and Other Essays* (New York: Harcourt Brace Jovanovich, 1978), 94–119, 97.

45. George Eliot, "The Sad Fortunes of the Reverend Amos Barton," in *Scenes of Clerical Life*, ed. Jennifer Gribble (New York: Penguin, 1998), 43.

46. On the range of ideological valences Victorians ascribed to character, see Stefan Collini, "The Idea of Character: Private Habits and Public Virtues," in *Public Moralists: Political Thought and Intellectual Life in Britain 1850–1930* (Oxford University Press, 1991), 91–118.

47. Stefan Collini, *Public Moralists: Political Thought and Intellectual Life in Britain, 1850-1930* (Oxford: Oxford University Press 1993), 105.

48. Lauren M. E. Goodlad, *Victorian Literature and the Victorian State: Character and Governance in a Liberal Society* (Baltimore: Johns Hopkins University Press, 2003), ix.

49. I would add that ideology as a concept was a dialectical product of the contemporaneous depth episteme Foucault describes: the concept poses

ideology as an artificial consciousness over and against the material reality supposed to underwrite it. The epistemology of character was a complementary episteme that was not invested in the same equation of real/ ideal with the spatial metaphor of depth/surface. Working at the level of epistemology allows us to see the tropes by which things like ideology and the thematics of character become knowable as such. Michel Foucault, *Power/ Knowledge: Selected Interviews & Other Writings, 1972–1977*, ed. Colin Gordon (New York: Pantheon, 1980), 118.

50. Amanda Anderson, *The Way We Argue Now: A Study in the Culture of Theory* (Princeton University Press, 2006), 120.

51. Clifford Siskin, *The Historicity of Romantic Discourse* (Oxford University Press, 1988), 55 and *passim*. Siskin identifies such "lyric turns" across the Romantic period and subsequent history, during which their production of depth effects legitimate professional discourses. See *The Work of Writing: Literature and Social Change in Britain 1700–1830* (Baltimore: Johns Hopkins University Press, 1998).

52. Deidre Shauna Lynch, *The Economy of Character: Novels, Market Culture, and the Business of Inner Meaning* (University of Chicago Press, 1998), 29–47.

53. Elizabeth Deeds Ermarth, *Realism and Consensus in English Fiction* (Princeton University Press, 1983), 64.

54. "The stile [*sic*] of an author is generally of the same stamp as their character": Adam Smith, *Lectures on Rhetoric and Belles Lettres*, ed. J. C. Bryce (Indianapolis: Liberty Fund, 1985), 34–35.

55. William Wordsworth, *The Prelude 1799, 1805, 1850*, eds. Jonathan Wordsworth, M. H. Abrams, and Stephen Gill (Norton: New York, 1979), 6. I quote from the 1799 manuscript, but Wordsworth's usage of "impressed" and "characters" remains constant in the 1805 and the 1850.

56. Archibald Alison, "The Historical Romance," in *Victorian Criticism of the Novel*, eds. Eigner and Worth (Cambridge: Cambridge University Press, 1845), 58–83, 80.

57. Roland Barthes, *S/Z: An Essay*, trans. Richard Miller (New York: Macmillan, 1975), 67.

58. Matthew Arnold, *Culture and Anarchy*, ed. J. Dover Wilson (Cambridge University Press, 1996), 54.

59. Matthew Arnold, *Selected Prose*, ed. P. J. Keating (New York: Penguin, 1970), 349. Siskin, *The Work of Writing, passim*.

60. Fredric Jameson, *The Political Unconscious: Narrative as a Socially Symbolic Act* (Cornell University Press, 1981), 17–102, esp. 28–29, 58. Louis Althusser and Etienne Balibar, *Reading Capital*, trans. Ben Brewster (London: New Left Books, 1970), 28.

61. Amanda Anderson, *The Powers of Distance: Cosmopolitanism and the Cultivation of Detachment* (Princeton University Press, 2001), 115.

62. John Ruskin, *The Works of John Ruskin*, eds. E. T. Cook and Alexander Wedderburn. Library Edition. 39 vols. (London: George Allen, 1903–12), 3: 151, 152.

63. Ruskin says "Fielding has given us every character of the quiet lake, Robson of the mountain tarn, De Wint of the lowland river, Nesfield of the radiant cataract, Harding of the roaring torrent" (3: 814).

64. Harry E. Shaw, *Narrating Reality: Austen, Scott, Eliot* (Cornell University Press, 1999), 88. Shaw's interest in ordinary language supports his thesis that realism enacts an ethical process of metonymy, by which readers are accustomed to appreciate meaning from contingency and association rather than metaphoric transformation, narrative progress, or interpretation per se.

65. For the history of philology in this period, including Trench's role, see Hans Aarsleff, *The Study of Language in England, 1780–1860* (Princeton University Press, 1967).

66. See Julie Coleman, *A History of Cant and Slang Dictionaries, Volume 2: 1785–1858* (Oxford University Press, 2004). As Janet Sorensen shows, by the late eighteenth century this "vulgar" language had become coterminous with the "common" language of "the people: "at the same time as a wide set of popular practices and beliefs were criminalized and rendered invisible," Sorensen writes, "a set of 'criminal' linguistic practices became highly visible and came to be understood as an expression of popular British culture and a uniquely British liberty in a dialectic of social repression and rhetorical rehabilitation of the people." Janet Sorensen, "Vulgar Tongues: Canting Dictionaries and the Language of the People in Eighteenth-Century Britain," *Eighteenth-Century Studies* 37.3 (2004): 435–54; 438.

67. See Dennis Taylor, *Hardy's Literary Language and Victorian Philology* (Clarendon Press, 1993).

68. Richard Chenevix Trench, *On Some Deficiencies in Our English Dictionaries*, 2nd edn. (London: John W. Parker and Son, 1860). The book combines two lectures first delivered by Trench in 1857.

69. Richard Chenevix Trench, *On the Study of Words: Six Lectures Addressed (Originally) to the Pupils at the Diocesan Training School, Winchester* (London: John W. Parker and Son, 1856), 128. The first edition was 1852.

70. Pierce Egan and George Cruikshank, *Tom and Jerry: Life in London; Or the Day and Night Scenes of Jerry Hawthorne and His Elegant Friend, Corinthian Tom* (London: John Camden Hotten, 1869), 52 and *passim*.

71. Gary Dyer, "Thieves, Boxers, Sodomites, Poets: Being Flash to Byron's Don Juan," *PMLA* 116.3 (May 2001): 562–78, convincingly describes how flash like Egan's functioned as a language of encryption that enabled people to keep important private secrets about boxing, sodomy, and other then-illicit subjects, but the culture of everyday words begs us to reconsider the

historicist investment in secrecy fueled by our methodological investment in a hermeneutics of suspicion, and instead to see a language that worked less because of its potential to simultaneously conceal and convey meaning and more because of its facility with making meaning readily fungible.

72. George Orwell, "Charles Dickens," *A Collection of Essays* (London: Harvest, 1981), 48–104, 75.

73. Discriminating between "novels of character" and "novels of action," "incident," "plot," and, especially in the 1870s, "sensation," was a mainstay of Victorian criticism. One of the earliest, exemplary statements of this is [Bulwer Lytton], The Critic Nos. I and II, "On Art in Fiction" *Monthly Chronicle* I (March 1838): 42–51 and (April 1838): 138–49. In the first installment, Bulwer actually divides novels into "manners," "character" (as in fictional personages), and "passions," and thereby disassociates manners from personages and ascribes it to the style of novels as wholes.

74. David Masson, *British Novelists and Their Styles: Being a Critical Sketch of the History of British Prose Fiction* [1859] (Boston: D. Lothrop and Co., 1875), 243–58, 254–55.

75. John Cordy Jeaffreson, *Novels and Novelists: From Elizabeth to Victoria* (London: Hurst and Blackett, 1858), 326.

76. [Anon.] Art. IV. Review of "Oliver Twist; or, the Parish Boy's Progress. By Boz," *The Quarterly Review* 64.127 (June 1839): 83–102. His revisions also sought to make the novel more respectable. Notwithstanding his revisions to *Oliver Twist*, Dickens persistently wrote in a singularly heteroglossic style informed by a casual social philology and invested in a model of character generated by and condensed in everyday words, as a currency, if not always the dialects, criminal cant, sporting flash, and professional idiolects of *Oliver Twist* and *The Pickwick Papers*.

77. George Eliot, *Adam Bede*, ed. Stephen Gill, (New York: Penguin, 1985), 494.

78. Joseph Conrad, *The Heart of Darkness*, ed. Paul B. Armstrong (New York: W. W. Norton, 2005), 66.

79. *The Egoist* includes 50 "turned," 36 "turn," 14 "turning," and 4 "turns," plus 19 "returned," 36 "return," 7 "returning," and 4 "returns," for a total of 170 instances of the expression in the 190,673-word novel, nevermind any synonymous locutions

80. George Meredith, *The Egoist*, ed. Robert M. Adams (New York: W. W. Norton, 1979), 4.

81. Judith Wilt, *The Readable People of George Meredith* (Princeton University Press, 1975).

82. Dorothy Van Ghent, *The English Novel: Form and Function* (New York: Harper Perennial, 1967), 236, which mistakenly ascribes these lines to Dr. Middleton.

83. Oscar Wilde, "The Decay of Lying," in *De Profundis and Other Writings*, ed. Hesketh Pearson (New York: Penguin, 1986), 55–87, 72.

84. Nicholas Dames, *The Physiology of the Novel: Reading, Neural Science, and the Form of Victorian Fiction* (Oxford University Press, 2007), 193.

85. Sianne Ngai, *Our Aesthetic Categories: Zany, Cute, Interesting* (Harvard University Press, 2012), 125. See 110–73 on the interesting, which shares a history with character as I describe it.

2 Inductive "Attentions"

1. David Hume, *A Treatise of Human Nature* (London: John Noon, 1739), vol. I, 94.

2. *PP* 46

3. Michel Foucault, *The Order of Things: An Archaeology of the Human Sciences* (New York: Vintage, 1973).

4. Charlotte Brontë, *Selected Letters*, ed. Margaret Smith (Oxford World's Classics, 2010), 161–2.

5. Andrea K. Henderson, *Romantic Identities: Varieties of Subjectivity, 1774–1830* (Cambridge University Press, 1996).

6. Deidre Shauna Lynch, *The Economy of Character: Novels, Market Culture, and the Business of Inner Meaning* (University of Chicago Press, 1998).

7. "Particular," "particulars," and "especially" turn up the following times, respectively, in each novel: 46, 20, 18 in *Sense and Sensibility*; 27, 20, and 22 in *Pride and Prejudice*; 25, 9, and 22 in *Mansfield Park*; 41, 13, and 25 in *Emma*; 16, 11, and 9 in *Northanger Abbey*; 16, 6, and 13 in the shorter *Persuasion*. Of course these are just three bits of wider vocabulary of particularity that included other words, like "individual," and other techniques of scale (listing actual details). "General" appears the following times in each novel: 55 in *Sense and Sensibility*; 51 in *Pride and Prejudice*; 72 in *Mansfield Park*; 65 in *Emma*; 154 in *Northanger Abbey*; 34 in *Persuasion*. As with "particular," it is only one readily traceable term for abstraction.

8. Clifford Siskin, *The Historicity of Romantic Discourse* (Oxford University Press, 1988), 55.

9. William Whewell, *The Philosophy of the Inductive Sciences, Founded Upon Their History*. 2 vols. (London: John W. Parker, 1840), 1: xxxix. Emphasis in original.

10. Jonathan Crary, *Suspensions of Perception: Attention, Spectacle, and Modern Culture* (MIT Press, 2001).

11. Many have customarily taken for granted the epistemological triumph of the particular over the general. See Ian Watt, *The Rise of the Novel: Studies in Defoe, Richardson, and Fielding* (Berkeley: University of California Press,

2001 [1957]), 9–34; and Cynthia Wall, *The Prose of Things* (University of Chicago Press, 2006), 31–40. Paying lip-service to an ideology of particularity certainly triumphed, but a propensity to generalize and universalize survived all along in different forms; I think Wall's description of the "erosion of the universal" is immersed in and captivated by the very ideology it purports to historicize.

12. Frances Burney, *Evelina*, ed. Stewart J. Cooke (New York: W. W. Norton, 1998), 6. *Evelina*, for example, includes 66 instances of "attention" and 77 of "attend"; 61 instances of "particular/s/ity" and 53 of "general/s/ity" out of 158,620 words.

13. [Anon.], "War, in general, and modern French Wars in particular," *Fraser's Magazine for Town and Country* 60 (1859):71.

14. A. J. Ellis, "On a more general theory of Analytical Geometry, including the Cartesian as a particular case," *Reports of the British Association for the Advancement of Science* (May 7, 1855).

15. [Anon.], "British Association for the Advancement of Everything in General, and Nothing in Particular" *Punch* 3 (1842): 6–7. This was one of many *Punch* lampoons of the annual BAAS meetings and the many dutiful periodical reports of their proceedings.

16. Wilkie Collins, *Heart and Science*, ed. Steve Farmer (Peterborough: Broadview Press, 1996), 37–40. See Sue Lonoff, *Wilkie Collins and His Victorian Readers* (New York: AMS Press, 1982) for Collins's depiction of his readership.

17. Antonio Pérez-Ramos, *Francis Bacon's Idea of Science and the Maker's Knowledge Tradition* (Clarendon, 1988), 24. On interpretations and uses of Bacon in nineteenth-century literature, also Jonathan Smith, *Fact and Feeling: Baconian Science and the Nineteenth-Century Literary Imagination* (University of Wisconsin Press, 1994), 13–24.

18. David Simpson, *Romanticism, Nationalism, and the Revolt against Theory* (University of Chicago Press, 1993), 45; see 45–47 on invocations of Baconian induction for nationalist ends.

19. [G. H. Lewes], "French Romances," *Fraser's Magazine* 27 (February 1843), 184–94.

20. Ernst Cassirer, *The Philosophy of the Enlightenment*, trans. Fritz C. A. Koelln and James P. Pettegrove (Princeton University Press, 1951), 287.

21. M. H. Abrams, *The Mirror and the Lamp: Romantic Theory and the Critical Tradition* (Oxford University Press, 1953), 41.

22. The preference for generalizations is thoroughly documented. See, for example, Jerome Christensen, *Practicing Enlightenment: Hume and the Formation of a Literary Career* (Madison: University of Wisconsin Press, 1987).

23. Samuel Johnson, "Rasselas," in *The Major Works*, ed. Donald Greene (Oxford University Press, 1984), 352. Johnson's *Preface to Shakespeare* (*The Major Works*, ed. Donald Greene [Oxford: Oxford University Press, 1984] 419–56). applauds general characters: "His persons act and speak by the influence of those general passions and principles by which all minds are agitated, and the whole system of life is continued in motion. In the writings of other poets a character is too often an individual; in those of Shakespeare it is commonly a species" (421).

24. Joshua Reynolds, *Discourses on Art*, ed. Robert R. Wark (London: Paul Mellon Centre for Studies in British Art, 1997), 57 and *passim*. Naomi Schor, *Reading in Detail: Aesthetics and the Feminine* (New York: Routledge, 2007) demonstrates how detail and particularity are gendered as feminine and thus how the mainstream prioritization of generality represses, abases, or otherwise minimizes femininity (3–18).

25. William Hazlitt, "On the Imitation of Nature," *The Champion* (December 25, 1814): 216–22.

26. William Blake. *The Complete Poetry and Prose of William Blake*, ed. David V. Erdman (New York: Doubleday, 1988), 641.

27. See, for instance, Ian Duncan's discussion of Scott's attention to unassimilable particularity in *Scott's Shadow: the Novel in Romantic Edinburgh* (Princeton University Press, 2007), 70–77.

28. Adam Smith, *Lectures on Rhetoric and Belles Lettres*, 2 vols. (London and Edinburgh, 1783), II: 372.

29. William Hazlitt, *The Collected Works*, ed. P. P. Howe. 21 vols. (London: J. M. Dent and Sons, 1931–34), 12: 234.

30. See Brian Vickers, "The Emergence of Character Criticism, 1774–1800," *Shakespeare Survey: An Annual Survey of Shakespeare Studies and Production* 34 (1981): 11–21. See also Jonathan Bate, *Shakespeare and the English Romantic Imagination* (Oxford University Press, 1986) and Simpson, *Romanticism, Nationalism, and the Revolt against Theory*, 57–63.

31. [On Romeo and Juliet] (December 9, 1811), in *Coleridge's Poetry and Prose*, eds. Nicholas Halmi, Paul Magnuson, and Raimonda Modiano (New York: W. W. Norton, 2004), 310. As Seamus Perry explains, Coleridge's criticism of Shakespeare, Milton, and Wordsworth all pivots on the irreconcilable values of egotism and selflessness, and this paradoxical combination, I would add, is symptomatic of the amalgam of subjective and objective knowledge "character" reconciled. See Seamus Perry, *Coleridge and the Uses of Division* (Clarendon Press, 1999), 209–80, esp. 233–73.

32. On Theophrastan characters and the eighteenth-century "social goal of 'generalizability,'" see Lynch, *Economy of Character*, 29–47. On typological thought, see Paul J. Korshin, *Typologies in England, 1650–1820* (Princeton University Press, 1982).

33. As James Mulvihill explains, "Though it defies satisfying structural or thematic analysis – perhaps, indeed, *because* it does so – Hazlitt's epistemic model of the age displays the age's particular self-representations in their collective emergence as a 'conscious individuality,' a character." James Mulvihill, "Character and Culture in Hazlitt's Spirit of the Age," *Nineteenth-Century Literature* 45.3 (December 1990): 281–99.

34. James Chandler, *England in 1819: The Politics of Literary Culture and the Case of Romantic Historicism* (University of Chicago Press, 1998), 175; see 174–85 on the spirit-of-the-age genre.

35. Thomas Carlyle, *Critical and Miscellaneous Essays in Five Volumes* (New York: AMS Press, 1980), III: 44–61, 44.

36. George Eliot, *Impressions of Theophrastus Such*, ed. Nancy Henry (University of Iowa Press, 1994), 55. On "the nature of things," see Chapter 5 herein.

37. "Catalogue of Bemrose and Sons' Publications," in *British Books in Print*, ed. J. Whitaker & Sons, vol. 2 (London: Bemrose, 1880), 9.

38. Mary Poovey, *A History of the Modern Fact: Problems of Knowledge in the Sciences of Wealth and Society* (University of Chicago Press, 1998), 327; on Baconian induction, see xvii–xviii, 97–99, and 188–89.

39. See Book I, part III, section VI. For an exacting account of Hume's role in the history of induction, see Peter Dear, *Discipline and Experience: The Mathematical Way in the Scientific Revolution* (University of Chicago Press, 1995), 15–21.

40. Below I justify my correlation of induction and attention with textual analysis, but some nineteenth-century writers did made the connection explicitly. In the late 1860s, for instance, the American philosopher Charles Sanders Pierce – a founder of pragmatism and scholar of semiotics – thought of attention as a form of induction: see Crary, *Suspensions of Perception*, 57–58.

41. D. Rae Greiner makes this case most persuasively and eloquently in *Sympathetic Realism in Nineteenth-Century British Fiction* (Baltimore: Johns Hopkins University Press, 2012).

42. Erving Goffman makes similar claims about how the attention and inattention of others produces one's identity. See "The Insanity of Place," in *Relations in Public: Microstudies of the Public Order* (New York: Harper & Row/Colophon Books, 1972), 335–91.

43. Adam Smith, *The Theory of Moral Sentiments* (Amherst: Prometheus books, 2000), 403.

44. Steven Shapin and Simon Shaffer, *Leviathan and the Air-Pump: Hobbes, Boyle, and the Experimental Life* (Princeton University Press, 1985) and Steven Shapin, *A Social History of Truth: Civility and Science in Seventeenth-Century England* (University of Chicago Press, 1994). Jan Golinski, *Science as*

Public Culture: Chemistry and Enlightenment in Britain, 1760–1820 (Cambridge University Press, 1992). See also *Science and Beliefs: From Natural Philosophy to Natural Science, 1700–1900*, ed. David M. Knight and Matthew D. Eddy (Aldershot: Ashgate, 2005), 63–76; Peter Clark, *British Clubs and Societies, 1500–1800* (Oxford University Press, 2000).

45. The idiom of induction was by no means the only natural historical convention that novelists appropriated. See Karen Bloom Gevirtz, *Women, the Novel, and Natural Philosophy, 1660–1727* (New York: Palgrave, 2014).

46. Excluding variants, "particular" appears 92 times and "general" 108 times in the first edition.

47. Michael McKeon, *The Secret History of Domesticity: Public, Private, and the Division of Knowledge* (Baltimore: Johns Hopkins University Press, 2005), 109 and *passim*. Lennard J. Davis, *Factual Fictions: The Origins of the English Novel* (New York: Columbia University Press, 193), 213 and *passim*.

48. For William Galperin, the oppositional quality of Austen – noted by so many of even her most appreciative nineteenth-century critics – is an effect of superfluous details, recalcitrant particulars that gesture at an extra-discursive world of missed opportunities which are foreclosed by the generic, aesthetic parameters of the real by the didactic objectives or ideas of story or reality by which her critics judged her. William H. Galperin, *The Historical Austen* (Philadelphia: University of Pennsylvania Press, 2003), 59–72.

49. Susan Morgan, *In the Meantime: Character and Perception in Jane Austen's Fiction* (University of Chicago Press, 1980), 10. Morgan discusses how Austen's fiction exhibits an epistemology of perception mediated through character. She writes, for instance, that *Persuasion* thematizes – through Anne Eliot's focalization – how "the process of understanding [character] can itself shape character." "Anne's character – and through Anne, the ways of seeing other characters – is," Morgan explains, "the subject of *Persuasion*" (175).

50. Dorothy Van Ghent, *The English Novel: Form and Function* (New York: Harper Perennial, 1967), 235.

51. George Orwell, *A Collection of Essays* (London: Harvest, 1981), 63.

52. Franco Moretti, *The Bourgeois: Between History and Literature* (London: Verso, 2014), 130–44.

53. Elizabeth Deeds Ermarth, *Realism and Consensus in the English Novel* (Princeton University Press, 1983), 37, 24–54.

54. Nineteenth-century reviewers also made this connection: picking up an observation of Macaulay, G. H. Lewes, for instance, styles Austen a "Prose Shakespeare," on the basis of a mutual "power of constructing and animating character," in a review of *The Fair Carew* in *The Leader* (November 22, 1851),

115, qtd. In B. C. Southam, ed. *Jane Austen: The Critical Heritage, Volume I, 1811–1870* (New York: Routledge, 1979), 130.

55. Walter Scott, *Old Mortality*, ed. Douglas S. Mack (New York: Penguin, 1999), 323.

56. Thomas Hughes, *Tom Brown's Schooldays* (New York: Macmillan and Co., 1891), 5.

57. Catherine Gallagher, "George Eliot: Immanent Victorian," *Representations* 90 (Spring 2005), 61–74, 61.

58. See *The Affective Life of the Average Man: The Victorian Novel and the Stock Market Graph* (Columbus: Ohio University Press, 2010), 40, 27.

59. G. H. Lewes, "The Lady Novelists," *Westminster Review* lviii (July 18562): 134–35, quoted in Southam, 140.

60. [Thomas Babington Macaulay], "The Diary and Letters of Mme D'Arblay," *Edinburgh Review* lxxvi (January 1843): 561–62, quoted in Southam 122–23. See also [Anon.], "Female Novelists," *New Monthly Magazine* xcv (May 1852): 17–23.

61. William Galperin, *The Historical Austen*, 74, 66–67.

62. Richard Whately, "Review of *Northanger Abbey* and *Persuasion*," *Quarterly Review* xxiv (January 1821): 352–76; 352–53, emphasis in original.

63. Fredric Jameson, *The Antinomies of Realism* (London: Verso, 2013).

64. *MP* 507

65. John Aikin, *An Essay on the Application of Natural History to Poetry* (London: Joseph Johnson, 1777), 10.

66. On Smith and Austen, see Peter Knox-Shaw, *Jane Austen and the Enlightenment* (Cambridge University Press, 2004), 139–52.

67. Penny Gay, *Jane Austen and the Theatre* (Cambridge University Press, 2002) registers how Austen incorporates theatrical experience into her prose.

68. Following Dorothy Van Ghent and others, many scholars have recognized how Austen's prose integrates character with economic discourse. Debt, credit, interest, capital, exchange, commerce, traffic, and obligation: such terms were correlated to character through ideologies and institutions of credit, and, as Margot C. Finn shows, Austen thematizes the correlation of personal debt to moral character in figures such as Sir Walter Elliot of *Persuasion* and Eliza Brandon of *Sense and Sensibility*; see Finn, *The Character of Credit: Personal Debt in English Culture, 1740–1914* (Cambridge University Press, 2003), 48, 60. Personal credit was a necessary fiction for eighteenth- and nineteenth-century Britons, and as such credit was of course an essential component of the plot, characterization, and themes of most British novels. See Dorothy Van Ghent, *The English Novel*, 135–36; Raymond Williams, *The Country and the City* (Oxford University Press, 1973), 115–16; and Mark Schorer, "Fiction and the 'Analogical Matrix,'" in *Critiques and Essays on Modern Fiction*, ed. John

W. Aldridge (New York: The Ronald Press, 1952), 83–98. Notable accounts of Austen's vocabulary include Norman Page, "The Best Chosen Language" in *The Language of Jane Austen* (New York: Barnes & Noble, 1972), 54–89 and Stuart M. Tave, *Some Words of Jane Austen* (University of Chicago Press, 1973). None attend to my subject words.

69. Alex Woloch, *The One vs. the Many: Minor Characters and the Space of the Protagonist in the Novel* (Princeton University Press, 2003), 45, emphasis in original.

70. Eve Kosofsky Sedgwick, "Jane Austen and the Masturbating Girl," in *Questions of Evidence: Proof, Practice, and Persuasion across the Disciplines*, eds. James Chandler, Arnold. I. Davidson, and Harry Harootunian (University of Chicago Press, 1994), 105–24.

71. Jameson, *Antinomies of Realism*, 41–42.

72. On Austen and the picturesque, see Alistair M. Duckworth, *The Improvement of the Estate: A Study of Jane Austen's Novels* (Baltimore: Johns Hopkins University Press, 1971); William H. Galperin, *The Historical Austen*, 44–81; Jill Heydt-Stevenson, "Liberty, Connection, and Tyranny: The Novels of Jane Austen and the Aesthetic Movement of the Picturesque," in *Lessons of Romanticism: A Critical Companion*, eds. Thomas Pfau and Robert F. Glackner (Durham: Duke University Press, 1998), 261–79; and Alan Liu, *Wordsworth: The Sense of History* (Stanford University Press, 1989), 61–137.

73. William Galperin has described Austen's realism as the effect of missed opportunities, of persistent disavowals of possibilities foreclosed by the generic parameters Austen simultaneously embraces and critiques. See "'Describing What Never Happened': Jane Austen and the History of Missed Opportunities," *ELH* 73.2 (2006): 355–82.

74. I discuss this passage at greater length in Chapter 4.

75. Leah Price, "Reader's Block: Trollope and the Book as Prop," in *The Feeling of Reading*, ed. Rachel Ablow (Minneapolis: University of Minnesota Press, 2010), 47–68, describes reading as deliberately not paying attention.

76. John Stuart Mill later defined "all the world" in *On Liberty* (1859): "the world, to each individual, means the part of it with which he comes in contact; his party, his sect, his church, his class of society; the man may be called, by comparison, almost liberal and large-minded to whom it means anything so comprehensive as his own country or his own age." John Stuart Mill, *Mill: The Spirit of the Age, On Liberty, The Subjection of Women*, ed. Alan Ryan (New York: W. W. Norton, 1997), 54.

77. Mary Shelley, *Frankenstein 1818 Text*, ed. Marilyn Butler (Oxford University Press, 1994), 87, 138, 154.

78. Anthony Trollope's *The Last Chronicle of Barset*, for example, includes the phrase four times on one page (140), but it occurs throughout Trollope's oeuvre.

79. Adela Pinch, *Strange Fits of Passion: Epistemologies of Emotion, Hume to Austen* (Stanford University Press, 1996), 139.

80. Tony Tanner, "'In Between': *Persuasion*," in *Jane Austen* (Harvard University Press, 1986), 209. See also 208–49. Maurice Merleau-Ponty, *Phenomenology of Perception*, trans. Colin Smith (London: Routledge, 2002), proffers *attention* as a middle term for the perception of motivated and reflected objects, like the self, which have no concrete, objectively knowable existence but which cannot be said to be altogether fictions: his phenomenological account of attention aptly, if obscurely, describes Austen's usage, for attention articulates her character's in-between-ness (30–59).

81. On character, reading, and performance here, see Susan Harlan, "'Talking' and Reading Shakespeare in Jane Austen's *Mansfield Park*," *Wordsworth Circle* 39.1–2 (Winter–Spring 2008): 43–46.

82. Patricia Meyer Spacks, *Boredom: The Literary History of a State of Mind* (University of Chicago Press, 1995), 124–5.

83. Stephen Arata, "On Not Paying Attention," *Victorian Studies* 46 (2004): 193–205.

84. Nicholas Dames, *The Physiology of the Novel: Reading, Neural Science, and the Form of Victorian Fiction* (Oxford University Press, 2007), 77.

85. Michel de Certeau, *The Practice of Everyday Life*, trans. Steven Randall (Berkeley: University of California Press, 1988), xii–xvii.

86. The two tests of character presented here in *Mansfield Park* and *Pride and Prejudice* – reading aloud and rereading – resurface together in one of the most thoughtful, erudite encomiums for Austen's style: G. H. Lewes's 1859 "The Novels of Jane Austen." Lewes twice iterates that "the highest department of art" is "the representation of character," and he claims "a sympathy is induced" between the reader the ordinary, as if the reader became a character (Southam 152, 153, 155). Lewes describes the process of "dramatic impersonation" responsible for this characterization, presumably what we now call free indirect discourse, but he concludes that no single instance can adequately summarize the effect because it is diffused throughout the text, a property of the prose. Victorian literary reviews, as rule, feign to have no space to elaborate their most provocative claims, but Lewes's restraint also evokes an attitude of genteel inattentiveness, as if to exemplify would be to assume that the reader doubted him or required evidence for the self-evident and to be too professional. [G. H. Lewes], "The Novels of Jane Austen," *Blackwood's Edinburgh Magazine* lxxxvi (July 1859): 99–113, quoted in Southam 148–66.

87. John F. W. Herschel, *A Preliminary Discourse on the Study of Natural Philosophy*, with a new forward by Arthur Fine (University of Chicago Press, 1987).

88. Most prominent and protracted of these disputes was that between Mill, who maintained that induction was purely empirical (that generalizations became sensible through the cumulative experience of particulars), and Whewell, who maintained that knowledge was comprised by a "Fundamental Antithesis" of empirical perceptions and generalizations induced from these perceptions by means of "Fundamental Ideas" (a priori categories of perception like space, time, likeness, substance, weight, number, and causation). Whewell said that the Fundamental Ideas were "superinduced" upon observed particulars in a process called "colligation," which inferred a general law. See Laura J. Snyder, *Reforming Philosophy: A Victorian Debate on Science and Society* (University of Chicago Press, 2006), 75–76. Mill proposed a "psychological method" of tracing alleged intuitions to external causes, consonant with a positivist streak that impelled him to imagine a science of character formation, "ethology." See Snyder, esp. 40–42 and 331–32, and Menachem Fisch, *William Whewell, Philosopher of Science* (Oxford University Press, 1991).

89. See Laura J. Snyder, *The Philosophical Breakfast Club* (New York: Broadway, 2011), 99–127.

90. John Herschel, "Whewell on Inductive Sciences," *Quarterly Review* 68 (1841):177–238, and see Snyder, *Reforming Philosophy*, 81–82.

91. James A. Secord, *Victorian Sensation: The Extraordinary Publication, Reception, and Secret Authorship of* Vestiges of the Natural History of Creation (University of Chicago Press, 2000), 272–73.

92. James A. Secord, *Visions of Science: Books and Readers at the Dawn of the Victorian Age* (Oxford University Press, 2014), 81.

93. Matthew Arnold, "On the Modern Element in Literature," *Macmillan's Magazine* 19.112 (February 1869), 304–14; 305.

94. Joel Haefner considers Hazlitt's theory of character (as in people's identities) in "'The Soul Speaking in the Face': Hazlitt's Concept of Character," *SEL: Studies in English Literature, 1500–1900* 24, no. 4 (Summer 1984): 655–70.

95. Jules David Law, The Rhetoric of Empiricism: Language and Perception from Locke to I. A. Richards (Cornell University Press, 1993).

96. Smiles's *Character* (1871) says: "We have spoken of work as a discipline: it is also an educator of character. Even work that produces no results, because it is work, is better than torpor – inasmuch as it educates faculty, and is thus preparatory to successful work. The habit of working teaches method" (110). Smiles perhaps alludes to Coleridge's "Essay on the Principles of Method,"

introductory to the *Encyclopedia Metropolitana* (1818–45), which equates character and method based on their investment in orderly relations. Coleridge claims the "merit" of Method "is, that *everything is in its place*" (Halmi 560). "METHOD," he writes, "becomes natural to the mind which has been accustomed to contemplate not *things* only, or for their own sake alone, but likewise and chiefly the *relations* of things, either their relations to each other, or to the observer, or to the state and apprehension of the hearers. To enumerate and analyze these relations, with the conditions under which alone they are discoverable, is to teach the science of Method" (Halmi 560). For Coleridge, methodical individuals therefore characterize their experiences by apprehending them in relations: a "man of methodical industry and honourable pursuits ... realizes it ideal divisions, and gives a character and individuality to its moments" (Halmi 562).

97. The notion that reading ought to be a strenuous, repetitive work recurred throughout nineteenth-century criticism, prominently appearing in the Calvinist hermeneutic principles that Suzy Anger observes in Thomas Carlyle. Suzy Anger, *Victorian Interpretation* (Cornell University Press, 2005), 70.

98. *Table Talk*, ed. Carl Woodring, 2 vols, *The Collected Works of Samuel Taylor Coleridge* (New York and London: Routledge & Kegan Paul, Princeton University Press, 1990), I: 125. Coleridge's "Essays on the Principles of Method" in *The Friend* (1818) repeatedly discuss Shakespeare's fictional personages to illustrate the balanced particularity and generality of the ideal "Science of Method." On Coleridge's interpretation of Bacon, see Smith, *Fact and Feeling*, 62–77, esp. 68.

99. William Hazlitt, "On Knowledge of the World," *The London Weekly Review* (December 1827).

100. Roy Park *Hazlitt and the Spirit of the Age* (Oxford University Press, 1971) contends that Hazlitt objected to abstraction because he objected "to all closed systems of thought in which the whole of human experience was interpreted in light of the system's initial premise, empirical or metaphysical, with scant regard to the individuality, complexity and diversity of 'the truth of things.'" David Bromwich disagrees, however, and claims Hazlitt only perfunctorily objects to the adverse (French) connotations of abstract theory and lifeless systematization, but maintains abstraction is fundamental to all imagination (Bromwich 75–77).

101. Baden Powell, *The Unity of Worlds and of Nature* (Cambridge: Cambridge University Press, [1856] 2009), 3–179.

102. Richard Henry Horne, *A New Spirit of the Age* (New York: Harper & Brothers, 1844), 9–52.

103. See John Bowen, *Other Dickens: From Pickwick to Chuzzlewit*, Oxford University Press, 2000, 16–20, for a summary of this well-trodden issue.

104. See, for examples, George Henry Lewes, "Criticism in Relation to Novels," *Fortnightly Review* 3 (December 15, 1865), 352–61 and "Dickens in Relation to Criticism," *Fortnightly Review* n.s. 2 (February 1, 1872): 141–54.

105. "A New Spirit of the Age," *The Morning Chronicle* (April 12, 1844), in *The Works of W. M. Thackeray* (New York: Charles Scribner's Sons, 1904), *Miscellaneous Essays Sketches and Reviews*, XXX: 99.

106. On Dickens's "metonymic reciprocity," see J. Hillis Miller, "The Fiction of Realism: *Sketches by Boz, Oliver Twist,* and Cruikshank's Illustrations," *Dickens Centennial Essays*, eds. Ada Nesbit and Blake Nevius (Berkeley: University of California Press, 1971), 97.

107. *The Reflector* 3 (April–September 1811); citations are from E. V. Lucas, ed., *The Works of Charles and Mary Lamb*, 7 vols. (London: Methuen & Co., 1903–5), vol. 1, *Miscellaneous Prose, 1798–1834,* 91–112. Dickens read Lamb's essay. In *The Life of Charles Dickens* (London: Chapman and Hall, 1872–74), II: 382–33, John Forster quotes Dickens admiring Hogarth's prints and evaluating Lamb's critique. On the influence of Lamb's essay and its innovative stress on the "suggestive," see Frederick Burwick, "Lamb, Hazlitt, and De Quincey on Hogarth," *The Wordsworth Circle* 28.1 (Winter 1997): 59–69.

108. Nineteenth-century reviewers typically compared this prodigality of characters to Walter Scott and Shakespeare: see, for example, "A Review of *Oliver Twist*," *Literary Gazette* (November 24, 1838), quoted in Philip Collins, ed., *Dickens: The Critical Heritage* (London: Routledge and Kegan Paul, 1986), 741.

109. Crary, *Suspensions of Perception*, 17.

110. In "'Very Abstract and Terribly Concrete': Capitalism and *The Theory of the Novel*," *NOVEL: A Forum on Fiction* 42.2 (Summer 2009): 311–17, David Cunningham privileges passages suspended between concrete particularity and utter abstraction as the signature features of novelistic modernity: "It is the dialectic of abstraction and concretion unique to each work – the variable points at which a 'concretism,' as Adorno puts it, 'passes directly into the most extreme abstraction' [250–51] – that on this reading marks its own negotiation with the sociohistorical reality of capitalism it confronts and that should thus provide one key site of critical judgment and reflection" (315–16). Cunningham concludes, "The dialectic without synthesis between its abstract and concrete tendencies is, on this reading, the very condition of the modernity of the novel as such. . . . Very abstract and terribly concrete at the same time, the novel can be no less so than that sociohistorical reality of modern culture that it has always confronted" (316).

111. David Masson, *British Novelists and Their Styles: Being a Critical Sketch of the History of British Prose Fiction* [1859] (Boston: D. Lothrop and Co., 1875),

243–58, quotations from 254–55. On Masson's role in the history of novel theory and criticism, see Jonathan Farina, "David Masson's *British Novelists and Their Styles* (1859) and the Establishment of Novels as an Object of Academic Study," *BRANCH: Britain, Representation and Nineteenth-Century History*, ed. Dino Franco Felluga. Extension of *Romanticism and Victorianism on the Net*: www.branchcollective.org/?ps_articles=jonathan-farina-on-david-massons-british-novelists-and-their-styles-1859-and-the-establishment-of-novels-as-an-object-of-academic-study.

112. E. S. Dallas, *The Gay Science*. 2 vols. (London: Chapman and Hall, 1866), I:26.

113. Carolyn Williams, *Transfigured World: Walter Pater's Aesthetic Historicism* (Cornell University Press, 1989), 52.

114. Carolyn Williams, "Walter Pater's Impressionism and the Form of Historical Revival," in *Knowing the Past: Victorian Literature & Culture*, ed. Suzy Anger (Cornell University Press, 2001):77–99, 80–81. As George Levine puts it, "Pater is arguing for a way to be objective about subjectivity, to find a position outside experience from which to experience it and possess it" (249). Levine describes Pater's paradoxically impressionistic objectivist epistemology (Dying to Know: Scientific Epistemology and Narrative in Victorian England. University of Chicago Press, 2002, 244–67).

115. Teukolsky explains how this rationalization and abstraction of art is part of the history of formalism, as it extends the enlightenment project of rationalization, particularly in the work of Roger Fry and Clive Bell, who "argue for formalism as an intellectual purification of art, a conceptual abstraction that is the most sublime kind of thought and emotion. In this they were continuing the Enlightenment endeavor to rationalize form – a project that Victorians also engaged in, as we saw . . . with Ruskin's use of eighteenth-century modes of classification through form" (195–96).

116. Suzy Anger, *Victorian Interpretation* (Cornell University Press, 2005), 134; see 131–40 for more on the key issues in the "objectivity" of Victorian literary criticism.

117. Richard Green Moulton, *Shakespeare as a Dramatic Artist* (1893; New York: Dover, 1966), 25, emphasis in original.

3 "Our skeptical as if"

1. Charles Dickens, *David Copperfield*, ed. Jerome H. Buckley (New York: Norton, 1990), 54.

2. Joseph Hillis Miller notes in passing the "omnipresence of the locution 'as if' in Dickens' most brilliant metaphorical transformations. The 'as if' admits

the fictitious nature of a surrealist view of persons or things. It testifies to the copresence of Dickens' childish view and his mature, disillusioned view." *Charles Dickens: The World of His Novels* (Harvard University Press, 1958), 152. Michael Hollington, "*Dickens* the Flâneur," *Dickensian* 77 (1981): 71–87, explains the adequacy of analogic tropes such as simile to Dickens's London. See also Garrett Stewart, *Dickens and the Trials of the Imagination* (Harvard University Press, 1974), Robert Golding, *Idiolects in Dickens: The Major Techniques and Chronological Development* (New York: St. Martin's Press, 1985), 33–34; and David Parker, "Dickens's Archness," *Dickensian* 67 (1971): 149–58.

3. According to a search with Google Ngram.

4. "As if" appears 236 times in *Nicholas Nickleby*, 336 times in *Martin Chuzzlewit*, 348 in *Little Dorrit*. The frequency of "as if" in *Bleak House* is 0.001718, which means the two-word phrase constitutes 17 of every 1,000 words of the novel. "As if" appears at the following frequencies in these novels: *Nicholas Nickleby*, 0.001434; *Martin Chuzzlewit*, 0.001944; *Dombey and Son*, 0.001995; *David Copperfield*, 0.002162; *Little Dorrit*, 0.002017; *Our Mutual Friend*, 0.002348. It appears with the highest frequency in *Great Expectations*, 0.002812. "As if" is actually one of the strongest stylistic similarities between the prose of Dickens and George Eliot. With the exceptions of *Adam Bede* (244 instances/0.002189) and *Middlemarch* (284 instances/0.001755) and Gaskell, Dickens used "as if" a statistically significant frequency higher than all canonical Victorian novelists and nineteenth-century American novelists, including Hawthorne, Melville, James, Austen, Collins, the Brontës, Trollope, and Hardy.

5. Wolfgang Iser, *The Fictive and the Imaginary: Charting Literary Anthropology* (Baltimore: Johns Hopkins University Press, 1993), 130–152.

6. The best accounts remain Dorothy Van Ghent, "On *Great Expectations*," in *The English Novel: Form and Function* (New York: Harper Perennial, 1967) 154–70, and J. Hillis Miller, *Charles Dickens*. On the uncanny, see Robert Newsome, *Dickens on the Romantic Side of Familiar Things*: Bleak House *and the Novel Tradition* (New York: Columbia University Press, 1977). On Dickens's explicit animation of abstractions, particularly the zeitgeist, see Jonathan Arac, *Commissioned Spirits: The Shaping of Social Motion in Dickens, Carlyle, Melville, and Hawthorne* (Cornell University Press, 1989). Such readings focus on metaphorical passages like that in *Dombey and Son* (1846–48) where the narrator yearns for "a good spirit who would take the house-tops off, with a more potent and benignant hand than" Le Sage's Asmodeus, and "[rouse] some who never looked out upon the world of human life around them, to a knowledge of their own relation to it, and [make] them acquainted with a perversion of nature in their own contracted sympathies and estimates" (702).

These passages explicitly represent humans as secrets unto themselves who need the agency of a narrator-like spirit to know themselves; and therefore they displace the agency for self-knowledge into an abstract figure.

7. Garrett Stewart, "Dickens and Language," in *The Cambridge Companion to Charles Dickens*, ed. John O. Jordan (Cambridge University Press, 2001), 141–43.

8. Arthur O. Lovejoy sketches the history of this epistemology in *The Great Chain of Being* (Harvard University Press, 1964), 183–207.

9. Dahlia Porter, "Scientific Analogy and Literary Taxonomy in Darwin's *Loves of the Plants*," *European Romantic Review* 18.2 (April 2007): 216–17.

10. David Hartley, *Observations on Man, His Frame, His Duty, and His Expectations* [1749]. 3 vols. (Joseph Johnson: London, 1791), II: 160–61.

11. Edmund Burke, *A Philosophical Inquiry into the Origin of Our Ideas of the Sublime and the Beautiful*, ed. James T. Boulton (South Bend: Notre Dame University Press, 1968), 139.

12. Kant distinguishes between constitutive and regulative ideas in "Dialectic of the Teleological Judgment" and "Methodology of the Teleology of Judgment" in Immanuel Kant, *Critique of Judgment*, ed. Werner S. Pluhar (Indiana: Hackett, 1987), 384.

13. Steven Shapin, *A Social History of Truth: Civility and Science in Seventeenth-Century England* (University of Chicago Press, 1994), 125.

14. I discuss self-abnegation and "as if" further below, but see George Levine, *Dying to Know: Scientific Epistemology and Narrative in Victorian England* (University of Chicago Press, 2002).

15. On Christian comportment and the epistemic decorum of science, see Shapin 193–242.

16. On Butler's Victorian influence, see Jane Garnett, "Bishop Butler and the Zeitgeist: Butler and the Development of Christian Moral Philosophy in Victorian Britain," in *Joseph Butler's Moral and Religious Thought: Tercentenary Essays*, ed. Christopher Cunliffe (Oxford University Press, 1992), 63–96. R. C. Tennant usefully explains Butler's analogical adaptation of Locke's theory of personal identity (character) in "The Anglican Response to Locke's Theory of Personal Identity," *Journal of the History of Ideas* 43.1 (January–March 1982): 73–90.

17. On "conjectural history" in the eighteenth and nineteenth centuries, see Mary Poovey, *A History of the Modern Fact: Problems of Knowledge in the Sciences of Wealth and Society* (University of Chicago Press, 1998), 218–36 and *passim*.

18. On sympathy and British fiction, see Barbara M. Benedict, *Framing Feeling: Sentiment and Style in English Prose Fiction, 1745–1800* (New York: AMS Press, 1994); Catherine Gallagher, *Nobody's Story: The Vanishing Acts of Women*

Writers in the Marketplace, 1670–1820 (Berkeley: University of California Press, 1994); Julie K. Ellison, *Cato's Tears and the Making of Anglo-American Emotion* (University of Chicago Press, 1999); Audrey Jaffe, *Scenes of Sympathy: Identity and Representation in Victorian Fiction* (Cornell University Press, 2000); and Adela Pinch, *Strange Fits of Passion: Epistemologies of Emotion, Hume to Austen* (Stanford University Press, 1996).

19. Adam Smith, *The Theory of Moral Sentiments* (Amherst: Prometheus Books, 2000), 3.

20. David Hume, *A Treatise of Human Nature* (London: John Noon, 1739).

21. Coincident with these epistemic changes, blatant forms of personification such as James Thomson's infamous "finny tribe" swiftly lost credibility with natural philosophers and poets alike. Anthropomorphizing the world nevertheless remained an epistemic imperative. In place of apostrophe and the overt pathetic fallacies of Erasmus Darwin's chatty, conjugal, mythological plants, conditional analogies subtly characterized organisms, inanimate objects, and social abstractions with the definitive individuality and sympathetic agency that define human character in Smith's *Theory of Moral Sentiments*. Personification in all sorts of different modes was an accepted form of knowledge production and transmission in the eighteenth-century, especially in Lord Kames, Hugh Blair, Erasmus Darwin, and even – although he explicitly denies it in the Preface to *Lyrical Ballads* – Wordsworth. See Catherine Packham, "The Science and Poetry of Animation: Personification, Analogy, and Erasmus Darwin's *Loves of the Plants,*" *Romanticism* 10.2 (2004): 191–208.

22. On the relationship between fiction, conjecture, and probability, see Lennard J. Davis, *Factual Fictions: The Origins of the English Novel* (University of Pennsylvania Press, 1997), 212 and *passim*; Michael McKeon, *The Origins of the English Novel, 1600–1740* (Baltimore: Johns Hopkins University Press, 1987), 118–28; and Douglas Lane Patey, *Probability and Literary Form: Philosophic Theory and Literary Practice in the Augustan Age* (Cambridge University Press, 1984).

23. Michael McKeon, *The Secret History of Domesticity: Public, Private, and the Division of Knowledge* (Baltimore: Johns Hopkins University Press, 2005), 108–09.

24. William H. Galperin, *The Historical Austen* (University of Pennsylvania Press, 2003), 90.

25. Clara Reeve, *The Progress of Romance and the History of Charoba, Queen of Aegypt* (Colchester, 1785), 111. Quoted in Galperin, 90.

26. Charles Lyell, *Principles of Geology*, ed. Martin J. S. Rudwick, 3 vols. (University of Chicago Press, 1992), I:3, originally published by John Murray in three volumes from 1830–33.

27. [G. Maclaren], *Scotsman* (September 25, 1830): 1 and *Athenaeum* (December 6, 1834): 881, both quoted in Charles Lyell, *Principles of Geology*, ed. James Secord (New York: Penguin, 1997), xx.

28. Alan Rauch, *Useful Knowledge: The Victorians, Morality, and the March of Intellect* (Durham: Duke University Press, 2001), 1–59.

29. Foremost amongst these critics was Henry James, who pinned the morality of fiction to its execution or treatment instead of its content. See Rohan Amanda Maitzen, "'The Soul of Art': Understanding Victorian Ethical Criticism," *ESC: English Studies in Canada* 31.2/3 (2005): 151–86.

30. On the compatible work of new geology and scripture, see William Maginn, "Discoveries of Modern Geologists," *Fraser's Magazine* 6.31 (August 1832): 54–66; 6.33 (October 1832): 278–85; and 7.41 (May 1833): 578–85.

31. *Spectator* (January 14, 1832): 39, quoted in Secord 1997, xv. Dickens invoked the same Shakespeare quotation in his characterization of the agglomeration of "fact and fancy" that his journal *Household Words* would produce. See [Charles Dickens], "A Preliminary Word," *Household Words* 1 (March 30, 1850): 1.

32. See James A. Secord, *Victorian Sensation: The Extraordinary Publication, Reception, and Secret Authorship of Vestiges of the Natural History of Creation* (University of Chicago Press, 2000), 235, 240, and 397–400 on Victorian ideas about the character of scientific books.

33. Charles Lyell, *Principles of Geology*, ed. James Secord (New York: Penguin, 1997), xii, xiii.

34. Lyell discriminates between the two connotations of conjecture current at the turn of the nineteenth century. He denigrates the fantastic and mystical speculation of Paley's *Natural Theology*, even though his own work readily subscribes to many of Paley's assumptions, and instead aligns his analogy with the work of conjectural philosophers and historians such as Dugald Stewart, on whose *Elements of the Philosophy of the Human Mind* (1792–1827) he draws in *Principles of Geology*. On Lyell's relation to the Scottish Enlightenment, see Roy Porter, "Charles Lyell and the Principles of the History of Geology," *British Journal for the History of Science* 9 (1976): 91–103, and James Secord, "Introduction," in Charles Lyell, *Principles of Geology*, ed. James Secord (New York: Penguin, 1997), xxii.

35. William Whewell coined "uniformitarianism" to distinguish Lyell's argument from "Catastrophists" but we ought to be careful not conflate uniformitarianism and gradualism. The important point for me about Lyell is the assumption that changes are uniform and small, which is the point of gradualism, but that the natural laws governing change are uniform now and then, which is to say the abstract laws are the same, not the concrete material changes. Review of *Principles of Geology*, vol. 2, *Quarterly Review* 47 (1832), 126.

36. Charles Lyell, *Principles of Geology*, ed. James Secord (New York: Penguin, 1997), xix, emphasis in original

37. "To produce systematic knowledge about society, human nature, or the market, social scientists first had to generate an abstraction – 'society,' 'human nature,' or 'the market' – that somehow stood in for, but did not refer directly to, whatever material phenomena it was said to represent": Mary Poovey, "The Structure of Anxiety in Political Economy and *Hard Times*," in *Knowing the Past: Victorian Literature and Culture*, ed. Suzy Anger (Cornell University Press, 2001), 151.

38. On realist narrative as a mode of representing what cannot be seen, see Alexander Welsh, *Strong Representations: Narrative and Circumstantial Evidence in England* (Baltimore: Johns Hopkins University Press, 1992), 178–95.

39. Charles Lyell, *Principles of Geology*, ed. Martin J. S. Rudwick, vol. 1 (1833; University of Chicago Press, 1969), 83.

40. Andrew H. Miller, *The Burdens of Perfection: On Ethics and Reading in Nineteenth-Century British Literature* (Cornell University Press, 2008), xii.

41. Gowan Dawson, "Literary Megatheriums and Loose Baggy Monsters: Paleontology and the Victorian Novel," *Victorian Studies* 53.2 (Winter 2011): 203–30, 212–16. Dawson explains that the Megatherium came to prominence in William Buckland's Bridgewater Treatise, *Geology and Mineralogy Considered with Reference to Natural Theology* (1836), where it starred precisely because it seemed to differ from other quadrupeds. Taking the exception as the sign of the rule, Buckland interprets various features of the Megatherium as homologous to those of other quadrupeds. The Megatherium thus became a popular touchstone for synecdochic historiography, a mode of history that replaces missing evidence by assuming that it is analogous to known entities. While Thackeray used it to represent fiction, Thomas Carlyle employed it as a figure for characterizing historiography. John M. Ulrich, "Thomas Carlyle, Richard Owen, and the Paleontological Articulation of the Past," *Journal of Victorian Culture* 11.1 (2006): 30–58.

42. W. M. Thackeray, *The Newcomes*, ed. Andrew Sanders (Oxford University Press, 1995), 616.

43. Critics tend to ascribe this to the generic undermining of omniscience characteristic of omniscient narratives. See George Levine, *The Realistic Imagination: English Fiction from* Frankenstein *to* Lady Chatterley (University of Chicago Press, 1981), 164.

44. [Margaret Oliphant], "Mr. Thackeray and his Novels," *Blackwood's Edinburgh Magazine* 77.471 (January 1855): 86–96. Oliphant was one of many to level this judgment, which could be positive or negative.

45. Perhaps the most exemplary of these is [Whitwell Elwin], "The Newcomes. Memoirs of a Most Respectable Family," *The Quarterly Review* 97.194

(September 1855): 350–78: Elwin praises *The Newcomes* for "a rich, abundance of strong, idiomatic, sterling English" (358) with "a marvelous perception of truth of character" (352).

46. See Amanpal Garcha, *From Sketch to Novel: The Development of Victorian Fiction* (Cambridge University Press, 2009).

47. "Review of The Newcomes. Memoirs of a most Respectable Family," *The Quarterly Review* 97 (September 1855): 350–387, 352.

48. E. S. Dallas, *The Gay Science.* 2 vols. (London: Chapman and Hall, 1866), I: 303.

49. I take *Bleak House* as the model here, if only because the form of the detective novel "depends," as George Levine puts it, "on the assumption that the conditions of ordinary life constantly disguise (even if in a Holmesian world they leave many traces of) an authentic reality." *Dying to Know*, 148.

50. William Buckland popularized the Megalosaurus in "Notice on the Megalosaurus or Great Fossil Lizard of Stonesfield," *Transactions of the Geological Society of London* 2.1 (1824): 390–96. Dickens may have invoked I metaphorically for similar purposes as Thackeray, but he was scarcely as intimate with geology. Still, Levine notes that Dickens, if he did not write much directly about science, certainly "absorbed ... some of the key ideas issuing from contemporary developments in geology, astronomy, and physics." George Levine, *Darwin and the Novelists: Patterns of Science in Victorian Fiction* (University of Chicago Press, 1988), 124. Ann Y. Wilkinson calls Dickens a Neptunist, from this passage; on *Bleak House* and science, see her "*Bleak House*: From Faraday to Judgment Day," *ELH* 34.2 (June 1967): 225–47.

51. J. Hillis Miller, "The Fiction of Realism: Sketches by Boz, Oliver Twist, and Cruikshank's Illustrations," *Dickens Centennial Essays*, eds. Ada Nesbit and Blake Nevius (Berkeley: University of California Press, 1971), 97.

52. Harry E. Shaw, *Narrating Reality: Austen, Scott, Eliot* (Cornell University Press, 1999), 234–35, 234fn13.

53. Nancy Armstrong makes the case that realism was indeed a recognizable movement: "everyone knew what realism was; authors wrote in relation to it, and readers read with a standard in mind based on the fidelity of language to visual evidence" *Fiction in the Age of Photography: The Legacy of British Realism* (Harvard University Press, 1999), 10. John Romano makes the case that Dickens's realism is an effect of his manifest frustration with the fact that language cannot picture reality. See *Dickens and Reality* (New York: Columbia University Press, 1978).

54. The literature on this is profuse, but see David Wayne Thomas, *Cultivating Victorians: Liberal Culture and the Aesthetic* (University of Pennsylvania Press, 2004), 22–28 and *passim*.

55. On the nuances of the Victorian "culture of altruism," see Stefan Collini, *Public Moralists: Political Thought and Intellectual Life in Britain 1850–1930* (Oxford University Press, 1991), 60–90.

56. Roland Barthes discusses this function of the proper name in *S/Z*, trans. Richard Miller (New York: Hill and Wang, 1974), 94–7.

57. Nina Auerbach, "Alluring Vacancies in the Victorian Character," *The Kenyon Review* 8.3 (Summer 1986): 36.

58. The oft-quoted phrase, "the romantic side of familiar things," comes from the preface of *Bleak House*. Newsome addresses the phrase in terms of the uncanny, melancholy, and the grotesque in *Dickens on the Romantic Side of Familiar Things:* Bleak House *and the Novel Tradition*.

59. John Stuart Mill, *Autobiography and Other Writings*, ed. Jack Stillinger (Boston: Houghton Mifflin, 1969), 101–2.

60. Lionel Trilling, *Sincerity and Authenticity* (Harvard University Press, 1972), 7.

61. See *Knowing Dickens* (Cornell University Press, 2007), 94–95. See also *The Letters of Charles Dickens*, ed. Kathleen Tillotson (Clarendon Press, 1977), IV: 207, for one of many instances where Dickens imagines his novels themselves "as if" they were real.

62. Charles Dickens, *Our Mutual Friend*, ed. Adrian Poole (New York: Penguin, 1997), 143–44.

63. Both Elizabeth Ermarth, *Realism and Consensus in the English Novel* (Princeton University Press, 1983) and Audrey Jaffe, *Vanishing Points: Dickens, Narrative, and the Subject of Omniscience* (Berkeley: University of California Press, 1991) note that omniscience is always delimited or strategically partial.

64. J. A. V. Chapple and Arthur Pollard, eds. *The Letters of Mrs. Gaskell* (Manchester: Manchester University Press, 1997), 538.

65. "As if" appears 206 times in *North and South* (187, 414 words), 181 times in *Ruth* (164,647 words), 91 times in the much shorter *Cranford* (72,393 words), and 168 times in *Mary Barton* (165,797).

66. On ideology as the medium of "lived experience," see Louis Althusser, *Lenin and Philosophy, and Other Essays* (London: New Left Review Books, 1971), 204–5.

67. Slavoj Žižek, *The Sublime Object of Ideology* (New York: Verso, 1989), 18.

68. See Žižek 11–23 on the representation of the real or universal knowledge as an unconscious subject. Michel de Certeau posits "as if" as the paradoxical relation historiography establishes "between two antinomic terms, between the real and discourse. Its task is one of connecting them and, at the point where this link cannot be imagined, of working as if the two were being joined." *The Writing of History*, trans. Tom Conley (New York: Columbia University Press, 1988), xxvii, emphasis in original.

69. Catherine Gallagher, *The Industrial Reformation of English Fiction: Social Discourse and Narrative Form 1832–1867* (University of Chicago Press, 1985), 68.

70. Lukács writes: "in the created reality of the novel all that becomes visible is the distance separating the systematisation from concrete life: a systemisation which emphasises the conventionality of the objective world and the interiority of the subjective one." Georg Lukács, *The Theory of the Novel*, trans. Anna Bostock (Boston: The MIT Press, 1971), 70.

71. Raymond Williams, *Culture and Society, 1780–1950*. New York: Columbia University Press, 1983, 87–91.

72. Charles Dickens, *The Old Curiosity Shop*, ed. Norman Page (New York: Penguin, 2000), 247.

73. Viktor Shklovsky, "Art as Device," *The Theory of Prose*. Trans. Benjamin Sher (London: Dalkey Archive Press, [1990] 2014), 1–14.

74. Ian Duncan, *Scott's Shadow: The Novel in Romantic Edinburgh* (Princeton University Press, 2007), 29–30.

75. Mary Poovey, *Genres of the Credit Economy: Mediating Value in Eighteenth- and Nineteenth-Century Britain* (University of Chicago Press, 2008), 374.

76. John Tyndall, *Fragments of Science:* A Series of Detached Essays, Addresses, and Reviews. 2 vols. (London: Longmans, Green, and Co., 1892), II, 103.

77. Michel Foucault, *The Order of Things: An Archeology of the Human Sciences* (New York: Vintage, 1994),

78. The influential early nineteenth-century physiologist Thomas Brown explicitly argues for substituting "suggestion" for "association" in his 1820 A Sketch of a System of the Philosophy of the Human Mind, (Edinburgh: Bell and Bradfute, 1820).

79. Quoted in Christopher Herbert, "*The Golden Bough* and the Unknowable," in *Knowing the Past*, ed. Anger, 37.

80. Christopher Herbert, *Victorian Relativity, Victorian Relativity: Radical Thought and Scientific Discovery* (University of Chicago Press, 2001), 3.

81. See Peter Garratt, *Victorian Empiricism: Self, Knowledge, and Reality in Ruskin, Bain, Lewes, Spencer, and George Eliot*. Farleigh Dickinson University Press, 2010.

82. Levine, *Dying to Know*, 4–5.

83. On the colloquial conventions of epistemic decorum, see Shapin, *A Social History of Truth*, 65–125 and *passim*. Jan Golinski, *Science as Public Culture: Chemistry and Enlightenment in Britain, 1760–1820* (Cambridge University Press, 1992) registers the prevalence of these conventions in the turn-of-the-nineteenth-century work of Joseph Priestly, Humphry Davy, and others.

4 "Something" in the Way Realism Moves

1. Jane Austen, *Mansfield Park*, 334.
2. Charles Dickens, *David Copperfield*, 688.
3. George Eliot, *Middlemarch*, 499, 501.
4. Adela Pinch, *Strange Fits of Passion: Epistemologies of Emotion, Hume to Austen* (Stanford University Press, 1996), 165.
5. See Richard Scholar, *The Je-Ne-Sais-Quoi in Early Modern Europe: Encounters with a Certain Something* (Oxford University Press, 2005), 2, 25, 28.
6. [Anon.], "LE JE NE SAIS QUOI. The I know not what," Momus: or The Laughing Philosopher. Number XXIV, *Westminster Magazine* (December 1774), 618–19.
7. Pierce Egan and George Cruikshank, *Tom and Jerry: Life in London; Or the Day and Night Scenes of Jerry Hawthorne and His Elegant Friend, Corinthian Tom* [1821], ed. John Camden Hotten (London: John Camden Hotten, 1869), 196, emphases in original.
8. George Gordon Byron, *Lord Byron: The Major Works*, ed. Jerome J. McGann (New York: Oxford University Press, 1986), 811.
9. However common these variants of *things* might be in Victorian prose, except for *nothing* they appear significantly more frequently in *Middlemarch* than in a sample corpus of 105 novels by Dickens, Wilkie Collins, George Meredith, Trollope, Charlotte Brontë, William Makepeace Thackeray, and Eliot. The frequency per 10,000 words in the sample set and *Middlemarch*, respectively, is as follows: *thing*: 5.005 and 6.764; *things*: 4.7924 and 9.5454; *something*: 6.0488 and 9.0397; and *nothing*: 10.7273 and 8.7869.
10. Much criticism dismisses Brooke as a Dickensian caricature or an otherwise ancillary and what we might call "flat" character. U. C. Knoepflmacher's "*Middlemarch*: An Avuncular View," focuses on Brooke, but analyzes him as symptomatic of a lack of stable parental/authority figures and the order they would maintain. Catherine Gallagher uses Brooke as an example of a paradigmatic style of characterization in Eliot.
11. Walter E. Houghton, *The Victorian Frame of Mind, 1830–1870* (Yale University Press, 1985), 291–97.
12. Thomas Brown, *Sketch of a System of Philosophy of the Human Mind* (1820), particularly chapter 3, "Of Mental Identity," 29–39. On Associationism and Victorian psychology, see Rick Rylance, *Victorian Psychology and British Culture, 1850–1880* (Oxford University Press, 2000), 55–69, and Sarah Winter, *The Pleasures of Memory: Learning to Read with Charles Dickens* (New York: Fordham University Press, 2011), 31–78.
13. Thomas Brown, *Sketch of a System of the Philosophy of the Human Mind* (Edinburgh: Bell and Bradfute, 1820).

14. James Mill, *Analysis of the Phenomena of the Human Mind*, ed. John Stuart Mill. 2 vols. (London: Longmans, Green, Reader, and Dyer, 1869), I: 141. Mill uses "something more" 34 times in the first volume alone.

15. G. W. F. Hegel, *Hegel's Aesthetics: Lectures on Fine Art*, trans. T. M. Knox (Oxford University Press, 2010), II: 984.

16. Franco Moretti, *The Way of the World: The* Bildungsroman *in European Culture*, trans. Albert Sbragia (London: Verso, 2000), 5–6.

17. Catherine Gallagher, *The Industrial Reformation of English Fiction: Social Discourse and Narrative Form, 1832–1867* (University of Chicago Press, 1985), 252.

18. See Stephen Gill, *Wordsworth and the Victorians* (Oxford: Clarendon, 1998), 145–67.

19. Inflections of "thing" appear some 439 times in Wordsworth's poetry, far more than the word "nature" by which many caricaturize his verse. See Adam Potkay, "Wordsworth and the Ethics of Things," *PMLA* 123, no. 2 (March 2008): 390–404 and Jonathan Farina, "The Excursion and 'the Surfaces of Things,'" *The Wordsworth Circle* 45.2 (Spring 2014): 99–105. *Nature* only appears 305 times in Wordsworth's oeuvre. I quote from "'Tintern Abbey," *The Excursion*, and "The Old Cumberland Beggar," respectively.

20. David Masson, *British Novelists and Their Styles: Being a Critical Sketch of the History of British Prose Fiction* (Boston: D. Lothrop and Co., 1875), 26.

21. See Bill Brown, "Thing Theory," in *Things*, ed. Bill Brown (University of Chicago Press, 2004), 1–22.

22. John Keats, *Complete Poems*, ed. Jack Stillinger (Belknap/Harvard University Press, 1982), 357.

23. G. H. Lewes, "The Principles of Success in Literature," *Fortnightly Review* 1 (1865): 589, 588, emphasis in original.

24. Jules Law, however, makes a compelling case for *something* as the medium of Mr. Hyde's "thingness": "There's Something about Hyde," *Novel: A Forum on Fiction* 42.3 (Fall 2009): 504–10.

25. Virginia Woolf, "Mr. Bennett and Mrs. Brown," in *The Captain's Death Bed and Other Essays* (New York: A Harvest/HBJ Book, 1978), 112.

26. George Eliot, *Adam Bede*, ed. Stephen Gill (New York: Penguin, 1980), 97, 115, 182. George Eliot, *Adam Bede*, ed. Stephen Gill (New York: Penguin, 1980), 97, 115, 182. Eliot and Lewes reread Lucretius from August 1868 through July 3, 1869. J. W. Cross, ed., *The Writings of George Eliot Together with the Life* (New York: AMS Press, 1970). 25 vols. 25: 23, 47. On the grasp of things: "Adam knew a fine sight more o' the natur o' things than those as thought themselves his betters" (97), Mr. Poyser says. And in Carlylean fashion, Adam reassures himself, "There's nothing but what's bearable as

long as a man can work . . . the natur o' things doesn't change, though it seems
as if one's own life was nothing but change" and "the best o' working is, it
gives you a grip hold o' things outside your own lot" (115). The narrator says
Adam appreciates "knowing the bearing of things" (163), and affable
Mr. Irwine appreciates mornings because they present "a clear mirror to the
rays of things" (168). Even such lines that explicitly exalt particularity do so
with self-reflexive generalizations. On the function of ambiguity in *Adam
Bede*, see also James Eli Adams, "Gyp's Tale," 227–42. In a letter to her
publisher John Blackwood on January 18, 1872, Eliot refers to her purpose in
writing *Middlemarch* as "the sort of thing I want to do" (Cross 25: 97).

27. Roland Barthes, "The Reality Effect," 141–48. As I mentioned in the previous
chapter, this is not at all to disagree with how Barthes describes realism in *S/Z*
as a copy of a copy, a pastiche of representation. He maintained that realism
declaims reference and reflexively turns on itself.

28. This is analogous to what Wordsworth called "the mighty commonwealth of
things" in *The Excursion* (2:130), which Eliot reread as she commenced
Middlemarch. Suzanne Graver describes George Eliot and Wordsworth on
the related concept of a "community of feeling": see *George Eliot and
Community: A Study in Social Theory and Fictional Form* (Berkeley:
University of California Press, 1984), 10–13.

29. See, for example, Michael York Mason, "Middlemarch and Science: Problems
of Life and Mind," *Review of English Studies* N.S. 22 no. 86 (May 1971): 151–69,
and Diana Postlewaite, "George Eliot and Science," in *The Cambridge
Companion to George Eliot*, ed. George Levin (Cambridge University Press,
2001), 98–118.

30. Lydgate is "one of those rarer lads who early . . . make up their minds that
there is something particular in life which they would like to do for its own
sake" (9); he idealizes the microscopic "nature of things" and hopes to isolate
"hitherto hidden facts of structure . . . the very grain of things," "the
homogenous origin of all the tissues" (95, 282). His invocation of "things"
posits the existence of an atomistic unit of similarity, a type of tissue
correlating all organisms but invisible to the naked eye. Lydgate's emphasis
on "hitherto hidden facts of structure" (95) affirms Michel Foucault's point
about the epistemological shift to hidden grammars of organic function:
"Henceforth, character resumes its former role as a visible sign directing us
towards a buried depth; but what it indicates is not a secret text, a muffled
word, or a resemblance too precious to be revealed; it is the coherent totality
of an organic structure that weaves back into the unique fabric of its
sovereignty both the visible and the invisible" (Foucault 229).

31. This problem of particularity and over-focus has been discussed in terms of
Eliot's microscope metaphor: see Mark Wormald, "Microscopy and Semiotic

in *Middlemarch*," *Nineteenth-Century Literature* 50 (1996):501–24. Wormald writes in dialogue with J. Hillis Miller, "Optic and Semiotic in *Middlemarch*," in *The Worlds of Victorian Fiction*, ed. Jerome H. Buckley (Harvard University Press, 1975), 125–45.

32. See Elaine Hadley, *Living Liberalism: Practical Citizenship in Mid-Victorian Britain* (University of Chicago Press, 2010), 16–17, 104.

33. Steven Shapin, *A Social History of Truth: Civility and Science in Seventeenth-Century England* (University of Chicago Press, 1994), 193–242.

34. William Whewell, *On the Philosophy of Discovery* (London: John W. Parker and Son, 1860), 367; and *The Philosophy of the Inductive Sciences*, Founded Upon Their History. 2 vols. (London: John W. Parker, 1840), 2:370.

35. John Stuart Mill, *Collected Works of John Stuart Mill*, eds. John M. Robson and Jack Stillinger. 33 vols. (University of Toronto Press, 1963), 7.127.

36. See Kate Flint, *The Victorians and the Visual Imagination* (Cambridge University Press, 2000), which delineates how *Middlemarch* insists upon the inseparability of "the world of things and the life of the mind" (65–86). Eliot wrote that "Severing ideas from things is the fundamental error of philosophy" (qtd. in Ermarth 115). She also maintained an anti-dualist philosophy along the lines of Feuerbach and Spinoza (Ermarth 114–121).

37. On Ruskin's role in introducing "realism" to English readers, see Caroline Levine, *The Serious Pleasures of Suspense: Victorian Realism and Narrative Doubt* (University of Virginia Press, 2003), 25–26.

38. *Westminster Review* n. s. 19 (July 1856): 51–56; 71–72. As Suzanne Graver explains, this phrase "exemplifies one of the most important premises of 'natural history': that all knowledge is a knowledge of relations." See *George Eliot and Community*, 31–32.

39. G. H. Lewes, *Problems of Life and Mind. First series: Foundations of a Creed*. 2 vols. (London: Trübner & Co., 1875), II, 31.

40. George Levine, "George Eliot's Hypothesis of Reality," *Nineteenth-Century Fiction* 35: 1 (June 1980): 1–28, 4. See also Sally Shuttleworth, *George Eliot and Nineteenth-Century Science: The Make-Believe of a Beginning* (Cambridge University Press, 1984), x, 1–24, and, on *Middlemarch*, 142–174.

41. David Kurnick, *Empty Houses: Theatrical Failure and the Novel* (Princeton University Press, 2012), 73–74. As Ermarth notes, "Altruism in George Eliot has little to do with selflessness or lack of ego; instead, it has to do with balancing the conflicting claims of ego and community" (113); and such "balancing" is precisely the process of articulating deep characters. More recently, Fredric Jameson has described "a kind of narrative democratization, a waning of protagonicity and a foregrounding of secondary characters as such" (*The Antinomies of Realism* [London: Verso, 2013], 121), and this context certainly makes Brooke less fatuous and more politically relevant than he has otherwise seemed.

42. Helena Michie describes disappointment with Rome and with honeymoons as altogether typical in Victorian writing, See *Victorian Honeymoons: Journeys to the Conjugal* (Cambridge University Press, 2006), 78, 85–89.

43. Bram Stoker, *Dracula*, ed. Maurice Hindle (New York: Penguin, 2003), 45.

44. Matthew Arnold, *Culture and Anarchy*, ed. J. Dover Wilson (Cambridge University Press, 1996), 87. See David Wayne Thomas, 34–39.

45. John Henry Newman, *The Idea of a University*, ed. Frank M. Turner (Yale University Press, 1996).

46. J. G. A. Pocock details the historical development of this form of abstract, mobile property in "The Mobility of Property and the Rise of Eighteenth-Century Sociology," in *Virtue, Commerce, and History: Essays on Political Thought and History, Chiefly in the Eighteenth Century* (Cambridge University Press, 1985), 103–24.

47. If we can trust the affable Lord Peregrine in Anthony Trollope's *Orley Farm* (1862), Brooke's agricultural advice here is not altogether misguided (*Orley Farm*, ed. David Skilton [Oxford University Press, 2000], 40).

48. Hadley explains the paradox of liberal character: "Although Victorian liberalism celebrates individuality, it also privileges it as the 'type' of modern subjectivity – because all subjects in a liberal society eventually ought to become individuals – thereby necessarily exposing idiosyncratic specificity to the sameness of the general, an irresolvable fact inherent to the political terms of abstracted individuality that is repeatedly manifested as a fear of anonymity" (Hadley 121).

49. Eliot is uncannily prescient: Hansard's registers a dramatic rise in the frequency of the phrase "that sort of thing" in Parliamentary speech during the 1870s and climaxing in the early 1880s (before rising again in the 1930s through 1960s): http://hansard.millbanksystems.com/search/ that+sort+of+thing?century=C19.

50. The novel describes Brooke's speech as "fallings from us, vanishings" and thus alludes to Wordsworth's "Ode: Intimations of Immortality," which is equally awash with "things": "The things which I have seen I now can see no more . . . Both of them speak of something that is gone . . . something that doth live . . . Those obstinate questionings / Of sense and outward things, / Fallings from us, vanishings, / Blank misgivings of a creature / Moving about in worlds not realized, / High instincts before which our mortal nature / Did tremble like a guilty Thing surprised . . . Though nothing can bring back the hour."

51. Henry Fielding, *Tom Jones*, ed. Sheridan Baker (New York: W. W. Norton, 1973), 121.

52. A. R. Humphreys, "The Eternal Fitness of Things: An Aspect of Eighteenth-Century Thought," *The Modern Language Review* 42, no. 2 (April 1947): 188–98. *Middlemarch* alludes directly to Clarke with Fred Vincy's

Lamarkian disappointment with the one hundred pounds he receives from Featherstone: "[the bank notes] actually presented the absurdity of being less than his hopefulness had decided that they must be. What can the fitness of things mean, if not their fitness to a man's expectations? Failing this, absurdity and atheism gape behind him" (86).

53. George Eliot, "Silly Novels by Lady Novelists," *Westminster Review* 66 O.S. /10 N.S. (October 1856): 450.

54. See Joseph Butler, *Fifteen Sermons Preached at the Rolls Chapel* (London: J. and J. Knapton, 1726), Preface §39.

55. Leslie Stephen, *George Eliot* (London: Macmillan, 1902), 176–77.

56. Daniel Wright, "George Eliot's Vagueness," *Victorian Studies* 56.4 (Summer 2014): 625–48, 641.

57. James Ferrier, "An Introduction to the Philosophy of Consciousness," *Blackwood's Edinburgh Magazine* 43 (1838): 186–201, 437–52, 784–91; 44 (1838): 234–44, 539–52; 45 (1839): 201–11, 419–30. Quotation from Part II, *Blackwood's* 43 (1838): 447.

58. Alexander Bain, *The Emotions and the Will* (London: John W. Parker and Son, 1859), 566.

59. Ladislaw replicates in this respect another of Eliot's troubled lovers, Philip Wakem, who also praises ineffability. George Eliot, *The Mill on the Floss*, ed. Carol T. Christ (New York: W. W. Norton, 1994), 248.

60. Daniel Cottom, *Social Figures: George Eliot, Social History, and Literary Representation* (Minneapolis: University of Minnesota Press, 1987), 189.

61. John Kucich, *Repression in Victorian Fiction: Charlotte Brontë, George Eliot, and Charles Dickens* (Berkeley: University of California Press, 1987), 118.

62. In *The Historical Austen* (2003), William Galperin delineates how, in Austen's writing, "silence becomes a way of directing attention to the density or heterogeneity of the real"; "Austen's 'silent treatment'" registers for Galperin the way Austen inscribes opposition to the conventions of "probability" into her prose. Her silences stand in for an intractable, ineffable, inexplicable real that neither the plot, which Austen subordinates to description and character, nor the narrative voice can rationalize or otherwise reduce to the generic demands of probability. Galperin grounds Austen's silence in her revision of epistolary prose into (selectively) omniscient free indirect discourse, but such silence and the "possible" (as opposed to probable) real that it implies are grammatically instantiated in the stress Austen puts on everyday pronouns without clear, immediate antecedents – pronouns such as *something* and "nothing." See *The Historical Austen* (University of Pennsylvania Press, 2003), 8, 35.

63. Ian Duncan, *Scott's Shadow: The Novel in Romantic Edinburgh* (Princeton University Press, 2007), 116–19.

64. On detail registering a hierarchy of values and substantiating realism and character, see Susan Stewart, *On Longing: Narratives of the Miniature, the Gigantic, the Souvenir, the Collection* (Durham: Duke University Press, 1993), 27–28.

65. Charlotte Brontë, *Villette*, eds. Margaret Smith and Herbert Rosengarten (Oxford University Press, 1984), 29, 38, and elsewhere throughout.

66. As I note in the Introduction, Lewes writes in "Dickens in Relation to Criticism," the infamous essay that describes Dickensian insight as a form of sane hallucination, of "the 'catchwords' personified as characters," which remind Lewes of "the frogs whose brains have been taken out for physiological purposes, and whose actions henceforth want the distinctive peculiarity of organic action, that of fluctuating spontaneity" ("Dickens in Relation to Criticism," *Fortnightly Review* 11:62 [February 1872]: 148–49). David Masson also registers Dickens's use of phrases of labels by which ... characters are distinguished," including Micawber's "Something will turn up" (*British Novelists and Their Styles*, 256–57).

67. Dora fails because her ineptitude makes visible the economics of domestic economy; see Leonore Davidoff, *Worlds Between: Historical Perspectives on Gender and Class* (New York: Routledge, 1995), 60, and Chris R. Vanden Bossche, "Cookery, Not Rookery: Family and Class in *David Copperfield*," *Dickens Studies Annual* 15 (1986): 98. On the visibility and invisibility of servants, Bruce W. Robbins, *The Servant's Hand: English Fiction from Below* (Durham: Duke University Press, 1993), ix.

68. Gallagher, *Nobody's Story*, xiii–xxiv. For all his uniqueness, Copperfield corresponds also to Franco Moretti's notion of "unmarked" normal, prosaic characters known from within (Moretti 11).

69. Wilkie Collins, *The Woman in White*, ed. John Sutherland (Oxford University Press, 1998), 50–51, emphasis original.

70. D. A. Miller, *The Novel and the Police* (Berkeley: University of California Press, 1988), reads this passage with wit: 174.

71. Garrett Stewart, *Dickens and the Trials of Imagination* (Harvard University Press, 1974), 136, 138.

72. I elsewhere discuss how Dickens's capitalizes on miscommunication of this sort: see Jonathan Farina, "Mad Libs and Stupid Criticism," *Dickens Studies Annual* 46 (August 2015): 325–38. On Dickensian failures to communicate, see also Rae Greiner, "Dickensian Sympathy: Translation in the Proper Pitch," *Sympathetic Realism in Nineteenth-Century British Realism* (Baltimore: Johns Hopkins University Press, 2012), 86–121.

73. For many examples, see Anthony Trollope, *The Small House at Allington*, ed. Julian Thompson (New York: Penguin, 2005), 51, 78, 108, 150–51, 171, 192, 262–64, 271, 279, 297, 351–52, 391–92, 422, 455, 461, 476, 483, 515, 571, 622–23, 637, and 661.

74. George Meredith, *The Egoist*, ed. Robert M. Adams (New York: W. W. Norton, 1979), 154.

75. Some did make claims for axiomatic morals: see Anthony Trollope, "Novel Reading," *Nineteenth Century: A Monthly Review* 5:23 (January 1879): 24–43. But most preferred vagueness: see, for example, Leslie Stephen, "The Moral Element in Literature," *Cornhill Magazine* 43.253 (January 1881): 34–50, esp. 40–41.

76. Samuel Smiles, *Character* (New York: Harper & Brothers, 1872), 372–73.

77. Rachel Teukolsky, *The Literate Eye: Victorian Art Writing and Modernist Aesthetics* (Oxford University Press, 2009), 30.

78. John Ruskin, *The Complete Works of John Ruskin*, eds. E. T. Cook and Alexander Wedderburn. Library edition. 39 vols. (London: George Allen, 1903–12), 3: 537.

79. Jules David Law, *The Rhetoric of Empiricism: Language and Perception from Locke to I. A. Richards* (Cornell University Press, 1993), 206. Deidre S. Lynch, *The Economy of Character: Novels, Market Culture, and the Business of Inner Meaning* (University of Chicago Press, 1998), 141 and *passim*.

80. Shapin, *A Social History of Truth*, 193–242.

81. George Eliot, "Art and Belles Lettres: Review of Modern Painters III," *Westminster Review* 65 (April 1856): 625–50, 626 (my emphasis).

82. George Henry Lewes, "Realism in Art: Recent German Fiction," *The Westminster Review* 70:138 (October 1858), 488–518.

83. Walter Pater, "Style," in *Appreciations* (London: Macmillan and Co., 1889), 5.

84. E. S. Dallas, *The Gay Science*. 2 vols. (London: Chapman and Hall, 1866).

85. Dallas describes the "hidden soul" as an "automatic action," "special function," "immense involuntary life which we lead out of consciousness" (I: 194, 220); "There is," he says, "knowledge active within us of which we see nothing, know nothing, think nothing" (I: 217). Nicholas Dames describes Dallas's theory of the "hidden soul" as linking "Romantic theories of imagination to nascent Victorian theories of the unconscious" in *The Physiology of the Novel: Reading, Neural Science, and the Form of Victorian Fiction* (Oxford University Press, 2007), 186.

86. [Anon.], "Belles Lettres," *Westminster Review* 31.1 (January 1867): 257–58.

87. Catherine Gallagher, *Nobody's Story: The Vanishing Acts of Women Writers in the Marketplace, 1670–1820* (Berkeley: University of California Press, 1994), xiii–xxiv.

5 "Whoever explains a 'but'"

1. Anthony Trollope, *Doctor Thorne*, ed. David Skilton (Oxford University Press, 1985), 394.

2. [Anon.] "Tact," *Chambers' Edinburgh Journal* 12.573 (January 21, 1843): 1–2, 1.

3. Anthony Trollope, *Thackeray*. English Men of Letters, ed. John Morley London: Macmillan & Co., 1879. 185

4. N. John Hall, *Trollope: A Biography* (Oxford: Clarendon Press, 1991), 106–8; Richard Mullen, *Anthony Trollope: A Victorian in His World* (London: Duckworth, 1990), 229–32; R. C. Terry, *Trollope: Interviews and Recollections* (London: Palgrave Macmillan, 1987), 37–45.

5. Mary Laffan Hartley negatively portrays Butt as "Mr. Rebutter" in her novel *Christy Carew* (1880). Alas, Hartley does not inflect Mr. Rebutter's idiolect with the Trollopian adversative I describe herein. *Christy Carew: A Novel* (New York: Henry Holt, 1880), 255, 263–64, 269, 273, 279–80.

6. Trollope writes, for instance: "as you are a witness yourself, go down to the court and admire the ingenious manner in which the great barrister, Mr. Allewinde, is endeavouring to make that unfortunate and thoroughly disconcerted young man in the witness box, swear to a point diametrically opposite to another point to which he has already sworn at the instigation of counsel on the other side, – and thereby perjure himself" *Macdermots of Ballycloran* (London: Ward, Lock, and Co., 1866), 294.

7. For a general account of Trollope and the law, including his distaste for cross-examination, see R. D. McMaster, *Trollope and the Law* (New York: Palgrave Macmillan, 1986), and Ayelet Ben-Yishai, *Common Precedents: The Presentness of the Past in Victorian Law and Literature* (Oxford University Press, 2013). See also Martha C. Nussbaum, "The Stain of Illegitimacy: Gender, Law, and Trollopian Subversion" in *Subversion and Sympathy: Gender, Law, and the British Novel*, eds. Martha C. Nussbaum and Alison L. LaCroix (Oxford University Press, 2013), 150–75.

8. In *Doctor Thorne, but* comprises 2,159 out of 220,553 words, a frequency of 0.009789; in *Framley Parsonage* 2,097 out of 211,290 words, a frequency of 0.009924; in *The Small House at Allington*, 2,569 out of 263,246 words, a frequency of 0.009758; in *The Eustace Diamonds* 2,331 out of 274,376 words, a frequency of 0.008495. The standard frequency of *but* in a sample collection of 150 canonical and popular nineteenth-century British novels is 0.0064. The differences are statistically significant.

9. Hugh Sykes Davies, "Trollope and His Style," *A Review of English Studies* 1.4 (October 1960), 73–85. Davies identifies Trollope's structure of *but* and adversative *and* as the "cadence" of Trollope's prose and presciently anticipates the electronic revolution that would enable him to verify that hunch statistically (81–82).

10. On which, see Juliet McMaster, *Trollope's Palliser Novels: Theme and Pattern* (Oxford University Press, 1978).

11. Trollope's early critics consistently register Trollope's lack of depth, his insistent residence on the surface of characters and life, and we would do well to respect this superficiality without subordinating it to a depth model. Surface matters. See [R. H. Hutton], Obituary for Trollope, *The Spectator* lv (December 9, 1882): 1573–74.

12. Georg Lukács, *The Theory of the Novel*, trans. Anna Bostock (Boston: The MIT Press, 1999), 72.

13. Eve Kosofsky Sedgwick, *Touching Feeling: Affect, Pedagogy, Performativity* (Durham: Duke University Press, 2003), 143–51.

14. John Ruskin, *The Works of John Ruskin*, ed. E. T. Cook and Alexander Wedderburn. Library Edition. 39 vols. London: George Allen, 1903–12), 18: 80.

15. Theodor Adorno, *Minima Moralia: Reflections from Damaged Life*, trans. E. N. F. Jephcott (London: Verso, 1999), 36.

16. Trollope evidences a comparably ambivalent relation to professional authority in his discussion of his post office reports: "it was my principle always to obey authority in everything instantly, but never to allow my mouth to be closed as to the expression of my opinion" (*AA* 135).

17. Amanda Anderson, "Trollope's Modernity," *ELH* 74 (2007): 509–34, 531. See also, Regenia Gagnier, "Gender, Liberalism, Resentment," in *The Politics of Gender in Anthony Trollope's Novels: New Readings for the Twenty-First Century*, eds. Margaret Markwick, Deborah Denenholz Morse, and Regenia Gagnier (Burlington: Ashgate, 2009), 235–48.

18. Dugald Stewart, "On [The Faculty of] Taste," *The Collected Works of Dugald Stewart*, ed. Sir William Hamilton (Edinburgh: Thomas Constable and Co., 1855), v: 347.

19. "Tact," *Chambers' Edinburgh Journal*, 1.

20. Samuel Smiles, *Character* (New York: Harper & Brothers, 1872), 248.

21. [Anon.] "Tact," *The Saturday Review of Politics, Literature, Science, and Art* 22.568 (September 15, 1866): 324–25, 324.

22. Christopher Herbert, *Culture and Anomie: Ethnographic Imagination in the Nineteenth Century* (University of Chicago Press, 1991) 279.

23. George Levine, *Darwin and the Novelists: Patterns of Science in Victorian Fiction* (University of Chicago Press, 1991), 201.

24. This graduated reality corresponds to the didactic realist ideal that Trollope expresses in *The Eustace Diamonds*: he there writes that moral character improvement ensues from reading characters who are not exemplary ideals, or impeccable heroes, but who are subtly better or worse than readers: "The true picture of life as it is, if it could be adequately painted, would show men what they are, and how they might rise, not, indeed, to perfection, but one step first, and then another on the ladder" (*ED* 357). Roger L. Slakey

addresses graduated difference and history in Trollope's novels in "Anthony Trollope, Master of Gradualness," *VIJ: Victorians Institute Journal* 16 (1988), 27–35.

25. Max Horkheimer and Theodore Adorno, *Dialectic of Enlightenment*, trans. John Cumming (New York: Continuum, 2002), 134.

26. In writing of his career-long effort to "improve the style of official writing" for Post Office reports, he claims to have essayed "always to write them in the form in which they should be sent, – without a copy. It is by writing thus that a man can throw on to his paper the exact feeling with which his mind is impressed at the moment. A rough copy, or what is called a draft, is written in order that it may be touched and altered and put upon stilts" (*AA* 135). Yet Trollope appreciated the ability to revise his novels. He recalls his reluctance to publish in serial parts without first finishing a novel, because "an artist should keep in his hand the power of fitting the beginning of his work to the end" (139).

27. Anthony Trollope, *The Struggles of Brown, Jones, and Robinson*, ed. N. John Hall (Oxford University Press, 1992), 103 and *passim*.

28. Henry James, from *Partial Portraits* (1888) in N. John Hall, ed., *The Trollope Critics* (Totowa: Barnes & Noble, 1981), 1–20, 3, emphasis in original. The entry was first published in *Century Magazine* n.s. 4 (July 1883), 385–95.

29. Anthony Trollope, *Framley Parsonage*, ed. David Skilton and Peter Miles (New York: Penguin, 2004), 151.

30. Contrast this with Christopher Herbert, "Trollope and the Fixity of Self," *PMLA* 93.2 (March 1978): 228–39, which argues that some of Trollope's fictions, particularly *Orley Farm, He Knew He Was Right*, and *The Duke's Children*, plot characters' discovery that character is largely intractable and not free to develop or progress as many ideologues and novelists would have it.

31. Trollope's contemporaries consistently register his insistent residence on the surface, and many do so approvingly: see [R. H. Hutton], Obituary for Trollope, *The Spectator* lv (December 9, 1882): 1573–74.

32. Trollope, *Doctor Thorne*, 394.

33. Elizabeth Gaskell, *Cranford*, ed., Elizabeth Porges Watson (Oxford University Press, 1998), 107.

34. Mary Poovey, *A History of the Modern Fact: Problems of Knowledge in the Sciences of Wealth and Society* (University of Chicago Press, 1998), 35–38.

35. Walter M. Kendrick, *The Novel Machine: The Theory and Fiction of Anthony Trollope* (Baltimore: Johns Hopkins University Press, 1980), 35.

36. Frank O'Connor, "Trollope the Realist," in N. John Hall, ed., *The Trollope Critics* (Totowa: Barnes & Noble, 1981), 83–94, 84–85.

37. In *Framley Parsonage*, for example: "I may as well confess that of absolute, true heroism there was only a moderate admixture in Lord Lufton's composition;

but what would the world come to if none *but* absolute true heroes were to be thought worthy of women's love?" (*FP* 261; my emphasis).

38. "The narrative of scientific epistemology . . . implies a narrative of disciplined, self-denying progress through enormous difficulties toward a highly valued end, marked by constant repression of desire," George Levine, *Dying to Know: Scientific Epistemology and Narrative in Victorian England* (University of Chicago Press, 2002), 87.

39. Trollope, *Thackeray*, 185.

40. D. A. Miller, *The Novel and the Police* (Berkeley: University of California Press, 1988), 107.

41. Laurie Langbauer, *Novels of Everyday Life: The Series in English Fiction, 1850–1930* (Cornell University Press, 1999), 19. Langbauer and Christopher Herbert claim in different ways that the expansiveness of Trollope's oeuvre bespeaks some sort of comprehensive register or "cultural repository," as Langbauer puts it, of everyday life. Christopher Herbert, *Culture and Anomie*, 253–299, and Langbauer 14.

42. Jenny Bourne-Taylor explains this inadequacy of this statement in "Trollope and the Sensation Novel," in *The Cambridge Companion to Anthony Trollope*, ed. Carolyn Dever and Lisa Niles (Cambridge University Press, 2011), 85–98.

43. Ruth apRoberts summarizes the issue in "Anthony Trollope, or the Man with No Style at All" *Victorian Newsletter* (Spring 1969): 10–13, but nearly everyone who writes about Trollope mentions the phenomenon. The second quotation is from J. A., notice in *Sharpe's London Magazine* n.s. xix (July 1861): 103–5, qtd. in Donald Smalley, ed., *Trollope: The Critical Heritage* (New York: Barnes & Noble, 1969), p. 131.

44. [Anon.], Notice for *An Old Man's Love, The Times* (April 14, 1884): 3, qtd. in Smalley 523.

45. Studies of Trollope's novels and epistemology include David Skilton, "Trollopian Realism," in *The Trollope Critics*, ed. N. John Hall (Totowa: Barnes & Noble, 1981), 160–69; George Levine, *The Realistic Imagination: English Fiction from* Frankenstein *to* Lady Chatterley (University of Chicago Press, 1981), 181–226; Ayelet Ben-Yishai, "The Fact of a Rumor: Anthony Trollope's *The Eustace Diamonds,*" *Nineteenth-Century Literature* 62.1 (2007): 88–120; Christopher Herbert, "The Novel of Cultural Symbolism: *Doctor Thorne,*" in *Culture and Anomie*, 253–99. On realism as epistemology, see also Alexander Welsh, *Strong Representations: Narrative and Circumstantial Evidence in England* (Baltimore: Johns Hopkins University Press, 1992). Herbert makes a similar methodological point that Trollope's "power lay in things in his work that have become at many points invisible to us" (268) and that these invisible things more legitimately evidence cultural assumptions than any intentional metaphor.

46. On the technical inadequacy of Victorian critical categories to comprehend Trollope, see Mary Poovey, *Genres of the Credit Economy: Mediating Value in Eighteenth- and Nineteenth-Century Britain* (University of Chicago Press, 2008), 404–11.

47. In practice, Trollope's prose is highly idiosyncratic and attentive to style. In theory, however – as he expressed it in *An Autobiography* – Trollope claims to have wished to erase the signs of his writing as writing, rather than draw attention to it with "conceits that smell of the oil" (*AA* 65). Kendrick thus remarks that "realism is a rhetorical discourse committed to the endless repetition of the assertion that it is not rhetorical. Beyond a certain cultural faith on which the realistic writer can depend without mentioning it, there is nothing to tell a reader what to do with realism except realism itself" (7). On Trollope and "the exclusion of writing from reality," see Kendrick 32–47.

48. Jerome Christensen, *Lord Byron's Strength: Romantic Writing and Commercial Society* (Baltimore: Johns Hopkins University Press, 1993), 220, 230. See "The Circumstantial Gravity of *Don Juan*," 214–257.

49. On Trollope's "Romantic" incorporation of the dialectic, see L. J. Swingle, *Romanticism and Anthony Trollope: A Study in the Continuities of Nineteenth-Century Thought* (University of Michigan, 1991).

50. Mary Shelley, *Frankenstein or the Modern Prometheus* (1818 Text), ed. Marilyn Butler (Oxford University Press, 1998), 20. Louisa Gradgrind is similar: "She was so constrained, and yet so careless; so reserved, and yet so watchful; so cold and proud, and yet so sensitively ashamed of her husband's braggart humility . . . Her features were handsome; but their natural play was so locked up, that it seemed impossible to guess at their genuine expression, Utterly indifferent, perfectly self-reliant, never at a loss, and yet never at her ease . . . she baffled all penetration," Charles Dickens, *Hard Times*, ed. Kate Flint (New York: Penguin, 2003), 127.

51. L. J. Swingle makes a related point that "fundamental differences of mind among people constitute one of the primary laws of Trollopian [fiction]" (26). See 23–58 on disjunctions of perspective, party, generation, and mentality in Trollope's fiction in relation to Romantic-era poetry and aesthetics.

52. Mary Poovey, *Genres of the Credit Economy: Mediating Value in Eighteenth- and Nineteenth-Century Britain* (University of Chicago Press, 2008), 396–97.

53. Alex Woloch, *The One vs. the Many: Minor Characters and the Space of the Protagonist in the Novel* (Princeton University Press, 2003).

54. On Palliser, see Anthony Trollope, *Can You Forgive Her?* ed. Stephen Wall (New York: Penguin, 1896), 250–51. On Chiltern, see *Phineas Finn*, I: 98–104.

55. Michel de Certeau, *The Practice of Everyday Life*, trans. Steven Randall (Berkeley: University of California Press, 1988), 91–110, 96.

56. Herbert shows how many Trollope novels, including *Orley Farm, He Knew He Was Right,* and *The Duke's Children,* plot the discovery that character is intractable and not subject to the growth or development of *Bildungsroman.*

57. W. M. Thackeray, *Vanity Fair,* ed. Peter Shillingsburg (New York: Norton, 1994), 391, 396.

58. See Jenny Davidson, *Hypocrisy and the Politics of Politeness: Manners and Morals from Locke to Austen* (Cambridge University Press, 2004).

59. On aphasic, incomplete utterances as solicitations of sympathetic imagination in nineteenth-century fiction, see Rae Greiner, *Sympathetic Realism in Nineteenth-Century Fiction* (Baltimore: Johns Hopkins University Press, 2012).

60. On the equanimity, politics of character, and reification of gentlemanliness in the Woodward home in *The Three Clerks,* see Lauren Goodlad, *Victorian Literature and the Victorian State: Character and Governance in a Liberal Society* (Baltimore: Johns Hopkins University Press, 2003).118–58.

61. Audrey Jaffe, *The Affective Life of the Average Man: The Victorian Novel and the Stock Market Graph* (Ohio State University Press, 2010), 71.

62. Anthony Trollope, *The Eustace Diamonds,* ed. John Sutherland (New York: Penguin, 2004), 190.

63. On the epistemological history of "giving the lie," see Steven Shapin, *A Social History of Truth: Civility and Science in Seventeenth-Century England* (University of Chicago Press, 1994), 107–19.

64. Such passages are fairly common, as in *Framley Parsonage* when Lady Lufton wants to underscore Lily's social insignificance. She engages Fanny Robarts with "'something that is important and necessary to mention, and yet it is a very delicate affair to speak of." Lucy, Lady Lufton continues, "must be a very pleasant companion to you, and so useful about the children; but – ' And then Lady Lufton paused for a moment; for she, eloquent and discreet as she always was, felt herself rather at a loss for words to express her exact meaning" (*FP* 172–73).

65. Anthony Trollope, *Phineas Finn,* ed. Jacques Berthoud (Oxford University Press, 1982), II:33.

66. Langbauer attends to Trollope's "loosely proverbial" admixture of "colloquialisms, mottoes, maxims, platitudes, clichés, and tag lines" (97), but the colloquialisms she discusses are even less ordinary than the conjunctions that connect the class- and locally specific sociolects of characters.

67. Ayelet Ben-Yishai, "The Fact of a Rumor," 102.

68. Stefan Collini, *Public Moralists: Political Thought and Intellectual Life in Britain 1850–1930* (Oxford University Press, 1991), 113.

69. [Alexander Smith], "Novels and Novelists of the Day," *North British Review* 38 (February 1863): 170–71 (emphasis added).

70. On character, credit, and correspondence, see Margot C. Finn, *The Character of Credit: Personal Debt in English Culture, 1740–1914* (Cambridge University Press, 2008).

71. W. M. Thackeray, *The History of Pendennis*, ed. Donald Hawes, (New York: Penguin, 1972), 737–38.

72. W. M. Thackeray, *The Newcomes*, ed. Andrew Sanders (Oxford University Press, 1995), 494–95.

73. Michael Sadleir, "The Books," in N. John Hall, ed., *The Trollope Critics* (Totowa: Barnes & Noble, 1981), 34–45, 34.

74. Sianne Ngai, *Our Aesthetic Categories: Zany, Cute, Interesting* (Harvard University Press, 2012), 17.

Afterword: The Fate of Character and the Philology of Everyday Life

1. Franco Moretti, *The Bourgeois: Between History and Literature* (London: Verso, 2014).

2. Michael McKeon, *The Secret History of Domesticity* (Baltimore: Johns Hopkins University Press, 2005), xix.

3. Henri Lefebvre, *Critique of Everyday Life*, trans. John Moore. 3 vols. (London: Verso: 2008), I: 132–36 and *passim*.

4. Andrew H. Miller, *The Burdens of Perfection: On Ethics and Reading in Nineteenth-Century British Literature* (Cornell University Press, 2008), 30, 118.

Bibliography

Aarsleff, Hans. *The Study of Language in England, 1780–1860*. Princeton: Princeton University Press, 1967.

Abrams, M. H. *The Mirror and the Lamp: Romantic Theory and the Critical Tradition*. New York: Oxford University Press, 1953.

Adams, James Eli. "Gyp's Tale: On Sympathy, Silence, and Realism in *Adam Bede*," *Dickens Studies Annual* 20 (1991): 227–42.

Adorno, Theodor. *Minima Moralia: Reflections from Damaged Life*, trans. E. N. F. Jephcott. London: Verso, 1999.

Adorno, Theodor and Max Horkheimer. *Dialectic of Enlightenment*, trans. John Cumming. New York: Continuum, 2002.

Aikin, John. *An Essay on the Application of Natural History to Poetry*. London: Joseph Johnson, 1777.

Althusser, Louis and Étienne Balibar. *Reading Capital*, trans. Ben Brewster. New York: New Left Books, 1970.

Anderson, Amanda. *The Powers of Distance: Cosmopolitanism and the Cultivation of Detachment*. Princeton: Princeton University Press, 2001.

The Way We Argue Now: A Study in the Cultures of Theory. Princeton: Princeton University Press, 2006.

"Trollope's Modernity," *ELH* 74 (2007): 509–34.

Anger, Suzy, ed. *Knowing the Past: Victorian Literature and Culture*. Ithaca: Cornell University Press, 2001.

Victorian Interpretation. Ithaca: Cornell University Press, 2005.

[Anon.]. "LE JE NE SAIS QUOI. The I know not what," Momus: or The Laughing Philosopher. Number XXIV, *Westminster Magazine* (December 1774), 618–19.

[Anon.]. "Advertisements Extraordinary," *New Monthly Magazine* 23 (September 1828): 209.

[Anon.]. "On Character in Architecture," *Architectural Magazine, and Journal of Improvement in Architecture, Building, and Furnishing and in the Various Arts and Trades Connected Therewith* 1.9 (November 1834): 324–28.

[Anon.]. "A Review of Oliver Twist," *Literary Gazette* (November 24, 1838): 741.

[Anon.]. "Character," *Chambers' Edinburgh Journal* 471 (February 6, 1841): 17–18.

[Anon.]. "British Association for the Advancement of Everything in General, and Nothing in Particular," *Punch* 3 (1842): 6–7.

[Anon.]. "Tact," *Chambers' Edinburgh Journal* 12.573 (January 21, 1843): 1–2.

[Anon.]. "*Balzac and his Writing,*" *Westminster Review* LX (July 1853): 199–214.

[Anon.]. "Character Is Everything," *Sunday at Home* 463 (March 14, 1863): 164–67.

[Anon.]. "Complexion of Character," *National Magazine* 15.90 (April 1864): 220–24.

[Anon.]. "Tact," *The Saturday Review of Politics, Literature, Science, and Art* 22.568 (September 15, 1866): 324–25.

apRoberts, Ruth. *Trollope: Artist and Moralist.* London: Chatto & Windus, 1971.

Arac, Jonathan. *Commissioned Spirits: The Shaping of Social Motion in Dickens, Carlyle, Melville, and Hawthorne.* New York: Columbia University Press, 1989.

Arata, Stephen. "On Not Paying Attention," *Victorian Studies* 46, no. 2 (Winter 2004): 193–205.

Aristotle. *On Rhetoric: A Theory of Civic Discourse,* trans. George A. Kennedy. New York: Oxford University Press, 1991.

Armstrong, Nancy. *Fiction in the Age of Photography: The Legacy of British Realism.* Cambridge, MA: Harvard University Press, 1999.

Arnold, Matthew. "The Modern Element in Literature," *Macmillan's Magazine* 19.112 (February 1869), 304–14.

Selected Prose, ed. P. J. Keating. Harmondsworth: Penguin, 1970.

Culture and Anarchy, ed. J. Dover Wilson. Cambridge, UK: Cambridge University Press, 1996.

Auerbach, Nina. "Alluring Vacancies in the Victorian Character," *The Kenyon Review* 8.3 (Summer 1986): 36–48.

"Dorothea's Lost Dog," in *Middlemarch in the 21st Century,* ed. Karen Chase. New York: Oxford University Press, 2006. 87–106.

Austen, Jane. *Emma,* eds. Richard Cronin and Dorothy McMillan. *Cambridge Edition of the Works of Jane Austen.* Cambridge: Cambridge University Press, [1815] 2005.

Mansfield Park, ed. John Wiltshire. *Cambridge Edition of the Works of Jane Austen.* Cambridge: Cambridge University Press, [1814] 2005.

Northanger Abbey, eds. Barbara M. Benedict and Deidre Le Faye. *Cambridge Edition of the Works of Jane Austen.* Cambridge: Cambridge University Press, [1817] 2006.

Persuasion, eds. Janet Todd and Antje Blank. *Cambridge Edition of the Works of Jane Austen.* Cambridge: Cambridge University Press, [1818] 2006.

Pride and Prejudice, ed. Pat Rogers. *Cambridge Edition of the Works of Jane Austen.* Cambridge: Cambridge University Press, [1813] 2006.

Sense and Sensibility, ed. Edward Copeland. *Cambridge Edition of the Works of Jane Austen.* Cambridge: Cambridge University Press, [1811] 2006.

Bailey, Samuel. *Letters on the Philosophy of the Human Mind.* London: Longmans, 1855.

Bain, Alexander. *The Emotions and the Will.* London: John W. Parker and Son, 1859.

Barthes, Roland. *S/Z,* trans. Richard Miller. New York: Hill and Wang, 1974.

"The Reality Effect," in *The Rustle of Language,* trans. Richard Howard. Berkeley: University of California Press, 1986. 141–48.

Bate, Jonathan. *Shakespeare and the English Romantic Imagination*. Oxford: Oxford University Press, 1986.

Baucom, Ian. *Specters of the Atlantic: Finance Capital, Slavery, and the Philosophy of History*. Durham: Duke University Press, 2005.

Beer, Gillian. *Darwin's Plots: Evolutionary Narrative in Darwin, George Eliot, and Nineteenth-Century Fiction*. Cambridge: Cambridge University Press, 2000.

Benedict, Barbara M. *Framing Feeling: Sentiment and Style in English Prose Fiction, 1745–1800*. New York: AMS Press, 1994.

Ben-Yishai, Ayelet. "The Fact of a Rumor: Anthony Trollope's *The Eustace Diamonds*," *Nineteenth-Century Literature* 62.1 (2007): 88–120.

Common Precedents: The Presentness of the Past in Victorian Law and Literature. Oxford: Oxford University Press, 2013.

Best, Stephen and Sharon Marcus. "The Way We Read Now: An Introduction," *Representations* 108.1 (2009): 1–21.

Birch, Dinah, ed. *John Ruskin: Selected Writings*. Oxford: Oxford University Press, 2004.

Blair, Hugh. *Lectures on Rhetoric and Belles Lettres*. 2 vols. London and Edinburgh, 1783.

Blake, William. *The Complete Poetry and Prose of William Blake*, ed. David V. Erdman. New York: Doubleday, 1988.

Bodenheimer, Rosemarie. *The Real Life of Mary Ann Evans: George Eliot, Her Letters and Fiction*. Ithaca: Cornell University Press, 1994.

Knowing Dickens. Ithaca: Cornell University Press, 2007.

Bourdieu, Pierre. *Distinction: A Social Critique of the Judgment of Taste*, trans. Richard Nice. Cambridge, MA: Harvard University Press, 1984.

Bourne-Taylor, Jenny. "Trollope and the Sensation Novel," in *The Cambridge Companion to Anthony Trollope*, eds. Carolyn Dever and Lisa Niles. Cambridge: Cambridge University Press, 2011. 85–98.

Bowen, John. *Other Dickens: From Pickwick to Chuzzlewit*. Oxford: Oxford University Press, 2000.

Brewer, David A. *The Afterlife of Character, 1726–1825*. Philadelphia: University of Pennsylvania Press, 2005.

Bromwich, David. *Hazlitt: The Mind of a Critic*. New Haven: Yale University Press, 1999.

Brontë, Charlotte. *Jane Eyre*, ed. Michael Mason. New York: Penguin, [1847] 1996.

Selected Letters, ed. Margaret Smith. Oxford: Oxford University Press, 2010.

Brown, Bill. *A Sense of Things: The Object Matter of American Literature*. Chicago: University of Chicago Press, 2003.

"Thing Theory," in *Things*, ed. Bill Brown. Chicago: University of Chicago Press, 2004. 1–22.

Brown, Thomas. *Sketch of a System of the Philosophy of the Human Mind*. Edinburgh: Bell and Bradfute, 1820.

Browning, Elizabeth Barrett. *Aurora Leigh*, ed. Margaret Reynolds. New York: Norton, [1856] 1996.

Buckland, William. "Notice on the Megalosaurus or Great Fossil Lizard of Stonesfield," *Transactions of the Geological Society of London* 2.1 (1824): 390–96.

Bulwer-Lytton, Edward. The Critic Nos. 1 and 2, "On Art in Fiction" *Monthly Chronicle* I (March 1838): 42–51 and (April 1838): 138–49.

England and the English, ed. Standish Meacham. Chicago: University of Chicago Press, 1970.

Burke, Edmund. *A Philosophical Inquiry into the Origin of Our Ideas of the Sublime and the Beautiful*, ed. James T. Boulton. South Bend: Notre Dame University Press, 1968.

Burney, Frances. *Evelina*, ed. Stewart J. Cooke. New York: W. W. Norton, [1778] 1998.

Burwick, Frederick. "Lamb, Hazlitt, and De Quincey on Hogarth." *The Wordsworth Circle* 28, no. 1 (Winter 1997): 59–69.

Butler, Joseph. *Fifteen Sermons Preached at the Rolls Chapel*. London: J. and J. Knapton, 1726.

Buzard, James. *Disorienting Fiction: The Autoethnographic Work of Nineteenth-Century British Novels*. Princeton: Princeton University Press, 2005.

Byron, George Gordon. *Lord Byron: The Major Works*, ed. Jerome J. McGann. New York: Oxford University Press, 1986.

Carlyle, Thomas. *Past and Present*, ed. Richard D. Altick. New York: New York University Press, [1843] 1965.

Critical and Miscellaneous Essays in Five Volumes. New York: AMS Press, 1980.

"Signs of the Times," in *A Carlyle Reader*, ed. G. B. Tennyson. Cambridge: Cambridge University Press, 1984. 31–55.

Sartor Resartus, eds. Kerry McSweeney and Peter Sabor. New York: Oxford University Press, [1833–34] 1999.

On Heroes, Hero-Worship, and the Heroic in History, eds. David R. Sorensen and Brent E. Kinser. New Haven: Yale University Press, [1841] 2013.

Carroll, David, ed. *George Eliot: The Critical Heritage*. New York: Barnes and Noble, 1971.

Cassirer, Ernst. *The Philosophy of the Enlightenment*, trans. Fritz C. A. Koelln and James P. Pettegrove. Princeton: Princeton University Press, 1951.

Chambers, Robert [ed., James, A. Secord]. *Vestiges of the Natural History of Creation*. Chicago: University of Chicago Press, [1844] 1994.

Chandler, David. "A Sign's Progress: Lamb on Hogarth," *The Charles Lamb Bulletin*, n.s. 94 (1996): 50–63.

Chandler, James. *England in 1819: The Politics of Literary Culture and the Case of Romantic Historicism*. Chicago: University of Chicago Press, 1998.

Chase, Karen, ed. *Middlemarch in the Twenty-First Century*. New York: Oxford University Press, 2006.

Christensen, Jerome. *Practicing Enlightenment: Hume and the Formation of a Literary Career*. Madison: University of Wisconsin Press, 1987.

Lord Byron's Strength: Romantic Writing and Commercial Society. Baltimore: Johns Hopkins University Press, 1993.

Cixous, Hélène and Keith Cohen. "The Character of 'Character.'" *New Literary History* 5 (Winter 1974): 383–402.

Claggett, Shalyn. "The Science of Character in Victorian Literature and Culture," *Dissertation Abstracts International, Section A: The Humanities and Social Sciences 67*, no. 5 (Nov. 2006; Vanderbilt University, 2005).

Clark, Peter. *British Clubs and Societies, 1500–1800*. Oxford: Oxford University Press, 2000.

Coleman, Julie. *A History of Cant and Slang Dictionaries, Volume 2: 1785–1858*. Oxford: Oxford University Press, 2004.

Coleridge, Samuel Taylor. *Table Talk*, ed. Carl Woodring. *The Collected Works of Samuel Taylor Coleridge*. 2 vols. New York and London: Routledge & Kegan Paul, Princeton University Press, 1990.

Coleridge's Poetry and Prose, eds. Nicholas Halmi, Paul Magnuson, and Raimonda Modiano. New York: Norton, 2004.

Collini, Stefan. *Public Moralists: Political Thought and Intellectual Life in Britain, 1850–1930*. Oxford: Clarendon, 1991.

Collins, Philip, ed. *Dickens: The Critical Heritage*. London: Routledge and Kegan Paul, 1986.

Collins, Wilkie. *Heart and Science*, ed. Steve Farmer. Peterborough: Broadview Press, [1883] 1996.

Colvin, Sidney. "[Review of *Middlemarch*]," *Fortnightly Review* XIII (January 19, 1873): 142–47.

Combe, George. *A System of Phrenology*. London: Longman, 1830.

Conrad, Joseph. *The Heart of Darkness*, ed. Paul B. Armstrong. New York: Norton, [1899] 2005.

Cottom, Daniel. *Social Figures: George Eliot, Social History, and Literary Representation*. Minneapolis: University of Minnesota Press, 1987.

Crary, Jonathan. *Suspensions of Perception: Attention, Spectacle, and Modern Culture*. Boston: MIT Press, 2001.

Cross, J. W. ed. *The Writings of George Eliot Together with the Life*. New York: AMS Press, 1970.

Culler, Jonathan. "Apostrophe," in *The Pursuit of Signs: Semiotics, Literature, Deconstruction*. Ithaca: Cornell University Press, 1981. 135–54.

Cunningham, David. "'Very Abstract and Terribly Concrete': Capitalism and *The Theory of the Novel*," *NOVEL: A Forum on Fiction* 42.2 (Summer 2009): 311–17.

Dallas, E. S. *The Gay Science*. 2 vols. London: Chapman and Hall, 1866.

Dames, Nicholas. *The Physiology of the Novel: Reading, Neural Science, and the Form of Victorian Fiction*. New York: Oxford University Press, 2007.

Darwin, Charles. *The Descent of Man*, ed. Adrian Desmond. New York: Penguin, [1871] 2004.

The Origin of Species, ed. George Levine. New York: Barnes and Noble, [1859] 2004.

Daston, Lorraine, ed. *Biographies of Scientific Objects*. Chicago: University of Chicago Press, 2000.

Daston, Lorraine and Peter Galison. "The Image of Objectivity," *Representations* 40 (Fall 1992): 81–127.

Davidoff, Leonore. *Worlds Between: Historical Perspectives on Gender and Class.* New York: Routledge, 1995.

Davidson, Jenny. *Hypocrisy and the Politics of Politeness: Manners and Morals from Locke to Austen.* Cambridge: Cambridge University Press, 2004.

Davies, Hugh Sykes. "Trollope and His Style," *A Review of English Literature* 1.4 (October 1960): 73–85.

Davis, Lennard J. *Factual Fictions: The Origins of the English Novel.* Philadelphia: University of Pennsylvania Press, 1997.

Dawson, Gowan. "Literary Megatheriums and Loose Baggy Monsters: Paleontology and the Victorian Novel," *Victorian Studies* 53.2 (Winter 2011): 203–30.

Dear, Peter. *Discipline and Experience: The Mathematical Way in the Scientific Revolution.* Chicago: University of Chicago Press, 1995.

De Certeau, Michel. *The Practice of Everyday Life,* trans. Steven Rendall. Berkeley: University of California Press, 1988.

The Writing of History, trans. Tom Conley. New York: Columbia University Press, 1988.

Derrida, Jacques. *Of Grammatology,* trans. Gayatri Chakravorty Spivak. Baltimore: Johns Hopkins University Press, 1997.

Dickens, Charles. *Bleak House,* eds. George Ford and Sylvère Monod. New York: Norton, [1852–53] 1977.

The Letters of Charles Dickens, ed. Kathleen Tillotson. Oxford: Clarendon Press, 1977.

David Copperfield, ed. Jerome H. Buckley. New York: Norton, [1849–50] 1990.

Great Expectations, ed. Janie Carlyle. New York: Bedford/St. Martin's, [1860–61] 1996.

Our Mutual Friend, ed. Adrian Poole. New York: Penguin, [1864–65] 1997.

The Old Curiosity Shop, ed. Norman Page. New York: Penguin, [1840–41] 2000.

Dombey and Son, ed. Andrew Saunders. New York: Penguin, [1846–48] 2002.

Hard Times, ed. Kate Flint. New York: Penguin, [1854] 2003.

D'Israeli, Isaac. *The Literary Character: or, The History of Men of Genius, Drawn from Their Own Feelings and Confessions; Literary Miscellanies; and, An Inquiry into the Character of James the First,* ed. Benjamin Disraeli. New York: Routledge, Warne, and Routledge, [1795] 1863.

Duckworth, Alistair M. *The Improvement of the Estate: A Study of Jane Austen's Novels.* Baltimore: Johns Hopkins University Press, 1971.

Duncan, Ian. *Scott's Shadow: The Novel in Romantic Edinburgh.* Princeton: Princeton University Press, 2008.

Dyer, Gary. "Thieves, Boxers, Sodomites, Poets: Being Flash to Byron's *Don Juan,*" *PMLA* 116.3 (May 2001): 562–78.

Egan, Pierce. *Tom and Jerry: Life in London; Or the Day and Night Scenes of Jerry Hawthorne and His Elegant Friend, Corinthian Tom.* London: John Camden Hotten, [1821] 1869.

Eigner, Edwin M. and George J. Worth, eds. *Victorian Criticism of the Novel*. New York: Cambridge University Press, 1985.

Eliot, George. "Silly Novels by Lady Novelists," *Westminster Review* 66 O.S./10 N.S. (October 1856): 442–61.

The Writings of George Eliot Together with the Life by J. W. Cross. 25 vols. New York: AMS Press, 1970.

Adam Bede, ed. Stephen Gill. New York: Penguin, [1859] 1985.

Characters of Theophrastus Such, ed. Nancy Henry. Iowa City: University of Iowa Press, [1879] 1994.

The Mill on the Floss, ed. Carol T. Christ. New York: Norton, [1860] 1994.

Daniel Deronda, ed. Terence Cave. New York: Penguin, [1876] 1995.

Felix Holt, the Radical, ed. Lynda Mugglestone. London: Penguin, [1866] 1995.

Scenes of Clerical Life, ed. Jennifer Gribble. New York: Penguin, [1857] 1998.

Middlemarch, ed. Bert G. Hornbeck. New York: Norton, [1871–72] 2000.

Eliot, T. S. "Hamlet and His Problems" (1919), in *Selected Essays*. New York: Harcourt Brace and World, Inc., 1932. 121–26.

Ellison, Julie K. *Cato's Tears and the Making of Anglo-American Emotion*. Chicago: University of Chicago Press, 1999.

Ermarth, Elizabeth Deeds. *Realism and Consensus in English Fiction*. Princeton: Princeton University Press, 1983.

"Negotiating *Middlemarch*," in *Middlemarch in the Twenty-First Century*, ed. Karen Chase. New York: Oxford University Press, 2006. 107–31.

Farina, Jonathan. "Characterizing the Factory System: Factory Subjectivity in *Household Words*," *Victorian Literature and Culture* 35, no. 1 (March 2007): 41–56.

"'The New Science of Literary Mensuration': Accounting for Reading, Then and Now," *Victorians Institute Journal Digital Annex* 38 (2010): www.nines .org/exhibits/Literary_Mensuration

"*The Excursion* and 'the Surfaces of Things,'" *The Wordsworth Circle* 45.2 (Spring 2014): 99–105.

"Mad Libs and Stupid Criticism," *Dickens Studies Annual* 46 (August 2015): 325–38.

Felski, Rita., ed. and intro. "Character" [Special Issue], *New Literary History: A Journal of Theory and Interpretation* 42.2 (Spring 2011): v–ix, 209–360.

Ferris, Ina. "Melancholy, Memory, and the 'Narrative Situation' of History in Post-Enlightenment Scotland," in *Scotland and the Borders of Romanticism*, eds. Leith Davis, Ian Duncan, and Janet Sorensen. Cambridge: Cambridge University Press, 2004. 77–93.

"Antiquarian Authorship: D'Israeli's Miscellany of Literary Curiosity and the Question of Secondary Genres," *Studies in Romanticism* 45 (Winter 2006): 523–42.

Fielding, Henry. *Tom Jones*, ed. Sheridan Baker. New York: Norton, [1749] 1973.

Finn, Margot C. *The Character of Credit: Personal Debt in English Culture, 1740–1914*. Cambridge: Cambridge University Press, 2003.

Fisch, Menachem. "Necessary and Contingent Truth in William Whewell's Antithetical Theory of Knowledge," *Studies in History and Philosophy of Science* 16 (1985): 275–314.

William Whewell, Philosopher of Science. Oxford: Oxford University Press, 1991.

Flint, Kate. *The Victorians and the Visual Imagination*. Cambridge: Cambridge University Press, 2000.

"The Materiality of *Middlemarch*," in *Middlemarch in the Twenty-First Century*, ed. Karen Chase. New York: Oxford University Press, 2006. 65–86.

Forster, John. *The Life of Charles Dickens*. 2 vols. London: Chapman and Hall, 1872–74.

Foucault, Michel. *The Archaeology of Knowledge and The Discourse on Language*, trans. A. M. Sheridan Smith. New York: Pantheon Books, 1972.

Power/Knowledge: Selected Interviews and Other Writings, 1972–1977, ed. Colin Gordon. New York: Pantheon, 1980.

The Order of Things: An Archaeology of the Human Sciences. New York: Vintage, 1994.

Fourier, Charles. *The Theory of the Four Movements*, eds. Gareth Stedman Jones and Ian Patterson. Cambridge: Cambridge University Press, 1996.

Gagnier, Regenia. "Gender, Liberalism, Resentment," in *The Politics of Gender in Anthony Trollope's Novels: New Readings for the Twenty-First Century*, eds. Margaret Markwick, Deborah Denenholz Morse, and Regenia Gagnier. Burlington: Ashgate, 2009.

Gallagher, Catherine. *The Industrial Reformation of English Fiction: Social Discourse and Narrative Form, 1832–1867*. Chicago: University of Chicago Press, 1985.

Nobody's Story: The Vanishing Acts of Women Writers in the Marketplace, 1670–1820. Berkeley: University of California Press, 1994.

"George Eliot: Immanent Victorian," *Representations* 90 (Spring 2005), 61–74.

Galperin, William H. *The Historical Austen*. Philadelphia: University of Pennsylvania Press, 2003.

"'Describing What Never Happened': Jane Austen and the History of Missed Opportunities," *ELH* 73.2 (2006): 355–82.

Galton, Francis. "Hereditary Talent and Character," *Macmillan's Magazine* 12 (1865): 157–66 (Part I); 318–27 (Part II).

Garcha, Amanpal. *From Sketch to Novel: The Development of Victorian Fiction*. Cambridge: Cambridge University Press, 2009.

Garnett, Jane. "Bishop Butler and the Zeitgeist: Butler and the Development of Christian Moral Philosophy in Victorian Britain," in *Joseph Butler's Moral and Religious Thought: Tercentenary Essays*, ed. Christopher Cunliffe. Oxford: Oxford University Press, 1992.

Garratt, Peter. *Victorian Empiricism: Self, Knowledge, and Reality in Ruskin, Bain, Lewes, Spencer, and George Eliot*. Madison: Farleigh Dickinson University Press, 2010.

Gaskell, Elizabeth. *The Letters of Mrs. Gaskell*, eds. J. A. V. Chapple and Arthur Pollard. Manchester: Manchester University Press, 1997.

Cranford, ed. Elizabeth Porges Watson. Oxford: Oxford University Press, [1851–53] 1998.

Mary Barton, ed. Thomas Recchio. New York: Norton, [1848] 2008.

Gay, Penny. *Jane Austen and the Theatre*. Cambridge: Cambridge University Press, 2002.

Gevirtz, Karen Bloom. *Women, the Novel, and Natural Philosophy, 1660–1727*. New York: Palgrave, 2014.

Gill, Stephen. *Wordsworth and the Victorians*. Oxford: Clarendon, 1998.

Goffman, Erving. *Relations in Public: Microstudies of the Public Order*. New York: Harper & Row/Colophon Books, 1972.

Goldberg, Michael K. *Carlyle and Dickens*. Athens: University of Georgia Press, 1972.

Golinski, Jan. *Science as Public Culture: Chemistry and Enlightenment in Britain, 1760–1820*. Cambridge: Cambridge University Press, 1992.

Goodlad, Lauren. *Victorian Literature and the Victorian State: Character and Governance in a Liberal Society*. Baltimore: Johns Hopkins University Press, 2003.

Graver, Suzanne. *George Eliot and Community: A Study in Social Theory and Fictional Form*. Berkeley: University of California Press, 1984.

Green, T. H. *Lectures on the Principles of Political Obligation and Other Writings*, eds. Paul Harris and John Morrow. Cambridge: Cambridge University Press, 1986.

Greiner, Rae. *Sympathetic Realism in Nineteenth-Century British Fiction*. Baltimore: Johns Hopkins University Press, 2012.

Guillory, John. *Cultural Capital: Literary Study and the Problem of Canon Formation*. Chicago: University of Chicago Press, 1994.

Hack, Daniel. *The Material Interests of the Victorian Novel*. Charlottesville: University of Virginia Press, 2005.

Hadley, Elaine. *Living Liberalism: Practical Citizenship in Mid-Victorian Britain*. Chicago: University of Chicago Press, 2010.

Haefner, Joel. "'The Soul Speaking in the Face': Hazlitt's Concept of Character," *SEL: Studies in English Literature, 1500–1900* 24, no. 4 (Summer 1984): 655–70.

Hall, N. John, ed. *The Trollope Critics*. Totowa: Barnes & Noble, 1981.

Trollope: A Biography. Oxford: Clarendon Press, 1991.

Harding, D. W. "Character and Caricature in Jane Austen," in *Critical Essays on Jane Austen*, ed. B. C. Southam. London: Routledge and Kegan Paul, 1968. 83–105.

Harlan, Susan. "'Talking' and Reading Shakespeare in Jane Austen's *Mansfield Park*," *Wordsworth Circle* 39.1–2 (Winter–Spring 2008): 43–46.

Hartley, Mary Laffan. *Christy Carew: A Novel*. New York: Henry Holt, 1880.

Hazlitt, William. *The Collected Works of William Hazlitt*, ed. P. P. Howe. 21 vols. London: J. M. Dent & Sons, 1930–1934.

Selected Essays, 1778–1830, ed. Geoffrey Keynes. London: The Nonesuch Press, 1948.

Selected Writings, ed. Jon Cook. Oxford: Oxford University Press, 1998.

Hegel, G. W. F. *Hegel's Aesthetics: Lectures on Fine Art*, trans. T. M. Knox. 2 vols. Oxford: Oxford University Press, [1835] 2010.

Henderson, Andrea K. *Romantic Identities: Varieties of Subjectivity, 1774–1830*. New York: Cambridge University Press, 1996.

Herbert, Christopher. "Trollope and the Fixity of Self," *PMLA* 93.2 (March 1978): 228–39.

Culture and Anomie: Ethnographic Imagination in the Nineteenth Century. Chicago: University of Chicago Press, 1991.

"*The Golden Bough* and the Unknowable," in *Knowing the Past: Victorian Literature and Culture*, ed. Suzy Anger. Ithaca: Cornell University Press, 2001. 32–51.

Victorian Relativity: Radical Thought and Scientific Discovery. Chicago: University of Chicago Press, 2001.

Herschel, John. "Whewell on Inductive Sciences," *Quarterly Review* 68 (1841): 177–238.

A Preliminary Discourse on the Study of Natural Philosophy, with a new forward by Arthur Fine. Chicago: University of Chicago Press, 1987.

Heydt-Stevenson, Jill. "Liberty, Connection, and Tyranny: The Novels of Jane Austen and the Aesthetic Movement of the Picturesque," in *Lessons of Romanticism: A Critical Companion*, eds. Thomas Pfau and Robert F. Glackner. Durham: Duke University Press, 1998.

Hill, Jr., Robert W, ed. *Tennyson's Poetry*. New York: Norton, 1999.

Horne, Richard Henry. *A New Spirit of the Age*, ed. R. H. Horne. New York: Harper & Brothers, 1844.

Houghton, Walter E. *The Victorian Frame of Mind, 1830–1870*. New Haven: Yale University Press, 1985.

Hughes, Thomas. *Tom Brown's Schooldays*. New York: Macmillan and Co., [1857] 1891.

Hume, David. *A Treatise of Human Nature*. 2 vols. London: John Noon, 1739.

Humphreys, A. R. "The Eternal Fitness of Things: An Aspect of Eighteenth-Century Thought," *The Modern Language Review* 42, no. 2 (April 1947): 188–98.

[Hutton, Richard Holt] [Obituary]. *The Spectator* lv (December 9, 1882): 1573–74.

[Inglis, Catherine Hartland]. "The Universal 'But,'" *Dublin University Magazine* (January 1874): 58–63.

Iser, Wolfgang. *The Fictive and the Imaginary: Charting Literary Anthropology*. Baltimore: Johns Hopkins University Press, 1993.

Jaffe, Audrey. *Vanishing Points: Dickens, Narrative, and the Subject of Omniscience*. Berkeley: University of California Press, 1991.

Scenes of Sympathy: Identity and Representation in Victorian Fiction. Ithaca: Cornell University Press, 2000.

The Affective Life of the Average Man: The Victorian Novel and the Stock Market Graph. Athens: Ohio State University Press, 2010.

Jameson, Fredric. *The Political Unconscious: Narrative as a Socially Symbolic Act*. Ithaca: Cornell University Press, 1981.

The Antinomies of Realism. London: Verso, 2013.

Jeaffreson, John Cordy. *Novels and Novelists: From Elizabeth to Victoria*. London: Hurst and Blackett, 1858.

Johnson, Samuel. *The Major Works*, ed. Donald Greene. Oxford: Oxford University Press, 1984.

Jones, Richard. *An Essay on the Distribution of Wealth and on the Sources of Taxation*. London: John Murray, 1831.

Kant, Immanuel. *Critique of Judgment*, ed. Werner S. Pluhar. Indiana: Hackett, [1790] 1987.

Keats, John. *Complete Poems*, ed. Jack Stillinger. Cambridge: Belknap/Harvard University Press, 1982.

Kendrick, Walter M. *The Novel Machine: The Theory and Fiction of Anthony Trollope*. Baltimore: Johns Hopkins University Press, 1980.

Khalip, Jacques. "Virtual Conduct: Disinterested Agency in Hazlitt and Keats," *ELH* 73, no. 4 (2006): 885–912.

Klancher, Jon P. *The Making of English Reading Audiences, 1790–1832*. Madison: University of Wisconsin Press, 1987.

Knight, David M. and Matthew D. Eddy, eds. *Science and Beliefs: From Natural Philosophy to Natural Science, 1700–1900*. Aldershot: Ashgate, 2005.

Knoepflmacher, U. C. "*Middlemarch*: An Avuncular View," *Nineteenth-Century Fiction* 30.1 (June 1975): 53–81.

Knox-Shaw, Peter. *Jane Austen and the Enlightenment*. Cambridge: Cambridge University Press, 2004.

Korshin, Paul J. *Typologies in England, 1650–1820*. Princeton: Princeton University Press, 1982.

Kraft, Elizabeth. *Character and Consciousness in Eighteenth-Century Comic Fiction*. Athens: University of Georgia Press, 1992.

Kramnick, Jonathan Brody. *Making the English Canon: Print-Capitalism and the Cultural Past, 1700–1770*. Cambridge: Cambridge University Press, 1999.

Kucich, John. *Repression in Victorian Fiction: Charlotte Brontë, George Eliot, and Charles Dickens*. Berkeley: University of California Press, 1987.

The Power of Lies: Transgression in Victorian Fiction. Ithaca: Cornell University Press, 1994.

Kurnick, David. *Empty Houses: Theatrical Failure and the Novel*. Princeton: Princeton University Press, 2012.

Lamb, Charles. "On the Genius and Character of Hogarth." *The Reflector* No. 3 (April–September 1811).

Langbauer, Laurie. *Novels of Everyday Life: The Series in English Fiction, 1850–1930*. Ithaca: Cornell University Press, 1999.

The Works of Charles and Mary Lamb, ed. E. V. Lucas. 7 vols. London: Methuen & Co., 1903–5.

Latour, Bruno. *We Have Never Been Modern*, trans. Catherine Porter. Cambridge: Harvard University Press, 1993.

Law, Jules David. *The Rhetoric of Empiricism: Language and Perception from Locke to I. A. Richards*. Ithaca: Cornell University Press, 1993.

"There's Something about Hyde," *Novel: A Forum on Fiction* 42.3 (Fall 2009): 504–510.

Leech, John. *John Leech's Pictures of Life and Character*, ed. W. M. Thackeray. London: Bradbury & Agnew, 1886.

Lefebvre, Henri. *Critique of Everyday Life*, trans. John Moore. 3 vols. London: Verso: 2008.

Levine, Caroline. *The Serious Pleasures of Suspense: Victorian Realism and Narrative Doubt*. Charolottesville: University of Virginia Press, 2003.

Forms: Whole, Rhythm, Hierarchy, Network. Princeton: Princeton University Press, 2015.

Levine, George. "George Eliot's Hypothesis of Reality," *Nineteenth-Century Fiction* 35.1 (June 1980): 1–28.

The Realistic Imagination: English Fiction from Frankenstein to Lady Chatterley. Chicago: University of Chicago Press, 1981. Rpt. 1983.

Darwin and the Novelists: Patterns of Science in Victorian Fiction. Chicago: University of Chicago Press, 1988.

Dying to Know: Scientific Epistemology and Narrative in Victorian England. Chicago: University of Chicago Press, 2002.

Darwin the Writer. New York: Oxford University Press, 2011.

Lewes, George H. "French Romances," *Fraser's Magazine* 27 (February 1843), 184–94.

The Life and Works of Goethe with Sketches of His Age and Contemporaries. 2 vols. London: David Nutt, 1855.

"Criticism in Relation to Novels," *Fortnightly Review* 3 (December 15, 1865), 352–61.

"The Principles of Success in Literature," *Fortnightly Review* 1 (1865): 572–89.

"Dickens in Relation to Criticism," *Fortnightly Review* 11.62 (February 1872): 141–54.

Problems of Life and Mind. 2 vols. London: Trübner, 1874.

Liu, Alan. *Wordsworth: The Sense of History*. Stanford: Stanford University Press, 1989.

Lonoff, Sue. *Wilkie Collins and His Victorian Readers*. New York: AMS Press, 1982.

Love, Heather. "Close but not Deep: Literary Ethics and the Descriptive Turn," *New Literary History* 41.2 (Spring 2010): 371–91.

Lukács, Georg. *The Theory of the Novel*, trans. Anna Bostock. Cambridge: MIT Press, 1971.

Lyell, Charles. *Principles of Geology*, ed. Martin J. S. Rudwick. 3 vols. Chicago: University of Chicago Press, [1830–33] 1990–92.

Lynch, Deidre Shauna. *The Economy of Character: Novels, Market Culture, and the Business of Inner Meaning*. Chicago: University of Chicago Press, 1998.

Maitzen, Rohan Amanda. "'The Soul of Art': Understanding Victorian Ethical Criticism," *ESC: English Studies in Canada* 31.2/3 (2005): 151–86.

Manning, Susan. *Poetics of Character: Transatlantic Encounters 1700–1900*. Cambridge: Cambridge University Press, 2013.

Marcus, Sharon. *Between Women: Friendship, Desire, and Marriage in Victorian England.* Princeton: Princeton University Press, 2007.

Marcus, Steven. *Dickens: From Pickwick to Dombey.* London: Chatto and Windus, 1965.

Mason, Michael York. "Middlemarch and Science: Problems of Life and Mind," *Review of English Studies* 22 (May 1971): 151–69.

Masson, David. *British Novelists and Their Styles: Being a Critical Sketch of the History of British Prose Fiction.* Boston: D. Lothrop and Co., 1875.

McGowan, John P. "The Turn of George Eliot's Realism," *Nineteenth-Century Fiction* 35 (1980): 171–92.

McKeon, Michael. *The Origins of the English Novel, 1600–1740.* Baltimore: Johns Hopkins University Press, 1987.

The Secret History of Domesticity: Public, Private, and the Division of Knowledge. Baltimore: Johns Hopkins University Press, 2005.

McMaster, Juliet. *Trollope's Palliser Novels: Theme and Pattern.* London: Macmillan, 1978.

McMaster, R. D. *Trollope and the Law.* New York: Palgrave Macmillan, 1986.

Meredith, George. *The Egoist,* ed. Robert M. Adams. New York: Norton, [1879] 1979.

Merleau-Ponty, Maurice. *Phenomenology of Perception,* trans. Colin Smith. London: Routledge, 2002.

Michie, Elsie B. *Outside the Pale: Cultural Exclusion, Gender Difference, and the Victorian Woman Writer.* Ithaca: Cornell University Press, 1993.

Michie, Helena. *Victorian Honeymoons: Journeys to the Conjugal.* Cambridge: Cambridge University Press, 2006.

Mill, James. *Analysis of the Phenomena of the Human Mind,* ed. John Stuart Mill. 2 vols. London: Longmans, Green, Reader, and Dyer, 1869.

Mill, John Stuart. *Collected Works of John Stuart Mill,* eds. John M. Robson and Jack Stillinger. 33 vols. Toronto: University of Toronto Press, 1963.

Autobiography and Other Writings, ed. Jack Stillinger. Boston: Houghton Mifflin, 1969.

Mill: The Spirit of the Age, On Liberty, The Subjection of Women, ed. Alan Ryan. New York: Norton, 1997.

Miller, Andrew H. *Novels Behind Glass: Commodity Culture and Victorian Narrative.* Cambridge: Cambridge University Press, 1995.

The Burdens of Perfection: On Ethics and Reading in Nineteenth-Century British Literature. Ithaca: Cornell University Press, 2008.

Miller, D. A. *The Novel and the Police.* Berkeley: University of California Press, 1988.

Miller, J. Hillis. *Charles Dickens: The World of His Novels.* Cambridge: Harvard University Press, 1958.

"The Fiction of Realism: *Sketches by Boz, Oliver Twist,* and Cruikshank's Illustrations," in *Victorian Subjects.* Durham: Duke University Press, 1991.

Montaigne, Michel de. *The Complete Essays of Montaigne,* trans. Donald M. Frame. Stanford: Stanford University Press, 1976.

Moretti, Franco. *The Way of the World: The Bildungsroman in European Culture,* trans. Albert Sbragia. London: Verso, 2000.

The Bourgeois: Between History and Literature. London: Verso, 2014.

Morgan, Susan. *In the Meantime: Character and Perception in Jane Austen's Fiction.* Chicago: University of Chicago Press, 1980.

Morley, Henry. *Character Writings of the 17th Century.* London: Ballantyne, Hanson, and Co., 1891.

Moulton, Richard Green. *Shakespeare as a Dramatic Artist.* New York: Dover, [1885/88] 1966.

Mullen, Richard. *Anthony Trollope: A Victorian in His World.* London: Duckworth, 1990.

Mulvihill, James. "Character and Culture in Hazlitt's Spirit of the Age," *Nineteenth-Century Literature* 45, no. 3 (December 1990), 281–99.

Newman, John Henry. *The Idea of a University,* ed. Frank M. Turner. New Haven: Yale University Press, [1854] 1996.

Newsome, Robert. *Dickens on the Romantic Side of Familiar Things: Bleak House and the Novel Tradition.* New York: Columbia University Press, 1977.

Ngai, Sianne. *Our Aesthetic Categories: Zany, Cute, Interesting.* Cambridge: Harvard University Press, 2012.

Nietzsche, Friedrich. *Daybreak: Thoughts on the Prejudices of Morality,* eds. Maudemarie Clark and Brian Leiter. Cambridge: Cambridge University Press, [1881] 1997.

Nussbaum, Martha and Alison L. LaCroix, eds. *Subversion and Sympathy: Gender, Law, and the British Novel.* Oxford: Oxford University Press, 2013.

Orwell, George. "Charles Dickens," *A Collection of Essays.* London: Harvest, 1981. 48–104.

Owen, Robert. *A New View of Society and Other Writings,* ed. Gregory Claeys. New York: Penguin, 1991.

Packham, Catherine. "The Science and Poetry of Animation: Personification, Analogy, and Erasmus Darwin's *Loves of the Plants,*" *Romanticism* 10.2 (2004): 191–208.

Page, Norman. *The Language of Jane Austen.* New York: Barnes & Noble, 1972.

Park, Roy. *Hazlitt and the Spirit of the Age.* Oxford: Oxford University Press, 1971.

Parker, David. "Dickens's Archness," *Dickensian* 67 (1971): 149–58.

Pater, Walter. *The Renaissance: Studies in Art and Poetry,* ed. Donald L. Hill. Berkeley: University of California Press, 1980.

Patey, Douglas Lane. *Probability and Literary Form: Philosophic Theory and Literary Practice in the Augustan Age.* Cambridge: Cambridge University Press, 1984.

Pérez-Ramos, Antonio. *Francis Bacon's Idea of Science and the Maker's Knowledge Tradition.* Oxford: Clarendon, 1988.

Perry, Seamus. *Coleridge and the Uses of Division.* Oxford: Clarendon Press, 1999.

Pinch, Adela. *Strange Fits of Passion: Epistemologies of Emotion, Hume to Austen.* Stanford: Stanford University Press, 1996.

Plotz, John. "Mediated Involvement: John Stuart Mill's Antisocial Sociability," in *The Feeling of Reading: Affective Experience & Victorian Literature*, ed. Rachel Ablow. Ann Arbor: University of Michigan Press, 2010, 69–92.

"The Semi-Detached Provincial Novel," *Victorian Studies* 53.3 (Spring 2011): 405–16.

Pocock, J. G. A. *Virtue, Commerce, and History: Essays on Political Thought and History, Chiefly in the Eighteenth Century*. Cambridge: Cambridge University Press, 1985.

Poovey, Mary. *Uneven Developments: The Ideological Work of Gender in Mid-Victorian England*. Chicago: University of Chicago Press, 1988.

Making a Social Body: British Cultural Formation, 1830–1864. Chicago: University of Chicago Press, 1995.

A History of the Modern Fact: Problems of Knowledge in the Sciences of Wealth and Society. Chicago: University of Chicago Press, 1998.

"The Structure of Anxiety in Political Economy and *Hard Times*," in *Knowing the Past: Victorian Literature and Culture*, ed. Suzy Anger. Ithaca: Cornell University Press, 2001. 151–71.

Genres of the Credit Economy: Mediating Value in Eighteenth- and Nineteenth-Century Britain. Chicago: University of Chicago Press, 2008.

Porter, Dahlia. "Scientific Analogy and Literary Taxonomy in Darwin's *Loves of the Plants*," *European Romantic Review* 18:2 (April 2007): 213–21.

Porter, Roy. "Charles Lyell and the Principles of the History of Geology," *British Journal for the History of Science* 9 (1976): 91–103.

Postlewaite, Diana. "George Eliot and Science," in *The Cambridge Companion to George Eliot*, ed. George Levine. Cambridge: Cambridge University Press, 2001.

Potkay, Adam. "Wordsworth and the Ethics of Things," *PMLA* 123, no. 2 (March 2008): 390–404.

Powell, Baden. *The Unity of Worlds and of Nature: Three Essays on the Spirit of Inductive Philosophy; the Plurality of Worlds; and the Philosophy of Creation*. Cambridge: Cambridge University Press, [1855] 2009.

Puckett, Kent. *Bad Form: Social Mistakes and the Nineteenth-Century Novel*. Oxford: Oxford University Press, 2008.

Price, Leah. *The Anthology and the Rise of the Novel: From Richardson to George Eliot*. Cambridge: Cambridge University Press, 2000.

"Reader's Block: Trollope and the Book as Prop," in *The Feeling of Reading*, ed. Rachel Ablow. Minneapolis: University of Minnesota Press, 2010. 47–68.

Rauch, Alan. *Useful Knowledge: The Victorians, Morality, and the March of Intellect*. Durham: Duke University Press, 2001.

Ready, Robert. "Hazlitt: In and Out of 'Gusto,'" *SEL: Studies in English Literature, 1500–1900* 14, no. 4 (Autumn 1974): 537–46.

Reynolds, Joshua. *Discourses on Art*, ed. Robert R. Wark. London: Paul Mellon Centre for Studies in British Art, 1997.

Ricouer, Paul. *Freud and Philosophy: An Essay on Interpretation*. New Haven: Yale University Press, 1970.

Robbins, Bruce. *The Servant's Hand: English Fiction from Below*. Durham: Duke University Press, 1993.

Robles, Mario Ortiz. *The Novel as Event*. Ann Arbor: University of Michigan Press, 2010.

Romano, John. *Dickens and Reality*. New York: Columbia University Press, 1978.

Ruskin, John. *The Works of John Ruskin*, eds. E. T. Cook and Alexander Wedderburn. Library Edition. 39 vols. London: George Allen, 1903–12.

Rylance, Rick. *Victorian Psychology and British Culture, 1850–1880*. Oxford: Oxford University Press, 2000.

Sadleir, Michael. "The Books," in *The Trollope Critics*, ed. N. John Hall. Totowa: Barnes & Noble, 1981. 34–45.

Schaffer, Simon. "The History and Geography of the Intellectual World," in *William Whewell, A Composite Portrait*, eds. Menachem Fisch and Simon Schaffer. Oxford: Oxford University Press, 1991. 201–31.

Schlicke, Paul. "Hazlitt, Horne, and the Spirit of the Age," *SEL: Studies in English Literature, 1500–1900* 45, no. 4 (Autumn 2005): 829–51.

Schoenfield, Mark. *The Professional Wordsworth: Law, Labor, and the Poet's Contract*. Athens: University of Georgia Press, 1996.

Scholar, Richard. *The Je-Ne-Sais-Quoi in Early Modern Europe: Encounters with a Certain Something*. Oxford: Oxford University Press, 2005.

Schor, Naomi. *Reading in Detail: Aesthetics and the Feminine*. New York: Routledge, 2007.

Schorer, Mark. "Fiction and the 'Analogical Matrix,'" in *Critiques and Essays on Modern Fiction*, ed. John W. Aldridge. New York: The Ronald Press, 1952. 83–98.

Scott, Walter. *Old Mortality*, ed. Douglas S. Mack. New York: Penguin, [1816] 1999.

Secord, James A. *Visions of Science: Books and Readers at the Dawn of the Victorian Age*. Oxford: Oxford University Press, 2014.

Victorian Sensation: The Extraordinary Publication, Reception, and Secret Authorship of Vestiges of the Natural History of Creation. Chicago: University of Chicago Press, 2000.

Sedgwick, Eve Kosofsky. "Jane Austen and the Masturbating Girl," in *Questions of Evidence: Proof, Practice, and Persuasion across the Disciplines*, eds. James Chandler, Arnold I. Davidson, and Harry Harootunian. Chicago: Chicago University Press, 1994. 105–24.

Touching Feeling: Affect, Pedagogy, Performativity. Durham: Duke University Press, 2003.

Serres, Michel. *Parasite*, trans. Lawrence R. Schehr. Minneapolis: University of Minnesota Press, 2007.

Shaftesbury (3rd Earl of), Anthony Ashley Cooper. *Characteristicks of Men, Manners, Opinions, Times*, ed. Philip Ayres. 2 vols. Oxford: Oxford University Press, [1711] 1999.

Shapin, Steven. *A Social History of Truth: Civility and Science in Seventeenth-Century England*. Chicago: University of Chicago Press, 1994.

Shapin, Steven and Simon Schaffer. *Leviathan and the Air-Pump: Hobbes, Boyle, and the Experimental Life*. Princeton: Princeton University Press, 1989.

Shaw, Harry E. *Narrating Reality: Austen, Scott, Eliot*. Ithaca: Cornell University Press, 1999.

Shelley, Mary. *Frankenstein 1818 Text*, ed. Marilyn Butler. Oxford: Oxford University Press, [1818] 1994.

Shuttleworth, Sally. *George Eliot and Nineteenth-Century Science: The Make-Believe of a Beginning*. Cambridge: Cambridge University Press, 1984.

Simpson, David. *Romanticism, Nationalism, and the Revolt against Theory*. Chicago: Chicago University Press, 1993.

Siskin, Clifford. *The Historicity of Romantic Discourse*. Oxford: Oxford University Press, 1988.

The Work of Writing: Literature and Social Change in Britain, 1700–1830. Baltimore: Johns Hopkins University Press, 1998.

Slakey, Roger L. "Anthony Trollope, Master of Gradualness," *VIJ: Victorians Institute Journal* 16 (1988): 27–35.

Smalley, Donald, ed. *Trollope: The Critical Heritage*. New York: Barnes & Noble Inc., 1969.

Smiles, Samuel. *Character*. New York: Harper & Brothers, 1872.

Self-Help, ed. Peter W. Sinnema. Oxford: Oxford University Press, [1859] 2002.

Smith, Adam. *An Inquiry into the Nature and Causes of the Wealth of Nations*, eds. R. H. Campbell and A. S. Skinner. 2 vols. Oxford: Clarendon Press, [1776] 1976.

Lectures on Rhetoric and Belles Lettres, ed. J. C. Bryce. Indianapolis: Liberty Fund, [c. 1762–63] 1985.

The Theory of Moral Sentiments. Amherst: Prometheus Books, [1759] 2000.

[Smith, Alexander]. "Novels and Novelists of the Day," *North British Review* 38 (February 1863): 170–71.

Smith, Jonathan. *Fact and Feeling: Baconian Science and the Nineteenth-Century Literary Imagination*. Science and Literature Series. Madison: University of Wisconsin Press, 1994.

Sneed, J. W. *The Theophrastan Character*. Oxford: Clarendon Press, 1985.

Snyder, Laura J. *Reforming Philosophy: A Victorian Debate on Science and Society*. Chicago: University of Chicago Press, 2006.

The Philosophical Breakfast Club. New York: Broadway, 2011.

Sorensen, Janet. "Vulgar Tongues: Canting Dictionaries and the Language of the People in Eighteenth-Century Britain," *Eighteenth-Century Studies* 37.3 (2004): 435–54.

Southam, B. C., ed. *Jane Austen: The Critical Heritage*. New York: Routledge, 1979.

Spacks, Patricia Meyer. *Boredom: The Literary History of a State of Mind*. Chicago: University of Chicago Press, 1995.

Stanford, W. B. *The Ulysses Theme: A Study in the Adaptability of a Traditional Hero*. 2nd edn. Ann Arbor: University of Michigan Press, 1968.

Stephen, Leslie. "The Moral Element in Literature," *Cornhill Magazine* 43.253 (January 1881): 34–50.

Stewart, Dugald. *The Collected Works of Dugald Stewart*, ed. Sir William Hamilton. 11 vols. Edinburgh: Thomas Constable and Co., 1854–60.

Stewart, Garrett. *Dickens and the Trials of the Imagination*. Cambridge: Harvard University Press, 1974.

"Dickens and Language," in *The Cambridge Companion to Charles Dickens*, ed. John O. Jordan. Cambridge: Cambridge University Press, 2001. 141–43.

Stewart, Susan. *On Longing: Narratives of the Gigantic, the Miniature, the Souvenir, the Collection*. Durham: Duke University Press, 1993.

Stoker, Bram. *Dracula*, ed. Maurice Hindle. New York: Penguin, [1897] 2003.

Sussman, Matthew. "Stylistic Virtue in Nineteenth-Century Criticism." *Victorian Studies* 56.2 (Winter 2014): 225–49.

Swingle, L. J. *Romanticism and Anthony Trollope: A Study in the Continuities of Nineteenth-Century Thought*. Ann Arbor: University of Michigan Press, 1990.

Tanner, Tony. *Jane Austen*. Cambridge: Harvard University Press, 1986.

Tave, Stuart M. *Some Words of Jane Austen*. Chicago: University of Chicago Press, 1973.

Taylor, Charles. *Sources of the Self: The Making of Modern Identity*. Cambridge: Cambridge University Press, 1989.

Taylor, Dennis. *Hardy's Literary Language and Victorian Philology*. Oxford: Clarendon Press, 1993.

Tennant, R. C. "The Anglican Response to Locke's Theory of Personal Identity," *Journal of the History of Ideas* 43.1 (January–March 1982): 73–90.

Terry, R. C. *Trollope: Interviews and Recollections*. London: Palgrave Macmillan, 1987.

Teukolsky, Rachel. *The Literate Eye: Victorian Art Writing and Modernist Aesthetics*. Oxford: Oxford University Press, 2009.

Thackeray, William Makepeace. "George Cruikshank," *Westminster Review* 66 (June 1840).

"A New Spirit of the Age," in *The Works of W. M. Thackeray*. New York: Charles Scribner's Sons, 1904. XXX: 99.

The History of Pendennis, ed. Donald Hawes. New York: Penguin, [1848–50] 1972.

Vanity Fair, ed. Peter Shillingsburg. New York: Norton, [1847–48] 1994.

The Newcomes, ed. Andrew Sanders. Oxford: Oxford University Press, [1855] 1995.

Thomas, David Wayne. *Cultivating Victorians: Liberal culture and the Aesthetic*. Philadelphia: University of Pennsylvania Press, 2004.

Trench, Richard Chenevix. *On the Study of Words: Six Lectures Addressed (Originally) to the Pupils at the Diocesan Training School, Winchester*. London: John W. Parker and Son, 1856.

On Some Deficiencies in Our English Dictionaries. 2nd edn. London: John W. Parker and Son, 1860.

Trilling, Lionel. *Sincerity and Authenticity*. Cambridge: Harvard University Press, 1972.

"The Liberal Imagination." *New York Review Books*, 2008.

Trollope, Anthony. *Thackeray*. English Men of Letters [series], ed. John Morley. London: Macmillan, 1879.

Macdermots of Ballycloran. London: Ward, Lock, and Co., 1866.

"Novel Reading," *Nineteenth Century: A Monthly Review* 5:23 (January 1879): 24–43.

Phineas Finn, ed. Jacques Berthoud. Oxford: Oxford University Press, [1869] 1982.

Doctor Thorne, ed. David Skilton. Oxford: Oxford University Press, [1858] 1985.

The Last Chronicle of Barset, ed. Sophie Gilmartin. New York: Penguin, [1867] 1986.

The Three Clerks, ed. Graham Handley. Oxford: Oxford University Press, [1858] 1989.

Orley Farm, ed. David Skilton. Oxford: Oxford University Press, [1862] 1991.

Rachel Ray, ed. P. D. Edwards. Oxford: Oxford University Press, [1863] 1991.

The Small House at Allington, ed. Julian Thompson. New York: Penguin, [1864] 1991.

The Struggles of Brown, Jones, and Robinson: By One of the Firm, ed. N. John Hall. Oxford: Oxford University Press, [1862] 1992.

Barchester Towers, ed. Robin Gilmour. New York: Penguin, [1857] 1994.

An Autobiography, eds. Michael Sadleir and Frederick Page. Oxford: Oxford University Press, [1883] 1999.

The Eustace Diamonds, eds. John Sutherland and Stephen Gill. New York: Penguin, [1873] 2004.

Framley Parsonage, eds. David Skilton and Peter Miles. New York: Penguin, [1861] 2004.

The Warden, ed. Robin Gilmour. New York: Penguin, [1855] 2004.

The Way We Live Now, ed. Karen Odden. New York: Barnes and Noble Press, [1875] 2005.

Tyndall, John. *Fragments of Science: A Series of Detached Essays, Addresses, and Reviews*. 2 vols. London: Longmans, Green, and Co., 1892; repr. by Westmead: Gregg International Publishers Ltd., 1970.

Ulrich, John M. "Thomas Carlyle, Richard Owen, and the Paleontological Articulation of the Past," *Journal of Victorian Culture* 11.1 (2006): 30–58.

Vanden Bossche, Chris R. "Cookery, Not Rookery: Family and Class in *David Copperfield*," *Dickens Studies Annual* 15 (1986): 98.

Van Ghent, Dorothy. *The English Novel: Form and Function*. Perennial Library. New York: Harper & Row Publishers, 1953.

Vickers, Brian. "The Emergence of Character Criticism, 1774–1800," *Shakespeare Survey: An Annual Survey of Shakespeare Studies and Production* 34 (1981): 11–21.

Wall, Cynthia Sundberg. *The Prose of Things: Transformations of Description in the Eighteenth Century*. Chicago: University of Chicago Press, 2006.

Watt, Ian. *The Rise of the Novel: Studies in Defoe, Richardson, and Fielding.* Berkeley: University of California Press, 2001.

Welsh, Alexander. *Strong Representations: Narrative and Circumstantial Evidence in England.* Baltimore: Johns Hopkins University Press, 1992.

Whately, George. "Review of *Northanger Abbey* and *Persuasion*," *Quarterly Review* xxiv (January 1821): 352–76.

Whewell, William. "Modern Science–Inductive Philosophy," *Quarterly Review* 45 (1831): 374–407.

The Philosophy of the Inductive Sciences, Founded Upon Their History.* 2 vols. London: John W. Parker, 1840.

On the Philosophy of Discovery: Chapters Historical and Critical. London: John W. Parker and Sons, 1860.

Whiting, Mary Bradford. "George Eliot as a Character Artist," *Westminster Review* 138 (October 1892): 406–15.

Wilde, Oscar. *De Profundis and Other Writings*, ed. Hesketh Pearson. New York: Penguin, 1986.

Wilkinson, Ann Y. "*Bleak House*: From Faraday to Judgment Day," *ELH* 34.2 (June 1967): 225–47.

Williams, Carolyn. *Transfigured World: Walter Pater's Aesthetic Historicism.* Ithaca: Cornell University Press, 1989.

"Walter Pater's Impressionism and the Form of Historical Revival," in *Knowing the Past: Victorian Literature & Culture*, ed. Suzy Anger. Ithaca: Cornell University Press, 2001. 77–99.

Gilbert and Sullivan: Gender, Genre, Parody. New York: Columbia University Press, 2012.

Williams, Raymond. *The Country and the City.* Oxford: Oxford University Press, 1975.

Marxism and Literature. Oxford: Oxford University Press, 1977.

Culture and Society, 1780–1950. New York: Columbia University Press, 1983.

Keywords: A Vocabulary of Culture and Society. Revd edn. Oxford: Oxford University Press, 1983.

Wilt, Judith. *The Readable People of George Meredith.* Princeton: Princeton University Press, 1975.

Winter, Sarah. *The Pleasures of Memory: Learning to Read with Charles Dickens.* New York: Fordham University Press, 2011.

Woloch, Alex. *The One vs. the Many: Minor Characters and the Space of the Protagonist in the Novel.* Princeton: Princeton University Press, 2003.

Woolf, Virginia. "Mr. Bennett and Mrs. Brown," in *The Captain's Death Bed and Other Essays.* New York: Harcourt Brace Jovanovich, 1978. 94–119.

Wordsworth, William. *The Prelude: 1799, 1805, 1850*, eds. Jonathan Wordsworth, M. H. Abrams, and Stephen Gill. New York: Norton, 1979.

The Poems, ed. John O. Hayden. 2 vols. New Haven: Yale University Press, 1981.

The Major Works, ed. Stephen Gill. Oxford: Oxford University Press, 2000.

Wormald, Mark. "Microscopy and Semiotic in *Middlemarch*," *Nineteenth-Century Literature* 50, no. 4 (March 1996): 501–24.

Wright, Daniel. "George Eliot's Vagueness," *Victorian Studies* 56.4 (Summer 2014): 625–48.

Yeo, Richard. *Defining Science: William Whewell, Natural Knowledge, and Public Debate in Early Victorian Britain*. Cambridge: Cambridge University Press, 1994.

Žižek, Slavoj. *The Sublime Object of Ideology*. New York: Verso, 1989.

Index

Cambridge Studies in Nineteenth-Century Literature and Culture

General Editor

Gillian Beer, *University of Cambridge*

Titles Published

1. The Sickroom in Victorian Fiction: The Art of Being Ill
   Miriam Bailin, *Washington University*

2. Muscular Christianity: Embodying the Victorian Age edited by
   Donald E. Hall, *California State University, Northridge*

3. Victorian Masculinities: Manhood and Masculine Poetics in Early Victorian
   Literature and Art
   Herbert Sussman, *Northeastern University, Boston*

4. Byron and the Victorians
   Andrew Elfenbein, *University of Minnesota*

5. Literature in the Marketplace: Nineteenth-Century British Publishing and the
   Circulation of Books edited by
   John O. Jordan, *University of California, Santa Cruz* and Robert L. Patten, *Rice
   University, Houston*

6. Victorian Photography, Painting and Poetry
   Lindsay Smith, *University of Sussex*

7. Charlotte Brontë and Victorian Psychology
   Sally Shuttleworth, *University of Sheffield*

8. The Gothic Body: Sexuality, Materialism and Degeneration at the *Fin de Siècle*
   Kelly Hurley, *University of Colorado at Boulder*

9. Rereading Walter Pater
   William F. Shuter, *Eastern Michigan University*